pulling the pieces together

PMP® EXAM
Simplified
5th Edition (5.1)

Completely Revised for 11 January 2016 PMP® Exam Update

© Jan 2016 AME Group, Inc. author Aileen Ellis, PMP, PgMP
aileen@amegroupinc.com 719-659-3658

Published by

AME Group Inc.
Aileen Ellis, PMP, PgMP
175 Palm Springs Drive
Colorado Springs, CO 80921
Phone: 719-659-3658
www.amegroupinc.com
aileen@amegroupinc.com

© Jan 2016 AME Group, Inc.

Fifth Edition (5.1d)

ISBN – 978-152289448

© January 2016 AME Group, Inc. author Aileen Ellis, PMP, PgMP
aileen@amegroupinc.com 719-659-3658

About the Author

Aileen Ellis, PgMP®, PMP®, is The PMP® Expert. She personally instructs project managers to gain the confidence and knowledge to pass the CAPM® Exam and the PMP® Exam. She has helped more than 1,000 professionals obtain their CAPM® and over 10,000 professionals obtain those coveted letters: PMP®. Working with thousands of students from dozens of countries, Ms. Ellis has gained a thorough understanding of the ins and outs of the PMBOK® Guide, the exam content, and proven test-taking strategies.

Ms. Ellis began teaching Exam Preparation Courses in 1998. Over the years she has mastered how students learn best and has incorporated those lessons and methods into her books. Her approach is focused on understanding the Project Management Processes and their interactions, with limited memorization. Along with teaching Project Management courses around the world, Ms. Ellis also leads workshops to help students study for and pass the CAPM®, PMP®, and PgMP® exams through review of content and hundreds of sample questions.

Ms. Ellis lives in Colorado Springs with her husband, Terry, and their two children, Nick and Alex. When not teaching, coaching, or writing, Ms. Ellis spends her days hiking the Colorado mountains.

Disclaimer: The purpose of this book is to help guide your study efforts. AME Group guarantees that every attempt has been made to check the accuracy of all information presented. Project Management is both an art and a science. You may at times find a difference of opinion on the information presented in this and other review books. In the end, your experience, education, test-taking ability, and dedication will determine your probability of passing the CAPM® and the PMP® exam.

© January 2016 AME Group, Inc. author Aileen Ellis, PMP, PgMP
aileen@amegroupinc.com 719-659-3658

PMP® EXAM - OVERVIEW

The PMP® Exam is based on the PMBOK® Guide 5th Edition as well as other current project management references. This does not mean that if someone reads the PMBOK® Guide that they will pass the exam. It is not that simple. To pass the exam, a person needs a detailed understanding of the PMBOK® Guide including how to take the information found in the PMBOK® Guide and use it to answer multiple choice questions.

While the goal of the book is to help you pass the PMP® EXAM, most people also learn a lot about being a good project manager. Pass the exam first, then go back through the book again to help you improve in your role as a project manager.

This book is for you if you want to:

- Pass the exam on the first try by practicing hundreds of sample exam questions
- Access a complete sample exam including detailed explanations of the right and wrong answers:
    - Understand why the best answer is best
    - Review detailed explanations of why the wrong answers are wrong
    - Practice systematically eliminating the wrong answers
- Reinforce your learning experience by utilizing sample questions continuously

Joining PMI (the Project Management Institute): Many people will decide to join PMI before applying for the exam. There are several reasons one may want to do this including a discount on the exam. We at AME Group believe in PMI membership, but that is completely up to you. If you are going to join PMI, we strongly suggest that you join PMI before you apply for the exam so as to obtain the PMI membership discount on the price of the exam. Make sure you retain your PMI membership number as you will need it on your application.

To join PMI, go to www.pmi.org and click on the pull down menu for membership.

To apply for the PMP® Exam: Go to www.pmi.org. Click on the pull down menu for certification. Then click on the link for the PMP® Exam. You will be instructed on how to open a PMP® online application. If you are a member of PMI®, make sure you have your membership number available. If you have applied for the PMP® exam but not paid for the exam realize that you are still at risk for the audit. You are notified of the audit after you make payment. Build this potential delay time into your schedule.

Qualifying for the PMP® Exam: You need at a minimum a secondary diploma (high school or the global equivalent), 35 hours of project management training/education and:

- Three (3) years of project management experience with a bachelor's degree

or

- Five (5) years of project management experience without a bachelor's degree

© January 2016 AME Group, Inc. author Aileen Ellis, PMP, PgMP
aileen@amegroupinc.com 719-659-3658

What you should expect when taking the exam:

Time- You have up to four hours to complete the exam. You may take a break at any time. Realize that the clock keeps going, even if you are taking a break.
Strategy on time- Make sure you are completing at least 50 questions each hour.

Number of questions- There are 200 questions total on your exam. Only 175 of these questions figure into your exam pass/fail calculation. The other 25 questions are considered pre-release questions. The pre-release questions are on the exam so that PMI can collect data of questions before they become official questions. These pre-release questions are placed randomly throughout the exam.
Strategy for pre-release questions- Assume every question on your exam counts. Don't think about which questions count and which are pre-release.

Organization of questions- The questions will appear in random order on your exam. They are not grouped by process group or by knowledge area.
Strategy for random questions- While studying for this exam, use the sample exam in the back of this book to get used to questions appearing in a random fashion.

Question format- Some of the questions on the exam will be short, just a sentence, others will be multiple sentences. There are no answers such as "all of the above" or "none of the above". The directions will tell you to pick the best answer.

Strategy for picking the best answer- Throughout this book we will discuss this strategy. In summary, focus as much on eliminating the wrong answers as on picking the best answer. More to come later in the book.

Passing the exam- To pass the exam you must get a certain number of the scored questions correct. You receive credit for each question you get correct. There are no subtractions for wrong answers.

Strategy- Make sure you answer every question on the exam. Use the strategy you learned in the book related to eliminating the wrong answers to increase the probability of you passing the exam on the first try.

The Exam Blue Print

The exam has 200 total questions of which 175 count toward pass-fail. The table below shows approximately the number of scored questions you will see from each of the five process groups.

Process Group	Approximate Percentage of Scored Questions	Approximate Number of Scored Questions
INITIATING	13%	23
PLANNING	24%	42
EXECUTING	31%	54
MONITORING AND CONTROLLING	25%	44
CLOSING	7%	12
TOTAL	100%	175 (Scored)

© January 2016 AME Group, Inc. author Aileen Ellis, PMP, PgMP
aileen@amegroupinc.com 719-659-3658

AILEEN'S Materials to help you Pass the PMP® EXAM

BOOKs written by Aileen:

All of Aileen's Books are available at Amazon.com in both print and e-book format and are appropriate for those testing January 12, 2016 or later.
- *PMP Exam Simplified 5th Edition* (5.1 Edition for post Jan 11, 2016 Exam)
- *How to get Every Earned Value Question right on the PMP Exam by Aileen*
- *How to get Every Network Diagram Question right on the PMP Exam by Aileen*
- *How to get Every Contract Math Question right on the PMP Exam by Aileen*

Let us know what content you would like to see next in a book by Aileen.

ONLINE COACHING for the PMP® EXAM with AILEEN:

Go to www.aileenellis.com for more information

- *BRONZE LEVEL*
    - o Step by Step guided Study
    - o Over 1,000 online sample questions and solutions

- *SILVER LEVEL-*
    - o Aileen's face to face program- but online
    - o Live and recorded videos of Aileen facilitating every aspect of Exam Preparation.
    - o Over 1,000 online sample questions and solutions

AILEEN's Live Face to Face Workshops:

Visit www.aileenellis.com for locations and dates.

Contact Aileen directly to bring her Face to Face Program to your location.
Aileen has taught on Five Continents and is eager to come to your location to work with you and your team.

Connect with AILEEN at:

LinkedIn: https://www.linkedin.com/in/pmpcertificationexpertaileen
Join Aileen's study group on LINKEDIN:
PMP Exam Prep Tribe
https://www.linkedin.com/grps?gid=6560819&trk=fulpro_grplogo

Twitter: @aileenellis
Follow Aileen on Twitter and subscribe to her Live Periscopes.

Website: www.aileenellis.com

Blogs: www.aileenellis.com/blogs

YouTube: subscribe to Aileen's Channel on YouTube for up to date PMP
Training Videos
https://www.youtube.com/user/aileenellis9

Email: aileen@aileenellis.com or aileen@amegroupinc.com

STUDYING FOR THE EXAM

The next few pages are the most important pages in this book. Do not take these ideas for granted. These pages represent a tremendous amount of work. This work often can make the difference between passing and failing the exam.

Before you go past the next few pages in the book, please purchase a set of index cards

List of equations- Use your index cards. Write the name of the equation on the front of the card and the actual equation on the back. Work these equations for five minutes of your studying every day. See the example below.

Front of Card	Back of Card
Cost Variance	CV= EV-AC

EQUATIONS TO KNOW FOR THE EXAM

Present Value	$PV = FV/(1+i)^t$ FV-future value, i= interest rate, t= time
PERT	$PERT = (P+4ML+O)/6$ P= pessimistic, ML=Most Likely, O= optimistic
One Standard Deviation	1 Standard Deviation= $\lvert(P-O)/6\rvert$
Variance	Variance= $(SD)^2$
Cost Variance (CV)	$CV = EV - AC$ EV=earned value AC= actual cost
Cost Performance Index (CPI)	$CPI = EV/AC$
Schedule Variance (SV)	$SV = EV - PV$ EV= earned value PV= planned value
Schedule Performance Index (SPI)	$SPI = EV/PV$
Estimate at Completion (EAC)- assume we will continue to spend at the same rate	$EAC = BAC/CPI$ BAC= budget at completion CPI= cost performance index
Estimate to Complete (ETC)- assume we will continue to spend at the same rate	$ETC = EAC - AC$ EAC= estimate at completion AC= actual cost
Variance at Completion (VAC)	$VAC = BAC - EAC$
TCPI-using BAC	$TCPI = (BAC-EV)/(BAC-AC)$
TCPI-using EAC	$TCPI = (BAC-EV)/(EAC-AC)$
Number of Communication Channels	# of channels= $n(n-1)/2$ n= number of people
Point of Total Assumption (PTA)	PTA= target cost+ ((ceiling price-target price)/buyer's share ratio)
Advanced equations	(it is less likely that the equations below will be needed on the exam.) ***Therefore I recommend most people not study these equations.***
EAC- assume the remaining work will be accomplished at the original planned rate	$EAC = AC + (BAC-EV)$
EAC- assume both CPI and SPI will influence the remaining work	$EAC = AC + ((BAC-EV)/(SPI*CPI))$
EAC- assume plan and current spending do not represent future	$EAC = AC +$ bottom-up ETC
ETC- assume need to re-estimate	$ETC =$ Bottom-up ETC

© January 2016 AME Group, Inc. author Aileen Ellis, PMP, PgMP
aileen@amegroupinc.com 719-659-3658

AILEEN's GAME ****(Extremely Important)****

Aileen's process game-. Follow the process game goal by goal. Start with goal one. Once you have achieved this move to goal two. Once this is easy then move to goal three. Goal four may take several weeks. Work this process game as the first ten minutes of your studying every day. After the process game work your equations for five minutes of every day.

First Goal (Part One of Game): 5 Process Groups

Use PMBOK® Guide: page 61 to help you.

Take five (5) index cards. Write the name of each process group on the front of one card and its definition on the back. See the Initiating Example below. Repeat for Planning, Executing, Monitoring and Controlling, and Closing. Note: For some of us, writing the definition on the back may be too detailed. If you do not want to write the definition, make sure you will recognize the definition.

Front of Card	Back of Card
INITIATING	Processes used to start a project or phase

Second Goal (PART TWO OF GAME): 10 Knowledge Areas

Take 10 index cards. Write the name of each knowledge area on the front of a card and its definition on the back. See the Integration example that follows. Also create cards for Scope, Time, Cost, Quality, HR, Communications, Risk, Procurement, and Stakeholder. Again, for some of us writing the definition will be too much detail. Just make sure you will recognize the definition.

Front of Card	Back of Card
INTEGRATION	Processes used to connect all the other project management processes

Practice taking cards and building the table in the PMBOK® Guide on page 61. After this is easy practice with a blank sheet of paper where you will write out knowledge areas and process groups in the correct spaces.

Third Goal (Part Three of Game) : Recognize 47 processes and be able to sort by process group or knowledge area.

Take 47 index cards. Write the name of each process on the front of one card. Leave the back of each card blank for now. See Collect Requirements example below. Do this for the other 46 processes.

Front of Card	Back of Card
Collect Requirements	(Leave blank for now.)

Practice sorting cards to build the table in the PMBOK® Guide Table page 61. Then start with a blank sheet of paper and try to write out the entire table in the PMBOK® Guide on page 61. Ignore the numbers on the table.

Fourth Goal (Part 4 of Game): Recognize the tools and techniques for each process

Take the 47 index cards. Write the names of the tools and techniques on the back of each card. You will need to get to the second or third page of chapter four through chapter thirteen of the PMBOK® Guide to find the tools and techniques. See the Collect Requirements Example below. This is from PMBOK® Guide Figure 5-1.

This goal may feel overwhelming. I suggest building just one card at a time as you go through each process.

Front of Card	Back of Card
Collect Requirements	Interviews, focus groups Facilitated workshops Group creativity techniques (brainstorming, etc.) Group decision making techniques (unanimity, etc.) Questionnaires and surveys Observations, prototypes Benchmarking, context diagrams Documentation analysis

Practice looking at the back of each card and being able to name the process. When that is easy, practice explaining to others how you could use each tool and technique during that process. Do not write down inputs or outputs. Inputs and outputs are important but if we have too much information on the cards they may become overwhelming.

☑ **EXAM TIP: Always have your cards with you. It is critical that you know the names of all 47 processes and can sort the processes by knowledge area and process group. It is also critical to recognize what tools and techniques go with what processes. Also know the examples listed in the PMBOK® Guide for each tool and technique.**

© January 2016 AME Group, Inc. author Aileen Ellis, PMP, PgMP
aileen@amegroupinc.com 719-659-3658

NAMES TO KNOW FOR THE EXAM

Goleman	Emotional Intelligence
Goldratt	Famous for Critical Chain Method.
Parkinson's Theory	Work expands so as to fill the time available for its completion.
Juran	Quality defined as fitness for use.
Crosby	Quality defined as conformance to requirements. Famous for ideas such as: Quality is free and zero defects are achievable.
Deming	Total Quality Management (TQM).
Shewhart and Deming	Plan-Do-Check-Act Cycle.
Ishikawa	Another name for cause and effect diagrams. The first seven tools of quality are known as the Ishikawa tools.
Taguchi	The lose function- "loss" in value progressively increases as variation increases from the intended condition.
Pareto	Italian economist. Pareto chart named after him.
Tuckman	Famous for 5 stages of team development.
Maslow	Hierarchy of needs.
McGregor	Theory X-Management has negative view of workers and Theory Y-management has positive view of workers.
Ouchi	Theory Z-increased employee loyalty by providing a job for life, etc.
McClelland	Acquired Needs Theory-Need for Achievement, Need for Power and Need for Affiliation.
Herzberg	Hygiene Factors not enough to motivate people. Most also address their motivators.
Vroom	Expectancy Theory- for people to be motivated they need to believe they can be successful, that they will be rewarded and that the reward is something they value.

List of names for the exam- Review this list once a day at the beginning of your study time. If you struggle with the list, you may need to build index cards similar to the index cards for the equations.

Organization of this Book

The book is organized by process group, not by knowledge area. The primary reasons:

- We manage projects by process group, not by knowledge area.
- On the exam you will see questions such as "what would you do next". These questions will be more logical and thus easier if you study by process group and not by knowledge area.

Sample questions will be provided throughout the material. The primary reason for this:

- o Very quickly you will be able to assess if you are understanding the PMBOK® Guide 5th Edition's point of view.
- o Sample questions make the material more interesting. If the material is more interesting you will be more involved and thus learn more.
- o To pass the exam, you not only need to understand (don't memorize) the material but you need to be able to determine the best answer. We can only do this by practicing on exam questions.

☑ **Exam tip**s will be provided throughout the materials.

PAIRS OF WORDS- We will often examine "pairs of words".

- o Often when one of the words in the pair is the correct idea in a question on the exam the other word represents the wrong answers.
- o See example below of how this idea will be presented hundreds of times.

INSPECTIONS	AUDITS
Related to deliverables and/or products.	Related to processes.
We inspect deliverables.	We audit processes.

Sample Question:
1. We are planning to have an outside organization come in and review our quality processes and recommend improvements. The tool and technique we will use is:
a. quality inspections
b. quality audits
c. process inspections
d. risk audits
Solution- hopefully you were able to eliminate answer d since this question is not about risk. Hopefully, you were able to eliminate answers a and c since the question is about processes and not deliverables. b is the correct answer.

FULL LENGTH EXAM- One full length exam may be found at the end of this book. More sample exams may be found at: www.aileenellis.com.

WRONG ANSWERS- We will discuss the "wrong answers" as much, if not even more than the "right answers" in the sample questions. If we are able to eliminate the wrong answers, it is easier to select the right answer.

© January 2016 AME Group, Inc. author Aileen Ellis, PMP, PgMP
aileen@amegroupinc.com 719-659-3658

EXAM QUESTION STRATEGY

1. Read the question and ask yourself: what process group am I in?   What knowledge area am I in? Once you can identify the knowledge area and the process group, you may then be able to identify the actual process (see PMBOK® Guide 5th Edition-Page 423).   Think of the objective of that process as well as the inputs/tools and techniques/outputs of this process to give you a clue.

2. Look for qualifier words in the question. Frequently used qualifier words include: every, always, never, all, etc.

Note: There are both "bad words" and "good words on the exam." For example:

Bad words	Good words
Frequently	Timely
Punish	Coach
Force	Encourage

3.   Identify the type of question.

- Input/output, tool and technique questions
- Definitional type questions

4. As you practice for the exam, read each question and write the question number on a piece of paper. Identify and eliminate any wrong answers. It is better to "guess" between two choices than four choices. When in doubt, remember that words from the PMBOK® Guide are more likely to be correct than non-PMBOK® Guide words. Use definitions, common sense, etc. Let's take a look at an example:

---

1. **What is the right answer?**
   - a. this answer I know is wrong, so I will put a line through "a"
   - b. this answer I am not sure of, so I will put a "?" next to "b"
   - c. this answer I know is wrong, so I will put a line through "c"
   - d. this answer I believe is the correct answer, so I will circle "d"

Your handwritten page should look something like this:
1. ~~a~~
   ? b
   ~~c~~
   d

Now go back and look at "b" and see if there is a way to eliminate this answer.

Special note on Input/Tool and Technique/Output Questions

The PMBOK® Guide 5ᵗʰ Edition uses terms such as inputs/tools and techniques/outputs. The outputs of one process are often the input to another process.

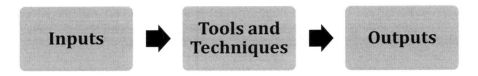

INPUTs and OUTPUTs are documents or documentable items. Learn to recognize this list of typical inputs and outputs. This list is not all inclusive, but gives you a good start.

- organizational process assets
- enterprise environmental factors
- policies and plans
- deliverables and product transition
- project documents
- constraints and assumptions
- PMIS
- change requests

- lesson learned
- reports and forecasts
- descriptions
- charter
- approved changes
- baselines
- lists
- diagrams
- estimates
- data and information
- formal acceptance

- registers
- requirements and matrixes
- calendars
- updates
- structures (WBS, RBS, OBS, etc.)
- checklists
- measurements
- metrics
- assessments
- communications
- logs (issue, change, etc.)

TOOLS and TECHNIQUES are mechanisms applied to the INPUTS to create OUTPUTS.

Tools and techniques are what we do or what we use on the inputs to create the outputs. Learn to recognize this list of typical tools and techniques. This list is not all inclusive but a good start.

- facilitation techniques
- PMIS (project management information system)
- techniques
- skills and knowledge
- estimating

- systems
- EVM
- meetings
- procedures
- management
- measurement
- analysis (any kind)
- identification
- flowcharts

- diagrams
- methods
- templates
- decomposition
- additional planning
- inspections
- simulation
- software

Many of these questions will ask: Which of the following is an input of ...? Or, which of the following is a tool and technique of...? If you can identify if each answer is an input (document) or tool and technique (things we do to documents to create other documents), you may easily be able to eliminate one, two, or three of the wrong answers.

Let's take some sample questions. Yes, you are going to do some questions and get them right without seeing the PMBOK® Guide content.

© January 2016 AME Group, Inc. author Aileen Ellis, PMP, PgMP
aileen@amegroupinc.com 719-659-3658

Input /T&T/ Output Sample Question #1

Which of the following is an input of control costs?

      a.   project management plan

      b.   reserve analysis

      c.   project management software

      d.   forecasting

Of course, we have not covered control costs yet, but use the ideas above to help you.

Step one: We are definitely in the control costs process because the question states "control costs." Control costs deals with controlling changes to the project budget.

Step two: There are no qualifying words like "not" or "only".

Step three: This is definitely an input/tool and techniques/output question. Knowing that, in general, inputs are documents, look for an answer that is a document.

In this example, "a" is a document. Answer "b", "c", and "d" are all tools and techniques. The book is using the word 'analysis' and the word 'forecasting' as verbs. We are doing analysis, we are forecasting, therefore these answers are tools and techniques. Software is always a tool and technique. Therefore, "a" must be the right answer.

Input/Tool and Technique/Output Question #2

Which of the following is a tool and technique of define scope?

      a.   product analysis

      b.   scope management plan

      c.   scope statement

      d.   communications methods

Again, we have not covered define scope yet, but let's give this a try.

Step one: We know we are in the planning process group because the question says "define scope." In fact, we are in the scope knowledge area, more specifically, the define scope process. Define scope deals with creating the scope statement.

Step two: There are no qualifying words like "not" or "only".

Step three: This is definitely an input/tool and tech/output question. Tools and techniques are things we do to documents to create other documents.

In this example, answers "a" and "d" are both tools and techniques; we will come back to them. Answer "b" and "c" are both documents and, therefore, not tools and techniques of any process. We are left with "a" and "d". Which one is more likely associated with scope? Hopefully you will select "a". Once we cover the material, "a" should be an easier answer to determine.

ASSUMPTIONS TO MAKE FOR THE EXAM:

- There is one project manager for the project
- The project manager will manage only one project at a time (not groups of projects)
- The project will span several years
- The team will have hundreds of members
- The project will cost millions of US Dollars or the equivalent
- The project manager has access to historical documents from previous projects
- The organization has documented processes that the project management team will use to guide the current project
- The customer is internal to your organization and most likely you have an internal agreement (not a contract) in place between your internal customer and your project team.

© January 2016 AME Group, Inc. author Aileen Ellis, PMP, PgMP
aileen@amegroupinc.com 719-659-3658

INTRODUCTION

The PMBOK® Guide provides ideas for managing a single project, not a group of related projects (called programs). For the exam, the focus is on a single project, and it is a big project. A project could be as simple as planning and hosting a party to as complicated as designing and constructing the Sydney Opera House. As you go through this material think of a project that you are currently involved in. Take the material and relate it to your work, and the work of others on the project.

Life Cycle:

Often there is confusion with the phrase "life cycle". In this book, we will actually discuss several life cycles. For now let's just focus on one. It is called the project management lifecycle. It is composed of the five process groups:

- Initiating
- Planning
- Executing
- Monitoring and Controlling
- Closing

Projects are often divided into phases. A simple project may have one phase and go through each of the process groups just once. A bigger project may have multiple phases and go through these process groups multiple times. More information on the project management life cycle, also known as the five process groups, will be given later.

The PMBOK® Guide contains the standard for our profession of managing projects. Most professions include standards. Standards often represent good practices for the profession. What might be a good practice for the medical profession? Interviewing a patient and performing tests before treatment. These might be standard good practices for the medical profession. Regulations are documents that must be followed. The PMBOK® Guide itself is not a regulation.

☑ **EXAM TIP:** Know the difference between standards and regulations.

STANDARD	REGULATION
Not mandatory to follow	Mandatory to follow
Represents good practice	Comes from Government

Purpose of the PMBOK® Guide

The PMBOK® Guide describes good practices for the profession of project management. This does not mean we should follow the book blindly. We should take the ideas of the book and tailor them so they make sense for our projects.

The PMBOK® Guide provides a lexicon (common vocabulary) for Project Management terminology. If, as a profession, we have a common vocabulary, communication will be clearer with less chance for misunderstanding.

The PMBOK® Guide is a guide not a methodology. As stated earlier, we should not follow the book process by process. We should evaluate each of our projects and select the appropriate processes. These processes should be used to the appropriate level of rigor that adds value, not adds busy work.

The PMBOK® Guide references the PMI Code of Ethics and Professional Conduct. This code
- describes the expectations for project managers as far as ethics
- mandates compliance with laws, regulations and organizational and professional practice

☐☑ **EXAM TIP**: Recognize the categories: responsibility, respect, fairness, and honesty.

What is a Project

Most organizations have an operations side to sustain the business, and a project side to change or grow the business.

☑ **EXAM TIP:** Know the difference between projects and operations.

PROJECTS	OPERATIONS
Temporary- beginning and an end	On-going
Unique Product(s), capabilities or results	Standard products or repetitive service
The end of the project- when objectives have been met or when the project is terminated	Generally repetitive process- follows organizations existing procedures
Purpose is to meet objectives and then terminate	Purpose is to sustain the business

© January 2016 AME Group, Inc. author Aileen Ellis, PMP, PgMP
aileen@amegroupinc.com 719-659-3658

What is Project Management

Think of project management as utilizing processes to accomplish the needs of the project stakeholders. A process is a group of related activities that we do in order to create a product or result. There are 47 processes in the PMBOK° Guide contained in five process groups. The five process groups are sometimes called the "project management lifecycle". Review PMBOK° Guide page 50, Figure 3-1.

Project management includes turning the needs of the project stakeholders into requirements and then planning and managing a project to meet those requirements. To do this, we must actively engage our stakeholders, including actively communicating with them.

On projects, we will run into things that constrain us in planning and executing the work. There are six (6) primary competing constraints on a project. If one of the six constraints change, others may (don't assume must) be affected.

- Scope
- Risk
- Resources
- Quality
- Schedule
- Budget

These **six constraints** are built on the original triple constraint - scope, time, and cost. Think about your current project. What would happen if a stakeholder wanted to add more scope? Would you need to increase the budget, extend the schedule, etc.? A big part of project management is managing change requests as they occur.

Progressive Elaboration- allows for improving and adding detail to the plan as more information becomes available. Adding additional objectives, requirements, or scope is not considered progressive elaboration. Progressive elaboration is adding detail to what we already have, not adding new objectives.

Relationship among Portfolio Management, etc.

Organizational Project Management (OPM)	Framework utilizing project, program, and portfolio management. Also links to organizational enablers.
Portfolio	Group of programs, projects, sub-portfolios, and operations (not necessarily interdependent). Focus is on achieving strategic objectives of the organization. Selects the right projects and programs, prioritizes the work, and provides the needed resources.
Program	Group of related projects and additional work. Goal is to obtain benefits and control not available if projects are managed separately. Manages the interdependencies between projects.
Project	Deliverable management.

Project Management Office (PMO)- The term PMO may have different meanings in different organizations. In general a PMO is a structure that may provide governance as well as helps the sharing of resources (people, knowledge, etc.) across projects. There are 3 categories of project management offices (PMOs) though certainly there may be overlap.

Supportive PMO	-provides low control. This structure provides the support the project needs including training, etc.
Controlling PMO	-provides moderate control. This structure provides support and requires compliance.
Directive PMO	-provides high control. This PMO actually manages the projects.

Relationship between Project Management and Operations Management- Projects and operations may interact in different ways.

PROJECTS	OPERATIONS
Requires project management	Requires business process management and operations management
Temporary	Permanent, process related work

Often, resources (including people) are transferred from the operations to the project at the beginning of the project or from the project to operations at the end of the project.

© January 2016 AME Group, Inc. author Aileen Ellis, PMP, PgMP
aileen@amegroupinc.com 719-659-3658

Operational stakeholders may be very important to project success.
Project objectives should always be aligned with the overall business objectives.

Role of the Project Manager

Know that good project managers must possess all of the following:

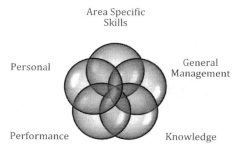

Area specific skills relate to the area of the project. As an example, if the project manager is managing a construction project, he should possess construction skills. General management proficiencies include accounting, marketing, and finance.

Project Management Body of Knowledge

The PMBOK® Guide contains a lot of useful information yet it is not all inclusive. Tailoring the ideas of the standard to our projects will increase the likelihood of success. Other standards exist related to program management and portfolio management.
An organization's project management process capabilities are addressed in PMI's Organizational Project Management Maturity Model (OPM3®).

INTRODUCTION – Sample Questions

1. You are managing the development of a new piece of exercise equipment that will require a person to exercise for only 30 minutes to achieve the same benefits that requires 60 minutes with other equipment. Now, there is discussion of terminating the project. Projects often terminate because:
a. the objectives have been met
b. additional stakeholders have been added to the stakeholder register
c. new customers have entered the market
d. the requirements are not achievable with current technology or funding

2. After a long day of work, you are socializing with other project managers in your organization. It seems that most of the other project managers are managing one large project. You, on the other hand, are managing a group of related projects. Your goal is to achieve certain benefits that could not be achieved if the projects were managed separately. Therefore, you:
a. should be paid more since you have more responsibility
b. are a portfolio manager since you are managing a group of related projects
c. should be promoted to senior management since you have so much responsibility
d. are a program manager since you are managing a group of related projects

3. The six competing constraints on a project include?
a. budget, quality, scope, resources risk and cost
b. quality, scope, budget, schedule, resources, time
c. budget, schedule, scope, quality, resources and risk
d. budget, scope, cost, quality, resources and risk

4. Managing a project usually includes:
a. identifying requirements
b. selecting the right project
c. prioritizing the work across multiple projects
d. controlling dependencies across projects

5. Projects within a program are related by:
a. shared client
b. common technology
c. shared supplier
d. common outcome

6. The PMBOK° Guide describes all of the following except:
a. integration management
b. operations management
c. project management processes
d. quality management

7. Your organization has a long and successful history as a manufacturing company. Project management is just being introduced and it is your responsibility to make sure everyone is clear on what project management is and is not. You explain that managing a project includes all the following except:
a. identifying requirements
b. addressing the needs, concerns, and expectations of the stakeholders
c. balancing the competing needs of the project constraints
d. on-going production of goods and services

© January 2016 AME Group, Inc. author Aileen Ellis, PMP, PgMP
aileen@amegroupinc.com 719-659-3658

8. All of the following are types of PMOs (project management offices) except:
a. analytical
b. supportive
c. controlling
d. directive

9. Your coffee distribution project was a huge success. The senior staff focused on the tangible elements of business value. For you, which of the following intangible elements of business value was most important?
a. monetary assets
b. stockholder equity
c. brand recognition
d. utility

10. An organization's project management process capabilities are addressed in:
a. Organizational Project Management Maturity Model (OPM3°)
b. PMBOK° Guide
c. The Standard for Program Management
d. The Standard for Portfolio Management

11. Projects and operations share which of the following characteristics?
a. planned, executed, and controlled
b. temporary
c. unique products
d. have a definite beginning and end

12. A portfolio is a:
a. group of related projects
b. group of related programs
c. group of related projects and programs that are managed together
d. group of projects or programs that may not necessarily be related

13. You have received acceptance of your last deliverable and are beginning to close out the project. Your sponsor now informs you that he wants you to add another phase to the project for operations and maintenance. Operations and maintenance should:
a. be the last phase of your project
b. be a separate project
c. be a new project
d. be considered work outside of the project

14. One of your fellow project managers comes to you for advice. Instead of managing one big project, he feels he is managing the same small project over and over again, sometimes over 100 a week. No planning is required and he struggles to follow the project management methodologies set-up by the PMO. Most likely he is struggling because:
a. he does not have the experience to be managing so many projects
b. project managers should only manage one project at a time
c. he is really involved in operations, not projects
d. the PMO has not developed a good methodology to support different projects

15. Your organization has been struggling with project management for years. Finally a PMO has been set-up and a project management methodology developed. You are a member of the PMO for your organization. Your project is to determine the maturity of your organization as it relates to project, program, and portfolio management. The standard(s) most likely to help you are:

a. *The Standard for Program Management*
b. *The Standard for Portfolio Management*
c. *The PMBOK® Guide*
d. *The Organizational Project Management Maturity Model*

© January 2016 AME Group, Inc. author Aileen Ellis, PMP, PgMP
aileen@amegroupinc.com 719-659-3658

INTRODUCTION - Solutions

1. d.   PMBOK° Guide: Section 1.2
Y   d. We terminate projects when the objectives cannot be met.
N   a. Projects successfully close when their objectives have been met.
N   b. Additional stakeholders may not be a reason to terminate a project.
N   c. Additional customers would not cause us to terminate.

2. d.   PMBOK° Guide: Section 1.4.1
Y   d. Program managers manage groups of related projects to obtain benefits that may not be obtained if the projects are managed separately.
N   a. and c. Answers related to being promoted or being paid more money generally will not be the right answers on the exam.
N   b. Since your focus is on benefits, most likely you are a program manager. If the question stated that your were managing a group of programs and that your focus was on achieving strategic objectives, the portfolio manager might be a better answer.

3. c.   PMBOK° Guide: Section 1.3
Y   c. The competing constraints are budget, schedule, scope, quality, resources, and risk.
N   a. and d. Schedule is missing.
N   b. Risk is missing.

4. a.   PMBOK° Guide: Section 1.3 and 1.4
Y   a. Identifying requirements is an early part of managing a project.
N   b. Selecting the right projects is part of portfolio management.
N   c. Prioritizing work across multiple projects is part of program management.
N   d. Controlling dependencies across projects is part of program management.

5. d.   PMBOK° Guide: Section 1.4.1
Y   d. We define related projects as projects with a common (or related) outcome.
N   a., b., and c. Having a shared client, common technology, or a shared supplier does not make projects related to each other.

6. b.   PMBOK° Guide: Section 1.5.1
Y   b. Operations management is not part of project management and therefore not contained in the PMBOK° Guide.
N   a. and d. Integration and Quality management are knowledge areas in the PMBOK® Guide.
N   c. Most of the PMBOK° Guide is a discussion of the 47 processes.

7. d.   PMBOK° Guide: Section 1.5.1.1
Y   d. On-going production is the objective of on-going operations, not projects.
N   a. Identifying requirements is an early part of managing a project.
N   b. Addressing the needs, concerns, and expectations of the stakeholders is a significant part of managing a project.
N   c. Balancing the competing constraints can be a very difficult part of project management.

8. a.   PMBOK° Guide: Section 1.4.4
Y   a. There is no such thing as an analytical PMO.
N   b. A supportive PMO provides training, templates, etc.

N   c. A controlling PMO ensures conformance to a project management methodology, etc.

N   d. A directive PMO manages the projects.

9. c. PMBOK® Guide: Section 1.6
Y   c. Brand recognition is an intangible example of business value.

N   a., b., and d. Monetary assets, stockholder equity, and utility are all tangible examples of business value.

10. a. PMBOK® Guide: Section 1.8
Y   a. Organizational Project Management Maturity Model (OPM3®) addresses process capabilities.

N   b. The PMBOK® Guide addresses project management processes.

N   c. The Standard for Program Management addresses program management processes.

N   d. The Standard for Portfolio Management addresses portfolio management processes.

11. a. PMBOK® Guide: Section 1.2 (implied)
Y   a. Projects and operations are performed by people, constrained by limited resources, and planned, executed, and controlled.

N   b. Projects are temporary; operations are on-going.

N   c. Projects produce unique products; operations produce multiple units of the same product.

N   d. Progressive elaboration is associated with project scope, product scope, and assumptions, not with operations.

12. d. PMBOK® Guide: Section 1.4.2
Y   d. A portfolio is a collection of projects or programs and other work that are grouped together to facilitate effective management of that work to meet strategic business objectives. The projects or programs of the portfolio may not necessarily be interdependent or directly related.

N   a. A program is a group of related projects managed in a coordinated way to obtain benefits and control not available from managing them individually. Programs may include elements of related work outside of the scope of the discrete projects in the program.

N   b. and c. The projects and programs in a portfolio may not necessarily be interdependent or directly related.

13. d. PMBOK® Guide: Section 1.5.1
Y   d. Operations and maintenance are not part of a project. They should be considered work outside of the project since they are not temporary.

14. c. PMBOK® Guide: Section 1.5.1
Y   c. Most likely your friend is involved in operations. There are two key ideas in the question that lead us to this conclusion. The first is that he is managing over 100 projects a week. Most likely they are not really projects. The second idea; the question states that no planning is required. If no planning is required then he is not managing projects.

15. d. PMBOK® Guide: Section 1.8
Y   *d. The Organizational Project Management Maturity Model* helps us understand the maturity of our organization as it relates to project, program, and portfolio management.

© January 2016 AME Group, Inc. author Aileen Ellis, PMP, PgMP
aileen@amegroupinc.com 719-659-3658

ORGANIZATIONAL INFLUENCES AND PROJECT LIFE CYCLE

The culture of your organization will influence your project and the success of your project. The organizational structure influences the culture and the culture influences the structure. Know the differences between these different structures.

Functional Structure	Weak Matrix	Balanced Matrix	Strong Matrix	Projectized
Hierarchy	Borrowed Resources	Borrowed Resources	Borrowed Resources	Full-time dedicated resources
People are grouped by specialty- ex. All engineers work in the engineering group	Complex Communication	Complex Communication	Complex Communication	Sometimes the team is co- located
	Project Manager is weaker than the Functional Manager	Project Manager and Functional Manager have balanced power	Project Manager is stronger than the Functional Manager	All resources report to the Project Manager, therefore the project manager has more authority than the functional manager
One clear supervisor who is the functional manager	**Coordinator**- reports to a higher–level manager and therefore has some authority.			
	Project Expeditor- this person is a communications link.			

© Jan 2016 AME Group, Inc. author Aileen Ellis, PMP, PgMP
aileen@amegroupinc.com 719-659-3658

Organizational Process Assets and Enterprise Environmental Factors

Enterprise Environmental Factors	Organizational Process Assets
Internal and external environmental factors	Plans, processes, policies, procedures, knowledge bases
Examples include: organizational culture, marketplace conditions, stakeholder risk tolerances, Project Management Information System (PMIS), systems	Examples include: processes, templates, guidelines, project files, historical information and lessons learned. Databases and knowledge bases that contain organizational... not commercial data.

Project Stakeholders

STAKEHOLDER	KEY WORDS
Customer/users	Will use the project's product, result, or service
Sponsor	Provides money, champions the project, navigates the political environment
Portfolio Managers/Review Board	High level governance, organizations executives, project selection committee
Program Manager	Manage group of interrelated projects- provide benefits not achievable if projects are managed separately
Project Management Office	Support and/or manage projects under the PMO's domain
Project Manager	Responsible for achieving project objectives
Functional Managers	Provides management oversight to an administrative area
Operational Management	Responsible for an area of the core business. Deals directly with the salable products or services
Sellers	External companies providing components or services
Business partners	External companies that fill a specified role such as installation, customization, training, or support

© January 2016 AME Group, Inc. author Aileen Ellis, PMP, PgMP
aileen@amegroupinc.com 719-659-3658

☑**EXAM TIP:** Questions may describe situations and you will need to be able to differentiate one stakeholder from another.

Project governance is the framework in which the project operates. It includes the structure, processes, and decision-making models for running a successful project. Governance should be described in the project management plan.

Project success should be measured against the most up-to-date baselines and include all of the project constraints.

Project Team
The project team includes:
- **The project manager**- always considered the leader of the team regardless of how much authority the project manager may exert
- **The project management staff**- this is a core team that helps the project manager manage the work of the project
- **Other team members**- these are the people who do the work of the project

There are several types of team compositions. Two to know for the exam:
- **Dedicated**- most if not all of the team members are full-time on the team. Reporting is clear for everyone, though this often is a more expensive structure since the project manager has all the resources full-time even if he does not need them all full-time.
  - Often we see dedicated team members in a projectized structure
  - Could also be used in a matrix structure though more likely in a strong matrix
- **Part-time**- most team members, including the project manager, are part-time. They may spend the rest of their time supporting operations and/or other projects.
  - Most often seen in functional organizations
  - Could be seen in a matrix structure though more likely in a weak matrix

Project Life Cycle

Cost and Staffing Levels	Low at the start, peak during intermediate phases, drops off quickly
Stakeholder influence, risk and uncertainly	High at the start and gets progressively lower
Cost of changes	Low at the start and gets progressively higher
Ability to influence product characteristics	High at the start and gets progressively lower

We want to try to identify and include stakeholders as early as possible.

If we do not identify the right stakeholders early enough and engage them enough we may see:

- More changes than expected
- Changes that cost more than expected
- Achieving requirements but the product/deliverables being rejected

☑ **EXAM TIPs:**

- If you get a question that states you are experiencing more changes than expected- look for an answer related to you not identifying stakeholders, not identifying stakeholders early enough, or not identifying the right stakeholders.

- If you get a question that states your changes are costing more than expected- look for an answer related to you not identifying stakeholders, not identifying stakeholders early enough, or not identifying the right stakeholders.

- If you get a question that states you have met the requirements but your product is still being rejected- look for an answer related to you not identifying stakeholders, not identifying stakeholders early enough, or not identifying the right stakeholders.

☑ **Exam Tip:** See and understand Figures 2-10. 2-11 and 2-12 of the PMBOK® Guide.

Project Phases and Project Process Groups are not the same thing. The five (5) process groups are repeated in each of the phases.

☑ **Exam Tip**: Know the difference between the five processes groups and the project life cycle. See Figures 2-8, 2-10, and 2-11 of the PMBOK° Guide.

Types of Life Cycles:

	Predictive	**Iterative and Incremental**	**Adaptive**
Other names	Fully plan-driven		Change driven or agile
Project scope	Defined as early as possible	Defined one iteration at a time	Will be decomposed into a list of requirements
			Are also considered iterative and incremental
Phases and iterations	Phases are sequential or over lapping	Iterations performed in a sequential or overlapping fashion	Each iteration is rapid and fixed in time and cost
Project Management Processes	Subset of activities and processes for each phase	During each iteration activities from all process groups performed	-Several processes are performed in each iteration -early iterations focus more on planning
When used	-the product to be delivered is well understood -there is a substantial base of industry practice -the product must be delivered in full to have value	-need to manage changing objectives and scope -reduce the complexity of a project -partial delivery of a product is beneficial and provides value	- in response to high level of change and stakeholder involvement

ORGANIZATIONAL INFLUENCES AND THE PROJECT LIFE CYCLE - Sample Questions

1. You have just been hired by a government agency. Your title is electronics systems engineer. It seems though that your primary role is to go to the different functional groups such as electrical engineering, mechanical engineering, and structural engineering and ensure they are communicating with each other. For the projects of this organization you really are operating as the:
a. project manager
b. project coordinator
c. project expeditor
d. functional manager

2. Your organization has been in the market of producing high sugar drinks for over 40 years. Now, people are putting more of a focus on health. Your project will be to develop and produce a product based on historical products though without the sugar. Many people will be involved with the project though the team make-up will change dramatically from phase to phase. Most likely you will use a(n):
a. predictive life cycle
b. iterative life cycle
c. incremental life cycle
d. adaptive life cycle

3. You have spent years managing small and midsize projects for your organization. Based on your success, you are managing your first large scale project with what seems like an unending list of project stakeholders. The number of change requests is so large it is hard to make progress. The most likely reason for this is:
a. not enough money in the budget
b. not enough time in the schedule
c. not enough focus on stakeholder identification and analysis
d. no quality assurance department assigned to the project

4. Your project is to design and build the stadium for a local university. The stadium will be used by both the university as well as local sports teams. It is important that the project set the tone of a modern city while not losing the charm of an established university. Suggestions have been made to overlap many of the project phases so as to save time and have the stadium ready for a critical soccer tournament. You realize that overlapping phases often leads to:
a. improved resource optimization
b. buffers to account for project uncertainty
c. activity rework
d. decreased risk

5. The framework that provides the project manager and the team with the structure, processes, decision-making models, and tools for managing the project is called:
a. the project management plan
b. project governance
c. change control system
d. project management information system

6. For years your organization has believed that project management is all about schedules and budgets. Based on many failed projects, stakeholder management is now being viewed as much more important. Management wants you to focus on the positive stakeholders who can aid in the success of the project. You remind management that a primary reason you must also focus on negative stakeholders is:
a. stakeholder classification can be very difficult
b. overlooking negative stakeholders can decrease the probability of project success
c. stakeholders must be identified and their requirements determined
d. society at large may be a stakeholder on your project

7. Part-time team members are most likely seen in all of the following structures except:
a. functional structure
b. balanced matrix
c. weak matrix
d. projectized structure

8. If a product is required to be delivered in full to have value to the stakeholder groups, we mostly will utilize what type of life cycle?
a. predictive
b. iterative
c. incremental
d. adaptive

9. To ensure benefits realization we often will include:
a. extra money in the budget
b. extra risk mitigation techniques
c. a test period, such as a soft launch in services
d. more monitoring during the execution phase

10. If our project requires very rapid iterations, on-going stakeholder involvement, and high levels of change, we most likely will utilize what type of life cycle?
a. predictive
b. iterative
c. incremental
d. adaptive

11. You have been hired to be the program manager over all of the project managers who work at the help desk. Most of the projects relate to technical issues and are resolved within a 24 hour period. Sometimes the solution to one problem leads to the solution of another problem. The projects managers usually do no planning and spend most of their time trouble shooting one technical problem after another. Their success rate is very high. The best way to describe this situation is a:
a. great example of a successful PMO
b. great example of successful program management on your part
c. great example of an operational type organization
d. great example of portfolio management since the solutions are often interrelated

12. The primary role of a project expeditor is to:
a. ensure communication happens quickly
b. set a good example for communication
c. bring parties together that need to communicate
d. escalate communication issues

ORG INFLUENCES AND LIFE CYCLES: Solutions

1. c. PMBOK® Guide: Section 2.1.3
Y   c. The project expeditor's role on a project is to serve as a communications link.
N   a. The project manager's role is to manage the project, not just serve as a communications link.
N   b. The project coordinator is similar to a project expeditor but has some authority.
N   d. The functional manager directs the work of the individuals in his functional area.

2. a. PMBOK® Guide: Section 2.4.2.2
Y   a. In a predictive life cycle the product to be delivered is often well understood and there is a base on industry practice. The work of each phase is usually different requiring a different team make-up for each phase.
N   b., c., and d. Interactive, incremental, and adaptive life cycles are not fully plan driven. Activities are intentionally repeated.

3. c. PMBOK® Guide: Section 2.4.1 (implied but not explicitly stated)
Y   c. Change requests are often initiated by stakeholders who were not involved in early project planning.
N   a. There is nothing in the question that states the project is in trouble from a cost standpoint. Don't draw conclusions that are not in the question.
N   b. There is nothing in the question that states the project is in trouble from a schedule standpoint. Don't draw conclusions that are not in the question.
N   d. Quality assurance is the application of quality activities to ensure the project will meet requirements. Quality assurance is about applying processes. This answer is not related to the question.

4. c. PMBOK® Guide: Section 2.4.2.1
Y   c. Fast tracking may increase the risk of rework.
N   a. Resource leveling and resource smoothing may lead to increased resource optimization.
N   b. The critical chain method may lead to the use of buffers to account for project uncertainty.
N   d. Fast tracking often leads to increased project risk as we are performing activities in parallel that we would prefer to perform in series.

5. b. PMBOK® Guide: Section 2.2.2
Y   b. Governance is a project framework in which decisions are made.
N   a. The project plan describes the plan and baselines for the project. As an example, it would not include the decision-making models. These more likely would be part of governance.
N   c. The change control system describes the process for making changes to the project.
N   d. The project management information system is an environmental factor that links us to other systems on the project such as the scheduling tool.

6. b. PMBOK® Guide: Section 2.2.1
Y   b. There must be a focus on negative stakeholders because ignoring these stakeholders can increase the risk of not achieving project success.
N   a. Stakeholder classification can be difficult but this does not explain why we need to put a focus on negative stakeholders.

N c. The statement that stakeholders must be identified and their requirements determined is true. This does not explain why we need to focus on negative stakeholders.

N d. Society at large may be a stakeholder on our project yet this does not explain why we need to put a focus on negative stakeholders.

7. d. PMBOK® Guide: Section 2.3.1

Y d. Notice that this question is asking for the exception. In a projectized structure team members are full-time.

N a., b., and c. In a functional, balanced matrix, and weak matrix, project team members are often only part-time. They spend their other time supporting other projects or performing non-project work.

8. a. PMBOK® Guide: Section 2.4.2.2

Y a. In a predictive (fully plan-driven) life cycle the project is often divided into sequential phases. The product is often delivered and ownership transitioned at the end of the last phase.

N b., c., and d. Interactive, incremental, and adaptive life cycles are not fully plan driven. Incremental deliverables are often useful to the project stakeholders. An incremental deliverable might be several pages for a website. These pages might be useful as other pages are being developed.

9. c. PMBOK® Guide: Section 2.2.3

Y c. A soft launch, such as the opening of a restaurant for only family members of the staff, is often used to ensure proper operation of a service.

N a. and b. "Extra" is not a good word from the standpoint of project management. We should develop the appropriate budget including contingency funds based on risk management, but this would not be considered extra.

N d. We should monitor and control appropriately. Think of the phrase "quality should be planned in, not inspected in." Even though this question is not directly about quality, the same ideas apply.

10. d. PMBOK® Guide: Section 2.4.2.4

Y d. The key phrase in the question is: rapid iterations. This leads us to an adaptive (Agile) life cycle.

N a. A predictive (fully plan-driven) life cycle is designed for projects in which we really understand the product and do not want rapid iterations.

N b. and c. While Interactive and incremental life cycles allow for many interactions it is the word "rapid" that makes these the wrong answers.

11. c. PMBOK® Guide: Section 1.5

Y c. The critical phrase in the question relates to "no planning". This phrase tells us we are not talking about project management, program management or portfolio management.

12. c. Verma, *Organizing Projects for Success*, page 148

Y c. A communications expeditor is one who brings parties together to communicate.

N a., b., and d. The expeditor may do all these things, but these are not the primary role of the expeditor.

PROJECT MANAGEMENT PROCESSES

This chapter is an overview of the PMBOK® Guide, including the five (5) process groups. Remember there are 47 processes in these five process groups. Many of these processes will be repeated in each of the phases of your project.

Types of processes: the book and the exam will focus on the project management processes.

- ***Project management processes*** - these are the 47 processes.

- ***Product-oriented processes*** - these processes are specific to the product, service, or result you are creating from the project. While these are important to your project, they are different from project to project, and therefore not on the exam and not covered in this book.

☑ **EXAM TIP:** Review and understand Figure 3-1 (page 50) of the PMBOK® Guide. Notice how the monitoring and controlling process group surrounds the other process groups. Visualize that monitoring and controlling is happening all the time (it is not a phase).

Process groups- we have already mentioned there are 5 process groups.

- ***Initiating process group*** - these are the processes to help us get a project or a phase of a project started. We have two initiating processes. The first initiating process, develop project charter, occurs outside the boundaries of the project.

- ***Planning process group*** - these are the processes used to develop a plan for the project including developing our project baselines (scope, time, and cost).

- ***Executing process group*** - these are the processes used to follow the plan and create the deliverables of the project. A majority of the project budget is spent during executing.

- ***Monitoring and Controlling process group*** - these are the processes used to track how we are doing on the project as well as initiate and manage changes. These processes are occurring all the time, even as the processes of the other groups are occurring. Notice in Figure 3-1 of the PMBOK® Guide how monitoring and controlling surrounds the other processes.

- ***Closing process group*** - these are the processes used to close out a project or a phase of the project.

Project Information - lots of data, information and reports will be collected and created on the project.

© Jan 2016 AME Group, Inc. author Aileen Ellis, PMP, PgMP
aileen@amegroupinc.com 719-659-3658

Work performance data	This is the raw data that comes from the process of direct and manage project work. No other process produces this data.
Work performance information	The data is analyzed and compared to the project baselines to create useful information. Decisions may be based off of information, not the raw data. Only monitoring and controlling processes transforms work performance data into work performance information.
Work performance reports	The product created (physical or electronic) from the work performance information. Realize that different stakeholders will need different reports.

☑ **EXAM TIP:** Review and understand Figure 3-5 (page 59) of the PMBOK® Guide. Know for example:
- work performance data is an output of project execution
- work performance data is an input to controlling processes
- etc.

Once this Figure makes sense, review and understand Figure X1-1 (page 467) of the PMBOK® Guide. Know for example:
- work performance information is an input of monitor and control project work
- work performance reports are an output of monitor and control project work
- etc.

Role of the knowledge areas- The 47 processes are not only grouped into the five (5) process groups but they are also grouped into ten (10) knowledge areas. See Table A1-1 from the PMBOK® Guide for the five process groups, the ten knowledge areas, and the 47 processes.

☑ **EXAM TIPS:** For the Exam:
- Be able to reproduce Table A1-1 from memory. This includes:
    - Names of ten (10) knowledge areas and what processes are in each knowledge area
    - Names of five (5) process groups and what processes are in each process group
- Know the tools and techniques (in detail) for each of the 47 processes
- Know the inputs and outputs (in less detail) for each of the 47 processes

PROJECT MANAGEMENT PROCESSES - Sample Questions

1. The five project management process groups include:
a. initiating, planning, executing, monitoring and controlling
b. integration, scope, time, cost, and quality
c. initiating, planning, executing, monitoring and controlling, and closing
d. concept, planning, execution, controlling, and closeout

2. Implementation status for change requests is an example of:
a. element of the project plan
b. work performance reports
c. work performance information
d. work performance data

3. Work performance data is:
a. an input to project execution
b. an output of project execution
c. an input into close project or phase
d. an output of overall project control

4. Large and complex projects are often separated into distinct phases. The five process groups are:
a. the same as these project phases
b. normally repeated in each of these phases
c. related to the product and, therefore, not related to the project phases
d. related to project management and therefore not related to the project phases

5. The processes of which process group are normally performed external to the project's level of control?
a. initiating
b. planning
c. executing
d. monitoring and controlling

6. In multi-phase projects, the initiating processes occur:
a. only during the concept phase
b. in every phase
c. only in the early phases
d. only when the sponsor requests them

7. The project becomes officially authorized through the:
a. approval of the concept phase gate
b. approval of the project charter
c. approval of the WBS
d. approval of the scope statement

8. Work performance information is often:
a. an input into project execution
b. an output of project execution
c. an output of controlling processes
d. an output of closing processes

© January 2016 AME Group, Inc. author Aileen Ellis, PMP, PgMP
aileen@amegroupinc.com 719-659-3658

9. The process group that must provide feedback to implement corrective or preventive action is:
a. planning
b. executing
c. monitoring and controlling
d. implementation

10. The processes that specify and create the project's product are called:
a. project management processes
b. scope management processes
c. product management processes
d. quality management processes

11. The processes of which process group occur at the same time as the processes of all the other process groups?
a. initiating
b. planning
c. executing
d. monitoring and controlling

12. The project statement of work is an input to which process group?
a. initiating
b. planning
c. executing
d. closing

13. The project charter is an input to which process group?
a. initiating
b. planning
c. executing
d. closing

14. Deliverables are an input to which process group?
a. monitoring and controlling
b. planning
c. executing
d. closing

15. Accepted deliverables are an input to which process group?
a. initiating
b. planning
c. executing
d. closing

16. Approved change requests are an input into which process group?
a. initiating
b. planning
c. executing
d. closing

17. Actual start and finish dates of schedule activities are an example of:
a. elements of the project plan
b. work performance reports
c. work performance information
d. work performance data

18. The stakeholder register is an input into which process group?
a. initiating
b. planning
c. executing
d. closing

19. The vast majority of the project budget is spent during which process group?
a. initiating
b. planning
c. executing
d. monitoring and controlling

20. Electronic dashboards are an example of:
a. deliverables
b. work performance reports
c. work performance information
d. work performance data

PROJECT MANAGEMENT PROCESSES: Solutions

1. c.   PMBOK° Guide: Chapter 3 - Introduction

Y   c. The five project management process groups are initiating, planning, executing, monitoring and controlling, and closing.

N   a. Monitoring and controlling together are the fourth process group; they are not two separate groups. Closing is not on this list.

N   b. Integration, scope, time, cost, and quality are knowledge areas, not process groups.

N   d. Concept, execution, and closeout are often names for phases of a project life cycle, not the five project management process groups.

2. c.   PMBOK° Guide: Section 3.8

Y   c. Work performance information includes performance data that has been analyzed.

N   a. The project plan includes sub-plans and baselines. It does not include the collected performance data.

N   b. The work performance reports are documents (physical or electronic).

N   d. The work performance data is raw observations and measurements, not in context to the performance set-up in the project plan.

3. b.   PMBOK° Guide: Figure 3-5

Y   b. Work performance data is the raw observations and measurements from executing. This is the data before it has been processed through the controlling processes and turned into work performance information.

4. b.   PMBOK° Guide: Section 3.2

Y   b. The five process groups are normally repeated in each project phase. The process groups are not the project phases themselves.

N   a. The project life cycle typically defines the product oriented processes.

N   c. The five project management process groups are related to the project, not the product.

N   d. Projects are managed through the five process groups, and the five process groups are repeated in each of the project phases.

5. a.   PMBOK° Guide: Section 3.3

Y   a. Initiating is about the formal authorization to start a new project or project phase. Initiating processes (specifically develop project charter) are often performed outside of the project's scope of control. This, at times, may blur the project boundaries.

N   b., c., and d. The planning, executing, and monitoring and controlling processes are all completed internal to the project's scope of control.

6. b.   PMBOK° Guide: Section 3.3

Y   b. The initiating processes are repeated at the start of every phase. Reviewing the initiating processes at the beginning of every phase helps to keep the project focused.

7. b.   PMBOK° Guide: Section 3.3

Y   b. The project charter authorizes the project or the project phase.

N   a. The approval of the concept phase gate signifies that the work of the concept phase is complete.

N   c. The approval of the WBS, and the scope statement before it, signifies that we have a scope baseline, which is completed after the project is authorized.

N   d. The scope statement is the definition of the project, which is completed after the project is authorized.

8. c. PMBOK® Guide: Figure 3-5

Y   c. Work performance information is the performance data that has been analyzed and integrated in context during many of the controlling processes. Therefore, it is an output of the controlling processes.

9. c. PMBOK® Guide: Section 3.6

Y   c. The monitoring and controlling process group provides feedback to implement corrective or preventive actions to bring the project into compliance with the project management plan or to appropriately modify the project management plan.

N   a. The planning process group defines the course of action required to attain the objectives and the scope the project was undertaken to address.

N   b. The executing process group integrates people and other resources to carry out the project management plan for the project.

N   d. There is no such thing as an implementation process group.

10. c. PMBOK® Guide: Chapter 3 - introduction

Y   c. The product management processes are the processes used to create the project's product.

N   a. The 47 project management processes are for the project. These 47 processes are often repeated in each of the project phases, regardless of the project's product.

N   b. The scope processes are used to ensure we perform all the work, and only the work required on the project.

N   d. The quality processes are used to ensure we achieve the project's objectives.

11. d. PMBOK® Guide: Section 3.1

Y   d. This may be a confusing idea. Lots of people think that we monitor and control only after executing. Don't think of monitoring as a phase of the project. It is not a phase. It is something that we are continuously doing.

12. a. PMBOK® Guide: Figure 3-3

Y   a. The project statement of work describes the output the customer (or sponsor) wants from the project. The document is written before the project begins. Therefore, it is an input to the initiating process group.

13. b. PMBOK® Guide: Figure 3-3

Y   b. The project charter is an output of the process develop project charter. It is an output of the initiating process group and therefore an input of the planning process group. The charter lists the project objectives. These objectives need to be defined before project planning may begin.

14. a. PMBOK® Guide: Figure 3-3

Y   a. The deliverables are an output of the executing process group. They are the reason we have projects. The deliverables lead to the objectives. The deliverables are an input to the monitoring and controlling process group. In the monitoring and controlling process group, they go to control quality to be tested for correctness. After that, they go to validate scope for the customer (or sponsor) to inspect them for acceptance. Accepted deliverables are an input to the closing process group.

15. d. PMBOK® Guide: Figure 3-3

Y   d. Accepted deliverables are an output of the process validate scope, which is part of the monitoring and controlling process group. Once the accepted deliverables leave the monitoring and controlling process group, they become an input to the closing process group. The output of the closing process group is final product, service, or result transition.

 © January 2016 AME Group, Inc. author Aileen Ellis, PMP, PgMP
aileen@amegroupinc.com 719-659-3658

16. c. PMBOK° Guide: Figure 3-3

Y   c. Change requests are an output of most of the executing processes and all of the monitoring and controlling processes. The change requests are an input to the integrated change control process. If the requests are approved, they are fed back into the direct and manage project work for implementation.

17. d. PMBOK° Guide: Section 3.8

Y   d. Actual start and finish dates are raw data.

N   a. The planned start and finish dates, not the actual start and finish dates are in the project plan.

N   b. Work performance reports are the physical representation of the work performance information.

N   c. Work performance information would contrast the actual start and finish dates in context against the planned start and finish dates.

18. b. PMBOK° Guide: Figure 3-3

Y   b. The stakeholder register is an output of the process identify stakeholders, which is part of the initiating process group. It becomes an input to the planning process group. As an example the stakeholder register becomes an input to the process collect requirements which is a process in the planning process group.

19. c. PMBOK° Guide: Section 3.5

Y   c. The executing process group is where a majority of the project budget is spent.

N   a. More money is spent during executing than during initiating.

N   b. The planning processes develop the project plan. More money is spent executing the project plan than developing the project plan.

N   d. The monitoring and controlling processes observe project execution. Potential problems are analyzed and corrective action taken. More money is spent in general on executing than monitoring and controlling.

20. b. PMBOK° Guide: Section 3.8

Y   b. Electronic dashboards are a way of reporting on information. Therefore, they are an example of work performance reports.

INITIATING PROCESSES

Initiating process group - these are the processes performed to help us get a project or a phase of a project started. We have two initiating processes. The work to develop the project charter, including the creation of the business case occurs outside of the boundaries of the project. The project becomes official once we have a project charter. The second process is identify stakeholders. We not only identify stakeholders in this process but we also analyze and prioritize the stakeholders. The primary outputs of the imitating process group are:
- The project charter
- The stakeholder register

Based on the PMP Examination Content outline published in June of 2015 by PMI there are eight (8) tasks of initiating. These processes represent 13% of your exam content. Key phrases associated with each task are:

Task	Key Words
Task 1	Perform project assessment
Task 2	Identify key stakeholders
Task 3	Perform stakeholder analysis
Task 4	Identify high level risks, assumptions and constraints
Task 5	Participate in the development of the project charter
Task 6	Obtain project charter approval from the sponsor
Task 7	Conduct benefit analysis
Task 8	Inform stakeholders of approved charter

The last table lists the key words for the tasks of the Initiating Process Group. These tasks are not listed in the PMBOK® Guide. These tasks come from the PMP® Exam Content Outline. You do not need to memorize these tasks for the exam. It is good though for you to review them from time to time because truly these 8 tasks are the basis for the questions on Initiating on the PMP® Exam. This Content Outline is absolutely an outline and therefore not robust enough to guide our studying in depth. Therefore almost everyone, if not everyone uses the PMBOK® Guide as their main reference when studying. The PMBOK® Guide includes processes not tasks. In the next few pages we cover the two processes of the Initiating Process Group based on the PMBOK® Guide. If you try you can see how these tasks relate well to the processes.

Develop Project Charter

☑ **Exam Tip:** Review Figure 4-3 of the PMBOK® Guide.

The charter is the document that formally shows we have an approved project. It should name the project manager and state what level of authority we have on this project. In general, the charter is signed by the project sponsor.

INPUTs of Develop Project Charter:

☑ **EXAM TIP:** The project statement of work (PSOW) is often confused with the scope statement. The scope statement is developed by the project manager along with members of the team to describe the work they are going to do on the project to deliver what is described in the PSOW.

Project Statement of Work (PSOW)- describes the output that someone wants from the project.
- For internal projects this document comes from the project sponsor
- For external projects this documents comes from the customer

The Business Case- this document describes the return on investment expected from the project. The return on investment may be in money or some other measure such as employee satisfaction.

Agreements- this document is between the organization and another group. As an example, if the customer is external, the agreement would be in the form of a contract.

Organizational process assets- these are the processes, etc. of the organization that help with the process of develop project charter. Examples include:
- Process- we have a process that tells us how to develop a project charter
- Template- we have a template to complete, instead of writing the charter from scratch
- Historical information- we have past project charters, etc. to write the current charter

TOOLs and TECHNIQUEs of develop project charter

Expert Judgment- go out and seek expertise to help you with your work on projects. Experts can be anyone and everyone who has knowledge that may help you.

Facilitation techniques- use these techniques to help you work with stakeholders as you develop the charter. These techniques will be used in many other project management processes.

OUTPUTs of Develop Project Charter:

Project Charter- this is a critical document. The issuing of this document by the project sponsor tells the organization that we have an official project. It should list the project objectives as well as name the project manager. Most of the other information in this document will be high-level but it gives us enough to be able to start identifying the stakeholders and then begin planning.

☑ **EXAM TIP:** The work to develop the charter is completed outside of the boundaries of the project. The project manager is involved but usually does not own the development or the approval of the project charter.

A few other ideas that may be on the exam that are not found in the PMBOK® Guide.

Project Selection – may include:
Constrained optimization methods such as linear programming.

☑ **EXAM TIP:** Any project selection method that ends with the word "programming" is a constrained optimization method. You need to recognize the list only, not be able to explain them.

Project Selection – may also include:
Cost-benefit analysis- an accounting idea used to determine if it is worthwhile to invest in a project and also used to compare projects.

☑ **EXAM TIP:** For the exam we need to know that the higher the benefit/cost ratio is the better. Benefit/cost ratio is sometimes abbreviated as B/C.

Internal Rate of Return (IRR)- an accounting idea used to compare the profitability of investments.

☑ **EXAM TIP:** For the exam we need to know the higher the IRR the better.

Payback period- an accounting idea used to determine the breakeven point on a project.

☑ **EXAM TIP:** For the exam we need to know the shorter the payback period the better.

© January 2016 AME Group, Inc. author Aileen Ellis, PMP, PgMP
aileen@amegroupinc.com 719-659-3658

Economic value added (EVA)- EVA is the profit earned by the firm less the cost of financing the firm's capital. (likely as a wrong answer on the exam).

Present Value (PV)- an accounting idea used to determine the value today of future cash flows.

> ☑ **EXAM TIP:** For the exam we need to know that the higher the present value the better. We may also need an equation:
>
> $PV = FV/(1+i)^t$
> FV-future value, i= interest rate, t= time

Net Present Value (PV)- The word net here means difference. The net present value looks at the difference (the net) between the project benefits and the project investment.

> ☑ **EXAM TIP:** For the exam we need to know that the higher the net present value the better. We may also need to use the present value equation.
>
> **NPV Example:**
> Project A has an initial investment at the start of the project of $100,000. At the end of year one there is a benefit of $50,000 and at the end of year two there is another benefit of $50,000. There are no other benefits. Use a discount rate (interest rate) of 10%.
>
> What is the Net Present Value of Project A?
>
> NPV Solution.
> The investment was made at the start of the project. Therefore, the present value (PV) of the investment is a negative $100,000.
> The Present Value of $50,000 received at the end of year 1:
> $PV = FV/(1+i)^t$
> $PV = \$50,000/(1.1)^1$
> $PV = \$45,454.55$
>
> The Present Value of $50,000 received at the end of year 2:
> $PV = FV/(1+i)^t$
> $PV = \$50,000/(1.1)^2$
> $PV = \$41,322.31$
>
> Therefore, the NPV for Project A= $45,454.55+$41,322.31-$100,000
> NPV for Project A= -$13,223.14
> The answer is negative because the benefits are of less value than the investment.
> Realize that Net Present Value is the difference between the benefits received and the investment made.

Develop Project Charter – Sample Questions

1. What document formally authorizes the project?
a. the project statement of work
b. the contract
c. the project charter
d. the business case

2. Who authorizes the project?
a. the project manager
b. the project sponsor
c. the project stakeholders
d. the customer

3. Which of the following is usually included in a project charter?
a. project risk register
b. project work breakdown structure
c. detailed project deliverables
d. project objectives

4. If someone requests a change to the project charter who most likely would need to approve this change?
a. the project manager
b. the project sponsor
c. the project stakeholders
d. the customer

5. Which document is a narrative description of the products or services to be delivered by the project?
a. the project statement of work
b. the contract
c. the project charter
d. the business case

6. The cost-benefit analysis is usually contained in what document?
a. the project statement of work
b. the contract
c. the project charter
d. the business case

7. Which of the following is a legal document between the organization performing the work and the external customer?
a. the organizational process assets
b. the contract
c. the project charter
d. the business case

8. The project charter includes:
a. the project objectives
b. detailed cost estimates
c. the risk management methodology
d. a list of project team members

© January 2016 AME Group, Inc. author Aileen Ellis, PMP, PgMP
aileen@amegroupinc.com 719-659-3658

9. Which of the following is an organizational asset?
a. government standards
b. industry standards
c. marketplace conditions
d. lessons learned knowledge base

10. Which of the following is an enterprise environmental factor?
a. government standards
b. organizational processes
c. templates
d. historical information

11. All of the following are examples of facilitation techniques except:
a. expert judgment
b. brainstorming
c. conflict resolution
d. problem solving

12. When a project is being performed for an outside customer the most likely form of agreement is?
a. service level agreement
b. memorandum of understanding
c. letter of intent
d. contract

13. The portfolio review board is conducting its yearly project selection meeting. Which of the following projects is the review board most likely to choose? Project A with an IRR of 12%, Project B with an IRR of 18%, Project C with an IRR of 9%, or Project D with an IRR of 14%?
a. Project A
b. Project B
c. Project C
d. Project D

14. The portfolio review board is conducting its yearly project selection meeting. Which of the following projects is the review board most likely to choose? Project F with a NPV (net present value) of $235Mil, Project G with a NPV of $282Mil, Project H with a NPV of $821Mil, or Project I with an NPV of $183Mil?
a. Project F
b. Project G
c. Project H
d. Project I

15. The portfolio review board is conducting its yearly project selection meeting. Which of the following projects is the review board most likely to choose? Project J with a payback period of 23 months, Project K with a payback period of 18 months, Project L with a payback period of 42 months, or Project M with a payback period of 38 months?
a. Project J
b. Project K
c. Project L
d. Project M

16. The portfolio review board is conducting its yearly project selection meeting. Which of the following projects is the review board most likely to choose? Project N with a benefit cost ratio of 1.2, Project M with a benefit cost ratio of 1.5, Project P with a benefit cost ratio of .8, or Project Q with a benefit cost ratio of .92?
a. Project N
b. Project M
c. Project P
d. Project Q

17. The portfolio review board is conducting its yearly project selection meeting. The most likely item not to be reviewed during selection is:
a. sunk costs
b. benefit–cost analysis
c. net present value
d. payback period

18. The portfolio steering committee is considering selecting Project A. The committee expects the project will produce a one-time benefit of $900,000 three years from now. The interest rate at a local bank is 10% per year. How much would need to be invested in the bank now to obtain the same benefit?
a. $ 900,000
b. $ 676,183
c. $ 1,197,900
d. $ 743,801

19. The portfolio review board is conducting a project selection review. They are going to make their decision based on the Net Present Value (NPV) Estimates for the projects. The organization has only $100,000 available for investment. Based on the following information which project should they select?
Assume an interest rate of 5%.
Project A- initial investment of $100,000.   Benefit at end of year 1 of $40,000. Additional benefit at end of year 2 of $70,000. No other benefits.
Project B- initial investment of $100,000. No benefit at the end of year 1. Benefit of $42,000 at end of year 2. Additional benefit of $70,000 at end of year 3.
a. Project A
b. Project B
c. Both projects since they each have a positive net present value.
d. Neither project since they each have a negative net present value.

© January 2016 AME Group, Inc. author Aileen Ellis, PMP, PgMP
aileen@amegroupinc.com 719-659-3658

DEVELOP PROJECT CHARTER - Solutions

1. c. PMBOK° Guide: Section 4.1.3.1

Y   c. The charter is the official document that signifies we have an approved project.

N   a. The project statement of work is a narrative description of the output the customer would like from the project.

N   b. The contract is a legal document between our external customer and our organization. We still need an internal document (the charter) to show we have an approved project. A contract many be split into many projects.

N   d. The business case shows the return on investment for the project. It still does not signify that a project has been approved.

2. b. PMBOK° Guide: Section 4.1

Y   b. The sponsor is the best answer.

N   a. The project manager can not authorize his/her own project. It must be someone higher up in the organization.

N   c. The answer project stakeholders is too broad. Yes, the sponsor is a stakeholder but that does not make this a good answer.

N   d. The customer may be external. They would not be able to authorize the project. Even if the customer is internal, they most likely could not authorize the project.

3. d. PMBOK° Guide: Section 4.1.3.1

Y   d. The primary item documented in the charter is the project objective(s).

N   a., b., and c. These documents are too detailed. They would be created later during planning.

4. b. PMBOK° Guide: Section 4.1 (not explicitly stated)

Y   b. Think of the sponsor as the owner of the charter. He is the only one who could approve changes to the charter.

N   a. The charter names the project manager and describes the level of authority of the project manager. Therefore, the project manager could not authorize changes to it.

N   c. The answer project stakeholders is too broad. Yes, the sponsor is a stakeholder but that does not make this a good answer.

N   d. The customer most likely would never even see the project charter, let alone be able to approve changes to it. (For the exam, make sure you understand the difference between the sponsor and the customer).

5. a. PMBOK° Guide: Section 4.1.1.1

Y   a. The project statement of work is a narrative description of the output the customer would like from the project.

N   b. The contract is a legal document between our external customer and our organization. It may reference the project statement of work.

N   c. The charter is the official document that signifies we have an approved project. It should contain the project objectives.

N   d. The business case shows the return on investment for the project.

6. d. PMBOK° Guide: Section 4.1.1.2

Y   d. The business case shows the return on investment for the project. This may include: cost-benefit analysis, payback period, net present value, etc.

N   a. The project statement of work is a narrative description of the output (products or services) the customer expects from the project.

N   b. The contract is a legal document between our external customer and our organization. It will include the contract price but not the cost-benefit analysis.

N   c. The charter is the official document that signifies we have an approved project. It may include a summary budget but not the cost-benefit analysis.

7. b. PMBOK® Guide: Sections 4.1 and 4.1.1.3

Y   b. The contract is the official, legal document between our organization and our external customer.

N   a., c., and d. These documents are internal documents and not legal documents.

8. a. PMBOK® Guide: Section 4.1.3.1

Y   a. The primary item documented in the charter is the project objective(s).

N   b., c., and d. These ideas are too detailed. They would be created later during planning.

9. d. PMBOK® Guide: Section 4.1.1.5

Y   d. Organizational assets are assets owned by the organization that help us manage processes. Examples include processes, templates, past project documents, and lessons learned.

N   a., b., and c. These examples are enterprise environmental factors, not organizational process assets.

10. a. PMBOK® Guide: Section 4.1.1.4

Y   a. Government standards exist in the environment and do not belong to the organization. Therefore, they are considered enterprise environmental factors.

N   b., c., and d. These are organizational process assets, not enterprise environmental factors.

11. a. PMBOK® Guide: Sections 4.1.2.1 - 4.1.2.2

Y   a. Expert judgment is used to help with many processes, though it is not considered a facilitation technique. A facilitation technique helps us design and run our meetings so they are more successful.

N   b., c., and d. These are all facilitation techniques.

12. d. PMBOK® Guide: Section 4.1.1.3

Y   d. A contract is a legal document between an external customer and our organization.

N   a. Service level agreements may be both legally binding or not (for internal relationships).

N   b. In general a memorandum of understanding defines a future relationship or a relationship when the parties do not want (or need) a legal agreement (a contract).

N   c. Letters of intent are often considered pre-contracts. In general, only some of the elements of the letters are legally enforceable.

13. b. Any accounting book

Y   b. Pick the project with the highest IRR (internal rate of return).

14. c. Any accounting book

Y   c. Pick the project with the highest NPV (net present value).

15. b. Any accounting book

Y   b. Pick the project with the shortest payback period

16. b. Any accounting book

Y   b. Pick the project with the highest benefit cost ratio.

© January 2016 AME Group, Inc. author Aileen Ellis, PMP, PgMP
aileen@amegroupinc.com 719-659-3658

17. a. Any accounting textbook or web search

Y   a. Sunk costs are costs that have already been expended but cannot be recouped. We should not take these into account during project selection.

N   b. We would normally select the projects with the highest benefit-cost ratio. We should take these into account during project selection.

N   c. In general, we want the present value of inflows to be greater than the present value of outflows (a positive net present value) when selecting projects. Thus, we should take into account net present value.

N   d. In general, we want the payback period (the time required for the project to repay its initial investments) to be as short as possible. Thus, we should take into account the payback period.

18. b. Any accounting textbook or web search

Y   b. This question is actually asking us to determine the present value of $900,000.
$PV=FV/(1+i)t$
Present Value= (Future Value) divided by ((one plus the interest rate) to the t power). t equals the number of time periods.
$PV= \$900,000/(1+.1)3 = \$900,000/(1.1) 3 = \$676,183$. The question is asking us about present value (PV), though nowhere in the question is the term present value (PV) used.

19. a. Any accounting textbook or web search

Y   a. Project A has a higher NPV than Project B. The NPV of Project A is a positive number. This means our estimates show we forecast to make money on this project.

Project A
The Present Value of $40,000 received at the end of year 1:
$PV= FV/(1+i)^t$
$PV= \$40,000/(1.05)^1$
$PV= \$38,095.23$
The Present Value of $70,000 received at the end of year 2:
$PV= FV/(1+i)^t$
$PV= \$70,000/(1.05)^2$
$PV= \$63,492.06$
Therefore, the NPV for Project A= $38,095.23+$63,492.06 -$100,000= +$1,587.29

Project B
The Present Value of $42,000 received at the end of year 2:
$PV= FV/(1+i)^t$
$PV= \$42,000/(1.05)^2$
$PV= \$38.095.23$
The Present Value of $70,000 received at the end of year 3:
$PV= FV/(1+i)^t$
$PV= \$70,000/(1.05)^3$
$PV= \$60,468.61$
Therefore, the NPV for Project B= $38,095.23+$60,468.61-$100,000= -$1,436.16

Identify Stakeholders

(Some of you are wondering why this process in next in the book. Remember the book is organized by process group not knowledge area). Go to the PMBOK Guide page 61. This study guide is organized by column not row. We have organized this study guide by process group for several reasons. The primary reason is to make the material in the study guide more realistic and more representative of your real projects and the Exam. We manage projects my process group, not knowledge area.)

☑ **Exam Tip:** Review Figure 13-3 of the PMBOK® Guide.

We want to identify and analyze our project stakeholders early so that we can develop a plan that puts the appropriate amount of focus on each stakeholder(s). Not all stakeholders are the same. We must focus on the most important relationships driving project success.

INPUTs of identify stakeholders (not all listed)

Project charter- the charter will list the name of the sponsor, the project manager, and may list names of other key stakeholders. This is a great place to start as far as identifying stakeholders.

Procurement documents- these documents are an output of plan procurement management. They may list key project stakeholders, specifically vendors, contractors, etc. If our customer is external, the contract may list key stakeholders from within our customer organization.

TOOLs and TECHNIQUEs of identify stakeholders (not all listed)

Stakeholder analysis- this is a way to gather and analyze data about our stakeholders so that we know which stakeholders should have the most focus. At the same time, we want to think about existing relationships and how we can use those relationships to the benefit of the project.

Often this stakeholder analysis is a three (3) step process:
1. Identify all stakeholders and everything we know about them
2. Analyze the impact or support each stakeholder could provide
3. Perform scenario planning- thinking about how each stakeholder would react if different situations occur.

There are several models that may help us with this. As an example: Salience model based on three factors:
- Power- level of authority of each stakeholder
- Urgency- need for immediate attention
- Legitimacy- whether the level of involvement of the stakeholder is appropriate

Where the three (3) circles cross we have our definitive stakeholder.

© January 2016 AME Group, Inc. author Aileen Ellis, PMP, PgMP
aileen@amegroupinc.com 719-659-3658

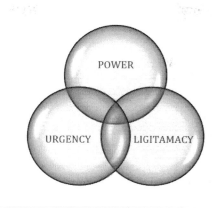

☑ **Exam Tips:** Recognize the three factors.

OUTPUTs of identify stakeholders

Stakeholder register: please see below a simple stakeholder register. Based on your project some elements may be more important than others. This register is a living register. It may need to be updated on a very regular basis as stakeholders join and leave the project or their level of interest and influence changes.

Name	Position	Department	Contact Info	Type	Requirements/ Expectations	Influence Level (1-5)	Interest Level (1-5)	Classification
John Jonathan	VP of Finance	Finance	John@AE.org	Internal	Stay on budget	3	1	neutral
Max Maxwell	Contracting Officer	Contracts	Max@us.gov	External	Deliver on time and on budget	5	2	resistor

IDENTIFY STAKEHOLDERS - Sample Questions

1. Which of the following statements is true about stakeholders?
a. all stakeholders are customers
b. all stakeholders are positive
c. all stakeholders should be classified
d. all stakeholders should be treated the same

2. Stakeholders not being identified or not being identified early enough on a project may increase the risk of all of the following except:
a. more requested changes
b. changes costing more money than they should
c. the deliverable or product being rejected by the customer
d. a smoother running project

3. The project sponsor is usually identified in what document:
a. the project statement of work
b. the project scope statement
c. the project charter
d. the project management plan

4. Which of the following is an organizational process asset?
a. government standards
b. industry standards
c. organizational culture
d. stakeholder register templates

5. Which of the following is an enterprise environmental factor?
a. company culture
b. lessons learned
c. stakeholder register templates
d. historical information from previous projects

6. Which of the following is an input to identify stakeholders:
a. project statement of work
b. business case
c. procurement documents
d. stakeholder register

7. A stakeholder register includes all of the following except:
a. strategy to interact with stakeholders
b. stakeholder classification
c. assessment information
d. identification information

8. Which of the following is a tool and technique of identify stakeholders:
a. stakeholder analysis
b. communications methods
c. organizational theory
d. negotiations

© January 2016 AME Group, Inc. author Aileen Ellis, PMP, PgMP
aileen@amegroupinc.com 719-659-3658

9. One of the key reasons to prioritize stakeholders is to ensure:
a. all stakeholders are treated the same
b. efficient use of effort when communicating with stakeholders
c. each stakeholder gets the same amount of focus
d. no stakeholders are overlooked

10. Which classification model describes classes of stakeholders based on the power, urgency, and legitimacy?
a. power/interest grid
b. power/influence grid
c. influence/impact grid
d. salience model

11. The legitimacy of a stakeholder is often defined as:
a. their ability to impose their will
b. their need for immediate attention
c. their involvement is appropriate
d. their level of concern

IDENTIFY STAKEHOLDERS - Solutions

1. c. PMBOK° Guide: Section 13.1
Y   c. All stakeholders should be classified so as to better manage their expectations.
N   a. All customers are stakeholders but not all stakeholders are customers.
N   b. We wish all stakeholders would be positive but reality tells us differently.
N   d. We want to treat all stakeholders fairly. They may have different needs and different impact and therefore we should not treat them all the same.

2. d. PMBOK° Guide: Section 2.4.1 (implied though not explicitly stated)
Y   d. The earlier we identify and involve our stakeholders, the more likely our project will run more smoothly.
N   a. The earlier we identify and involve our stakeholders, the fewer requested changes we should expect.
N   b. The earlier we identify and involve our stakeholders, the less likely changes will cost more than expected.
N   c. The earlier we identify and involve our stakeholders, the less likely the product will be rejected.

3. c. PMBOK° Guide: Section 13.1.1.1
Y   c. The project charter is issued by the sponsor and should identify both the sponsor and the project manager.
N   a. The project statement of work defines the output the customer is looking for from the project.
N   b. The scope statement describes both the product and the project scope.
N   d. The project management plan includes the baselines as well as the management plans.

4. d. PMBOK° Guide: Sections 13.1.1.3 and 13.1.1.4
Y   d. In general, templates are considered organizational process assets.
N   a., b., and c. Standards and culture are considered enterprise environmental factors.

5. a. PMBOK° Guide: Sections 13.1.1.3 and 13.1.1.4
Y   a. Company culture is an enterprise environmental factor.
N   b., c., and d. Lessons learned: stakeholder register templates and historical information are considered organizational process assets.

6. c. PMBOK° Guide: Section 13.1.1.2
Y   c. Procurement documents are an input of identify stakeholders.
N   a. and b. The project statement of work and the business case are an input to develop project charter.
N   d. The stakeholder register is an output of identify stakeholders.

7. a. PMBOK° Guide: Section 13.1.3.1
Y   a. The stakeholder management plan, not the stakeholder register, describes the strategy for interaction with the project stakeholders.
N   b., c., and d. The stakeholder register addresses: classification, assessment, and identification information.

8. a. PMBOK° Guide: Section 13.1.2.1
Y   a. Stakeholder analysis is a tool and technique of identify stakeholders.
N   b. Communication methods is a tool and technique of both plan communications and manage communications.

N   c. Organizational theory is a tool and technique of plan human resource management.

N   d. Negotiation is a tool and technique of acquire project team.

9. b. PMBOK° Guide: Section 13.1

Y   b. We want to prioritize our stakeholders to ensure each stakeholder gets the appropriate amount of attention.

N   a. and c. We want to treat all stakeholders fairly. They may have different needs and different impacts and therefore we should not treat them the same or give them the same amount of focus.

N   d. We identify all stakeholders to ensure that no one is overlooked. We prioritize stakeholders to ensure each gets the appropriate amount of focus.

10. d. PMBOK° Guide: Section 13.1.2.1

Y   d. The salience model prioritizes based on power, urgency, and legitimacy.

N   a. The power/interest grid prioritizes based on power and interest.

N   b. The power/influence grid prioritizes based on power and influence.

N   c. The influence/impact grid prioritizes based influence and impact.

11. c. PMBOK° Guide: Section 13..1.2.1

Y   c. Legitimacy of stakeholders is defined as whether their involvement is appropriate.

N   a. Power is defined as their ability to impose their will.

N   b. Urgency is defined as their need for immediate attention.

N   d. Interest is defined as their level of concern.

INITIATING-other ideas

These ideas are based on information in the PMP® Exam Content Outline published by PMI® on June 2015 for inclusion on the PMP® Exam beginning January 12, 2016. For the exam you do not need to know which tasks or which knowledge and skills have been added. The information in the tasks and knowledge and skills may be on your PMP® exam.

Initiating Task 2: Identify key deliverables based on business requirements in order to manage customer expectations and direct the achievement of project goals.
Keep in mind that key deliverables should now be listed in the Project Charter.

Initiating Task 7: Conduct Benefit Analysis with relevant stakeholders to validate project alignment with organizational strategy and expected business value.
See Initiating Knowledge and skills below for more on benefits management.

Initiating Task 8: Inform stakeholders of the approved project charter to ensure common understanding of the key deliverables, milestones, and their roles and responsibilities.
While this is a new task in the exam content outline this task has been part of this study guide for years.

Initiating Knowledge and Skills

Analytical skills:
Analytical skill is the ability to visualize, articulate, conceptualize or solve both complex and uncomplicated problems by making decisions that are sensible given the available information. Such skills include demonstration of the ability to apply logical thinking to gathering and analyzing information, designing and testing solutions to problems, and formulating plans.
One use of analytical techniques is to forecast potential outcomes. Analytical techniques are used in many project management processes.

Benefits analysis techniques:
Benefits management may be thought as a five step process though this process is not found in the PMBOK® Guide.
.

1. Benefits identification. Key output is the benefits register. The benefits register should list the planned benefits and is used to communicate and measure the delivery of benefits throughout the project (and or program).
2. Benefits analysis and planning. Key outputs include:
   a. Benefits realization plan- documents the strategy to achieve benefits.
   b. Benefits metrics- may be included in the benefits realization plan. The metrics should include the key performance indicators (KPIs).
3. Benefits delivery. Benefits may be delivered during the life of the project, the program or after the project and program have completed.
4. Benefits transition. The objective is to ensure that the benefits are transitioned to operational areas and can be sustained. Value is only obtained when the intended recipients are able to utilize the benefits.
5. Benefits sustainment. The objective is to ensure that the intended recipients have full responsibility for the ongoing benefits.

© January 2016 AME Group, Inc. author Aileen Ellis, PMP, PgMP
aileen@amegroupinc.com 719-659-3658

Elements of a project charter:

The following are typical elements found in the project charter.
- Project purpose and justification
- Measurable project objectives
- Key Deliverables – this may be a new item in your list
- Project manager- name and authority level
- Sponsor- name and authority level
- Many other elements- most of the other elements are at a high or summary level and will become more detailed during project planning

Remember that the project manager participates in the development of the project charter but usually the project manager does not own the development or the approval of the project charter.

Estimating tools and techniques:

An estimate is a quantitative assessment of the likely amount or outcome. Estimates are outputs of many project processes specifically in the cost and time knowledge areas. Estimates should always include some indication of accuracy.

Based on the *Practice Standard for Project Estimating* published by PMI® in 2011 there is a four stage life cycle for project estimating:
1. Prepare to estimate – includes items such as determining the estimating approach, the estimating team, constraints to the estimates, etc.
2. Create estimates – includes estimating costs, resources, durations
3. Manage estimates – after the project work has started, the stage may include change control, comparing actuals to baseline estimates, calibrating the forecast
4. Improve estimating process- applying lessons learned to the project estimating life cycle

Strategic Alignment: ensuring the organization's strategic objectives are achieved through program and project implementation.

Other critical ideas:

Vision: the desired future state of an organization, program or project

Mission: the purpose of an organization, program or project

Values: important and lasting beliefs. Often an organization's values are a critical input to decision making.

MINI TEST after INITIATING PROCESSES - Sample Questions

Strong suggestion: Do not write on these questions so you may attempt them again later. Realize these questions are coming from all areas of the PMP® Exam and many are coming from outside of the PMBOK® Guide. After you have completed each of the other process groups come back and try these questions again.

1. As a young and inexperienced project manager you work very hard to follow your organization's policies and procedures. It seems though that not all work follows according to policy. You are working to understand the organization's culture and style. To do this well it very importantly for you to identify:
a. who are the most experienced technical people in the organization
b. who are the decision makers and influencers in the organization
c. who sits where on the organizational chart
d. who sits where on the organizational breakdown structure

2. Many models exist for stakeholder analysis. It has been requested by the sponsor that we should use the salience model as part of initiating the project. The model looks at stakeholders from the views of :
a. legitimacy, power and influence
b. power, interest and impact
c. influence, impact and power
d. power, urgency and legitimacy

3. The document that lists the project's planned benefits including a status or progress indicator for each benefit is:
a. benefits realization plan
b. benefits register
c. benefits transition plan
d. benefits sustainment plan

4. During project initiating a project assessment should be performed based upon available information including lessons learned from previous projects. These lessons learned are often found in the:
a. organizational process assets
b. enterprise environmental factors
c. project charter
d. stakeholder register

5. All of the following are examples of benefits except:
a. improved moral
b. market share increased
c. training class delivered
d. strength of competitor reduced

6. Kanban is based on a pull system. One of the characteristics of a pull system as opposed to a push system is:
a. less inventory on hand
b. inventory based on historical ordering patterns instead of demand driven
c. longer time to respond to changing market demands
d. more likely to deal with product obsolescence issues

© January 2016 AME Group, Inc. author Aileen Ellis, PMP, PgMP
aileen@amegroupinc.com 719-659-3658

7. During the implementation phase of your project many deliverables have been produced on time and on budget. At this point it is important that the deliverables are tested to determine if we are building the correct product. Most likely we determine this during which process?
a. collect requirements
b. perform quality assurance
c. control quality
d. validate scope

8. Knowledge transfer can be a very costly and time-consuming activity. It is important to assess the benefits of the knowledge transferred. One way to assess the benefits is:
a. HR systems tracking of competence, expertise, etc.
b. knowledge transfer-related software resources
c. inventory of knowledge assets
d. project success rates

9. While using key performance indicators (KPI), many organizations focus on how many issues are found by our customers. This KPI would be considered a:
a. qualitative indicator
b. financial indicator
c. leading indicator
d. lagging indicator

10. Active listening is simple in theory but in reality may be a very difficult task. When active listening is used properly there may be many benefits excluding:
a. a shift response
b. a resolved conflict
c. avoiding misunderstanding
d. building trust

11. Alexandra has been working very successfully as a project manager for over ten years. Alexandra's mentor wants her to continue to progress and therefore has recommended she develop more skills related to business acumen. An example of business acumen is:
a. spending time with business leaders as social event
b. cutting project costs so as to protect the business
c. learning more about the organization's financial goals
d. using "business buzz words" when interacting with members of the business units

12. An organization scoring low on Hofstede's dimension for masculinity believes in:
a. equal opportunities in jobs and education
b. need to be in charge
c. more job stress
d. traditional sex roles

13. Your organization provides 360 degree feedback for all project managers. This means that not only is your manager reviewing you but that your team members also have an opportunity to provide feedback to you. Your team tells you that at times you do not consider their feelings, especially when you are making decisions. Based on Daniel Goleman's mixed model for emotional intelligence you need to work more on:
a. self-awareness
b. self-regulation
c. social skills
d. empathy

14. You are working to establish essential practices for decisions. In simplistic terms you want to ensure all of the following except:
a. decision makers have the right information to make decisions
b. all project stakeholders have a voice in project decisions
c. organizations provide adequate attention to risk management
d. decision makers are familiar with organizational strategy

15. You and your project management team are deep into project planning. You have decided to bring in a facilitator from another part of the organization to facilitate a critical meeting. Often we use a facilitator in order to:
a. have a outside party support our position
b. allow us be an active participant in the meeting
c. force the use of meeting tools such as nominal group technique
d. ensure we mix meeting types to save time and effort

16. In our project management office is has been determined that collectively we have a lot of experience but individually we are lacking. Therefore peer-reviews will be held before important reports are published. One of the primary outcomes of a peer-review is:
a. the project manager feels threatened
b. discussions become very defensive
c. comments are taken personally
d. documents or projects continue to improve with each implementation

17. Which of the following is true about the project processes?
a. all processes should be repeated in every project phase
b. the level of rigor applied for each process may be adjusted for different projects
c. the project charter is the first of seven processes of the initiating process group
d. work performance reports are an input to monitor and control project work

18. Work performance data is an output of which process?
a. develop project management plan
b. direct and manage project work
c. monitor and control project work
d. perform integrated change control

19. Work performance reports are an output of which process?
a. develop project management plan
b. direct and manage project work
c. monitor and control project work
d. perform integrated change control

© January 2016 AME Group, Inc. author Aileen Ellis, PMP, PgMP
aileen@amegroupinc.com 719-659-3658

20. Expert judgment is:
a. an input to all integration processes
b. an output of all integration processes
c. a tool and technique of all integration processes
d. an input and an output of all integration processes

21. The project management information system is a tool and technique of which process(es)?
a. develop project charter and develop project management plan
b. develop project management plan and direct and manage project work
c. direct and manage project work and monitor and control project work
d. monitor and control project work and close project or phase

22. Change control tools are a tool and technique of which process?
a. develop project management plan
b. direct and manage project work
c. monitor and control project work
d. perform integrated change control

23. Historically, your organization has struggled with scope management. While running projects it is often confusing to the team what work will be part of the project and what work will not be part of the project. Therefore, you have decided on your current project to put a much stronger focus on scope management. At an early team meeting the members of the core team are arguing as to what is really the first thing to do to address this issue. You tell them we must focus first on:
a. working with stakeholders to understand their real needs before we develop requirements
b. developing a scope management plan
c. defining in detail what is in scope and what is out of scope
d. building a solid work breakdown structure that represents 100% of the project work

24. The deliverables are accepted by the customer as part of what process?
a. plan scope management
b. validate scope
c. define scope
d. create WBS

25. Variance analysis is a tool and technique of which process?
a. plan scope management
b. validate scope
c. define scope
d. control scope

26. Completion of project scope is measured against:
a. the project charter
b. the project management plan
c. the schedule
d. the budget

27. Product analysis is a tool and technique of which process?
a. plan scope management
b. validate scope
c. define scope
d. create WBS

28. Completion of the product scope is measured against?
a. the scope management plan
b. the requirements management plan
c. the project management plan
d. the product requirements

29. Historically, your organization has struggled with schedule management. While running projects it is often confusing to the team what work should begin when and how the activities interact with each other. Therefore, you have decided on your current project to put a much stronger focus on schedule management. At an early team meeting the members of the core team are arguing as to what is really the first thing to do to address this issue. You tell them we must focus first on:
a. developing a strong schedule model using schedule data and a scheduling tool
b. understanding dependencies between schedule activities
c. assigning resources to schedule activities
d. building the schedule management plan

30. Example of scheduling methods include:
a. activity list, bar chart, network diagram
b. WBS, activities, resources, dependencies
c. critical path method, critical chain method
d. define activities, sequence activities, estimate activity resources

31. Examples of project schedule presentations include:
a. activity list, bar chart, network diagram
b. WBS, activities, resources, dependencies
c. critical path method, critical chain method
d. define activities, sequence activities, estimate activity resources

32. Examples of project schedule data or information include:
a. activity list, bar chart, network diagram
b. WBS, activities, resources, dependencies
c. critical path method, critical chain method
d. define activities, sequence activities, estimate activity resources

33. The document that defines the scheduling method and scheduling tool, as well as sets the format for the schedule is called:
a. the activity list
b. the project schedule network diagram
c. the schedule baseline
d. the schedule management plan

34. The schedule model:
a. is the scheduling tool populated with project data
b. identifies the scheduling method and scheduling tool
c. is the same as the schedule presentation
d. is developed from the project schedule

© January 2016 AME Group, Inc. author Aileen Ellis, PMP, PgMP
aileen@amegroupinc.com 719-659-3658

MINI TEST after INITIATING PROCESSES - Solutions

1. b. *PMBOK® Guide Section 2.1.1*
Y   b. As the project manager we should identify who are the decision makers and influencers in the organization and work with them to increase the probability of project success.

2. d. *PMBOK® Guide* section 13.1.2.1
Y   d. The salience model analyzes stakeholders based on power (ability to impose their will), urgency (need for immediate attention) and legitimacy (the involvement is appropriate).

3. b.
Y   b. The benefits register lists the project's planned benefits including a status or progress indicator for each benefit. Not all projects have a benefits register. The benefits register is often maintained at the program level.
a. The benefits realization plan describes our strategy to realize the benefits.
c. The benefits transition plan describes our strategy to transition ownership of the benefits to another organization.
d. The benefits sustainment plan describes the strategy to maintain the benefits long-term.

4. a. *PMBOK® Guide Section 2.1.4*
Y   a. Lessons learned are part of the organization's knowledge base and should be included in the organizational process assets.

5. c
Y   c. A training class delivered is an example of a deliverable not a benefit.

6. a.
Y   a. With a pull system we carry less inventory as inventory is based on demand instead of history.

7. d. *PMBOK Guide Section 5.5*
Y   d. During validate scope the customer tests the product to determine if we have built the right product.
N   c. During control quality we test to determine if we built the product correctly.

8 d.
Y   d. Project success rates are one way to measure the benefits of knowledge transfer.
N   a, b and c are all technologies used to apply transferred knowledge. These are not methods for assessing the value or benefits of the knowledge transfer.

9. d.
Y   d. How many issues our customers find each month is a lagging indicator. A lagging indicator tells us what has already occurred.
N   a. A qualitative indicator is an indicator that cannot be measured numerically. Often they are a descriptive or an opinion.
N   b. A financial indicator is measured in monetary terms.
N   c. A leading indicator is forward looking and helps predict the future.

10. a.
Y   a. A shift response is the tendency of a listener to turn the conversation to a focus on them without showing sustained interest in the speaker. This should not occur if active listening is used correctly.

11. c. Web search on Business Acumen
Y   c. An example of business acumen is learning more about the organization including financial goals.

12. a. Web search on Geert Hofstede
Y   a. A low score on Hofstede's dimension for masculinity means we support more stereotypical feminine ideas.
N   b. c. and d. A high score on Hofstede's dimension for masculinity means we support more stereotypical masculine ideas.

13. d. Wikipedia on Emotional Intelligence
Y   d. Empathy is the ability to understand and share the feelings of others. In this example our team is telling us that we do not demonstrate empathy.

14. b. *PMBOK® Guide Section X3.6*
Y   b. This question is asking for the exception. There are times when the project manager should make certain decisions alone and there are times when certain stakeholders should have a voice in project decisions. I would eliminate this answer specifically because it uses the word "all". All is an extreme word. We may have thousands of stakeholders on our projects.

15. b.
Y   b. We use facilitators so that we the project manager may be an active participant in meetings.
N   a. The facilitator should be neutral and not support or weaken our positions.
N   c. I would eliminate this answer because of the word "force". Nominal group technique is not appropriate in every meeting.
N   d. We should not mix meeting types. This is a standard rule for meetings. (*PMBOK® Guide Section 4.3.2.3*).

16. d.
Y   d. The goal of a peer review is for the project manager to learn from his peers and thus improve the documents or the projects.
N   a., b. and c. All three of these answers are negatives. On the exam if you are asked about the outcome of implementing a best practice look for the positive answer.

17. b. PMBOK˚ Guide: Chapter 4 - Introduction
Y   b. The project manager and the project management team should decide how much rigor to apply for each process.
N   a. We should use only the processes we need. As an example, we may not need all the procurement processes in every phase.
N   c. The project charter is the first of two (not seven) processes in the initiating process group.
N   d. Work performance reports are an output (not an input) to monitor and control project work.

18. b. PMBOK˚ Guide: Figure 4-1
Y   b. As we perform the work of the project (direct and manage project work) work performance data becomes an output.

19. c. PMBOK˚ Guide: Figure 4-1
Y   c. During the process of monitor and control project work, the work performance information is an input. During this process that information is turned into the work performance reports.

© January 2016 AME Group, Inc. author Aileen Ellis, PMP, PgMP
aileen@amegroupinc.com 719-659-3658

20. c. PMBOK° Guide: Figure 4-1
Y   c. If expert judgment is part of a process it is always a tool and technique and never (never ever) an input or an output.

21. c. PMBOK° Guide: Figure 4-1
Y   c. This is a harder question. Remember the PMIS helps us execute and control the plan, not write the charter or identify stakeholders (initiating) and not set-up the plan (planning).

22. d. PMBOK° Guide: Figure 4-1
Y   d. Even if you don't remember the answer to this question, use common sense. The tool and technique is about change control and one of the answers is about change control. All change requests become an input into perform integrated change control. In this process, we use change control tools to help us approve or reject change requests.

23. b. PMBOK° Guide: Figure 5-1
Y   b. We need a scope management plan to tell us how to collect requirements, set project boundaries, build the WBS, etc.
N   a., c., and d. The scope management plan is an input to each of the processes described.

24. b. PMBOK° Guide: Figure 5-1
Y   b. After the deliverables have been tested for correctness as part of control quality they are sent to the customer as part of validate scope. The customer accepts or rejects the deliverables as part of validate scope.
N   a. The scope management plan is the output of plan scope management.
N   c. The scope statement is the output of define scope. This document may define some of the deliverables.
N   d. The WBS and WBS dictionary and eventually the scope baseline are outputs of create WBS. The WBS will contain (list) what we plan the deliverables of the projects will be.

25. d. PMBOK° Guide: Figure 5-1
Y   d. Variance analysis is a tool and technique of control scope and control cost. Variance and trend analysis is a tool and technique of control risks.
N   a. and c. Variance analysis is a tool and technique of only monitoring and controlling processes, never planning processes. This eliminates answer a. and c.
N   b. During validate scope the customer (or sponsor) inspects the deliverables for acceptance. Inspections, not variance analysis is the tool and technique.

26. b. PMBOK° Guide: Chapter 5 - Introduction (top of page 106)
Y   b. Since the question is asking about project scope the best answer is the project plan.
N   a. Completion of the project objectives would be measured against the project charter.
N   c. Performance, from a time standpoint would be measured against the schedule.
N   d. How the project performed from a cost standpoint would be measured against the budget.

27. c. PMBOK° Guide: Figure 5-1
Y   c. During define scope we analyze what the product needs to be so as to meet the requirements.
N   a. Expert judgment and meetings are tools and techniques of plan scope management.

N   b. Inspections and group decision-making techniques are tools and techniques of validate scope.

N   d. Decomposition and expert judgment are the tools and techniques of create WBS.

28. d. PMBOK® Guide: Chapter 5 - Introduction

Y   d. Completion of product scope is measured against the product requirements.

N   a. The scope management plan describes the scope processes. There are no product requirements listed in this document.

N   b. The requirements management plan describes the plan for the collecting and managing the requirements. The are no product requirements listed in this plan.

N   c. The project management plan describes the plan for the project. There are no product requirements listed in this plan.

29. d. PMBOK® Guide: Chapter 6 - Introduction

Y   d. The schedule management plan guides us on all the other schedule processes.

N   a., b., and c. The schedule management plan guides us in accomplishing each of these activities. Therefore, we must have the schedule management plan first.

30. c. PMBOK® Guide : Chapter 6 - Introduction

Y   c. These are examples of scheduling methods.

N   a. These are examples of scheduling presentations.

N   b. These are examples of project information.

N   d. These are examples of processes in the project time management knowledge area.

31. a. PMBOK® Guide: Figure 6-2

Y   a. These are examples of scheduling presentations.

N   b. These are examples of project information.

N   c. These are examples of scheduling methods.

N   d. These are examples of processes in the project time management knowledge area.

32. b. PMBOK® Guide: Figure 6-2

Y   b. These are examples of project information.

N   a. These are examples of scheduling presentations.

N   c. These are examples of scheduling methods.

N   d. These are examples of processes in the project time management knowledge area.

33. d. PMBOK® Guide: Chapter 6 - Introduction

Y   d. This is a definition of the schedule management plan.

N   a. The activity list is the output of define activities. It is a list of activities that we will use to build the schedule.

N   b. The network diagram is a diagram that shows the logical relationships between activities.

N   c. The schedule baseline is the approved version of the project schedule.

34. a. PMBOK® Guide: Chapter 6 - Introduction

Y   a. The schedule model is the scheduling tool populated with the schedule data.

N   b. This is a definition of the schedule management plan.

N   c. The schedule model generates the schedule, of which the schedule presentation is a depiction.

N   d. The project schedule presentations are developed from the project schedule.

© January 2016 AME Group, Inc. author Aileen Ellis, PMP, PgMP
aileen@amegroupinc.com 719-659-3658

PLANNING PROCESSES

There are 24 planning processes. These processes are performed to define the total scope of the project and refine the objectives. These processes develop the complete project management plan required to meet the project objectives. There are two primary outputs of the planning process group:

- The project management plan (includes the management plans as well as the project baselines)
- The project documents (examples include the risk register, the issue log, etc.)

Based on the PMP Examination Content outline published in June of 2015 by PMI there are thirteen (13) tasks of planning. These processes represent 24% of your exam content. Key phrases associated with each task are:

Task	Key Words
Task 1	Review and assess detailed project requirements, constraints and assumptions with stakeholders
Task 2	Develop a scope management plan
Task 3	Develop a cost management plan
Task 4	Develop the project schedule
Task 5	Develop the human resource plan
Task 6	Develop the communications management plan
Task 7	Develop the procurement management plan
Task 8	Develop the quality management plan and the quality standards
Task 9	Develop the change management plan
Task 10	Plan for risk management
Task 11	Present the project management plan to relevant stakeholders and obtain approval
Task 12	Conduct a kick-off meeting
Task 13	Develop the stakeholder management plan

© Jan 2016 AME Group, Inc. author Aileen Ellis, PMP, PgMP
aileen@amegroupinc.com 719-659-3658

The last table lists the key words for the tasks of the Planning Process Group. These tasks are not listed in the PMBOK° Guide. These tasks come from the PMP° Exam Content Outline. You do not need to memorize these tasks for the exam. It is good though for you to review them from time to time because these 13 tasks are the basis for the questions on Planning on the PMP° Exam. This Content Outline is absolutely an outline and therefore not robust enough to guide our studying in depth. Therefore almost everyone, if not everyone uses the PMBOK° Guide as their main reference when studying. The PMBOK° Guide includes processes not tasks. In the next few pages we cover the 24 processes of the Planning Process Group based on the PMBOK° Guide. If you try you could see how the tasks relate well to the processes. The planning processes are listed in the approximate sequence we would use them on our real projects. Realize though that this processes are very iterative.

Develop Project Management Plan

> ☑ **Exam Tip:** Review Figure 4-5 of the PMBOK° Guide.

Think of this process as integrating the other 23 planning processes. The project plan should include the project baselines, the subsidiary plans, as well as other items such as the project life cycle, the change management plan, and the configuration management plan. The first time we go through this process we are planning how to plan. As we go through the other planning processes we will pull outputs from those other processes into our project plan. The further we get with the planning processes the more robust our project plan will become.

INPUTs of develop project management plan

Project charter- this is the initial data to help us build the project plan.

Outputs from other planning processes- this includes the management plans (scope management plan, schedule management plan, etc.) and baselines (scope baseline, schedule baseline, cost baseline) developed in the other planning processes. Later, we will discuss each of the subsidiary plans and baselines. The first time we go through this process we don't have the other documents but eventually they all will be pulled together in this process to create a comprehensive project management plan. Also, as these documents are updated, the updates are incorporated into the project management plan so as to keep the project management plan up-to-date.

Enterprise environmental factors- this is your project environment. A great example is the PMIS (project management information system). This system includes our configuration management system, our change management system, our project management software tool, etc.

Organizational assets- hopefully we have a documented process, templates, and lessons learned to help us build our project plan.

TOOLs and TECHNIQUEs of develop project management plan

© January 2016 AME Group, Inc. author Aileen Ellis, PMP, PgMP
aileen@amegroupinc.com 719-659-3658

Expert judgment- go out and seek expertise to help you with your work on projects. Experts can be anyone and everyone who has knowledge that may help you.

Facilitation Techniques- use these techniques to help you develop the project plan.

OUTPUTs of develop project management plan

Project Management Plan- this is the plan that you use to guide all the work of the project. It should include many items. The level of detail in each of these items depends on the complexity of your project.

- ***Management plans***- every knowledge area has at least one management plan and some knowledge areas have two. The management plans describe how the work of the knowledge area will be defined and managed.
- ***Baselines***- your project should have at least three (3) baselines:
  - Scope baseline- made up of the scope statement, WBS, and WBS dictionary
  - Schedule baseline
  - Cost baseline
- ***Other important sections include:***
  - Project life cycle selected – how many phases and what processes in each phase
  - Change management plan
  - Configuration management plan

☑ **EXAM TIP:** Make sure you have a basic understanding of what the elements are of the project plan versus what documents are considered project documents. Please review Table 4-1 of the PMBOK® Guide. The left column of this table lists the documents that are usually considered part of the project plan. The right two columns are project documents not usually considered part of the project plan. The rows of this table have no meaning.

DEVELOP PROJECT MANAGEMENT PLAN - Sample Questions

1. As a project manager, you have learned that technology can be both a positive and a negative on projects. You need an automated tool that will help you to be successful. Which enterprise environmental factor might you focus on as you are developing your project plan?
a. configuration management knowledge base
b. change control procedures
c. guidelines and criteria for tailoring the organizations set of standard processes
d. project management information system (PMIS)

2. Typical items found in the project management plan include all of the following except:
a. the contract
b. the schedule baseline
c. the procurement management plan
d. the process improvement plan

3. The project plan should contain at least 3 baselines. Which baseline below is not typically one of the three?
a. scope baseline
b. risk baseline
c. schedule baseline
d. cost baseline

4. The configuration management system is an example of a(n):
a. enterprise environmental factor
b. organizational process asset
c. government standard
d. industry standard

5. The configuration management knowledge base is an example of a(n):
a. enterprise environmental factor
b. organizational process asset
c. government standard
d. industry standard

6. You have been very successful as a project manager. You have been asked to move into an organization that struggles to maintain accurate versions and baselines of official organizational standards, policies, and project documents. History tells you that version control of these documents is critical for project success. As you develop your project management plan, which organizational asset may help you the most:
a. project management body of knowledge for your vertical market
b. project management information system
c. organizational infrastructure
d. configuration management knowledge base

© January 2016 AME Group, Inc. author Aileen Ellis, PMP, PgMP
aileen@amegroupinc.com 719-659-3658

DEVELOP PROJECT MANAGEMENT PLAN – Solutions

1. d. PMBOK° Guide: Section 4.2.1.3 and 4.2.1.4
Y   d. The PMIS is an enterprise environmental factor. It may be an automated tool such as scheduling software.
N   a., b., and c. These examples are all organizational process assets not enterprise environmental factors.

2. a. PMBOK° Guide: Section 4.2.3.1
Y   a. The contract is a stand-alone document between our external customer and our organization. It would not be part of the project plan. It is a legal document.
N   a., b., and c. These are likely elements of the project plan.

3. b. PMBOK° Guide: Section 4.2.3.1
Y   b. There are normally three baselines on our project: scope, schedule, and cost.

4. a. PMBOK° Guide: Section 4.2.1.3 and 4.2.1.4
Y   a. The PMIS (project management information system) is considered an enterprise environmental factor (EEF). The configuration management system is a subset of the PMIS.
N   b. Systems are usually considered EEFs. The databases inside of these systems are usually considered the organizational assets.

5. b. PMBOK° Guide: Section 4.2.1.3 and 4.2.1.4
Y   b. Databases and knowledge bases belonging to the organization (containing organizational data, not commercial data) are usually considered the organizational assets (OPAs).

6. d. PMBOK° Guide: Section 4.2.1.3 and 4.2.1.4
Y   d. The configuration management knowledge base contains versions and baselines of critical documents.
N   a., b., and c. These examples are usually considered enterprise environmental factors (EEFs).

Plan Scope Management

> ☑ **Exam Tip:** Review Figure 5-3 of the PMBOK® Guide.

In this process the scope management plan and the requirements management plan are developed.

INPUTs of plan scope management

Project management plan- the project plan most likely is not fully developed yet. Elements of the project plan though may help develop the scope management plan.

Project charter- this document provides high level information including the project context to help start planning for scope.

Enterprise environmental factors- ex. Organizational culture- the culture of our organization may affect the process we use to define scope. As an example, a culture that is dominated by functional groups and not project teams may lead the work breakdown structure to be organized by function.

Organizational process assets- ex. Templates- our organization may have work breakdown structure templates that organize the WBS by phases and therefore we are more likely to organize the current WBS by phases.

TOOLs and TECHNIQUEs of plan scope management

Expert judgment- go out and seek expertise to help you with your work on projects. Experts can be anyone and everyone who has knowledge that may help you.

Meetings- held to develop the scope management plan and the requirements management plan

OUTPUTs of plan scope management

Scope Management Plan	Provides guidance on how the project scope will be defined, validated, and controlled.
	☑EXAM TIP: It does not describe what is in or out of scope.
	☑EXAM TIP: It is not the scope baseline or part of the scope baseline.
	It is a subset plan of the project management plan.

© January 2016 AME Group, Inc. author Aileen Ellis, PMP, PgMP
aileen@amegroupinc.com 719-659-3658

Requirements Management Plan	Provides guidance on how the requirements will be analyzed, documented, and managed.
	Defines configuration management of the product.
	Defines traceability structure.
	☑EXAM TIP: It does not describe what is in or out of scope.
	☑EXAM TIP: It is not the scope baseline or part of the scope baseline.
	It is a subset plan of the project management plan.

☑ **EXAM TIP:** This process is one of only two processes that has two plans as outputs.

Product Scope	Project Scope
Features and functions of the product	The work to deliver the product
Measured against the product requirements	Measured against the project plan
Defined before the project scope	Defined after the product scope

☑ **EXAM TIP:** Know the difference between project and product scope.

PLAN SCOPE MANAGEMENT - Sample Questions

1. The scope management plan is an input to all of the following processes except?
a. collect requirements
b. define scope
c. create WBS
d. develop schedule

2. The requirements management plan is an input into which of the following processes?
a. collect requirements
b. define scope
c. create WBS
d. develop schedule

3. The requirements management plan describes:
a. process for preparing a detailed project scope statement
b. process that enables the creation of the WBS
c. configuration management activities
d. marketplace conditions

4. The scope management plan describes:
a. requirements prioritization process
b. process that enables the creation of the WBS
c. configuration management activities
d. marketplace conditions

5. Completion of the project scope is measured against?
a. the scope management plan
b. the requirements management plan
c. the project management plan
d. the product requirements

© January 2016 AME Group, Inc. author Aileen Ellis, PMP, PgMP
aileen@amegroupinc.com 719-659-3658

PLAN SCOPE MANAGEMENT- Solutions

1. d. PMBOK° Guide: Figure 5-3
Y   d. The scope management plan will be input to scope processes, not schedule processes.

2. a. PMBOK° Guide: Figure 5-3
Y   a. The requirements management plan describes how we will collect and manage the requirements.

3. c. PMBOK° Guide: Section 5.1.3.2
Y   c. Configuration management is a process for setting up and maintaining consistency related to the product. It includes the management of system information and changes to that information. Configuration management is used to manage requirements and therefore it may be addressed in the requirements management plan.
N   a. The scope management plan describes the process for preparing a scope statement.
N   b. The scope management plan describes the processes for creating the WBS.
N   d. Marketplace conditions are examples of enterprise environmental factors.

4. b. PMBOK° Guide: Section 5.1.3.1
Y   b. The scope management plan describes the processes for creating the WBS.
N   a. The requirements prioritization process is described in the requirements management plan.
N   c. Configuration management is used to manage requirements and therefore it may be addressed in the requirements management plan.
N   d. Marketplace conditions are examples of enterprise environmental factors.

5. c. PMBOK° Guide: Chapter 5 - Introduction
Y   c. Completion on the project scope is measured against the project plan.
N   a. The scope management plan describes the processes to define the scope, create the WBS, validate scope, and control scope.
N   b. The requirements management plan describes how we will collect and manage the requirements.
N   d. Completion of the product scope is measured against the product requirements.

Collect Requirements

☑ **Exam Tip:** Review Figure 5-5 of the PMBOK° Guide.

This is the process of turning the needs of the project stakeholders into requirements. This process has 11 tools and techniques. As you study each tool and technique make sure you know when you would want to use one versus another.

Project requirements and project failure:

Early and frequent involvement with stakeholders is needed for accurate requirements collection. On some projects the requirements are met but the project still fails, because:
- the wrong requirements were collected
- the requirements were collected from the wrong stakeholders
- many other reasons

INPUTs of collect requirements

Scope management plan- this plan describes the process for knowing which requirements to collect and not collect

Requirements management plan- this plan describes the process for collecting requirements

Stakeholder management plan- this plan describes the process to engage stakeholders. It may describe how to engage stakeholders to participate in collecting requirements

Project charter- contains high level project requirements

Stakeholder register- organizes the information you currently have about your project stakeholders. Remember the requirements on the project come from the project stakeholders

TOOLs and TECHNIQUEs of collect requirements

There are eleven tools and techniques. It is important to understand each tool and technique as well as be able to differentiate one tool and technique from another.

Interviews- this is you or your team members talking to stakeholders one-on-one (though could be more than one-on-one). This process is slow, time consuming, and would not make sense if you had a lot of stakeholders or a lot of information to collect.

© January 2016 AME Group, Inc. author Aileen Ellis, PMP, PgMP
aileen@amegroupinc.com 719-659-3658

Focus groups- similar to interviews from the standpoint that this technique involves talking with your stakeholders. With this technique we are working on expectations, attitudes, and not usually the requirements themselves.

Facilitated workshops- usually more technical than focus groups as you are now working on developing the requirements. Examples include:

- JAD sessions- joint application design/development sessions- associated with software industry
- QFD- quality function deployment- associated with manufacturing-begins with understanding the VOC- voice of the customer
- Agile method- utilizes collecting user stories- short descriptions of the user's requirements

Group Creativity Techniques

- Brainstorming- group of people share ideas with no prioritization
  - A positive of this technique is that lots of ideas are collected.
  - Potential negative-group think
- Nominal group technique- voting technique to rank ideas. Usually used after brainstorming.
- Ideas/mind maps- visual of ideas generated during brainstorming
- Affinity diagrams- these diagrams sort or group "like" ideas
- Multi-criteria decision analysis (MCDA)- explicitly considers multiple criteria in decision-making environments.

Group Decision-making techniques- when making decisions make sure the decision-making process is clear to all stakeholders before work begins on requirements.

- Unanimity- In this decision-making technique everyone agrees to the same course. Often the Delphi method (we will discuss this later) is used to reach this type of decision.
- Majority- In this decision-making technique the option that has over 50% support will be chosen. Be careful not to have an even number of members voting as you risk a tie.
- Plurality- In this decision-making technique the option that has the most support wins, even if that option does not have over 50% of the support. This does not make sense when deciding between only 2 options and therefore we must have 3 or more options for this technique to make sense.
- Dictatorship- in this decision-making technique only one person makes the decision for the group.

Questionnaires and surveys- we use this technique if we need to collect large quantities of information or we are collecting information from a large number of respondents. A key idea here is the ability to perform statistical analysis on the information. Questionnaires are different from interviews in several ways.

INTERVIEWS	QUESTIONAIRES
Face-to-face, verbal	Written- statistical analysis often performed
Used when only a limited number of respondents	Used when lots of respondents and/or lots of information to be collected

Observations- job shadowing. Used when:
- The person has a hard time describing their requirements
- The person does not want to describe their requirements
  The person collecting the observations may be:
  - Watching someone else perform the work- job shadowing
  - Performing the work themselves- participant observer

Prototypes- we use this method when we want to capture requirements as early as possible from our stakeholders. The stakeholders really feel they are part of defining the requirements. A prototype is a mock-up of the actual product. It is not the actual product. One of the risks with prototypes is that stakeholders often want to take the prototype and begin using it as a real product. This is not possible. Key words:
- Tangible- the prototype is something the stakeholders may be able to touch and manipulate
- Progressive elaboration- the requirements are elaborated through a series of prototypes
- Story boards- used to navigate through a series of interfaces (think agile PM).

Benchmarking- we use this method to compare our practices to other organizations. The goal is to help us set standards and identify strategies to reach those standards.

Context diagrams- show the relationship between the business system, and the relationship of everything and everyone who interacts with the system.

Documentation analysis- at this point we should evaluate the documents that we have related to the project.

OUTPUTs of collect requirements

Requirements documentation- These documents contain the requirements and supporting detail for the requirements.
Key words:
Unambiguous- meaning the requirements should be measureable and testable
Progressive elaboration- the requirements may be more detailed as the project moves forward

Requirements traceability matrix- (see PMBOK° Guide: Figure 5-6). The primary purpose of this matrix is to ensure that only requirements that add business value are included in the project.

☑ **EXAM TIP:** There are many tools and techniques in this process. Make sure you understand why you would use one over another when collecting requirements.

© January 2016 AME Group, Inc. author Aileen Ellis, PMP, PgMP
aileen@amegroupinc.com 719-659-3658

COLLECT REQUIREMENTS - Sample Questions

1. One of the reasons to use prototypes when collecting requirements is:
a. provide the customer with a tangible mock-up to collect early feedback
b. provide the customer with the actual product to collect early feedback
c. provide the customer with statistical outputs to collect early feedback
d. provide the customer with abstract representations to collect early feedback

2. Functional requirements describe:
a. the behaviors of the product
b. security
c. safety
d. level of service

3. What document is used to identify the people who can provide information to help develop detailed requirements:
a. the requirements documentation
b. the stakeholder register
c. the work breakdown structure
d. the project charter

4. We often talk with stakeholders one-on-one to help collect requirements. This is called:
a. interviews
b. questionnaires
c. facilitated workshops
d. prototypes

5. A Joint Application Development (JAD) session is an example of what tool and technique:
a. interviews
b. focus groups
c. facilitated workshops
d. benchmarking

6. Configuration management activities such as how changes to the product will be initiated are found in what document:
a. requirements management plan
b. requirements traceability matrix
c. scope management plan
d. requirements documentation

7. There are many group creativity techniques used to collect requirements. The technique that groups like ideas is called:
a. brainstorming
b. the Delphi method
c. nominal group technique
d. affinity diagrams

8. While collecting requirements we realize that a statistical analysis needs to be performed. We are most likely to use what method below:
a. prototypes
b. questionnaires
c. observations
d. brainstorming

9. Joint Application Development (JAD) sessions are most often associated with what industry:
a. construction
b. marketing
c. software
d. manufacturing

10. Another name for job shadowing when collecting requirements is:
a. observations
b. prototypes
c. questionnaires
d. focus groups

11. The document that demonstrates that each requirement adds business value is:
a. the requirements documentation
b. the stakeholder register
c. the work breakdown structure
d. the requirements traceability matrix

12. Quality Function Deployment (QFD) sessions are most often associated with what industry:
a. construction
b. marketing
c. software
d. manufacturing

13. Transition requirements include:
a. data conversion and training requirements
b. security requirements
c. safety requirements
d. supportability requirements

14. A trained moderator is often used to guide a group of people through a discussion on their expectations of a proposed product. This method is called:
a. interviews
b. focus groups
c. facilitated workshops
d. prototypes

15. High level requirements are included in what document:
a. the requirements management plan
b. the stakeholder register
c. the work breakdown structure
d. the project charter

© January 2016 AME Group, Inc. author Aileen Ellis, PMP, PgMP
aileen@amegroupinc.com 719-659-3658

16.   Your project management team is working with the stakeholders to generate, classify, and prioritize product requirements. Decisions are being reached based on the opinions that receive more support than other opinions. This method is called:
a. unanimity
b. majority
c. plurality
d. dictatorship

17. The project team is working with stakeholders to identify product and project requirements. You are using a voting process to rank the most useful ideas. This voting process is called:
a. brainstorming
b. nominal group technique
c. the Delphi technique
d. idea/mind mapping

18. An example of a scope model is:
a. prototype
b. questionnaire
c. context diagram
d. job shadowing

19.   The process of comparing planned or actual practices to those of other organizations is:
a. context diagrams
b. job shadowing
c. benchmarking
d. prototypes

20. The requirements traceability matrix is an input to:
a. define scope and validate scope
b. validate scope and control scope
c. control scope and create WBS
d. create WBS and define scope

COLLECT REQUIREMENTS - Solutions

1. a. PMBOK® Guide: Section 5.2.2.8

Y   a. A prototype is a tangible mock-up that customers may try out in order to give us early feedback on a product.

N   b. A prototype is not the actual product. It is a working model of the product.

N   c. A prototype does not contain statistical outputs. It is a mock-up.

N   d. A prototype is not an abstract representation. It is a mock-up.

2. a. PMBOK® Guide: Section 5.2

Y   a. The functional requirements describe the intended behavior we want from the product.

N   b. Security is a nonfunctional requirement.

N   c. Safety is a nonfunctional requirement.

N   d. Level of service is a nonfunctional requirement.

3. b. PMBOK® Guide: Section 5.2.1.5

Y   b. The stakeholder register identifies the stakeholders for the project, including those stakeholders who need to be involved with collect requirements.

N   a. The requirements documentation describes the requirements, not the people who are involved in defining the requirements.

N   c. The work breakdown structure organizes the deliverables of the project. It does not provide a stakeholder list.

N   d. The project charter will list the sponsor and the project manager. This is not a complete list of people who need to be involved in collecting the requirements.

4. a. PMBOK® Guide: Section 5.2.2.1

Y   a. Interviews are talking with stakeholders one-on-one.

N   b. Questionnaires are documents. They do not involve talking with the stakeholders.

N   c. Facilitated workshops include groups of people, not talking one-on-one like interviews.

N   d. Focus groups include groups of people, not talking one-on-one like interviews.

5. c. PMBOK® Guide: Section 5.2.2.3

Y   c. A JAD session is a meeting, or series of meetings, where knowledge workers, often IT professionals work together to develop the requirements.

N   a. Interviews are conducted one-on-one. JAD sessions are always are a group setting.

N   b. A focus group is often considered less technical than a JAD session. With a focus group, people are asked their opinion on some aspect of the product.

N   d. Benchmarking is looking at another organization to get ideas on where to set our quality standards or how to achieve our quality standards.

6. a. PMBOK® Guide: Section 5.1.3.2

Y   a. Configuration management ideas are found in the requirements management plan, and the configuration managements plan.

N   b. The requirements traceability matrix ensures that every requirement adds business value. We do not want to have requirements, and complete the work to meet those requirements, if it does not provide business value.

N   c. The scope management plan does not address configuration management. The scope plan describes the processes to define the scope, create the WBS, validate scope, and control scope.

N   d. The requirements documentation describes the requirements, not configuration management.

© January 2016 AME Group, Inc. author Aileen Ellis, PMP, PgMP
aileen@amegroupinc.com 719-659-3658

7. d. PMBOK° Guide: Section 5.2.2.4

Y   d. Affinity diagrams sort similar ideas together into groups.

N   a. Brainstorming generates ideas, though it does not group like ideas together.

N   b. The Delphi method is used to help us reach a consensus.

N   c. Nominal group technique ranks ideas.

8. b. PMBOK° Guide: Section 5.2.2.6

Y   b. Questionnaires are often used when we want to collect lots of information or collect information from lots of people so as to perform a statistical analysis.

N   a. Prototypes are not about statistics. They are mock-ups so we may collect early feedback on requirements.

N   c. Observations are used to collect data as someone is using, or needs to use a product.

N   d. Brainstorming is used to collect lots of ideas, but not to perform a statistical analysis.

9. c. PMBOK° Guide: Section 5.2.2.3

Y   c. JAD sessions are most often associated with developing an information system for an organization.

N   a. While JAD sessions may have many applications, we most often associate JAD with software, not construction.

N   b. While JAD sessions may have many applications, we most often associate JAD with software, not marketing.

N   d. QFD (quality function deployment) is more often associated with manufacturing than a JAD session.

10. a. PMBOK° Guide: Section 5.2.2.7

Y   a. Observation is the method of watching someone as they perform their job (job shadowing) so as to collect requirements.

N   b. A prototype is a tangible mock-up that customers may try out in order to give us early feedback on a product.

N   c. Questionnaires are often used when we want to collect lots of information or collect information from lots of people so as to perform a statistical analysis. They are in written form.

N   d. A focus group is often considered less technical than a JAD session. With a focus group, people are asked their opinion on some aspect of the product.

11. d. PMBOK° Guide: Section 5.2.3.2

Y   d. The requirements traceability matrix is critical. Its role is to ensure that we have no requirements that do not add business value.

N   a. The requirements documentation list and describe the requirements.

N   b. The stakeholder register lists and organizes our project stakeholders.

N   c. The work breakdown structure organizes the deliverables for the project in a hierarchical format.

12. d. PMBOK° Guide: Section 5.2.2.3

Y   d. QFD (quality function deployment) is more often associated with manufacturing than a JAD session.

N   a. While QFD may have many applications, we most often associate QFD with manufacturing, not construction.

N   b. While QFD may have many applications, we most often associate QFD with manufacturing, not marketing.

N   c. JAD sessions are most often associated with developing an information system for an organization.

13. a. PMBOK® Guide: Section 5.2

Y   a. Transitional requirements describe the requirements to move us from where we are to where we want to be.

N   b. Security is a nonfunctional requirement.

N   c. Safety is a nonfunctional requirement.

N   d. Supportability is a nonfunctional requirement.

14. b. PMBOK® Guide: Section 5.2.2.2

Y   b. With focus groups a moderator asks a group of people questions to understand their expectations of a product.

N   a. With interviews we meet with the stakeholders one-on-one to ask them questions.

N   c. Think of a facilitated workshop as being much more technical than a focus group. It is truly developing the product requirements.

N   d. A prototype is a tangible mock-up that customers may try out in order to give us early feedback on a product.

15. d. PMBOK® Guide: Section 4.1.3.1

Y   d. This is a trickier question. The high level requirements are in the project charter. The detailed requirements are in the requirements documentation.

N   a. There are no requirements listed in the requirements management plan. It is a plan of how to collect and manage the requirements.

N   b. The stakeholder register is an organized list of project stakeholders.

N   c. The WBS is a structure that shows the project deliverables in a hierarchical format.

16. c. PMBOK® Guide: Section 5.2.2.5

Y   c. Plurality is a decision-making technique where we pick the option that has the most votes, even if it is not the majority.

N   a. Unanimity is a decision-making technique in which all voters must agree on the same option.

N   b. Majority is a decision-making technique in which we pick that option that receives more than 50% of the votes.

N   d. Dictatorship is a decision-making technique in which only one person gets to decide for a group of people.

17. b. PMBOK® Guide: Section 5.2.2.4

Y   b. Nominal group technique is a voting technique often used after brainstorming.

N   a. Brainstorming is a method to obtain many ideas. Voting is not considered part of brainstorming.

N   c. The Delphi technique involves working with experts in an anonymous way to reach a consensus.

N   d. Idea/mind mapping is a way to visualize ideas from brainstorming. It often leads to new ideas.

18. c. PMBOK® Guide: Section 5.2.2.10

Y   c. A context diagram is a visual of the product scope.

N   a. A prototype is a tangible mock-up that customers may try out in order to give us early feedback on a product.

N   b. Questionnaires allow us to perform statistical analysis when we collect lots of information or collect information from lots of people.

N   d. Job shadowing is the method of watching someone as they perform their job so as to collect requirements.

19. c. PMBOK® Guide: Section 5.2.2.9

© January 2016 AME Group, Inc. author Aileen Ellis, PMP, PgMP
aileen@amegroupinc.com 719-659-3658

Y c. Benchmarking is used to identify new ideas as well as best practices. We often associate benchmarking with the quality processes. We do this by comparing our processes to those of other organizations.

N a. A context diagram is a visual of the product scope, often depicting an entire system.

N b. Job shadowing is the method of watching someone as they perform their job so as to collect requirements.

N d. A prototype is a tangible mock-up that customers may try out in order to give us early feedback on a product.

20. b. PMBOK° Guide: Figure 5-5

Y b. The traceability matrix is an input to validate scope and control scope.

N a., c., and d. The matrix is not an input to create WBS or define scope.

Define Scope

Define scope is the process of creating the project scope statement. Another key element of this process is that the final project requirements are selected from the project requirements list generated during the previous process (collect requirements).

Think of define scope and collect requirements (the last process we discussed) as being very iterative. As we get into the details of defining scope, this may lead us back to the requirements we have just collected.

☑ **EXAM TIP:** It is a best practice when we are defining scope to be explicit about what is out of scope. Better to be proactive in letting the stakeholders know what not to expect than to have them expect something and we not deliver.

INPUTs of define scope

Scope management plan- this plan describes how the scope statement (as well as other scope documents) will be developed and managed.

☑ **EXAM TIP:** Since we are in the scope knowledge area it is a good assumption that the scope (not time, not cost, etc.) management plan will be an input.

Project charter- the charter may describe the product and the project at a high level. We will use this now to create the details of the project scope statement.

Requirements documentation- remember that not all the requirements that were just developed will become part of the project. In the process of define scope we need to determine what requirements the project will satisfy and what requirements the project will not satisfy.

Organizational process assets- these assets will continue to be inputs during planning. We will not highlight them each time. As we are preparing a scope statement it makes sense to look back at the assets for processes, templates, previous project scope statements and lessons learned that will help us develop the current scope statement.

TOOLs and TECHNIQUEs of define scope

Expert judgment- is a tool of many though not all planning processes. On the project it makes sense to connect with experts who can make our work easier and our output better.

© January 2016 AME Group, Inc. author Aileen Ellis, PMP, PgMP
aileen@amegroupinc.com 719-659-3658

Product analysis- we have no product yet. We are analyzing what our product (or service) needs to be, including the deliverables, to meet the requirements identified.

Alternative generation- there are often multiple ways to do the work on the project to get to the same result (product). Of course, each option has its own risks and rewards. Different ways to generate alternatives include:
- Brainstorming- sharing lots of ideas
- Lateral thinking- solving problems through a unique and/or creative approach. Looking at problem solving from a different angle.

Facilitated workshops- this is also a tool and technique of collect requirements. These sessions may be very technical and very intense.

OUTPUTs of define scope

Project scope statement- this document is usually in paragraph form (not a hierarchy). It describes both the project and product scope. A good practice is to also describe what work will be considered out of scope.

☑ **EXAM TIP:** At this point in your studying, make sure you can differentiate between the project charter and the project scope statement. (See PMBOK® Guide: Table 5-1 to help). If a question is asking about something high level (or summary level) most likely they are asking about the project charter.

CHARTER	SCOPE STATEMENT
High level	Detailed
Comes from sponsor	Comes from project manager and key members of team
Describes project output	Describes work to achieve output
Output of develop project charter INTEGRATION Knowledge area INITIATING Process group	Output of define scope SCOPE Knowledge area PLANNING Process group

Project documents updates- this will be an output of many planning processes. Remember that nothing is under baseline control yet. As we create one document (ex. scope statement), this may lead us back to updating other documents (requirements documentation).

DEFINE SCOPE - Sample Questions

1. The detailed descriptions of the product and project scope can be found in what document:
a. the scope statement
b. the requirements documentation
c. the work breakdown structure
d. the scope management plan

2. An example of a product analysis technique is:
a. brainstorming
b. lateral thinking
c. pair wise comparisons
d. systems engineering

3. Which of the following is a tool and technique of define scope?
a. interviews
b. focus groups
c. facilitated workshops
d. prototypes

4. Product acceptance criteria is found in what document?
a. the scope statement
b. the requirements documentation
c. the work breakdown structure
d. the scope management plan

5. An example of an alternative generation technique is:
a. value engineering
b. lateral thinking
c. systems analysis
d. functional analysis

6. Your product development project is wrapping up and your management asks where you stand as far as product scope. Completion of product scope is measured against the:
a. project management plan
b. scope statement
c. WBS
d. product requirements

7. Which management plan is an input into define scope?
a. requirements management plan
b. scope management plan
c. schedule management plan
d. configuration management plan

8. In iterative life cycles the project's detailed scope is determined:
a. as an output of the concept phase
b. as part of the develop project charter process
c. one iteration at a time
d. never

9. There is often confusion between the project charter and the project scope statement. Which overall statement is true?
a. the project charter contains more high level information, the project scope statement contains more detailed information
b. the project scope statement contains more high level information, the project charter statement contains more detailed information
c. the project charter is developed after the project scope statement
d. the project scope statement gives the project manager authority to utilize project resources

10. Measurable project objectives are included in which document?
a. the project scope statement
b. the project charter
c. the work breakdown structure
d. the scope management plan

DEFINE SCOPE - Solutions

1. a. PMBOK® Guide: Section 5.3.3.1
Y   a. The scope statement describes both the project and the product scope.
N   b. The requirements documentation describe the requirements, not the scope.
N   c. The WBS is a structure that organizes the deliverables in a hierarchical form.
N   d. The scope management plan describes the processes to define and manage scope. The scope itself is not in the plan.

2. d. PMBOK® Guide: Section 5.3.2.2
Y   d. There are many examples of product analysis including system engineering, value engineering, etc.
N   a. Brainstorming is a group creativity technique.
N   b. Lateral thinking is an example of an alternative generation technique.
N   c. Pair wise comparisons is a technique that compares ideas in pairs, to decide which is the preferred idea.

3. c. PMBOK® Guide: Section 5.3.2.4
Y   c. Facilitated workshops are a tool and technique of both collect requirements and define scope.
N   a. Interviews are a tool and technique of collect requirements.
N   b. Focus groups are a tool and technique of collect requirements.
N   d. Prototypes are a tool and technique of collect requirements.

4. a. PMBOK® Guide: Section 5.3.3.1
Y   a. The scope statement describes the project scope, the product scope, the acceptance criteria, etc.
N   b. The requirements documentation describe the project and product requirements, etc.
N   c. The WBS is a structure that organizes the deliverables in a hierarchical form.
N   d. The scope management plan describes the processes to define and manage scope.

5. b. PMBOK® Guide: Section 5.3.2.3
Y   b. Lateral thinking is an example of an alternative generation technique. It includes solving problems in an indirect way.
N   a. Value engineering is a product analysis technique that optimizes the value of a product.
N   c. Systems analysis is a product analysis technique that studies interacting entities.
N   d. Functional analysis is a product analysis technique.

6. d. PMBOK® Guide: Chapter 5 - Introduction
Y   d. Product scope is measured against the product requirements.
N   a. The project scope is measured against the project management plan.
N   b. The project scope is measured against the project management plan including the scope statement.
N   c. The project scope is measured against the project management plan including the WBS.

7. b. PMBOK® Guide: Figure 5-6 and Section 5.3.1.1
Y   b. Since the process is called define scope, it makes sense that the scope management plan is the input.
N   a. The requirements management plan is an input to collect requirements.
N   c. The schedule management plan is an input into several processes in the time knowledge area.

© January 2016 AME Group, Inc. author Aileen Ellis, PMP, PgMP
aileen@amegroupinc.com 719-659-3658

N   d. The configuration management plan is a subset of the project management plan.

8. c. PMBOK° Guide: Section 5.3

Y   c. In iterative life cycles the scope is not all developed upfront, but one iteration at time.

N   a. In a predictive life cycle, the detailed scope may be an output of an earlier phase.

N   b. Usually the project objectives, not the project scope are part of the project charter process.

N   d. At some point on every project the scope needs to be defined.

9. a. PMBOK° Guide: Table 5-1 and Section 5.3.3.1

Y   a. The charter is more high level, the scope statement is more detailed.

N   b. This statement is reversed.

N   c. This charter is developed before the scope statement.

N   d. The charter gives the project manager authority to use project resources.

10. b. PMBOK° Guide: Table 5-1

Y   b. The charter contains the project objectives.

N   a. The scope statement describes the project and product scope.

N   c. The WBS is a structure that shows the project deliverables in a hierarchical format.

N   d. The scope management plan describes the processes to define and manage scope.

Create WBS

Create WBS (work breakdown structure) is the process of taking the deliverables listed in the scope statement and subdividing them into small deliverables. This is a critical process of planning as much of the other work in planning is based off of the WBS. Put a real focus on understanding the ideas surrounding the WBS.

Work package level - the lowest level of the WBS

Control account (cost account) - the level above the work package level

INPUTs of create WBS (not all listed)

Scope management plan - this plan describes how the WBS (and other scope documents) will be defined and managed.

Project scope statement - this document lists in paragraph form the deliverables of the project. In create WBS we will take these deliverables and subdivide them into smaller more manageable deliverables.

Requirements documentation - as we develop the WBS we need to ensure that we have all the deliverables needed to meet the requirements.

TOOLs and TECHNIQUEs of create WBS

Decomposition - we use this tool to break larger deliverables into smaller more manageable deliverables. The WBS should be decomposed to the appropriate level. Excessive decomposition of the WBS is bad. It may lead to:
- wasted management effort
- inefficient use of resources
- decreased efficiency in performing the work

Expert judgment - this tool may be referring to people who can provide the details to breakdown deliverables into even smaller deliverables or the use of templates to help us do this.

100% rule - the WBS should represent all the work for the project. If a deliverable is not in the WBS, there is no plan to create it.

☑ **EXAM TIP:** The most likely question on this relates to project management work. Make sure that you list all your project management deliverables in the WBS.

OUTPUTs of create WBS (not all listed)

Scope baseline- the timing of this output may be a little confusing. We do not have a scope baseline yet, at least not in its approved form. After we finish planning we will get approval on our documents and baseline the following scope documents. All three should exist, just not in their approved form yet.

- ***Project scope statement***- describes project and product scope
- ***Work breakdown structure (WBS***)- the work breakdown structure will be a critical input to future planning processes. The WBS is a deliverable-oriented hierarchical decomposition of the work to be performed by the project team so as to meet the objectives of the project charter and the deliverables of the project scope statement. Below is a sample WBS.

☑ **EXAM TIP:** The control account is not always the second level, it is always the level above the work package level. The work package level is not always the third level, it is always the lowest level.

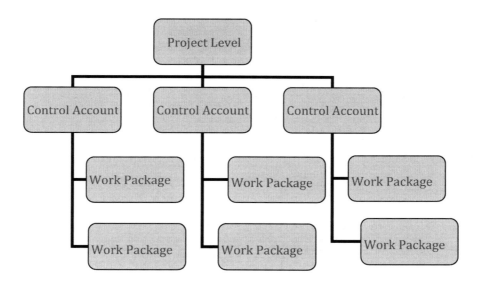

WBS dictionary- provides details about each control account or work package in the WBS. Here is an example of one page from a dictionary.

*WBS Number: 1.5	*WBS Name: Design deck	*WBS Owner: Engineer # 3
WBS Predecessor(s): Concept	**WBS Description:** Design deck including 50% drawings, 90% drawings, and 100% drawings.	
WBS Successor(s): Construction		
Resource effort: 30 person hours		
Cost estimate: $12,000 loaded	**Assumptions and Constraints:** Assume concept sketch acceptable to customer.	

☑ **EXAM TIP:** At this point we may not have all the information that goes into the WBS dictionary. As an example we may not have estimated resource effort or costs.

© January 2016 AME Group, Inc. author Aileen Ellis, PMP, PgMP
aileen@amegroupinc.com 719-659-3658

CREATE WBS - Sample Questions

1. The WBS should be :
a. a list of activities
b. a hierarchy of activities
c. a list of deliverables
d. a hierarchy of deliverables

2. Planning the near term deliverables in more detail and the far term deliverables in less detail or waiting until later to plan the far term deliverables is called:
a. rolling wave planning
b. 100% rule
c. 80 hour rule
d. scope creep

3. The 100% rule for WBSs includes all of the following except:
a. the WBS represents all the project management work
b. the WBS represents all the product work
c. nothing extra is in the WBS
d. the WBS includes planned start and finish dates for all deliverables

4. The lowest level of the WBS is called:
a. the work package level
b. the activity level
c. the control account level
d. the cost account level

5. A WBS is used for all of the following except:
a. to help us communicate
b. to help us build the team
c. to show planned start and finish dates
d. to organize the project deliverables

6. The level above the work package level is called:
a. the work package level
b. the activity level
c. the control account level
d. the dictionary level

7. The Work Breakdown Structure (WBS) should be:
a. deliverable oriented
b. activity oriented
c. both deliverable and activity oriented
d. neither deliverable or activity oriented

8. The document that provides details of the WBS components is called:
a. the scope statement
b. the WBS dictionary
c. the control account
d. the requirements document

9. The scope baseline includes:
a. the project scope statement
b. the scope management plan
c. the requirements management plan
d. the requirements traceability matrix

10. The WBS level used for earned value management is:
a. the work package level
b. the activity level
c. the control account level
d. the planning package level

11. The project manager has been busy with the core team developing all of the baselines required to manage the project. A status meeting is being held and the customer is reviewing all of the baselines. One reason to review the scope baseline is to see:
a. the planning dates for each of the work packages
b. the sequencing of the activities of the project
c. the estimated cost broken down by deliverable
d. the deliverables of the project

12. The code of accounts is:
a. a numbering system used to uniquely identify each component of the WBS
b. a numbering system used to monitor project costs by category
c. based on the corporate chart of accounts of the performing organization
d. the level of the WBS above the work package level

13. The WBS should be decomposed to as detailed a level as:
a. possible based on the scope of the work
b. money allows in the project budget
c. time allows in the project schedule
d. the ability to plan, manage, and control the work is enhanced

© January 2016 AME Group, Inc. author Aileen Ellis, PMP, PgMP
aileen@amegroupinc.com 719-659-3658

CREATE WBS - Solutions

1. d. PMBOK® Guide: Section 5.4
Y   d. The WBS is a hierarchy of deliverables.
N   a. The WBS is not a list and does not include activities.
N   b. The WBS is a hierarchy but not of activities.
N   c. The WBS is not a list.

2. a. PMBOK® Guide: Section 5.4.2.2
Y   a. Rolling wave planning is planning the near term activities in great detail and activities further out with a lot less detail.
N   b. The 100% rule states that the WBS should represent 100% of the work of the project.
N   c. The 80 hour rule is a rule of thumb that states no activity should be more than 80 hours of effort.
N   d. Scope creep is another name for uncontrolled scope growth.

3. d. PMBOK® Guide: Section 5.4.2.2
Y   d. The WBS does not include dates. The schedule includes dates.
N   a. All the project management deliverables should be included in the WBS.
N   b. All the product deliverables should be included in the WBS.
N   c. The WBS should include only the planned deliverables. Nothing else should be included in the WBS.

4. a. PMBOK® Guide: Section 5.4
Y   a. The work package level is the lowest level of the WBS.
N   b. There is no activity level in the WBS. In the process define activities we take the work packages of the WBS and turn them into small components called activities.
N   c. The control account level is the level in the WBS above the work package level. It is sometimes called the cost account level.
N   d. The control account level is the level in the WBS above the work package level. It is sometimes called the cost account level.

5. c. PMBOK® Guide: Section 5.4 (implied though not explicitly stated)
Y   c. The WBS does not include dates. The schedule includes dates.
N   a. The WBS may help us communicate with many of the project stakeholders.
N   b. Building the WBS is a great team building activity.
N   d. The WBS organizes the project deliverables. They may be organized by phase, etc.

6. c. PMBOK® Guide: Section 5.4.3.1
Y   c. The control account level is the level in the WBS above the work package level. It is sometimes called the cost account level.
N   a. The work package level is the lowest level of the WBS.
N   b. There is no activity level in the WBS. In the process define activities we take the work packages of the WBS and turn them into small components called activities.
N   d. There is no such thing as the dictionary level of the WBS.

7. a. PMBOK® Guide: Section 5.4
Y   a. The WBS should be deliverable oriented.
N   b. and c. The activity list, not the WBS, should be activity oriented.
N   d. The WBS should be deliverable oriented.

8. b. PMBOK® Guide: Section 5.4.3.1

Y   b. The WBS dictionary describes in detail the work packages in the WBS.

N   a. The scope statement describes the project and the product scope.

N   c. The control account level is the level in the WBS above the work package level. It is sometimes called the cost account level.

N   d. The requirement documents describe the requirements.

9. a. PMBOK° Guide: Section 5.4.3.1

Y   a. The scope baseline includes three documents: the scope statement, the WBS, and the WBS dictionary.

N   b. The project scope is not described in the scope management plan. The plan describes how to define and manage the scope.

N   c. The requirements management plan describes how to collect and manage the requirements.

N   d. The requirements traceability matrix ensures that all the requirements provide business value.

10. c. PMBOK° Guide: Section 5.4.3.1

Y   c. The control account level integrates scope, time, and cost and is the level used for earned value management.

N   a. The work package level is too detailed to be the level for earned value management.

N   b. There is no activity level in the WBS. In the process define activities we take the work packages of the WBS and turn them into small components called activities.

N   d. The planning package level is below the control account level and is a holding bucket for future work.

11. d. PMBOK° Guide: Section 5.4

Y   d. The scope baseline includes the project deliverables.

N   a. The schedule baseline includes the planning dates.

N   b. The schedule baseline includes the sequencing of activities.

N   c. The cost estimates include the estimated costs for each work package.

12. a. PMBOK° Guide: Section 5.4.3.1

Y   a. The code of accounts assigns a unique number to each and every component of the WBS.

N   b. This is the definition of the chart of accounts. It is another WBS idea that assigns categories to costs so as to keep track of them.

N   c. The corporation, or the organization may have a chart of accounts. This is a numbering system that keeps track of costs by category, not by WBS component.

N   d. The cost account level, sometimes called the control account level, is the level above the work package level.

13. d. PMBOK° Guide: Section 5.4.2.2

Y   d. We should decompose to a level that adds value, and no further.

N   a. We may be able to decompose to a high level of detail, but we only want to decompose to a level that adds value.

N   b. We may have money available to allow us to decompose to a high level of detail, but we only want to decompose to a level that adds value.

N   c. We may have time available to allow us to decompose to a high level of detail, but we only want to decompose to a level that adds value.

Plan Schedule Management

> ☑ **Exam Tip:** Review Figure 6-4 of the PMBOK° Guide.

In this process the schedule management plan is created.

INPUTs of plan schedule management

Project management plan- the project plan most likely is not fully developed yet. Elements of the project plan though may help develop the schedule management plan.

Project charter- this document provides high level information including the summary milestone schedule to help start planning for the schedule.

Enterprise environmental factors- ex. Organizational culture- the culture of our organization may affect the process we use to plan for the schedule. As an example, a culture that is very detail oriented may lead us to develop a schedule plan that is very detail oriented.

Organizational process assets- ex. Templates- our organization may have templates for the schedule management plan, the activity list, etc. These templates may make developing the schedule a much quicker process.

TOOLs and TECHNIQUEs of plan schedule management

Expert judgment, **Analytical techniques** and **Meetings**-

OUTPUTs of plan schedule management

Schedule Management Plan	Selects a scheduling methodology, a scheduling tool, and sets formats and criteria for the project schedule.
	It does not describe or list the planned start and finish dates for project activities. (The schedule does this).
	It is not part of the schedule baseline.
	It is contained in or a subsidiary plan of the project management plan.

PLAN SCHEDULE MANAGEMENT - Sample Questions

1. An example of an enterprise environmental factor is:
a. historical information
b. templates
c. change control procedures
d. project management software

2. An example of an organizational process asset is:
a. change control procedures
b. project management software
c. organizational work authorization system
d. organizational culture

3. The schedule management plan establishes:
a. the planned start and finish dates for all activities
b. the dependencies for project activities
c. the units of measure (staff hours, staff days) for project activities
d. the leads and lags for project activities

© January 2016 AME Group, Inc. author Aileen Ellis, PMP, PgMP
aileen@amegroupinc.com 719-659-3658

PLAN SCHEDULE MANAGEMENT - Solutions

1. d. PMBOK° Guide: Section 6.1.1.3
Y   d. Software in general is an enterprise environmental factor.
N   a., b., and c. Templates, change control procedures, and historical information are organizational process assets, not enterprise environmental factors.

2. a. PMBOK° Guide: Section 6.1.1.4
Y   a. Change control procedures are organizational assets.
N   b., c., and d. Software, organizational work authorization systems, and organizational culture are all examples of enterprise environmental factors not organizational process assets.

3. c. PMBOK° Guide: Section 6.1.3.1
Y   c. The schedule management plan describes how we will create and manage the schedule. This includes information about units of measure.
N   a. The schedule includes the planned start and finish dates for all activities.
N   b. The network diagram and the schedule show the dependencies for project activities.
N   d. The network diagram and the schedule show the leads and lags for activities.

Define Activities

☑ **Exam Tip:** Review Figure 6-6 of the PMBOK° Guide.

In this process we take the lowest level deliverables of the Work Breakdown Structure and break them down into even smaller components called activities.

☑ **EXAM TIP:** Know the difference between the WBS and the activity list.

WBS	ACTIVITY LIST
Made up of deliverables (nouns)	Made up of activities (verbs)
Output of Create WBS	Output of define activities

INPUTs of define activities (not all listed)

Schedule management plan- the schedule management plan may describe the process for developing the activity list.

Scope baseline- the scope baseline contains the WBS (work breakdown structure). The lowest level of the WBS are the work packages. During define activities we take these work packages and break them down even further into activities.

☑ **EXAM TIP:** The scope baseline contains: Scope statement, WBS, and WBS Dictionary.

TOOLs and TECHNIQUEs of define activities (not all listed)

Decomposition- we use this tool to break the work packages (in deliverable format) into smaller more manageable items (activities –in action format).

Rolling wave planning- we plan the near term work in great detail and the far term work in much less detail. This is a type of progressive elaboration.

OUTPUTs of define activities

Activity list- this is a list of all the activities we need for the project. Of course, if we are doing rolling wave planning, we will only have the activities for the near term work.

© January 2016 AME Group, Inc. author Aileen Ellis, PMP, PgMP
aileen@amegroupinc.com 719-659-3658

Activity attributes- this is a complete description of the activity including activity ID and WBS ID, etc. Also included is the type of activity. Examples of types of activities include:
- Level of effort
- Discrete effort
- Apportioned effort

Milestone list- this is a list of milestones for the project. Milestones may be:
- Mandatory- required by physical nature of work or by a contract (hard logic)
- Discretionary- based on best practices but not mandatory (soft logic)

☑ **EXAM TIP:** Milestones have zero cost and zero duration.

DEFINE ACTIVITIES - Sample Questions

1. In the process of define activities we:
a. decompose the work packages into a list of activities
b. decompose the activities into a list of work packages
c. decompose the work packages into a hierarchy of activities
d. decompose the activities into a hierarchy of work packages

2. Milestones:
a. have zero duration
b. are always mandatory
c. have a planned start and finish date
d. are an input to define activities

3. The scope baseline is made up of all the following documents except:
a. the WBS
b. the WBS dictionary
c. the schedule
d. the scope statement

4. Decomposition is a tool and technique of what process(es)?
a. define activities
b. define activities and create WBS
c. define activities and define scope
d. define activities and collect requirements

5. Based on your success on small projects you now have been made the project manager of a large, complex, multi-year project. In the past, you have planned out all the details of the activities early in the project. For your current project you are more likely to do progressive elaboration through:
a. rolling wave planning
b. scope changes
c. WBS dictionary
d. templates

6. Your project team is new to project management. They are struggling with the idea of a WBS versus an activity list. You explain that:
a. the activity list is really the lowest level of the WBS
b. the WBS shows the sequence of activities
c. the activity list drives the creation of the WBS
d. the WBS is deliverable oriented whereas the activity list is action oriented

© January 2016 AME Group, Inc. author Aileen Ellis, PMP, PgMP
aileen@amegroupinc.com 719-659-3658

DEFINE ACTIVITIES - Solutions

1. a. **PMBOK° Guide: Section 6.2**
Y   a. Define activities is the process in which we take the work packages of the WBS and break them down into smaller components called activities.
N   b. The activities are smaller than the work packages. We decompose the work packages into activities, not the activities into work packages.
N   c. We do decompose the work packages into activities but not a hierarchy of activities. The output is a list.
N   d. The activities are smaller than the work packages. We decompose the work packages into activities, not the activities into work packages.

2. a. **PMBOK° Guide: Section 6.2.3.3**
Y   a. Milestones have zero duration.
N   b. Milestones may be mandatory or discretionary.
N   c. Since milestones have zero duration they have only one date, not a planned start and a planned finish date.
N   d. Milestones are an output of define activities, not an input.

3. c. **PMBOK° Guide: Section 5.4.3.1**
Y   c. The schedule, once approved, will become the schedule baseline, not the scope baseline.
N   a., b., and d. The scope baseline is made up of 3 documents: the scope statement, the WBS, and the WBS dictionary.

4. b. **PMBOK° Guide: Sections 5.4.2.1 and 6.2.2.1**
Y   b. This is the best answer. Decomposition is a tool and technique of both of these processes.
N   a. This is a true answer but look for a better one.
N   c. Decomposition is not a tool and technique of define scope.
N   d. Decomposition is not a tool and technique of collect requirements.

5. a. **PMBOK° Guide: Section 6.2.2.2**
Y   a. Rolling wave planning means we plan the near term activities in detail and the activates further out in much less detail.
N   b. Scope changes should be processed through the perform integrated change control process.
N   c. The WBS dictionary is created before the activities. It is related to the work packages.
N   d. Templates help us know what activities may be associated with what work packages. This activity does not fit in the context of the question.

6. d. **PMBOK° Guide: Section 6.2**
Y   d. The WBS is deliverable oriented (the components of the WBS are deliverables), whereas the activity list is action oriented (the components of the activity list are activities- actions).
N   a. The lowest level of the WBS is the work package level. The activities are not in the WBS.
N   b. The network diagram, not the WBS, shows the sequence of activities.
N   c. The WBS drives the creation of the activity list.

After we define activities we may begin sequencing activities and/or estimating activity resources. These two processes may occur in parallel.

Sequence Activities

☑ **Exam Tip:** Review Figure 6-8 of the PMBOK® Guide.

During sequence activities we want to create a network diagram that visualizes the logical relationships between all the activities. All activities should have a predecessor (only exception- the first activity has no predecessor) and a successor (only exception- the last activity has no successor.)
- Predecessor- an activity that comes before (precedes) another activity
- Successor- an activity that comes after (succeeds) another activity

INPUTs of sequence activities (not all listed)

Schedule management plan- the schedule management plan describes the process for sequencing the activities found in the list. It may include the name of the scheduling tool (ex. Microsoft Project) and the scheduling method (ex. critical path method).

Activity list -these are the activities we need to sequence. At this point we will be thinking about predecessors and successors.

Activity attributes- details about mandatory or discretionary relationships may be included in the attributes.

Milestone list- these milestones may need to occur before or after specific activities or at certain dates (monthly status reviews).

Project Scope Statement- includes the constraints and assumptions that we need to consider as we sequence the activities.

TOOLs AND TECHNIQUEs of sequence activities

Precedence diagramming method (PDM)- most common method of sequencing activities
- Nodes (boxes)- represent activities
- Lines (arrows)- represent relationships

There are four types of **relationships** represented in the precedence diagramming method. (see **PMBOK® Guide: Figure 6-9**)

Finish to start (FS)- this is the most common relationship. If a relationship is not specifically listed on a diagram assume it is finish to start.

Finish to finish (FF)- the finish of one activity is driving the finish of another.

Start to start (SS)- the start of one activity is driving the start of another.

© January 2016 AME Group, Inc. author Aileen Ellis, PMP, PgMP
aileen@amegroupinc.com 719-659-3658

Start to Finish (SF)- this is the least common of all the relationships- the start of one activity is driving the finish of another.

Other methods of depicting relationships include:
Arrow Diagramming Method (ADM): (not in PMBOK® Guide)
- used less often than the PDM
- activities are placed on arrows (not in boxes)
- the arrows represent both the activities and the relationships
- diagram called "activity-on-arrow" or "activity-on-line" diagram
- only uses finish to start relationships
- uses dummy activities to show dummy relationships. There are no cost and no duration for dummy activities

GERT- graphical evaluation and review technique (not in PMBOK® Guide)
- Allows for probabilistic treatment of the network diagram
- Very complex and thus not common
- Allows loops between activities

Dependency determination- the type of dependency has a huge impact on the amount of flexibility the project manager may use when managing the schedule.
- Mandatory dependency- required by the physical nature of work or by a contract (hard logic)
- Discretionary- based on best practices but not mandatory (soft logic)
- External- something outside the project is driving something inside the project
- Internal- a dependency that is within the control of the project team members

☑ **EXAM TIP:** Recognize the phrases: hard logic and soft logic.

Leads and Lags- (see PMBOK® Guide: Figure 6-10)
- Project Leads- leads allow a successor activity to advance as it is related to a predecessor. Ex. When we are writing code we may be able to start testing some code even before we finish writing all the code.
- Project Lags- lags forces a delay in a relationship. Ex. When painting a room we often want a lag after painting the walls before we will hang artwork on the walls.

☑ **EXAM TIP:** Be careful on the exam with these ideas. Leads only advance the project when the lead falls on the critical path. Lags only delay a project schedule when the lag is on the critical path.

OUTPUTs of sequence activities (not all listed)

Project schedule network diagrams (see PMBOK® Guide: Figure 6-11) -this diagram is a physical representation of the logical relationships of the project activities. Notice at this point there are no dates, no durations, etc. on the diagram. This will come later when we get to develop schedule.

SEQUENCE ACTIVITIES - Sample Questions

1. In the precedence diagramming method which relationship is most common:
a. finish to start
b. finish to finish
c. start to start
d. start to finish

2. Another name for the precedence diagramming method is:
a. activity on arrow
b. arrow diagramming
c. activity on node
d. activity on line

3. The nodes (boxes) in a precedence diagram represent:
a. the activity
b. the relationship
c. the duration
d. the cost

4. Soft logic is another name for:
a. discretionary dependency
b. mandatory dependency
c. external dependency
d. internal dependency

5. We show the delay of a successor activity on a network diagram through:
a. leads
b. lags
c. milestones
d. arrows

6. The arrows in a precedence diagram represent:
a. the activity
b. the relationship
c. the duration
d. the cost

7. Hard logic is another name for:
a. discretionary dependency
b. mandatory dependency
c. external dependency
d. preferential dependency

8. We show the acceleration of a successor activity on a network diagram through:
a. leads
b. lags
c. milestones
d. arrows

© January 2016 AME Group, Inc. author Aileen Ellis, PMP, PgMP
aileen@amegroupinc.com 719-659-3658

9. In the Precedence Diagramming method which relationship is least common:
a. finish to start
b. finish to finish
c. start to start
d. start to finish

10. You are working with your core team developing the network diagram for your map making project. Your team member tells you that they suggest you plan in your schedule that you will do a fly over of the area before researching the geography. You ask them why and they tell you it is a best practice. This is an example of a(n):
a. mandatory dependency
b. discretionary dependency
c. hard logic
d. external dependency

11. The schedule network diagrams are an output of sequence activities. This output becomes an input to which process?
a. estimate activity resources
b. estimate activity durations
c. develop schedule
d. plan schedule management

SEQUENCE ACTIVITIES - Solutions

1. a. PMBOK° Guide: Section 6.3.2.1
Y a. If you think about the schedules that you now use, most likely the most common relationship is finish to start.
N b. Finish to finish means the finish of one activity drives the finish of another. This is not nearly as common as finish to start.
N c. Start to start means the start of one activity drives the start of another. This is not nearly as common as finish to start.
N d. Start to finish is the least common relationship. It means the start of one activity drives the finish of another.

2. c. PMBOK° Guide: Section 6.3.2.1
Y c. Another name for the precedence diagramming method (PDM) is activity on node.
N a., b., and d. Activity on arrow, arrow diagramming, and activity on line are all another way of representing logical relationships. These diagrams are limited to finish to start relationships and therefore are not as common as the precedence diagramming method.

3. a. PMBOK° Guide: Section 6.3.2.1
Y a. The boxes represent the activity.
N b. The lines (or the arrows) represent the relationship.
N c. The duration is not represented in the diagram. In this context the diagram is only showing the activities and the relationships. All the boxes are the same size. (See PMBOK° Guide: Figure 6-11.)
N d. The cost is not represented in the diagram.

4. a. PMBOK° Guide: Section 6.3.2.2
Y a. Another name for discretionary logic is soft logic. It is based on good practice.
N b. Hard logic is another name for mandatory dependencies.
N c. External dependencies are normally outside the control of the project team. They may use hard or soft logic.
N d. Internal dependencies are normally inside the control of the project team. They may use hard or soft logic.

5. b. PMBOK° Guide: Section 6.3.2.3
Y b. Lags show the delay of a successor activity.
N a. Leads show the advancement (acceleration) of a successor activity. The successor activity begins before the predecessor has completed.
N c. Milestones are events with zero duration.
N d. Arrows (or lines) represent relationships in precedence diagrams.

6. b. PMBOK° Guide: Section 6.3.2.1
Y b. The arrows (or lines) represents the relationships.
N a. The boxes represent the activity.
N c. The duration is not represented in the diagram. In this context the diagram is only showing the activities and the relationships. All the boxes are the same size. (See PMBOK° Guide: Figure 6-11.)
N d. The project cost is not represented in the diagram.

7. b. PMBOK° Guide: Section 6.3.2.2
Y b. Hard logic is another name for mandatory dependencies.
N a. Another name for discretionary logic is soft logic. It is based on good practice.

© January 2016 AME Group, Inc. author Aileen Ellis, PMP, PgMP
aileen@amegroupinc.com 719-659-3658

N   c. External dependencies are normally outside the control of the project team. They may use hard or soft logic.

N   d. Internal dependencies are normally inside the control of the project team. They may use hard or soft logic.

8. a.   PMBOK° Guide: Section 6.3.2.3

Y   a. Leads show the advancement (acceleration) of a successor activity. The successor activity begins before the predecessor has completed.

N   b. Lags show the delay of a successor activity.

N   c. Milestones are events with zero duration.

N   d. Arrows (or lines) represent relationships in precedence diagrams.

9. d.   PMBOK° Guide: Section 6.3.2.1

Y   d. Start to finish is the least common relationship. It means the start of one activity drives the finish of another.

N   a. If you think about the schedules that you now use, most likely the most common relationship is finish to start.

N   b. Finish to finish means the finish of one activity drives the finish of another. This is not nearly as common as finish to start.

N   c. Start to start means the start of one activity drives the start of another. This is not nearly as common as finish to start.

10. b. PMBOK° Guide: Section 6.3.2.2

Y   b. Discretionary dependencies are based on best practices.

N   a. This is not a mandatory dependency because we do not have to use this sequence.

N   c. Hard logic is mandatory logic. This is not mandatory. We do not have to do it this way.

N   d. Both of the activities are related to the project and therefore would not be considered external.

11. c. PMBOK° Guide: Figure 6-8

Y   c. This diagram shows the logical relationships between activities. This is needed to develop a schedule.

N   a. We do not need the network diagram to estimate activity resources.

N   b. We do not need the network diagram to estimate activity durations.

N   d. The schedule management plan is used to help sequence activities. Therefore, the schedule management plan is an input to sequence the activities, not the other way around.

Estimate Activity Resources

☑ **Exam Tip:** Review Figure 6-13 of the PMBOK® Guide.

In this process we estimate the number of resources (material, people, equipment, and supplies) needed for each activity. With human resources we often estimate in terms of person hours or person days. Realize we are not determining the durations of the activities yet, just how many resources are needed for each activity.

INPUTS of estimate activity resources (not all listed)

Schedule management plan- the schedule management plan may describe the process for estimating activity resources. As an example the plan should define what units of measure are acceptable. Maybe you want all labor hours estimated in work hours, or work days, or work weeks. The plan will specify this.

Activity list- we will estimate how many resources (material, people, equipment, and supplies) we need for each activity.

Activity attributes- details listed in the attributes may help with estimating resources.

Resource calendars- you may be wondering about this input. It is actually an output of acquire project team and conduct procurements. Think of the current process as being iterative. We may not have resource calendars the first time we estimate our resources, but eventually we will need these calendars to do a good job of estimating.

Risk register- again you may be wondering about this input. We may not have a risk register the first time we estimate resources but eventually we will want to include risk in all of our planning. Think of the risk register as a spreadsheet or a database that includes all of our current risk information.

Activity cost estimates- one more time you may be wondering where this input came from. It is an output of estimate costs. The cost of resources may be something we want to think about as we consider different resource options.

TOOLS and TECHNIQUES of estimate activity resources (not all listed)

Alternative analysis- there may be different options as far as resources. Ex. – maybe you would prefer to have 100 hours of a senior engineer on a particular activity but you know you will not be able to acquire that many hours from a senior engineer. Another option would be 20 hours of a senior engineer and 150 hours of a junior engineer.

Published estimating data- in some industries there are published unit costs, etc. for labor, material, etc. In this technique, the activity is compared to the

© January 2016 AME Group, Inc. author Aileen Ellis, PMP, PgMP
aileen@amegroupinc.com 719-659-3658

activities for which data exists and the actual cost or durations or resources of the closest comparable activity is selected from the data and used as the estimate. This only works if there is published estimated data available.

Ex.- when you take your automobile in for service the service organization often obtains labor requirements for the required service from a book or database.

Bottom-up estimating- after the resources are estimated for all the activities these estimates are aggregated (added together) so as to develop an estimate for the entire project.

Project management software- this software is often used to help improve resource utilization. Examples of items to help with this include: resource breakdown structures, etc.

OUTPUTs of estimate activity resources (not all listed)

Activity resource requirements- based on the information we have, this is what we require as far as type and quantity of resources for each activity. Documentation should include not just the requirements but how you came up with those requirements (basis of estimate and assumptions).

Resource Breakdown Structure- this is one way to visualize resource requirements.

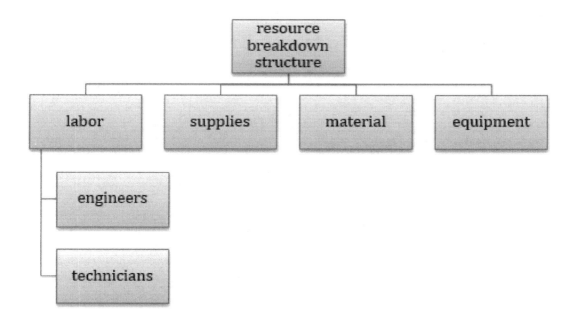

ESTIMATE ACTIVITY RESOURCES - Sample Questions

1. During estimate activity resources we should estimate the type and quantities of all of the following resources except:
a. material
b. money
c. people
d. equipment

2. Examples of alternative analysis include all of the following except:
a. using different levels of people (20 hours of a senior engineer may be equivalent in output to 5 hours of a senior engineer and 40 hours of a junior engineer)
b. different machines or tools
c. in-house labor versus contractors
d. analogous versus parametric estimating

3. Which of the following is a tool and technique of estimate activity resources:
a. published estimating data
b. precedence diagramming method
c. critical path method
d. resource leveling

4. All of the following are outputs of estimate activity resources except:
a. activity resource requirements
b. activity duration estimates
c. resource breakdown structure
d. project documentation updates

5. Optimizing resource utilization often uses what tool and technique:
a. bottom-up estimating
b. project management software
c. precedence diagramming method
d. critical path method

© January 2016 AME Group, Inc. author Aileen Ellis, PMP, PgMP
aileen@amegroupinc.com 719-659-3658

ESTIMATE ACTIVITY RESOURCES - Solutions

1. b. PMBOK® Guide: Section 6.4
Y   b. We estimate money during the process estimate costs.

N   a., c., and d. Estimating resources includes estimating equipment, materials, labor (people hours, not the actual people we will use - that comes later).

2. d. PMBOK® Guide: Section 6.4.2.2
Y   d. Alternative analysis is a tool and technique we use to look at different alternatives from a resource standpoint to get us to the same output. Analogous versus parametric estimating are two estimating techniques, not two alternative uses of resources.

N   a., b., and c. These are examples of alternative resources that may be analyzed as we estimate our resources.

3. a. PMBOK® Guide: Section 6.4.2.3
Y   a. Published estimating data may be used to help speed up the process of estimating resources.

N   b. The precedence diagramming method is a tool and technique of sequence activities.

N   c. The critical path method is a tool and technique of develop schedule.

N   d. Resource leveling is a tool and technique of develop schedule.

4. b. PMBOK® Guide: Section 6.4.3
Y   b. The activity duration estimates are an output of estimate activity durations.

N   a., c., and d. Estimate activity resources has several outputs including activity resource requirements, resource breakdown structure, and project documentation updates.

5. b. PMBOK® Guide: Section 6.4.2.5
Y   b. Project management software, with the appropriate data entered may be used to optimize resource allocation.

N   a. Bottom-up estimating is used a tool and technique of both estimate activity resources and estimate costs.

N   c. The precedence diagramming method is a tool and technique of sequence activities and is used to show logical relationships among the schedule activities.

N   d. The critical path method is a tool and technique of develop schedule and is used to calculate the early start and finish dates, the late start and finish dates, as well as the float of activities and project duration.

Estimate Activity Durations

In this process we estimate the number of work periods (not the number of person hours) required to complete each activity. Example- Activity A will take 80 person hours to complete. We have one person available half time and therefore we will estimate four weeks to complete the activity.

INPUTs of estimate activity durations (not all listed)

Schedule management plan- the schedule management plan describes the process for estimating activity resources. As an example the plan should define what units of measure are acceptable.

Activity list- we will estimate the duration needed for each activity.

Activity attributes- details listed in the attributes may help with estimating durations.

Activity resource requirements- if we believe an activity will take 80 hours of a standard senior engineer and an above average senior engineer becomes available we may not have to estimate 2 full weeks of duration but maybe something less.
Efficiency and productivity must be taken into account when moving from resource requirements to duration estimates.

Resource calendars- we review these calendars to check availability of desired resources. As an example, we require 40 hours of a junior engineer. The calendar shows us that the engineer will only be available half time. Therefore, we may estimate a duration of 2 weeks (the engineer can work 20 hours per week).

Project scope statement- constraints and assumptions will be listed in the scope statement that may affect activity durations.
Example related to assumptions- we may assume that the project team will be projectized and that all resources will be available full-time.
Example related to constraints- we may have a constraint that all electrical work will be performed by union labor and that labor is allowed to work no more than 35 hours/week.

Risk register- this is the spreadsheet or database that contains our list of risks, etc. Based on the risks, we may add contingency to our duration estimates.

© January 2016 AME Group, Inc. author Aileen Ellis, PMP, PgMP
aileen@amegroupinc.com 719-659-3658

TOOLs and TECHNIQUEs of estimate activity durations (not all listed)

☑ **EXAM TIP:** Know the difference between analogous and parametric estimating.

ANALOGOUS ESTIMATING	PARAMETRIC ESTIMATING
Based on one past project	Based on statistics
Limited amount of data available	Enough data to create statistics
Less costly	More costly
Quicker	Slower- because we need to develop the statistics
Less accurate	More accurate

Three-Point Estimating- to increase the accuracy of an estimate we may go from just asking for the most likely result to asking for 3 estimates/activity. The three estimates are:
P- pessimistic (worst case scenario)
ML- most likely
O- optimistic (best case scenario).

PERT- Program Evaluation and Review Technique: Used to define the range of activity's duration. Takes 3 estimates and provides weighted average. Know the equations below for the exam.

PERT Estimate= $(P + 4ML + O)/6$.
P= pessimistic
ML= most likely
O= optimistic

One Standard Deviation= $|(P - O)/6|$
P= pessimistic
O= optimistic

Variance = $(1 SD)^2$

☑ **EXAM TIP:** PERT stands for: Program Evaluation and Review Technique.

Group decision-making techniques- more accurate estimates, and greater commitment to the project, may be obtained by working as a team on estimates. Examples of these techniques include:

Delphi technique- a technique in which we only work with experts in an anonymous fashion to reach a consensus.

Nominal group technique- a voting technique used after brainstorming to rank the most important ideas.

Brainstorming- a technique in which many ideas are generated often from lots of people.

Reserve analysis- there are two types of reserves: contingency and management.

Contingency reserves- at times we add a contingency reserve to our duration estimates. They are set-up for known unknowns. Contingency reserves are considered part of the project baseline.
The contingency reserve amount may be determined several different ways:
- it may be a percentage of the estimated duration
- it may be a fixed time
- it may be developed using other methods
- as we move through the project, we should have a better estimate of what contingency is required

Management reserves- these reserves are set-up for unknown-unknowns (unforeseen work that is within the scope of the project). These reserves are not in the schedule baseline but are considered part of the overall project duration estimates.

☑ **EXAM TIP:** Know the difference between contingency and management reserves.

OUTPUTs of estimate activity durations (not all listed)

Activity duration estimates- these are the estimates for each project activity. The estimates may include reserve but do not include leads and lags. It is always good to include a range with each estimate.

© January 2016 AME Group, Inc. author Aileen Ellis, PMP, PgMP
aileen@amegroupinc.com 719-659-3658

ESTIMATE ACTIVITY DURATIONS - Sample Questions

1. The purpose of estimating activity durations is to get an approximation on:
a. the amount of time it will take to complete the project
b. the number of work periods for each activity
c. the quantity of resources needed for the project
d. the amount of effort required for each activity

2. Your team is deciding between analogous estimating and parametric estimating to assist with estimating the activity durations. Which of the following is true of analogous estimating compared to parametric estimating:
a. analogous is a slower process
b. analogous is based on statistics
c. analogous is generally more costly to develop
d. analogous is based on one past project

3. The PERT (program evaluation and review technique) uses all of the following estimates except:
a. most likely
b. optimistic (best-case)
c. pessimistic (worst-case)
d. mean (average)

4. All of the following are true about a time reserve except:
a. it may be a percentage of the estimated duration
b. it may be a fixed time
c. it may be developed using other methods
d. it should be the same amount for each activity

5. Management reserves are set-up for:
a. known-unknowns
b. accepted risks
c. extra work to make the customer happy
d. unforeseen work that is within the scope of the project

6. The traditional PERT technique uses:
a. a triangular distribution
b. a beta distribution
c. mean
d. average

ESTIMATE ACTIVITY DURATIONS - Solutions

1. b. PMBOK° Guide: Section 6.5.3.1

Y   b. Estimating activity durations is estimating the durations of the activities, not of the project.

N   a. The word in this answer that makes it incorrect is project. Estimating activity durations is estimating the durations of the activities, not of the project.

N   c. Activity resource requirements is an estimate of the quantity of resources required for the project.

N   d. Estimating activity resources is estimating effort (for people) for each activity. Estimating activity durations is about estimating the durations of each activity. They are not the same thing. We may need 40 hours of effort on activity A. If we have 2 people available full-time the duration of the activity may be closer to 20 hours, not 40 hours.

2. d. PMBOK° Guide: Section 6.5.2.2

Y   d. Analogous estimates are based on one past project. Parametric estimates are based on the statistics developed from many past projects.

N   a. Parametric estimating is a slower process. The assumption is that we need to develop the statistics used in the parametric estimates.

N   b. Parametric estimating is based on statistics, analogous is not.

N   c. Parametric estimates are usually more costly to develop. The assumption is that we need to develop the statistics used in the parametric estimates.

3. d. PMBOK° Guide: Section 6.5.2.4

Y   d. The equation for PERT. PERT= PERT Estimate= $(P + 4ML + O)/6$.
P= pessimistic, ML= most likely, O= optimistic

4. d. PMBOK° Guide: Section 6.5.2.6

Y   d. The tricky part of this answer is the word "should". Be careful of words like should. The time reserve is what makes sense for the activity and the project.

N   a. A time reserve may be a percentage. Let's take the example of 10% reserve added. If the duration for activity A is 10 days we may then add 10% of 10 days =1 day. The new estimated duration for activity A =10 days + 1 day reserve = 11 days.

N   b. A time reserve may be a fixed amount of time.

N   c. A time reserve may be developed using risk management processes.

5. d. PMBOK° Guide: Section 6.5.2.6

Y   d. Management reserves may relate to cost or schedule. They are for unplanned work within the project scope.

N   a. Contingency reserves are for known-unknowns. An example would be rework. We know we are going to have rework though we don't know exactly how much.

N   b. Contingency reserves are for risks that have been accepted actively. More on this when we get to plan risk responses.

N   c. We do not do extra work to make the customer happy. We do the work to meet the project objectives, nothing more, nothing less.

6. b. PMBOK° Guide: Section 6.5.2.4

Y   b. PERT uses a beta distribution.

N   a. If we are going to use a triangular distribution we would use the equation: Duration estimate= $(P + ML + O)/3$. P= pessimistic. O= optimistic, ML= most likely.

N   c. and d. Mean and average have the same definition. Therefore, neither may be right. We use the most likely estimate not the mean (or average) in the PERT equation.

© January 2016 AME Group, Inc. author Aileen Ellis, PMP, PgMP
aileen@amegroupinc.com 719-659-3658

Develop Schedule

☑ **Exam Tip:** Review Figure 6-17 of the PMBOK® Guide.

In this process we enter the schedule data into the scheduling tool so a schedule model may be created. Each activity in the schedule should have a planned start and planned finish date.

INPUTS of develop schedule (not all listed)

Schedule management plan- the schedule management plan describes the process for developing the schedule. The plan will list the scheduling software to be used, as well as what methods (CPM, critical chain, etc.) will be used in what order. The plan may identify who owns the review for accuracy for each activity once the initial schedule is developed.

Activity list- each of these activities will be included in the schedule.

Activity attributes- the attributes provide finer detail of the activities on the list. This detail may help in developing the schedule.

Project schedule network diagrams- these diagrams show the relationships (predecessors and successors) for the activities on the activity list.

Activity resource requirements- provide information on the types and quantities of resources required. Tradeoffs may need to be made to optimize resource utilization.

Resource calendars- provide information on when each resource is, and is not, available to work on the project. Tradeoffs may need to be made to optimize resource utilization.

Activity duration estimates- these estimates of time periods required for each activity are a critical part to developing the schedule.

☑ **EXAM TIP:** The scope statement contains the constraints and assumptions for the project.

Project staff assignments- these are an output of the process acquire project team. We will get there later in this book. In simplistic terms, the staff assignments name the person who will perform each activity.

TOOLS and TECHNIQUES of develop schedule (not all listed)

Schedule network analysis- a group of techniques used to develop the schedule.
Important terms:

path convergence- two or more paths becoming one
path divergence- one path becoming two or more

The critical path method (CPM)- this is the method used to calculate
the theoretical early start, early finish, late start, and late finish for each activity on
the project schedule. These theoretical numbers tell us how much flexibility we have
on the schedule and also the minimum project duration.
Several important definitions:

The critical path:
- the longest path through the network
- the shortest amount of time to complete the project (the shortest project duration)
- with CPM (critical path method) the critical path normally has zero total float

Critical activity- any activity on the critical path.
Total float = float = total slack = slack- the amount of time an activity may be
delayed without delaying the project finish date. The equation: total float= late finish
– early finish.
Free float- the amount of time an activity may be delayed without delaying the
earliest start of any successor.
Project float- the amount of time the project may be delayed without impacting an
imposed end date.
Negative float- a project may have negative float. A negative float for the project
means the amount of time required for the project is greater than the amount of time
allocated.

Early start- theoretically the earliest an activity may start
Early finish- theoretically the earliest an activity may finish
Late start- theoretically the latest an activity may start
Late finish- theoretically the latest an activity may finish

☑ **EXAM TIP:** The critical path method assumes unlimited resources.

Often when we do critical path calculations we use the notation shown below.

Early Start	Duration	Early Finish
	Activity Name	
Late Start	Float	Late Finish

We suggest you go to YouTube and search for Aileen Ellis. You will find multiple free
videos to help you. Search for videos from Aileen Ellis on network diagrams.

Also if you need more help we suggest our book available at Amazon:
How to get Every Network Diagram Right on the PMP Exam (print and e-book
format).

A few ideas to help us contrast some project management terminology.

© January 2016 AME Group, Inc. author Aileen Ellis, PMP, PgMP
aileen@amegroupinc.com 719-659-3658

The critical chain method- in this method we place buffers along schedule paths. The buffers help us manage:

- limited resources
- project uncertainties

There are two types of buffers (see PMBOK® Guide: Figure 6-19):

- feeding buffer-
  - placed at the end of a path feeding into the critical chain
  - these buffers help protect the critical path from any slippages on the feeding path
- project buffer-
  - placed at the end of the critical chain
  - these buffers help protect the end date from any slippages on the critical chain
- developed by Dr. Goldratt (know this name for exam)
- Parkinson theory- expanding the work to fill the time
- Student syndrome- procrastination. Example- If we know it will take two weeks to complete an activity but we are given five weeks.....many of us will not start the activity for three weeks.

☑ **EXAM TIP:** The critical chain is the resource –constrained critical path.

	Critical Path Method	Critical Chain Method
Resource assumptions	Unlimited resources	Limited resources
Management of:	Total float of network paths	Remaining buffer durations
Activity duration estimates may include:	Contingency reserve (safety margins)	No contingency reserve (no safety margins)
When used:	Before critical chain method	After critical path method

Resource optimization techniques- two of several techniques are discussed.

RESOURCE LEVELING	RESOURCE SMOOTHING
GOAL: Balance demand for resources with supply	GOAL: Ensure demand for resources does not exceed certain limits
Critical path may change- usually get longer	Critical path not allowed to change
All resource issues resolved	Not all resources may be optimized

Modeling techniques- two of several techniques are discussed.

WHAT–IF Scenario Analysis	Simulation
GOAL: assess feasibility of schedule, preparing contingency plans	GOAL: understand probability of hitting project objectives
METHOD: evaluating scenarios to predict effect on project objectives	METHOD: using three-point estimates to simulate schedule (note: to simulate the schedule a network diagram is also required). Ex. Monte Carlo

LEADS	LAGS
Advance a successor activity in relationship to its predecessor	Delay an activity in relationship to its predecessor
Only affects project end date if on the critical path.	Only affects project end date if on the critical path
Ex.- allowing testing to begin even though we have not completed coding	Ex. Waiting a time period after painting a wall before hanging art work on the wall (the lag is required for the paint on the wall to dry)

Two types of schedule compression tools and techniques are listed

CRASHING	FAST TRACKING
GOAL: shorten the project duration	GOAL: shorten the project duration
METHOD: add more resources to the critical path activities	METHOD: overlap activities or phases that we would prefer to complete in sequence
EFFECT: increased cost to the project. The risk is also increased but not nearly as much as in Fast Tracking.	EFFECT: increased risk for the project. In simple terms, no increased cost unless a negative risk event occurs because of overlap.

© January 2016 AME Group, Inc. author Aileen Ellis, PMP, PgMP
aileen@amegroupinc.com 719-659-3658

☑ **EXAM TIP:** If the question states:
- You want to shorten the schedule but you have no money, what should you do? The answer is fast track. (We cannot crash since we have no money available).
- You want to shorten the schedule and you have money available, what should you do? The answer is Crash. Now of course you can also Fast Track but do not pick the answer Fast Track. If we have money we should crash since crashing raises our risk less than Fast Tracking.

Schedule tool- this is usually a software based tool that allows for scheduling.

OUTPUTS of develop schedule (not all listed)

Schedule baseline- this is the approved schedule. The schedule baseline is not normally created the first time through the process develop schedule. Only after several iterations do we normally have a schedule baseline. To change the schedule baseline, or any baseline, requested changes must be processed and approved through the integrated change control process.

Project schedule- this is your working schedule. It is expected to change and to be updated with actual data. May be expressed in several forms:
Bar chart- simple, easy to read, good to show progress
Milestone chart- simple, easy to read, good for management presentations
Project schedule network diagram- more complex, show logical relationships. Good for working with team.

Project Schedule	Schedule Baseline
Living document	Frozen document
Is a project document	Is a part of the project plan
Can be changed by the project manager (without formal change control)	Can only be changed through a formal change control process
	Schedule performance is always measured against the schedule baseline

For 50 more sample questions and solutions related to the critical path method please see Aileen's book: *How to get Every Network Diagram question right on the PMP Exam.* The book is available in both print and e-book format on Amazon. This book is much better in the print format.

DEVELOP SCHEDULE - Sample Questions

Use the following table for questions 1-4.

Activity	Predecessor	Duration
A	Start	2
B	A	5
C	B	6
D	B	3
E	C	8
F	C and D	7
G	E and F	4

1. The duration of the critical path in the above diagram is:
a. 20 days
b. 25 days
c. 35 days
d. 37 days

2. The total float of Activity C is:
a. 0 days
b. 9 days
c. 12 days
d. 24 days

3. The critical path activities are:
a. A, B, E, G
b. A, B, C, E, G
c. A, B, C, D, E, F, G
d. A, B, D, E, G

4. If management imposes an end time of 22 days the project float is:
a. 3 days
b. 4 days
c. -4 days
d. -3 days

5. In the critical chain method the project buffer:
a. protects the target finish date from slippage along the critical path
b. protects the critical chain from slippage along the feeding chains
c. is placed on the feeding chain
d. is placed at the beginning of the critical chain

6. In the critical chain method the feeding buffer:
a. protects the target finish date from slippage along the critical path
b. protects the critical chain from slippage along the feeding chains
c. is placed at the end of the critical chain
d. is placed at the beginning of the critical chain

© January 2016 AME Group, Inc. author Aileen Ellis, PMP, PgMP
aileen@amegroupinc.com 719-659-3658

7. Resource Leveling is used:
a. after the critical path method
b. before the critical path method
c. instead of the critical path method
d. instead of crashing

8. The most common type of simulation technique used to develop the schedule is:
a. earned value method
b. Monte Carlo Analysis
c. decision tree analysis
d. expected monetary value

9. The purpose of schedule compression is to:
a. shorten the project schedule
b. obtain a constant use of resources
c. overlap the project activities
d. add resources to the critical path

10. You are managing the development of a new medical device. Hitting the market window is critical for project success. To analyze the amount of float each activity has you will most likely use what method?
a. bottom-up estimating
b. expert judgment
c. critical path method
d. resource leveling

Develop Schedule - Solutions

1. The first thing we must do is draw out the diagram, showing the dependencies.

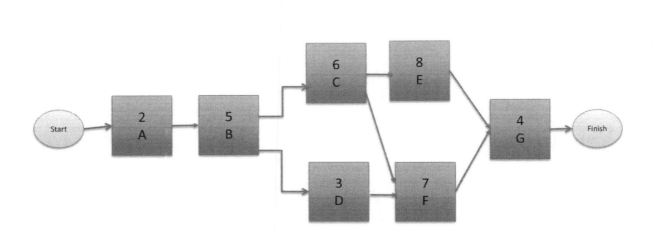

Now that we have the logic we will want to do a forward pass to identify the early start and early finish numbers for each activity. Try it on your own and then use the notes below to check your work.

© January 2016 AME Group, Inc. author Aileen Ellis, PMP, PgMP
aileen@amegroupinc.com 719-659-3658

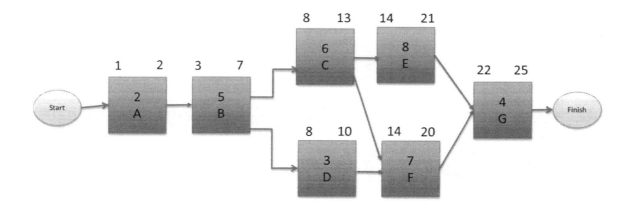

Since A is the first activity it begins on day 1 (early start). A is 2 days long. A's early finish= A's early start of 1 plus A's duration of 2 days minus 1= 1+2-1= 2.

B is the successor to A. The early start of B is the early finish of A (2 days) plus 1= 3. B's early finish= B's early start of 3 plus B's duration of 5 minus 1= 3+5-1= 7.

C is the successor to B. The early start of C is the early finish of B (7 days) plus 1= 8. C's early finish = C's early start of 8 plus C's duration of 6 minus 1= 8+6-1= 13.

D is also the successor of B. The early start of D is the early finish of B (7 days) plus 1= 8. D's early finish = D's early start of 8 plus D's duration of 3 minus 1= 8+3-1= 10.

E is the successor to C. The early start of E is the early finish of C (13 days) plus 1= 14. E's early finish = E's early start of 14 plus E's duration of 8 minus 1= 14+8-1= 21.

F is the successor to both C and D. We look at both of these predecessors to determine which has the largest early finish value. The early finish of C is 13 and of D is 10. Therefore, C has the largest early finish and that is the number we use. Therefore, the early start of F will be the early finish of C (13 days) plus 1= 14 days.
F's early finish = F's early start of 14 plus F's duration of 7 minus 1= 14+7-1= 20.

G is the successor to both E and F. We look at both these predecessors to determine which one has the largest early finish value. The early finish of E is 21 and of F is 20. Therefore, E has the largest early finish value and that is the number we use. Therefore, the early start of G will be the early finish of E (21 days) plus 1= 22 days.
G's early finish = G's early start of 22 plus G's duration of 4 minus 1= 22+4-1= 25.
The critical path duration is 25 days.

2.To calculate the float of activities we do a backward pass through the network.

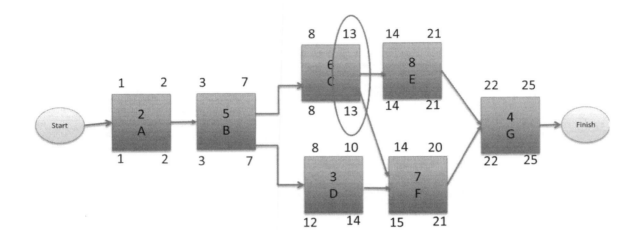

To do a backward pass we begin at the last activity which is G. We take the early finish of G (25 days) and bring that number down into the box for the late finish of G (now also 25 days).

Late start of G= late finish of G (25 days) – duration of G (4 days) plus 1= 25 - 4+1= 22 days.

Late finish of E= late start of G (22 days) minus 1= 22-1= 21 days.
Late start of E = late finish of E (21 days) – duration of E (8 days) plus 1= 21 – 8 + 1= 14 days.

Late finish of F = late start of G (22 days) minus 1= 22-1= 21 days.
Late start of F = late finish of F (21 days) – duration of F (7 days) plus 1= 21 – 7 + 1= 15 days.

Late finish of C is trickier. C is the predecessor for both E and F. We ask which successor to C (E or F) has the lower late start date. E has a late start of 14 days. F has a late start of 15 days. Therefore, E has the lower late start date.
Late finish of C= late start of E (14 days) minus 1= 14-1=13.
Late start of C= late finish of C (13 days) – duration of C (6 days) plus 1= 13 – 6 + 1= 8 days.

Late finish of D= late start of F (15 days) minus 1= 15-1+14.
Late start of D= late finish of D (14 days) – duration of D (3 days) plus 1= 14 – 3 + 1= 12 days.

© January 2016 AME Group, Inc. author Aileen Ellis, PMP, PgMP
aileen@amegroupinc.com 719-659-3658

Late finish of B is trickier. B is the predecessor for both C and D. We ask which immediate successor to B (C or D) has the lower late start date. C has a late start of 8 days. D has a late start of 12 days. Therefore, C has the lower late start date.
Late finish of B= late start of C (8 days) minus 1= 8-1= 7.
Late start of B= late finish of B (7 days) – duration of B (5 days) plus 1= 7 – 5 + 1 = 3 days.

The late finish of A now should be easier. Late finish of A = late start of B (3 days) -1 = 2 days.
The late start of A =late finish of A (2 days) – duration of A (2 days) +1= 2-2+1= 1.

The question is asking for the total float of C. Total Float of C= late finish of C (13 days) minus early finish of C (13 days)= 13-13= 0. Since this answer is 0 this also tells us that C is on the critical path.

3. b   PMBOK° Guide Section 6.6.2.3
To determine which activities are critical we calculate the total float for each activity.
Float of Activity A = 2-2 = 0
Float of Activity B = 7-7 = 0
Floact of Activity C =13-13 = 0
Float of Activity D = 14-10 = 4
Float of Activity E = 21-21 = 0
Float of Activity F = 21-20 = 1
Float of Activity G = 25-25 = 0.
Notice that Activity A, B, C, E and G all have zero total float. These activities are critical.
Activity D has a total float of 4. Activity F has a total float of 1. These two activities are not critical. We did a lot of math here. Hopefully it was easy to look at the diagram and easily know that Activity A, B, and G are critical.

4. d   PMBOK° Guide Section 6.6.2.3
If management imposes an end date of 22 days the project float = late finish of G (22 days) minus early finish of G (25 days) = - 3 days.

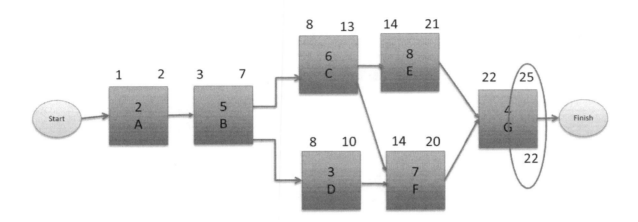

5. a. **PMBOK® Guide: Section 6.6.2.3**

Y   a. The project buffer is placed at the end of the critical chain to protect the project end date.

N   b. and c. Feeding buffers are placed at the end of the feeding chain before it hits the critical chain to protect the critical chain.

N   d. The project buffer is placed at the end of the critical chain to protect the project end date.

6. b. **PMBOK® Guide: Section 6.6.2.3**

Y   b. The feeding buffers are placed at the end of the feeding chain before it hits the critical chain to protect the critical chain.

N   a. and c. The project buffer is placed at the end of the critical chain to protect the project end date.

N   d. No buffers are placed at the beginning of chains.

7. a. **PMBOK® Guide: Section 6.6.2.4**

Y   a. There must be a schedule to resource level. Resource leveling occurs after the critical path method.

N   b. and c. There must be a schedule in place to resource level. Therefore, resource leveling occurs after the critical path method.

N   d. Resource leveling is used to ensure no resources are overcommitted. Fast tracking is used to shorten the schedule.

© January 2016 AME Group, Inc. author Aileen Ellis, PMP, PgMP
aileen@amegroupinc.com 719-659-3658

8. b. PMBOK° Guide: Section 6.6.2.5
Y   b. Monte Carlo analysis is the most common simulation technique used to develop the schedule.
N   a. Earned value method is not a simulation technique.
N   c. Decision tree analysis is not a simulation technique.
N   d. Expected monetary value is not a simulation technique.

9. a. PMBOK° Guide: Section 6.6.2.7
Y   a. The goal of schedule compression is to shorten the schedule.
N   b. The goal of resource leveling is to ensure we have no overcommitted resources.
N   c. With fast tracking we overlap activities or phases. The goal of fast tracking is to shorten the schedule. The method is overlapping the activities.
N   d. Crashing adds resources to the critical path. The goal of crashing is to shorten the schedule. The method is adding resources to the critical path.

10. c. PMBOK° Guide: Section 6.6.2.3
Y   c. The critical path method determines the float of each activity.
N   a. Bottom-up estimating determines the activity requirements.
N   b. Expert judgment may help with many processes.
N   d. Resource leveling helps ensure we have no overcommitted resources.

Plan Cost Management

> ☑ **Exam Tip:** Review Figure 7-3 of the PMBOK® Guide.

In this process we create the cost management plan.

INPUTs of plan cost management

Project management plan- the project plan most likely is not fully developed yet. Elements of the project plan though may help develop the cost management plan. Examples include:
Scope baseline- scope statement (contains constraints and assumptions), the WBS, and the WBS dictionary.
Schedule baseline- contains the approved start and finish dates for project activities.

Project charter- this document provides high level information including the summary budget to help start planning for costs.

Enterprise environmental factors- ex. Currency exchange rates. When we plan for costs we need to decide if we will accept cost estimates in multiple currencies or only one currency. Also, when we pay our internal labor and our vendors, we need to decide how we will deal with different currencies.

Organizational process assets- ex. Accounting codes most likely are standard for the organization. We need to ensure that we organize and collect cost information in a way that it is easy to move that data into the organization's accounting system.

TOOLs and TECHNIQUEs of plan cost management
Analytical techniques- these techniques may relate to project funding such as self-funding, etc. Other techniques may relate to how financial decisions are made such as: return on investment, cost–benefit analysis, net present value, opportunity cost, etc.
Expert judgment and meetings

OUTPUTS of plan cost management

Cost management plan	Defines- level of accuracy, units of measure, earned value rules, etc.
	It does not describe or list the planned costs for the project. (The cost estimate and cost baseline do this).
	It is not part of the cost baseline.

© January 2016 AME Group, Inc. author Aileen Ellis, PMP, PgMP
aileen@amegroupinc.com 719-659-3658

	It is contained in or a subsidiary plan of the project management plan.

A few other ideas:

DIRECT COST	INDIRECT COST
Directly related to the project	Not directly related to a project
Ex. Cost of full-time consultant on project	Ex. Building security, electricity

VARIABLE COST – UNIT COSTS	FIXED COST
Varies with output	Independent of output
Ex. Wages- the more people the more we spend in total on wages	Ex. Rent for building- the rent does not change based on the number of people

PLAN COST MANAGEMENT - Sample Questions

1. The degree of rounding allowed is called:
a. level of precision
b. level of accuracy
c. control thresholds
d. rules of performance measurement

2. Weighted milestones, percent complete, etc., are techniques used in:
a. units of measure
b. levels of precision
c. levels of accuracy
d. earned value measurement

3. All estimates must be within +/- 20 % is an example of:
a. control thresholds
b. levels of precision
c. levels of accuracy
d. earned value measurement

4. The amount we are allowed to deviate from the baselines without escalating is called:
a. control thresholds
b. levels of precision
c. levels of accuracy
d. earned value measurement

5. Currency exchange rates are an example of:
a. units of measure
b. enterprise environmental factors
c. levels of accuracy
d. organizational process assets

© January 2016 AME Group, Inc. author Aileen Ellis, PMP, PgMP
aileen@amegroupinc.com 719-659-3658

PLAN COST MANAGEMENT - Solutions

1. a. PMBOK® Guide: Section 7.1.3.1
Y a. The amount of rounding allowed with numbers is called the level of precision. This should be defined in the cost management plan.
N b. The level of accuracy defines the acceptable range on numbers. Maybe we will accept numbers that are +/- 50 % early in the project.
N c. Often we specify how much variance we will allow in actuals before escalation needs to occur. As an example we may say that if the project's CPI gets below .90 or above 1.1 the sponsor needs to be notified.
N d. Performance measurement rules relate to earned value. As an example the 0/100 rule states that an activity gets earned value credit only when the activity is 100% complete. The 50/50 rule states that an activity gets 50% earned value credit when it begins and 50% earned value credit when it completes.

2. d. PMBOK® Guide: Section 7.1.3.1
Y d. These are all examples of earned value measurement techniques which are a subset of the rules of performance measurement.
N a. Examples of units of measure include work hours, work days, work weeks, etc.
N b. The amount of rounding allowed with numbers is called the level of precision. As an example we want all costs rounded to US$1000.
N c. The level of accuracy defines the acceptable range on numbers. Ex. +/-50 %.

3. c. PMBOK® Guide: Section 7.1.3.1
Y c. The level of accuracy defines the acceptable range on numbers.
N a. Examples of units of measure include work hours, work days, work weeks, etc.
N b. The amount of rounding allowed with numbers is called the level of precision. As an example we want all costs rounded to US$1000.
N d. Performance measurement rules relate to earned value. Weighted milestones and percent complete are examples.

4. a. PMBOK® Guide: Section 7.1.3.1
Y a. Often we specify how much variance we will allow in actuals before escalation needs to occur. As an example we may say that if the project's CPI gets below .90 or above 1.1 the sponsor needs to be notified.
N b. The amount of rounding allowed with numbers is called the level of precision. As an example we want all costs rounded to US$1000.
N c. The level of accuracy defines the acceptable range on numbers. Maybe we will accept numbers that are +/- 50 % early in the project.
N d. Performance measurement rules relate to earned value. Weighted milestones and percent complete are examples.

5. b. PMBOK® Guide: Section 7.1.1.3
Y b. Currency rates relate to the project environment. Therefore, they are considered enterprise environmental factors.
N a. Examples of units of measure include work hours, work days, work weeks, etc.
N c. The level of accuracy defines the acceptable range on numbers. Ex. +/-50 % .
N d. Cost estimating policies, procedures, etc. are examples of organizational process assets.

Estimate Costs

In this process we determine what we think it will cost to complete the project. Usually, we estimate in some form of currency though terms like labor hours may be used. Cost estimates should improve over the life of the project.

Cost estimating accuracy:
During the initiation phase- Rough order of magnitude estimate of -25% -+75%
Later in project- definitive estimates of -5% -+10%

Cost estimates should include all costs billed to the project:
- Labor, equipment, materials, facilities
- Inflation allowance
- Contingency costs- from risk management

INPUTs of estimate costs (not all listed)

Cost management plan- this plan describes the process of estimating costs. It also may include guidelines for:
- Units of measure- should costs be estimated in labor hours, etc.
- Levels of accuracy- how much rounding will be allowed in the cost estimates (round to the $1, or $10,000?)

Human resource plan- we may not have created this plan yet but once we do we will need to update our cost estimates. This plan will include information on costs related to training, rewards, etc.

Scope baseline- is made up of three documents
- Scope statement- contains project constraints and assumptions. The most likely constraint is a predefined budget. Assumptions may relate to direct and indirect costs.
  - Direct costs- costs billed directly to the project (the cost of material)
  - Indirect costs- costs that often hit a project through an allocation (the cost of water or electricity in the building when the building houses multiple project teams)
- WBS and the WBS Dictionary- sometimes costs are estimated at the work package

Project schedule- tells us when we plan our activities and the type and amount of resources required for each activity. We may estimate costs at this level.

Risk register- contains both threats and opportunities. The responses to these risks may have a cost to the project.

TOOLs and TECHNIQUEs of estimate costs (not all listed)

☑ **EXAM TIP:** Know the difference between analogous and parametric estimating.

ANALOGOUS ESTIMATING	PARAMETRIC ESTIMATING
Based on one past project	Based on statistics
Limited amount of data available	Enough data needed to create statistics
Less costly	More costly
Quicker	Slower
Less accurate	More accurate

Bottom-up estimating- after the costs are estimated for all the activities these estimates are aggregated (added) so as to develop an estimate for the entire project.

Three-Point Estimating- to increase the accuracy of an estimate we may go from just asking for the most likely result to asking for 3 estimates/activity. The three estimates are:
> P- pessimistic (worst case scenario)
> ML- most likely
> O- optimistic (best case scenario)

PERT- Program Evaluation and Review Technique: Used to define range of activity's duration. Takes 3 estimates and provides weighted average. Know the equation below for the exam.

PERT Estimate= (P +4ML +O)/6.

Reserve analysis- There are two types of reserves: contingency and management.
    Contingency reserves- at times we add a contingency reserve to our cost estimates. They are set-up for known unknowns. Contingency reserves are considered part of the project baseline.
The contingency reserve amount may be determined several different ways:
- it may be a percentage of the estimated duration or cost
- it may be a fixed amount of time or cost
- it may be developed using other methods
- as we move through the project, we should have a better estimate of what contingency is required

    Management reserves- these reserves are set-up for unknown-unknowns (unforeseen work that is within the scope of the project). These reserves are not in the cost baseline but are considered part of the overall project budget.

☑ **EXAM TIP:** Know the difference between contingency and management reserves.

Cost of quality - often an organization will estimate the cost of the project and then add on a factor to cover the cost of quality. Much more on this when we get to plan quality.

Project Management software - may be used to simplify and speed up the estimate cost process.

Vendor bid analysis - often we may ask our vendors to submit bids, etc. that we may use in our cost estimating process.

Group decision-making techniques - more accurate estimates, and greater commitment to the project, may be obtained by working as a team on estimates. Examples of these techniques include:
Delphi technique- a technique in which we only work with experts in an anonymous fashion to reach a consensus
Nominal group technique- a voting technique used after brainstorming to rank the most important ideas
Brainstorming- a technique in which lots of ideas are generated often from lots of people

☑ **EXAM TIP:** Notice how many of the tools and techniques of estimate costs are also tools and techniques of estimate activity durations. Build a list of the T&T that these two processes have in common.

OUTPUTs of estimate costs (not all listed)

Activity cost estimates - these are the estimates of how much we believe the project will cost. It must be decided if these estimates include only direct costs or if indirect costs will also be estimated.

Basis of Estimates (BOEs) - this is all of your backup information to support how you came to the cost estimate you did. It should include constraints and assumptions, etc.

© January 2016 AME Group, Inc. author Aileen Ellis, PMP, PgMP
aileen@amegroupinc.com 719-659-3658

ESTIMATE COSTS - Sample Questions

1. All of the following are tools and techniques of estimate costs except:
a. cost of quality
b. project management software
c. vendor bid analysis
d. benefit cost analysis

2. Cost estimate tolerances should:
a. narrow over the life of the project
b. widen over the life of the project
c. stay approximately the same over the life of the project
d. increase over the life of the project

3. All of the following are true concerning the basis of estimate except:
a. supports the cost estimate backup information
b. should include ranges
c. describes how cost estimate was developed
d. is an input to estimate costs

4. As you are planning your project, your team members are asking about the amount of variance that will be allowed. They are really asking you about:
a. precision level
b. control thresholds
c. earned value rules
d. report formats

5. One way to get people more committed to meeting a cost estimate is to:
a. involve people doing the technical work in the estimating process
b. ensure the cost of quality is used as a tool and technique
c. utilize reserve analysis on the project
d. use project management software for all estimating

Estimate Costs - Solutions

1. d. PMBOK® Guide: Figure 7-4
Y   d. Benefit cost analysis may be used to create the business case before the project begins and as a tool in the quality project management processes.

N   a., b., and c. The cost of quality, project management software, and vendor bid analysis are all tools and techniques of estimate costs.

2. a. PMBOK® Guide: Section 7.2
Y   a. Cost estimate should be refined over the life of the project. This means that our cost estimates should get better, get more accurate over the life of the project.

N   b. Cost estimates should get better (narrower) over the life of the project not wider (worse).

N   c. The further we are in a project the more we know and the better (more accurate) the cost estimates should be.

N   d. Cost estimates should not increase (get higher) over the life of the project. They should get more accurate.

3. d. PMBOK® Guide: Section 7.2.3.2 (it is an output not an input)
Y   d. The basis of estimates is an output not an input to estimate costs.

N   a. The basis of estimate is the backup information to support the cost estimate.

N   b. The basis of estimates should include ranges. As an example, instead of saying we estimate the project will cost $100 we should say it will cost somewhere between $90-$125.

N   c. The basis of estimate should describe what methods we used for each estimate. As an example, we may state that our labor estimates were determined using bottom-up estimating.

4. b. PMBOK® Guide: Section 7.1.3.1
Y   b. Often we specify how much variance we allow in actuals before escalation needs to occur. As an example we may say that if the project's CPI gets below .90 or above 1.1 the sponsor needs to be notified. These levels are called our control thresholds.

N   a. The amount of rounding allowed with numbers is called the level of precision. As an example, we want all costs rounded to US$1000.

N   c. Performance measurement rules relate to earned value. As an example, the 0/100 rule states that an activity gets earned value credit only when the activity is 100% complete. The 50/50 rule states that an activity gets 50% earned value credit when it begins and 50% earned value credit when it completes.

N   d. We may specify the formats we want for all cost reports. By specifying the format it makes it easier to combine reports, etc.

5. a. PMBOK® Guide: Section 7.2.2.10
Y   a. Often the best way to get people committed is to get them involved.

N   b. Using the cost of quality it not likely to affect people's commitment.

N   c. Reserve analysis is a tool and technique of estimate costs. Using it though it not likely to affect people's commitment to the project.

N   d. Project management software is a tool and technique of estimate costs. Using it though it not likely to affect people's commitment to the project.

Determine Budget

> ☑ **Exam Tip:** Review Figure 7-7 of the PMBOK° Guide.

The cost baseline is the primary output of this process.

INPUTs of determine budget (not all listed)

Cost management plan- this plan describes the process of determine budget.

Scope baseline- is made up of three documents

- Scope statement- contains project constraints and assumptions. Constraints most likely would be related to the spending of money over time.
- WBS and the WBS Dictionary- sometimes costs are estimated at the work package level of the WBS.

Activity cost estimates and basis of estimates- these estimates will be aggregated into the cost baseline.

Project schedule- the cost baseline will show when we plan to spend money (over time). The schedule of activities is the driving force for this.

Risk register- responses to opportunities and threats may have a cost to the project.

Agreements- we may have agreements in place with our suppliers. The cost of these agreements should be in the cost baseline.

TOOLs and TECHNIQUEs of determine budget (not all listed)

Cost aggregation- the cost of the individual activities (or work packages) are aggregated (added up) to create the cost baseline.

Reserve analysis- the contingency reserve needs to be part of the cost baseline. The management reserve needs to be part of the project budget.

Funding limit reconciliation- when we plan to spend money (see the cost baseline) needs to be in line with when money will be available. If this does not reconcile, the timing of activities may need to be adjusted.

OUTPUTs of determine budget (not all listed)

Cost baseline- this is the approved time phased budget for the project. It should include contingency reserve but not management reserve.

☑ **EXAM TIP:** Review PMBOK® Guide: Figures 7-8 and 7-9 for understanding.

Project funding requirements - should match the cost baseline plus management reserve. Funding may occur all at once but more likely will occur incrementally over the life of the project.

DETERMINE BUDGET - Sample Questions

1. The total value of the control accounts is equal to:
a. value of work package cost estimates plus value of contingency reserve
b. value of the cost baseline plus the value of the management reserve
c. value of the activity cost estimates plus the value of the activity contingency reserve
d. value of the work package cost estimates plus value of the activity contingency reserve

2. Cost aggregation results in:
a. cost estimates allocated to each activity
b. cost estimates allocated to each work package
c. cost estimates added together to create an estimate for the entire project
d. cost estimates added together to create an estimate for the product life cycle

3. The project budget is equal to:
a. value of work package cost estimates plus value of contingency reserve
b. value of the cost baseline plus the value of the management reserve
c. value of the activity cost estimates plus the value of the activity contingency reserve
d. value of the work package cost estimates plus value of the activity contingency reserve

4. The project funding requirements should equal:
a. the cost baseline
b. value of work package cost estimates plus value of contingency reserve
c. the cost baseline plus the management reserve
d. the cost baseline plus the contingency reserve

5. Management is concerned about the practice of cost estimators and project managers inflating cost estimates. To deal with this practice in a positive way, management has told you that you will be allowed a contingency reserve on your project if you can support the reserve with real data. From your project management training, you realize that all the following are true about a contingency reserves except:
a. they are set-up for expected but not certain events
b. they are part of your project schedule and cost baselines
c. they are for unknown unknowns
d. they are under the control of the project manager

6. Your management has approved a contingency reserve for the project. There seems to be some confusion between contingency reserve and management reserve. You explain that management reserve is:
a. the difference between the maximum funding and the top end of the cost baseline
b. the same as contingency reserve
c. part of the cost baseline
d. under the discretion of the project manager

7. The output of determine budget is the:
a. cost estimate
b. basis of estimate
c. cost baseline
d. cost-benefit analysis

Determine Budget - Solutions

1. a. PMBOK® Guide: Figure 7-8
Y   a. The value of the control accounts = work package cost estimates + contingency reserve.
N   b. The project budget= cost baseline + management reserve.
N   c. Work package cost estimates= activity cost estimates + activity contingency reserve.
N   d. This definition has no real meaning.

2. c. PMBOK® Guide: Section 7.3
Y   c. Aggregation is adding together. Cost aggregation is adding the individual cost estimates together to get an estimate for the whole project.
N   a. and b. Aggregation is the opposite of allocation. Allocation is to distribute. Aggregate is to bring together.
N   d. The phrase "product life cycle" makes this answer wrong.

3. b. PMBOK® Guide: Figure 7-8
Y   b. The total project budget= cost baseline + management reserve.
N   a. The value of the control accounts= work package cost estimates + contingency resource.
N   c. Work package cost estimates= activity cost estimates + activity contingency reserve.
N   d. This definition has no real meaning.

4. c. PMBOK® Guide: Figure 7-9 (look at the top right of diagram)
Y   c. The project funding should equal the project budget = cost baseline + management reserve.
N   a. This answer is not complete. Need to add the management reserve.
N   b. The value of the control accounts = work package cost estimates + contingency reserve.
N   d. The word "contingency" makes this answer wrong. It should say "management."

5. c. PMBOK® Guide: Section 7.2.2.6
Y   c. Management reserve, not contingency reserve is for unknown unknowns.
N   a. Contingency reserve may be used for expected but not certain events.
N   b. Contingency reserve is part of the baselines, both cost and schedule.
N   d. Contingency reserve spending should be under the control of the project manager.

6. a. PMBOK® Guide: Figure 7-9
Y   a. Management reserve= project budget – cost baseline.
N   b. Management reserve is for unknown unknowns. Contingency reserve is for known unknowns.
N   c. Management reserve is not part of the cost baseline. Contingency reserve is.
N   d. Management reserve is not under the control of the project manager. Contingency reserve is under the control of the project manager.

7. c. PMBOK® Guide: Section 7.3.3.1
Y   c. The cost baseline is the output of determine budget.
N   a. The cost estimate is the output of estimate costs.
N   b. The basis of estimate is an output of estimate costs.
N   d. The cost-benefit analysis may be part of the business case (an input to develop project charter) and it is a tool and technique in quality management.

Plan Quality Management

> ☑ **Exam Tip:** Review Figure 8-4 of the PMBOK® Guide.

The outputs include the quality management plan and the process improvement plan.

INPUTs of plan quality management (not all listed)

Project management plan- the project plan most likely is not fully developed yet. Elements of the project plan though may help develop the quality management plan. Examples include:

Scope baseline- scope statement (contains information on acceptance criteria that may affect how we plan for quality), the WBS, and the WBS dictionary.

Schedule baseline- contains the approved start and finish dates for project activities. Schedule performance will be measured against this baseline.

Cost baseline- contains the approved cost information. Cost performance will be measured against this baseline.

Stakeholder register- may contain information on which stakeholders are most interested in quality.

Risk register- may contain information on what threats or opportunities may have the biggest impact on quality.

Requirements documentation- used to plan how to perform quality control.

TOOLs and TECHNIQUEs of plan quality management

There is a strong link between quality and cost.

> ☑ **EXAM TIP:** The first two tools and techniques have the word cost in their name. Remember they belong in Quality.

Cost-benefit analysis- some people will say that all money spent on quality is money well spent. That is not the view we want to take. We should only spend money on quality initiatives if the benefit is greater than the cost.

Cost of Quality- includes all money spent to ensure quality. The costs are often broken down into two categories (cost of conformance and the cost of non-conformance) and then sometimes even into two more subcategories under each category (**see PMBOK® Guide: Figure 8-5**). In theory we want to invest more in the cost of conformance (spend money proactively) and invest less in the cost of non-conformance (spend less money reactively).

☑ **EXAM TIP:** Make sure you recognize what costs fall into each of the categories of the cost of quality.

Seven basic quality tools (study PMBOK® Guide: Figure 8-7).

1. Cause and Effect diagrams (study PMBOK® Guide: Figure 8-7)
- sometimes called fishbone diagrams- because of the shape
- sometimes called Ishikawa diagrams- because he developed them

These diagrams show the causes of a specific result. Causes are usually grouped in a specific category to help identify sources of variation. Sometimes the 5 whys technique is used to trace the cause all the way back to the root cause. We don't just want to solve problems, we want to find their root cause so they do not occur again. In quality- cause and effect diagrams are often used in association with control charts. The control charts show if we have variation. The cause and effect diagram, along with the 5 whys, may lead us to the assignable cause for the variation.

2. Flowcharts (study PMBOK® Guide: Figure 8-7)
- sometimes called process maps

These diagrams show the steps in a process. Flowcharts are used to analyze, design, or document a process.

Boxes are often used to show the activities. Arrows are used to show the direction of flow.

In quality- flowcharts are often used to estimate the cost of quality in a process.

3. Check sheets (study PMBOK® Guide: Figure 8-7)
- Sometimes called Tally sheets

These sheets allow us to collect data in an organized way. Data is often recorded by making checks on it. The sheet may be divided into different areas where a check in one area has a different meaning than a check in another area. Ex. Let's assume you are having someone transport your car across the country. Sometimes you are asked to fill out a check sheet (the diagram on the check sheet looks like a car) and you check every place where there is a mark on your real car. You fill out the sheet before they move your car and then again afterwards, to note if any damage was done while the car was being moved.

In Quality- check sheets are often used to collect data while performing inspections on deliverables or products.

4. Pareto diagrams (study PMBOK® Guide: Figure 8-7)
These are vertical bar charts that also show a line. The bars often are listed in descending order (the highest at the left) and the line (curve) shows the cumulative total.

Pareto diagrams show what is most important (the highest bar) from multiple factors. In quality control, the bars often represent:
- the most common sources of defects
- the highest occurring type of defect
- the most frequent reasons for customer complaints

© January 2016 AME Group, Inc. author Aileen Ellis, PMP, PgMP
aileen@amegroupinc.com 719-659-3658

5. Histogram- is a vertical bar chart. It shows a visual impression of the distribution of data. Time is not an input to the histogram.

6. Control charts- show if a process is running in control and has stable performance. If the process is under control, there is variation but the variation is coming from sources common to the process. Often, control charts will have two sets of lines above and below the mean.

Control limits- these are the voice of the process. These limits are based on history. How well you control your process. Control limits are often set at +/- 3 SD. These limits inform us of when to take corrective action.

Out of control process-
- a data point is outside of a control limit (regardless of whether it is outside of the specification limit)
- the rule of seven- seven consecutive points are above or below the mean

Specification limits- (sometimes called tolerance limits)- these come from the customer and define the acceptable limits from the customer.

In operations environment- control charts are often used to track behavior on repetitive processes

In project management environment- control charts are often used to track items that let us know if our project management processes are running in control. Examples include:
- Schedule variance (SV)
- Cost variance (CV)

Also know: SD stands for standard deviation. (You need these numbers for the exam)
+/- 3 SD represents 99.7 % of the data
+/- 2 SD represents 95.5 % of the data
+/- 1 SD represents 68.3 % of the data

7. Scatter diagrams- Sometimes called correlation charts
X-Y chart that may suggest correlations between two variables.

Benchmarking- comparing your organization's practices to practices of other organizations.
The goals of benchmarking are to:
- generate quality standards for measurement
- identify best practices
- develop ideas for improvement

The biggest learning from benchmarking often comes when we benchmark outside of our industry.

Design of experiments- a statistical idea where we set-up an experiment to determine what factors have the most influence on a specific variable.

Statistical sampling- planning to test only part of a population. We often only test a sample of the population because it is:
- less expensive
- less time consuming
- and must be done if the testing is destructive (crash testing a car)

OUTPUTs of plan quality management (not all listed)

Quality management plan	Describes how the quality requirements will be met.
	Does not contain the quality standards.
	It is a subset of the project management plan.

Process Improvement plan	Describes how project management and product development processes will be analyzed and enhanced.
	It is a subset of the project management plan.

Quality metrics- a project or product attribute and how it will be measured. Examples- on time performance, etc.

Before we plan for quality, we need to review ideas from Chapter 8 – Introduction.

QUALITY	GRADE
Degree to which a product meets requirements	Category for products having the same use but different characteristics

PRECISION	ACCURACY
Value of results forms a cluster – little scatter	Value of results is close to true value
Not all precise measurements are accurate.	Not all accurate measurements are precise.

To achieve customer satisfaction we need both:

Conformance to requirements	Fitness for use
Ensure project produces what it said it would produce	The product satisfies a real need
Crosby's definition of quality	Juran's definition of quality

Continuous improvement- based off of the work of Shewhart and Deming

© January 2016 AME Group, Inc. author Aileen Ellis, PMP, PgMP
aileen@amegroupinc.com 719-659-3658

5 Process Groups	Shewhart and Deming
INITIATING	
PLANNING	PLAN
EXECUTING	DO
MONITORING AND CONTROLLING	CHECK-ACT
CLOSING	

Responsibility for quality:

- At the task level- the person performing the task (not the inspector).
- At the project level- the project manager (not the quality manager on the team) owns quality.
- At the organizational level- senior management (not the quality department) owns quality.

Kaizen- the ideas that focus on continuous process improvement.

Just-in-time- the goal is higher return on investment by reducing inventory and costs to carry that inventory.

Marginal analysis- optimal quality is reached when incremental revenue from improvements = incremental costs to secure it. (Stop spending more money).

Total Quality Management (TQM)- know the name Deming for this. Everyone inside and outside the organization has responsibility to continuously improve the quality of products and processes.

QCC- quality control circles- volunteer group with the purpose of identifying, analyzing, and solving problems in order to improve organizational performance.

QFD- quality function deployment- takes customer needs (VOC- voice of the customer) and transforms into product/service characteristics.

PLAN QUALITY – Sample Questions

1. Rework is an example of a(n):
a. prevention cost
b. appraisal cost
c. internal failure cost
d. external failure cost

2. Control limits are usually set at:
a. +/- 3 sigma
b. +/- 6 sigma
c. +/- 1 sigma
d. +/- 4 sigma

3. Comparing project practices to those of other organizations to identify best practices is known as:
a. the cost of quality
b. cost–benefit analysis
c. benchmarking
d. design of experiments

4. A statistical method used to determine optimal conditions for producing the product is called:
a. the cost of quality
b. cost-benefit analysis
c. benchmarking
d. design of experiments

5. Ensuring that each quality activity is worth the cost is confirmed through:
a. the cost of quality
b. cost-benefit analysis
c. benchmarking
d. design of experiments

6. Testing only part of a population that is representative of the whole is known as:
a. statistical sampling
b. benchmarking
c. design of experiments
d. the cost of quality

7. Training is an example of a(n):
a. prevention cost
b. appraisal cost
c. internal failure cost
d. external failure cost

8. You own an outdoor food stand where your main product is hamburgers. You want to collect data so you can understand the inherent limits of your process. To do this, you are most likely to use a:
a. Pareto chart
b. control chart
c. cause and effect diagram
d. trend analysis

© January 2016 AME Group, Inc. author Aileen Ellis, PMP, PgMP
aileen@amegroupinc.com 719-659-3658

9. A SIPOC (supplier, inputs, process, outputs, customers) model is an example of:
a. cause-and-effect diagram
b. check sheets
c. Pareto diagram
d. flowchart

10. A cause-and-effect diagram is also known as:
a. Ishikawa diagram
b. scatter diagram
c. Pareto diagram
d. flowchart

11. You are the project manager for a logging company. This month you are charted to deliver 10,000 units that are 60 centimeters each. Your upper control limit on your process is 63 centimeters. Your lower control limit on your process is 57 centimeters. Approximately what percentage of your units will be above 61 centimeters?
a. 68.3%
b. 31.7%
c. 95.5%
d. 15.9%

Plan Quality - Solutions

1. c. PMBOK® Guide: Figure 8-5
Y   c. Rework is an example of an internal failure cost.
N   a. Training is an example of a prevention cost.
N   b. Testing is an example of an appraisal cost.
N   d. Customer returns is an example of an external failure cost.

2. a. PMBOK® Guide: Section 8.1.2.3
Y   a. Control limits are usually set at +/- 3 sigma.
N   b., c., and d. Control limits are usually set at +/- 3 sigma. Realize your organization may use a different number.

3. c. PMBOK® Guide: Section 8.1.2.4
Y   c. We may benchmark with another organization for several reasons.
- To develop quality standards
- To gain ideas on how to achieve those quality standards
- To learn best practices

N   a. The cost of quality is the total cost spent to achieve quality.
N   b. Cost-benefit analysis is used in quality planning to ensure that money is only spent on quality where the benefit from the expenditure is greater than the cost.
N   d. Design of experiments is a statistical idea that helps us understand how varying certain factors leads to optimal results.

4. d. PMBOK® Guide: Section 8.1.2.5
Y   d. This is a definition of design of experiments.
N   a. The cost of quality is the total cost spent to achieve quality.
N   b. Cost-benefit analysis is used in quality planning to ensure that money is only spent on quality where the benefit from the expenditure is greater than the cost.
N   c. Benchmarking with another organization may be used to identify best practices.

5. b. PMBOK® Guide: Section 8.1.2.1
Y   b. Cost-benefit analysis is used in quality planning to ensure that money is only spent on quality where the benefit from the expenditure is greater than the cost.
N   a. The cost of quality is the total cost spent to achieve quality.
N   c. Benchmarking with another organization may be used to identify best practices.
N   d. Design of experiments is a statistical idea that helps us understand how varying certain factors leads to optimal results.

6. a. PMBOK® Guide: Section 8.1.2.6
Y   a. Statistical sampling is used to save both money and time. With this method we test only a representative sample of an entire population.
N   b. Benchmarking with another organization may be used to identify best practices.
N   c. Design of experiments is a statistical idea that helps us understand how varying certain factors leads to optimal results.
N   d. The cost of quality is the total cost spent to achieve quality.

7. a. PMBOK® Guide: Figure 8-5
Y   a. Training is an example of a prevention cost.
N   b. Testing is an example of an appraisal cost.
N   c. Rework is an example of an internal failure cost.
N   d. Customer returns is an example of an external failure cost.

8.   b.   PMBOK® Guide: Section 8.1.2.3
Y   b.   Control charts help us understand the inherent limits of our process.
N   a.   Pareto charts help us prioritize.
N   c.   Cause and effect diagrams help us see what inputs lead to what effects.
N   d.   Trend analysis uses history to predict the future.

9.   d.   PMBOK® Guide: Section 8.1.2.3
Y   d.   A SIPOC is an example of a flowchart.
N   a.   A fishbone diagram is another name for a cause and effect diagram.
N   b.   Check sheets are used to collect data, often by the collector making a check or a tally mark in a certain region of the sheet.
N   c.   Pareto diagrams are used to help us prioritize.

10.   a. PMBOK® Guide: Section 8.1.2.3
Y   a.   An Isikawa diagram and a fishbone diagram are the other names for a cause and effect diagram.
N   b.   A scatter diagram shows data for two variables using an X and Y plot.
N   c.   A Pareto chart helps us prioritize.
N   d.   A flowchart shows how elements in a system relate to each other.

11.   d. Statistical Process Control textbook or Web Search
☺   d.   15.9 % of the data will be above 61 centimeters. One standard deviation is equal to the absolute value of ((Upper control limit-Lower control limit)/6). Therefore, one standard deviation = (63-57)/6= 6/6= 1 centimeter. The mean is 60 centimeters. 61 centimeters is +1 standard deviation from the mean. and 59 centimeters is -1 standard deviation from the mean. Therefore, 68.3 % of the data will be between 59 and 61 centimeters. 100-68.3= 31.7 will be outside of 59 and 61. 31.7/2= 15.9 will be above 61 centimeters.
☹   a.   68.3 % of the data will be between 59 and 61 centimeters because this range represents +/- 1 standard deviations.
☹   b.   31.7% of the data will be outside the range of 59 and 61 centimeters because 100%-68.3% =31.7%.
☹   c.   95.5 % of the data will be between 58 and 62 centimeters because this range represents +/- 2 standard deviations.

Plan Human Resource Management

In this process we are planning for the team. This includes deciding what positions we need, what tasks people will perform in each position, how positions will report to each other, and when each position will join and leave the team.
Reality- we may not get the people we want in the positions we want. We need to plan for this reality and also think about using resources outside of the organization if skill sets cannot be found or are not available inside.

INPUTs of Plan Human Resource Management (not all listed)

Project management plan- the project plan is not complete yet. Still there are elements in the plan that may help us plan for human resources.

Activity resource requirements- most likely these requirements have been developed, at least a first draft, by the time we begin planning for human resources. These requirements are an output of the estimate activity resource process. These requirements tell us what type and quantity (by hour or day) of the different skill sets will be required on the project.

TOOLs and TECHNIQUEs of Plan Human Resource Management

Org charts and positional descriptions- the primary purpose of this tool and technique is to ensure that every team member understands explicitly their roles and responsibilities and that all project work is clearly owned by someone.

Hierarchical-type charts- there are several of these type charts that may be used to help plan for human resources.

Organizational chart: Shows reporting relationships on the team.

Organizational breakdown structure: shows what work packages (or activities) each existing department is responsible for.

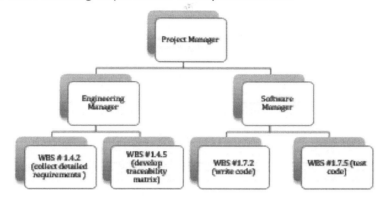

The resource breakdown structure (RBS)- groups resources by category for the project. The one below is very high level. In general you want the RBS to be detailed enough to be used with the WBS.

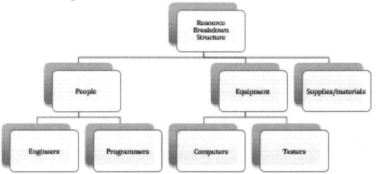

Matrix based charts- the most likely example of this will be a RAM (responsibility assignment matrix). This matrix shows who (by person, position, or group) is responsible for what activity (or work package).

ACTIVITY	Engineer #1	Engineer #2	Programmer #1	Programmer #2
Write requirements documentation	Accountable	Responsible	Inform	Consult
Develop traceability matrix	Inform	Accountable	Responsible	Consult
Develop requirements management plan	Consult	Inform	Accountable	Responsible
Develop scope statement exclusions	Consult	Responsible	Inform	Accountable

☑ **EXAM TIP:** Only one person is allowed to be accountable for each activity.

Text-oriented formats- here we are talking about a positional description. This is a document (may be electronic) that describes details of a particular position. These descriptions help the project manager when he goes out to recruit people to fill specific positions.

Networking- we want to network inside and outside of our organization. Networking helps us understand office politics but more importantly helps us understand how to best set-up our project organization to be successful. Networking may help us better understand where the skill sets exist that we need for the project, both internally and externally. Networking such as attending conferences, can help us grow professionally.

Organizational theory- is the study of organizations. We want to study how organizations work so as to have a positive effect on our project. As an example, by studying organizational theory we may learn the best organizational structure to set-up for the type of work and the individuals of our project. Also, this theory may help us with other elements of planning such as identifying resource requirements, etc.

Expert judgment- there are many details related to planning for human resources. If we utilize experts, both on and off the team, then most likely it will lead to a better human resource plan.

OUTPUTs of Plan human resources

Human Resource plan- this plan is a subset of the project plan and deals just with items affecting the project team (and not stakeholders as a whole). Most likely the plan will include:
- Roles and responsibilities by position- what position owns each work package
- Project organization chart- visual display of reporting relationships of the positions on the team
- Staffing management plan- the primary purpose of this plan, which is a subset of the human resource plan, is to define how and when people will be acquired and how long they will be needed, by position. Other elements relate to training, rewards and recognition, compliance, and safety.

☑ **EXAM TIP:** Know the difference between the human resource plan and the staffing management plan. Know the org chart is part of the human resource plan.

The halo effect:
- applied to project management: assuming that if someone is good at something.. they are good at everything.
- Ex. Assuming that because someone is a great engineer they will make a great project manager.

© January 2016 AME Group, Inc. author Aileen Ellis, PMP, PgMP
aileen@amegroupinc.com 719-659-3658

PLAN HUMAN RESOURCE MANAGEMENT - Sample Questions

1. The project organizational chart shows:
a. reporting relationships
b. the project deliverables
c. the communication protocols
d. the existing organizational departments with the project work packages listed under each department

2. The organizational breakdown structure shows:
a. reporting relationships
b. the project deliverables
c. the resources required for the project
d. the existing organizational departments with the project work packages listed under each department

3. The responsibility assignment matrix shows:
a. how many hours are required by resource category
b. who is responsible for what activities
c. the reporting relationships
d. the positional descriptions for team members

4. Information on how people, teams, and organizations behave is called:
a. roles and responsibilities
b. networking
c. organizational theory
d. human resource plan

5. All of the following are elements of the human resource management plan except:
a. project staff assignments
b. roles and responsibilities
c. project organization charts
d. staffing management plan

6. All of the following are reasons to document team member roles and responsibilities except:
a. ensure each work package has an owner
b. ensure each team member understands their role
c. ensure each team member understands the reporting relationships
d. ensure each team member understands the communication plan

7. The resource breakdown structure:
a. may contain multiple categories including human resources
b. shows the reporting relationships
c. shows the project deliverables
d. defines the communication protocols

8. When utilizing a RAM (responsibility assignment matrix) it is important to:
a. show reporting relationships
b. describe the way people and teams behave
c. ensure that only one person is accountable for each task
d. identify risks associated with staff acquisition

9. Exercising a flexible management style as the team matures is an example of:
a. networking
b. an organizational theory
c. enterprise environmental factors
d. organizational process assets

10. Geographical dispersion of team members is an example of:
a. networking
b. an organizational theory
c. enterprise environmental factors
d. organizational process assets

PLAN HUMAN RESOURCE MANAGEMENT - Solutions

1. a. PMBOK° Guide: Section 9.1.3.1
Y   a. The project organizational chart shows reporting relationships.
N   b. The WBS shows the project deliverables.
N   c. The communication plan would describe communication protocols.
N   d. The organizational breakdown structure (OBS) shows which work packages fall under which departments.

2. d. PMBOK° Guide: Section 9.1.2.1
Y   d. The organizational breakdown structure (OBS) shows which work packages fall under which departments.
N   a. The project organizational chart shows reporting relationships.
N   b. The WBS shows the project deliverables.
N   c. The resources required for the project are listed and organized in the resource breakdown structure.

3. b. PMBOK° Guide: Section 9.1.2.1
Y   b. The responsibility assignment matrix shows who is responsible for what activities (or work packages).
N   a. The resource histogram shows how many hours are required by resource category.
N   c. The project organizational chart shows reporting relationships.
N   d. The positional description forms, sometimes called the role-responsibility-authority forms, show the descriptions for each position.

4. c. PMBOK° Guide: Section 9.1.2.3
Y   c. Information on how people, teams, and organizations behave is called organizational theory.
N   a. The human resource plan describes roles and responsibilities.
N   b. Networking should be used inside and outside the organization for many reasons including understanding the politics. We need this knowledge to set-up a strong project organization.
N   d. The human resource plan includes the project organizational chart, roles, and responsibilities and the staffing management plan.

5. a. PMBOK° Guide: Section 9.1.3.1
Y   a. When we create the human resource plan we do not know the project staff assignments. The staff assignments are an output of acquire project team. These assignments tell us what person has what position on the project.
N   b., c., and d. The human resource plan includes the project organizational chart, roles and responsibilities, and the staffing management plan.

6. d. PMBOK° Guide: Section 9.1.2.1 (focus is not on communications)
Y   d. Communication protocols are described in the communications management plan.
N   a., b., and c. We document roles and responsibilities for many reasons including: to ensure each work package has an owner, to ensure each team member understands their roles, and to ensure each team member understands the reporting relationships.

7. a. PMBOK° Guide: Section 9.1.2.1

Y   a. The resources required for the project are listed and organized in the resource breakdown structure. Examples of resources include human resources, equipment, material, etc.

N   b. The project organizational chart shows reporting relationships.

N   c. The WBS shows the project deliverables.

N   d. The communications plan defines the communication protocols.

8. c. PMBOK° Guide: Section 9.1.2.1

Y   c. A RAM will allow only one person to be accountable for each task (or activity).

N   a. The project organizational chart shows reporting relationships.

N   b. Information on how people, teams, and organizations behave is called organizational theory.

N   d. RAMs are not used to identify risks associated with staff acquisition.

9. b. PMBOK° Guide: Section 9.1.2.3

Y   b. Organizational theory may tell us to be less flexible with a junior team and to be more flexible with a more mature team.

N   a. Networking may help us understand the project and organizational environment. It may also be a way to develop ourselves as a professional project manager.

N   c. Organizational culture is an example of an enterprise environmental factor that may be useful as we plan for human resource management.

N   d. Templates for positional descriptions are an example of an organizational process asset that may be useful as we plan for human resource management.

10. c. PMBOK° Guide: Section 9.1.1.3

Y   c. Geographical dispersion is an example of an enterprise environmental factor that may be useful as we plan for human resource management.

N   a. Networking may help us understand the project and organizational environment. It may also be a way to develop ourselves as a professional project manager.

N   b. Organizational theory provides information on how people behave.

N   d. Templates for organizational charts are an example of an organizational process asset that may be useful as we plan for human resource management.

© January 2016 AME Group, Inc. author Aileen Ellis, PMP, PgMP
aileen@amegroupinc.com 719-659-3658

Plan Communications

In this process we develop our plan for ensuring stakeholders have the information they need, when they need it, using a method that works for them, in a format that works for them, based on what assets we have available. **The project manager should spend 90% of his time communicating.** Communicating involves more than talking, it also involves listening.

INPUTs to plan communications management (not all listed)

Project management plan- this plan most likely is not complete when we enter plan communications. If fact, plan communications should occur very early in planning. At this point though, there may be elements of the project plan, such as the change control plan, etc. that may help with this process.

Stakeholder register- this register is an output of identify stakeholders. It lists the project stakeholders and what we know about them. This list as well as other data in the register can help us understand what stakeholders will require what information at what time, etc.

TOOLs and TECHNIQUEs of plan communications management

Communications requirements analysis- we want to analyze what the stakeholders truly need as far as communication. It is important to understand what value different types of information, in different formats provide to the stakeholders.
One specific question that may come up in this area relates to communication channels.

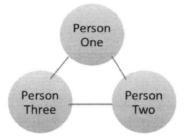

Let's assume there are three (3) stakeholders total on your project, including you. You could get a question asking how many communication channels you have. To solve:

☑ **EXAM TIP:** # of communication channels = $n(n-1)/2$ where n is the number of people.

For this problem we have 3 people therefore:
# of channels= $3(3-1)/2$= 3 channels.

Now let's say the question says you have 7 people total. We obviously do not want to draw 7 little heads and connect the heads. Therefore, we use the equation:

# of channels = $7(7-1)/2$= $(42)/2$= 21 channels.

☑ **EXAM TIP:** Be careful if the exam question states that you are interacting with 9 other stakeholders. This means there are 10 people and you need to solve the problem for n= 10 people.

☑ **EXAM TIP:** The question states there are 2 stakeholders on the project in total. (The 2 includes you). 5 more stakeholders are added. The question asks how many new channels are added. Now you need to solve the problem for n=2 people, again for n=7 people (we got 7 from 2+5) and then take the difference to get the number of new channels added. The answer is 20 new channels. See if you can get to that answer.

Communication technology- many factors affect the type of technology used for project communication. The project manager should select the technology that best fits the needs of the stakeholders based on certain factors:
- What technology is available to different stakeholders
- What level of knowledge, experience, and comfort do the stakeholders possess on the different technologies
- How quickly do stakeholders require information
- What is the project environment- do people meet face-to-face, is the team virtual, are people working on different shifts in different time zones, etc.

Communication Models- several different models exist related to communications.

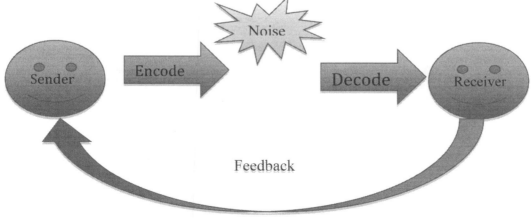

© January 2016 AME Group, Inc. author Aileen Ellis, PMP, PgMP
aileen@amegroupinc.com 719-659-3658

Sender- they encode the message based on who they are, their experiences, etc.

Receiver- they decode the message based on who they are, their experiences, etc.

The tricky part is the receiver may not decode the same way the sender encodes.

Acknowledgement- the receiver should acknowledge that he received the message.

The tricky part- acknowledgement does not mean understanding or agreement.

Medium- the message is sent through some medium (e-mail, face-to-face, etc.)

Noise- the message may experience noise (distance, etc.)

There should be a feedback loop. Remember in the feedback loop the original receiver will encode the message and the original sender will decode the message. Again, this provides a chance for miscommunication.

Communication Methods: Make sure you understand the difference between these three types of communication methods.

Interactive	Most efficient way to ensure a common understanding	Meetings, phone calls, video conferences, etc.
Push	Sent to specific recipients. Does not ensure receipt or understanding	Letters, memos, reports, e-mails, faxes, voice mails, press releases, etc.
Pull	Used for large volumes of info and/or large audiences. People may decide to access or not access information	Intranet sites, e-learning, knowledge repositories, etc.

Meetings- this is a tool and technique of many processes
- there are three types of meetings.
  - Information exchange- to give updates to other parties
  - Brainstorming, etc.- to generate ideas
  - Decision-making- to come to a decision
- Some general guidelines for meetings
  - Be clear on the type of meeting
  - Only call a meeting when a meeting is required
  - Have an agenda, follow an agenda
  - Make sure people know the items to be discussed before the meeting occurs
  - Collect action items- distribute action items in a timely manner
  - Have meeting rules (one person speaks at a time, etc.)
- Face-to-face vs. Virtual
  - Face-to-face- most effective – may not be practical
  - Virtual meetings- take more effort to achieve same result as face-to-face

OUTPUTs- Plan Communications (not all listed)

Communications management plan- this plan may be a simple spreadsheet for a small project to a very complex plan for bigger projects. The plan is a subset of the project management plan. Please see a high level example below.

Com Type	Objective	Medium	Frequency	Audience	Owner	Deliverables	Format
Team meeting	Update on status, team building	Preferred-Face-to-face Acceptable-phone conference	1x/week 2pm Thursday	Team members	Project Manager	Agenda Action items	Posted on team site (no e-mails)
Status reports	Communicate status to all interested parties	Soft copy	Weekly-5pm Friday	All stakeholders	Project coordinator	report	Posted on project site (no e-mails)

Other Ideas -Understand the following table.

	Written	Oral
Formal	Reports, memos	Briefing, speeches
Informal	E-mails	Ad-hoc conversations

☑ **EXAM TIP:** On the exam you may be given an example such as reports. You will then be asked if reports are formal or informal, written or oral.

When we communicate face-to-face with each other, much (more than 50%) of the meaning is communicated through our non-verbals. In simple terms, we trust what we see (non-verbals) and hear (para linguals such as pitch and tone), more than the actual words spoken.

© January 2016 AME Group, Inc. author Aileen Ellis, PMP, PgMP
aileen@amegroupinc.com 719-659-3658

Face to Face Communications

- non-verbals
- paralinguals
- words

☑ **EXAM TIP:** It is important to know that much of the meaning of what is communicated comes from the person's body language (such as gestures, is the person leaning forward or backward, etc.)

PLAN COMMUNICATIONS - Sample Questions

1. Which of the following is an input to plan communications?
a. stakeholder register
b. team directory
c. human resource plan
d. communications plan

2. In the communications model, translating the message back into meaningful thoughts is:
a. encoding
b. medium
c. noise
d. decoding

3. When sharing large amounts of information or information to a large group, we are most likely to use:
a. push communication
b. interactive communication
c. pull communication
d. communication model

4. You realize that as you increase the number of stakeholders, you increase the number of communication channels. Your current project has 10 stakeholders total. How many communications channels are there on this project?
a. 10
b. 45
c. 50
d. 100

5. In the communications model, distance is an example of:
a. encoding
b. the message
c. the medium
d. noise

6. Which plan is an input to plan communications management?
a. communications management plan
b. human resource plan
c. procurement management plan
d. project management plan

7. Video conferencing is an example of what communication method?
a. interactive communication
b. push communication
c. pull communication
d. silent communication

8. The most efficient way to ensure a common understanding is:
a. interactive communication
b. push communication
c. pull communication
d. silent communication

9. When the receiver acknowledges the message, he is really saying that he:
a. agrees with the message
b. understands the message
c. has received the message
d. comprehends the message

10. The communications plan is an output of plan communications management. This plan then becomes an input to:
a. manage communications and identify stakeholders
b. manage communications and manage stakeholder engagement
c. manage communications and plan stakeholder management
d. manage communications and control stakeholder engagement

11. The most efficient means for communicating and ensuring a common understanding with stakeholders is:
a. electronic mail
b. a face-to-face meeting
c. a report
d. a voice mail

PLAN COMMUNICATIONS - Solutions

1. a.   PMBOK® Guide: Section 10.1.1.2
Y   a.   The stakeholder register is an input to plan communication. It lists the stakeholders. It gives us details to help us begin to plan communication with these stakeholders.
N   b.   The team directory would be associated with processes in the human resource area, not the communication area.
N   c.   The human resource plan would be associated with processes in the human resource area, not the communication area.
N   d.   The communications plan is an output, not an input to plan communications.

☑ **EXAM TIP:** The human resource plan is associated with the team.

☑ **EXAM TIP:** The communication plan is associated with the stakeholders. The team is a subset of the project stakeholders.

2. d.   PMBOK® Guide: Section 10.1.2.3
Y   d.   Decoding is translating the message back into meaningful thoughts.
N   a.   Encoding is translating ideas into language.
N   b.   The medium is the transmission channel selected. Examples include e-mail, face-to-face, etc.
N   c.   Noise is anything that gets in the way of the transmission. Examples include: distance, etc.

3. c.   PMBOK® Guide: Section 10.1.2.4
Y   c.   The larger the audience or the bigger the volume of the information, the more likely we are to use pull communications. An example would be an intranet site.
N   a.   The amount of information may be too large to push. Examples of push include e-mails, voice mails, etc.
N   b.   Interactive communication is often used for smaller groups or smaller amounts of information.
N   d.   The communication model does not make sense in the context of this question.

4. b.   PMBOK® Guide: Section 10.1.2.1
Y   b.   The number (#) of communication channels = n(n-1)/2 where n is the number of people. For this problem we have 10 people therefore: # of channels= 10(10-1)/2= 45 channels.

5. d.   PMBOK® Guide: Section 10.1.2.3
Y   d.   Distance is an example of noise.
N   a.   Encoding is translating thoughts into language.
N   b.   The message is the information being sent.
N   c.   The medium is the transmission channel selected. Examples include e-mail, face-to-face, etc.

6. d.   PMBOK® Guide: Section 10.1.1.1
Y   d.   The project management plan is an input to plan communications.
N   a.   The communications management plan would be an output of, not an input of plan communications management.
N   b.   The human resource plan would be associated with processes in the human resource area, not the communication area.

N   c. The procurement plan would be associated with processes in the procurement area, not the communications area.

> ☑ **EXAM TIP:** The project management plan is an input of all processes that begin with the word "plan". Examples include but are not limited to: plan scope management, plan schedule management, etc.

7. a. PMBOK® Guide: Section 10.1.2.4
Y   a. Video conferences are an example of interactive communication.
N   b. E-mails are examples of push communications.
N   c. Lessons learned databases are examples of pull communications.
N   d. The PMBOK® Guide does not, in general, use the term silent communication.

8. a. PMBOK® Guide: Section 10.1.2.4
Y   a. Interactive communication is often the most efficient way to ensure that all parties have the same understanding on a particular idea.
N   b. Push communication is used when we want to ensure the message was sent.
N   c. Pull communication is used when we are providing a large amount of information or information to a large audience.
N   d. The PMBOK® Guide does not, in general, use the term silent communication.

9. c. PMBOK® Guide: Section 10.1.2.3
Y   c. Acknowledgement of the message from the receiver means he has received it.
N   a. Acknowledgement of the message from the receiver means he has received it. It does not mean he agrees, or disagrees, with it.
N   b. and d. Since answer b. and answer d. mean the same thing as each other they must both be wrong, since they cannot both be right. Regardless, acknowledgement does not mean understanding.

10. b. PMBOK® Guide: Figure 10-3
Y   b. The communications plan is an input to both manage communication and manage stakeholder engagement.
N   a. The communications plan would not be an input to identify stakeholders. The output of identify stakeholders, the stakeholder register helps us develop the communications plan.
N   c. The communications plan is not an input to plan stakeholder management. Since this process begins with the word "plan" we know the project management plan, not any other plan will be an input.
N   d. The project management plan, not the communications plan, is used to control stakeholder engagement.

11. b. PMBOK® Guide: 10.1.2.4
☺   b. Face-to-face meetings are the most effective means for communicating and gaining a common understanding. During a face-to-face meeting, verbals, non-verbals, and para linguals can all be transmitted.
N   a., c., and d. Notice the question uses the word effective, not the word practical. If a face-to-face meeting is not warranted or practical, telephone calls, electronic mail, and other electronic tools are useful for exchanging information and dialoguing.

Plan Risk Management

In this process we determine our strategy for the other risk management processes. This may include our risk methodology, roles and responsibilities, etc.

Some key terminology:
Opportunity - risk event that would lead to a positive outcome

Threat - risk event that would lead to a negative outcome

Known risks - those risks where it is possible to develop responses. Contingency reserves may be set for known risks that cannot (or we chose not to) be managed proactively.

Unknown risks - truly unknown risks that cannot be managed proactively. We may set-up management reserve for unknown risks.

A risk has **not** occurred yet. Once a negative risk (a threat) has occurred it is now called an issue. As a project manager we should be proactive. We want to spend time managing risks before they occur instead of dealing with issues after the fact.

There are two kinds of risks
- Pure (sometimes called insurable risk)- the effect of this risk can only be negative
- Business risk- the effect of this risk may be positive or negative

Uncertainty - every risk has some amount of uncertainty to it. If we are certain an event will occur, it is not a risk.

INPUTs of plan risk management (not all listed)

Project management plan - many areas of this plan may be reviewed to help plan for risk management. Most importantly we will review the information on the triple constraint of scope, time, and cost.

Project charter - the charter includes much information about the project. We will review the project objectives to think about how certain risks will effect these objectives. Also, we will look at the high level risks defined in the objectives as a starting point when we begin to identify risks.

© January 2016 AME Group, Inc. author Aileen Ellis, PMP, PgMP
aileen@amegroupinc.com 719-659-3658

Stakeholder register- as we think about risks we need to understand the risk attitudes of key stakeholders. Also the roles of the stakeholders are defined in the register. We need to consider who will own risk management for the project.

TOOLs and TECHNIQUEs of plan risk management (not all listed)

Analytical techniques- these are various techniques used to evaluate, analyze, or forecast potential outcomes based on possible variations and combinations of variations. These techniques may be used to help us understand the risk attitudes of key stakeholders or the total risk exposure.

OUTPUTs of plan risk management

Risk management plan- this is our strategy for all the risk management activities on the project. It may include:
- **Risk management methodology**- the principles and rules we will use to drive action in the area of risk.
- **Roles and responsibilities**- we want to answer the question: who owns risk on this project? Will we have a risk manager? Will we have a risk management team? Will risk management ownership be spread across all the team members?
- **Risk categories**- many organizations visualize their risk categories using a risk breakdown structure (see Figure in the PMBOK® Guide).
- **Definitions**- it is important to define our terms we will use in risk management analysis. See PMBOK® Guide: Table 11-1.

PLAN RISK MANAGEMENT – Sample Questions

1. What plan is an input to the plan risk management process?
a. risk management plan
b. stakeholder management plan
c. communications management plan
d. project management plan

2. The risk breakdown structure (RBS) is a hierarchical breakdown of risk by:
a. impact
b. probability
c. timing
d. category

3. Which of the following is developed as part of plan risk management:
a. a risk register
b. a list of risks
c. a risk methodology
d. a risk response plan

4. The tool and technique of plan risk management that is used to define the overall risk management context of the project is:
a. meetings
b. analytical techniques
c. stakeholder register
d. project charter

5. Which of the following is not developed as part of plan risk management:
a. a risk methodology
b. roles and responsibilities for risk management
c. risk register
d. risk definitions

© January 2016 AME Group, Inc. author Aileen Ellis, PMP, PgMP
aileen@amegroupinc.com 719-659-3658

PLAN RISK MANAGEMENT - Solutions

1. d. PMBOK° Guide: Section 11.1.1.1
Y   d. The project management plan is an input to plan risk management.
N   a. The risk management plan is an output of plan risk management.
N   b. The stakeholder management plan is associated with stakeholder processes, not risk processes.
N   c. The communications management plan is associated with communication processes not risk processes.

2. d. PMBOK° Guide: Section 11.1.3.1
Y   d. The risk breakdown structure (RBS) is set-up by risk category.
N   a., b., and c. The risk breakdown structure (RBS) is set-up by risk category not by impact, probability, or timing.

3. c. PMBOK° Guide: Section 11.1.3.1
Y   c. A risk methodology is developed as part of the risk management plan.
N   a. The risk register is an output of identify risks etc. It is not part of the risk management plan.
N   b. A list of risks is the early basis for the risk register. This list is not part of the risk management plan. The plan describes how to develop the risk register.
N   d. The risk responses are developed and become part of the risk register. They are not in the risk management plan.

4. b. PMBOK° Guide: Section 11.1.2.1
Y   b. These analytical techniques help define the risk context for the project. Ideas considered may include the risk attitudes of stakeholders as well as the overall risk exposure.
N   a. Meetings are used to develop the risk management plan.
N   c. The stakeholder register is an input not a tool and technique for plan risk management. It helps us understand the various roles the stakeholders will have in regards to risk management.
N   d. The project charter is an input not a tool and technique for plan risk management. It includes information on risk from a high level standpoint.

5. c. PMBOK° Guide: Section 11.1.3.1
Y   c. The risk register is an output of identify risks. The register gets updated in subsequent processes. It is not developed as part of plan risk management.
N   a., b., and d. The risk management plan includes the risk methodology, roles and responsibilities related to risk, as well as risk definitions.

☑ **EXAM TIP**: The project management plan is an input of all processes that begin with the word "plan". Examples include but are not limited to: plan scope management, plan schedule management, etc.

☑ **EXAM TIP**: Remember there are no risks listed in the risk management plan. The risk register is not an element of the risk management plan. The plan describes how to create the risk register, etc.

Identify Risks

> ☑ **Exam Tip:** Review Figure 11-6 of the PMBOK° Guide.

In the process identify risk we identify potential opportunities or threats that may affect the project objectives. Often, a large group of people may be involved in this process. Risk identification is so important that we may even include risk experts from outside of the team or even the project stakeholders.

INPUTs of identify risks (not all listed)

Risk management plan- this was the output of the last process. It includes our risk methodology, etc. It should include how we plan to conduct the identify risks process.

Scope baseline-
- **Scope statement**- includes the list of project constraints and assumptions. We need to ask what risks are present in the project assumptions.

- **WBS and WBS dictionary**- these are key inputs. We may look at each component of the WBS (at the control account level or the work package level) and ask: What risks might there be associated with this component?

Activity cost and activity duration estimates- each of these many contain ranges around the estimates. We may ask what risks are associated with these estimates and the ranges.

Stakeholder register- as we think about risks we need to understand the risk attitudes of key stakeholders. We may want to include key stakeholders in identify risks.

TOOLs and TECHNIQUEs of identify risks

Documentation review- we want to review the documents that already exist on the project to check for risks.
- Example- if you already have a contract in place with an external customer. First review the contract for threats (risks that if they occurred would have a negative outcome) and opportunities (risks that if they occurred would have a positive outcome).
- It is important to check documents for potential conflicts (one document conflicts another) or gaps (there is information required for the project that is not documented any place).

Information gathering techniques:
Make sure you know the difference between brainstorming and Delphi.

© January 2016 AME Group, Inc. author Aileen Ellis, PMP, PgMP
aileen@amegroupinc.com 719-659-3658

Brainstorming	Delphi technique
Goal- list of risks (no priority)	Goal- reach a consensus Includes reducing bias
May be free form or Nominal Group Technique, etc. RBS (risk breakdown structure) may be used Be careful of Group think	Only experts involved Anonymous Questionnaire Multiple rounds

Checklist analysis- we may have or may develop a checklist to help us identify risks. Sometimes we use the lowest level of the risk breakdown structure as our checklist. Be careful to not overly rely on the checklist.

Assumption analysis- assumptions are found in the scope statement. We need to evaluate these assumptions and ask how much risk is there associated with these assumptions.

Example- we assume that the human resources we need for the project will be available. We may need to ask, based on past experience and the current project context, what is the likelihood that assumption is true?

Diagramming techniques- we discussed several of these techniques in the quality chapter of this study guide. Think about how each one could be used to help us identify risk.

Cause and effect diagram- what causes lead to what effects. What causes would lead certain risks to occur.

System or process flow charts- these diagrams show how elements in a system relate to each other.

Influence diagrams- see PMBOK® Guide: Figure 11-7. These diagrams show influences. How one event or activity may influence another.

SWOT (strengths, weaknesses, opportunities, and threats) analysis

	Project opportunities	Project threats
Organizational strengths	What project opportunities may we have because of the organization's strengths	What project threats may be diminished because of the organization's strengths
Organizational weaknesses	What project opportunities may be diminished because of the organization's weaknesses	What project threats may we have because of the organization's weaknesses

Expert judgment- in all areas, but especially in risk we want to ensure our risk experts have current experience and that the experience is related to the risks we may experience on the project.

Ex. If we are managing a software project, bringing in a risk expert with experience in the construction industry may not be the best idea. While this person may help us think outside the box with risk, they may miss some common risks associated with software.

OUTPUTS of identify risks

The output is the risk register. At this point the register includes no priority, no probability, and no impact information for the risks.

Risk category	Risk Name	Priority	Probability	Impact	Potential responses	Owner	Comments
Technology	Late delivery of computer systems				last time we borrowed the systems we needed		
Resources	Terry moved off project- need replacement				Last time Terry was pulled off we got him 10% of the time to mentor his replacement		

© January 2016 AME Group, Inc. author Aileen Ellis, PMP, PgMP
aileen@amegroupinc.com 719-659-3658

IDENTIFY RISKS - Sample Questions

1. **Diagramming techniques to identify risks include the following except:**
a. Delphi
b. cause and effect
c. system or process
d. influence

2. **Who should be involved to help identify risks?**
a. the project manager
b. the project management team
c. all project personnel
d. the risk management team

3. **The goal of Delphi is:**
a. a long list of risks
b. a consensus
c. strengths, weaknesses, opportunities, and threats
d. group think

4. **All of the following are tools and techniques of identify risks except:**
a. brainstorming
b. the Delphi method
c. risk probability and impact
d. assumption analysis

5. **At the end of identify risks the risk register should include:**
a. a list of risks with relative ranking
b. a list of risks with probabilistic analysis
c. a list of risks
d. a list of risks and a watch list

IDENTIFY RISKS - Solutions

1. a. PMBOK° Guide: Section 11.2.2.5
Y   a. Delphi is not a diagramming technique.
N   b., c., and d. Cause and effect, system or process, and influence are all examples of diagramming techniques that may be used to identify risks.

2. c. PMBOK° Guide: Section 11.2
Y   c. Good ideas related to risks may come from any and all project personnel.
N   a. The project manager alone would not be the best option as far as identifying risk.
N   b. The project management team alone would not be the best option as far as identifying risk.
N   d. The risk management team alone would not be the best option as far as identifying risk.

3. b. PMBOK° Guide: Section 11.2.2.2
Y   b. The goal of Delphi is for a limited group of experts to reach a consensus.
N   a. From brainstorming we often have a long list of risks.
N   c. SWOT looks at: strengths, weaknesses, opportunities, and threats.
N   d. Group think is a negative outcome that occurs from brainstorming at times. It is often caused by a group's desire to get along with each other. They put this desire ahead of critical evaluation of different ideas.

4. c. PMBOK° Guide: Section 11.2.2
Y   c. Risk probability and impact is a tool and technique of qualitative risk analysis. You need a list of risks to use this tool. We would not have this list while identifying risks.
N   a. Brainstorming is used during identify risk as a way to come up with lots of ideas.
N   b. The Delphi method is used during identify risks so that a limited group of experts may reach a consensus.
N   d. During the process of identify risks we want to analyze our assumptions and ask: what risks do we see in our assumptions?

5. c. PMBOK° Guide: Section 11.2.3.1
Y   c. The output of identify risks is a risk register that includes a list of risks.
N   a. The risks of the risk register are not ranked until after qualitative risk analysis. This ranking may change after quantitative risk analysis.
N   b. The risks of the risk register do not include probabilistic analysis until quantitative risk analysis has been performed.
N   d. As part of qualitative risk analysis it is determined which risks are low priority and should be placed on a watch list.

© January 2016 AME Group, Inc. author Aileen Ellis, PMP, PgMP
aileen@amegroupinc.com 719-659-3658

Perform Qualitative Risk Analysis

☑ **Exam Tip:** Review Figure 11-9 of the PMBOK® Guide.

In the process perform qualitative risk analysis we analyze the risks from a qualitative (not quantitative) standpoint so as to prioritize them for quantitative analysis and planning responses.

Be sure to know THE difference between Qualitative risk and Quantitative risk analysis.

Qualitative Risk Analysis	Quantitative Risk Analysis
Goal- prioritize risks for quantitative analysis or developing responses	Goal- understand overall risk for project
Quick Cost effective Uses words like- low, moderate, high Can use numbers relative to each other	Slower More expensive Based on statistics Uses numbers

INPUTs of perform qualitative risk analysis

Risk management plan- This plan includes a description of how to perform qualitative risk analysis.

Scope baseline-
- **Scope statement**- includes the list of project constraints and assumptions.

- **WBS and WBS dictionary**- .We may look at each component of the WBS (at the control account level or the work package level) and ask about probability and impact of risks associated with this component.

Risk register- all the information we have so far on the project risks are in the risk register.

TOOLs and TECHNIQUEs of perform qualitative risk analysis

Risk probability and impact assessment: helps up prioritize our risks from a relative standpoint. We may use numbers like 1-10 or words like low, moderate, or high.

	Probability	Impact
RISK A	Low	Low
RISK B	Low	Moderate
RISK C	High	Moderate
RISK D	Moderate	Moderate
RISK E	High	High

Probability and impact matrix- see PMBOK® Guide: Figure 11-10. This matrix again helps us prioritize our risks:

Threats (negative risks) in the high risk zone:
- Have a higher probability of occurring and will have a higher impact
- Require more active management

Opportunities (positive risks) in the high risk zone:
- Have a higher probability of occurring and will have a higher impact (this is a good thing)
- We may want to put more focus on these opportunities because this is where we will get the biggest payback

Risk data quality assessment- we need to ask how good is the data we are using to perform risk analysis. What is the accuracy, quality, reliability, and integrity of the data.

Risk categorization- there are several ways to group our risks. It is a best practice to group them by root cause (not by their effects).

Risk urgency assessment- we often prioritize risks by impact and probability. In some cases there is another dimension to think about: urgency. Urgency is how quickly the risk requires a response. A risk that requires an immediate response may take a higher priority than one that does not.

OUTPUTs of perform qualitative risk analysis

Risk register updates- now we should have analyzed probability and impact qualitatively.

Risk category	Risk Name	Priority	Probability	Impact	Potential responses	Owner	Comments
Technology	Late delivery of computer systems	1	High	low		Nick	
Resources	Terry moved off project- need replacement	2	Moderate	low		Alex	

© January 2016 AME Group, Inc. author Aileen Ellis, PMP, PgMP
aileen@amegroupinc.com 719-659-3658

PERFORM QUALITATIVE RISK ANALYSIS - Sample Questions

1. A risk watch list is for:
a. all risks
b. low priority risks
c. high priority risks
d. all threats

2. At the end of perform qualitative risk analysis the risk register should include:
a. a list of risks with relative ranking
b. a list of risks with probabilistic analysis of the project
c. a list of risks with no ranking
d. a list of risks and fully developed risk responses

3. To develop a risk rating which of the following tools and techniques is used:
a. risk categorization
b. probability and impact matrix
c. risk data quality assessment
d. risk urgency assessment

4. Examining the level of our understanding of a risk is called:
a. risk probability and impact assessment
b. probability and impact matrix
c. risk data quality assessment
d. risk urgency assessment

5. If we hope to develop effective risk responses we may want to group our risks by:
a. the deliverable affected
b. the objective affected
c. the project phase
d. the root cause

PERFORM QUALITATIVE RISK ANALYSIS - Solutions

1. b. **PMBOK® Guide: Section 11.3.3.1**
Y   b. A risk watch list is for low priority risks.
N   a. Be careful of the word all.
N   c. High priority risks do not go on the watch list.
N   d. The watch list is for low priority risks, regardless if they are threats or opportunities.

2. a. **PMBOK® Guide: Section 11.3.3.1**
Y   a. As an output of qualitative analysis the risks should be ranked from a relative standpoint.
N   b. As an output of quantitative analysis the risks should include probabilistic analysis of the project.
N   c. As an output of identify risks, there should be a list of risks with no ranking.
N   d. As an output of plan risk responses the list of risks should include fully developed risk responses for the higher priority risks.

3. b. **PMBOK® Guide: Section 11.3.3.2**
Y   b. The risk rating may be developed by using the probability and impact matrix. This matrix develops the rating based on a risk's estimated impact and probability.
N   a. We use the tool risk categorization to group our risks by category.
N   c. We use the tool risk data quality assessment to ask: How useful is the data we have on risk? We may ask where did we get the data from? Is there bias in the data? Etc.
N   d. Many organizations look at estimated probability and impact to determine a risk score. At times though, risk urgency is evaluated to determine a risk severity rating. This rating takes into account impact, probability, and urgency. One aspect of urgency: How quickly must we respond if the risk occurs? Will there be any warning signs that the risk is about to occur?

4. c. **PMBOK® Guide: Section 11.3.2.3**
Y   c. Risk data quality assessment looks at how useful is the risk data to us. We may ask: How well do we understand this risk?
N   a. A risk probability and impact assessment looks at what is the probability the risk will occur and if it does, what effect is it likely to have on project objectives.
N   b. A risk probability and impact matrix helps us determine the risk rating based on estimated probability and impact.
N   d. Many organizations look at estimated probability and impact to determine a risk score. At times though, risk urgency is evaluated to determine a risk severity rating. This rating takes into account impact, probability, and urgency. One aspect of urgency: How quickly must we respond if the risk occurs? Will there be any warning signs that the risk is about to occur?

5. d. **PMBOK® Guide: Section 11.3.2.4**
Y   d. In general, to develop effective risk responses we may want to group our risks by root cause.
N   a. It is fine to group our risks by the deliverable affected. In general though, to develop effective risk responses we may want to group our risks by root cause.
N   b. It is fine to group our risks by the objective affected. To develop effective risk responses we may want to group our risks by root cause.
N   c. If it fine to group our risks by the project phase. To develop effective risk responses we may want to group our risks by root cause.

Perform Quantitative Risk Analysis

> ☑ **Exam Tip:** Review Figure 11-12 of the PMBOK® Guide.

At this point we want to take the higher priority risks and put them through quantitative analysis.

Be sure to know difference between Qualitative risk analysis and Quantitative risk analysis.

Qualitative Risk Analysis	Quantitative Risk Analysis
Goal- prioritize risks for Quantitative analysis or developing responses	Goal- understand overall risk for project
Quick Cost effective Uses words like: low, moderate, high Can use numbers relative to each other	Slower More expensive Based on statistics Uses numbers

INPUTs of perform quantitative risk analysis

Risk management plan- this plan includes a description to perform quantitative risk analysis

Cost and schedule management plan- both of these plans describe how risk reserves (cost and schedule) are set-up and managed

Risk register- all the information we have so far on the project risks are in the risk register.

TOOLs and TECHNIQUEs of perform quantitative risk analysis

Data gathering and representation techniques

Interviews and probability distributions- statisticians will develop interviews where the results may be plotted on probability distributions. Think of this as being based on statistics... not your normal interviews.

Quantitative risk analysis and modeling techniques:

Sensitivity analysis- a technique used to determine how different values for risks may effect project objectives. The results are plotted on a tornado diagram. See PMBOK® Guide: Figure 11-15.

> ☑ **EXAM TIP:** The word sensitivity makes us think of people. Be careful, make sure you associate sensitivity analysis with quantitative risk, not with the team or the stakeholders.

Expected monetary value: this is a complicated idea, easier to understand through an example:

> Your project has 30% probability of having to pay $20,000 in damages and a 40% probability of receiving $30,000 in damages. What is the expected monetary value of this situation?
> a. - $ 6,000
> b. + $ 6,000
> c. - $ 12,000
> d. + $ 12,000
>
> b.   PMBOK® Guide: Section 11.4.2.2 (theory)
>
> | Amount at Stake | Risk Probability | Expected Monetary Value |
> |---|---|---|
> | -$20,000 | 30% | -$20,000*30%= -$6,000 |
> | $30,000 | 40% | $30,000*40%=$12,000 |
> | | | EMV of Venture= +$6,000 |
>
> Think of expected monetary value as a statistical representation of a situation.

Modeling and simulation: often will use a model to simulate a particular risk and its effect on project objectives.

☑ **EXAM TIP:**
- When using a model to simulate a cost risk we need cost estimates.
- When using a model to simulate schedule risk we need activity durations as well as an activity network diagram.
- Most often we simulate using Monte Carlo.

OUTPUTs of perform quantitative risk analysis

Risk register with quantitative risk information:

Risk category	Risk Name	Priority	Probability	Impact	Potential responses	Owner	Comments
Technology	Late delivery of computer systems	1	95%	1 week to schedule		Nick	
Resources	Terry moved off project- need replacement	2	45%	4 weeks to schedule		Alex	

PERFORM QUANTITATIVE RISK ANALYSIS - Sample Questions

1. The tornado diagram is associated with:
a. sensitivity analysis
b. expected monetary value
c. decision tree analysis
d. simulations

2. The triangular distribution gathers information from all of the following scenarios except:
a. most likely
b. mean
c. optimistic
d. pessimistic

3. At the end of perform quantitative risk analysis the risk register should include:
a. a list of risks with relative ranking
b. a list of risks with probabilistic information
c. a list of risks
d. a list of risks and a watch list

4. Which of the following statements is true about quantitative risk analysis?
a. all risks should go through quantitative analysis
b. only the risks on the watch list should go through quantitative analysis
c. quantitative risk analysis is a quick low cost process
d. the effect of identified risks on project objectives can be quantified

5. To simulate the project schedule what information is required:
a. cost estimates
b. the schedule network diagram and the duration estimates
c. the schedule management plan
d. the cost management plan

6. To perform a cost risk analysis what information is required:
a. cost estimates
b. the schedule network diagram and the duration estimates
c. the schedule management plan
d. the cost management plan

PERFORM QUANTITATIVE RISK ANALYSIS - Solutions

1. a.   PMBOK° Guide: Section 11.4.2.2

Y   a. The tornado diagram is often associated with sensitivity analysis. See PMBOK° Guide: Figure 11-15.

N   b. and c. Sometimes expected monetary value is applied to decision tree analysis. See PMBOK° Guide: Figure 11-16.

N   d. Simulations are often performed using the Monte Carlo technique. See PMBOK° Guide: Figure 11-17.

2. b.   PMBOK° Guide: Section 11.4.2.1

Y   b. The triangular distribution uses the low (pessimistic), most likely, and high (optimistic) values for the calculation. The mean is not used.

3. b.   PMBOK° Guide: Section 11.4.3.1

Y   b. As an output of quantitative analysis the risks should include probabilistic analysis of the project.

N   a. and d. As an output of qualitative analysis the risks should be ranked from a relative standpoint and include a watch list.

N   c. As an output of identify risks, there should be a list of risks with no ranking.

4. d.   PMBOK° Guide: Section 11.4

Y   d. Perform quantitative risk analysis should be used to understand the potential effect of identified risks on project objectives.

N   a. Not all risks should go through quantitative risk analysis. It is not worth the time and money for low priority risks.

N   b. In general, the risks on the watch list are the lower priority risks and therefore they are the least likely to go through quantitative analysis.

N   c. Qualitative risk analysis, not quantitative risk analysis, is a quicker low cost process.

5. b.   PMBOK° Guide: Section 11.4.2.2

Y   b. We need a schedule network diagram to show path conformance and path divergence as well as the activity duration estimates to simulate the schedule.

N   a. The cost estimates are needed to simulate the project budget.

N   c. The schedule management plan does not contain the network diagram or duration estimates and therefore would not be used to simulate the schedule.

N   d. The cost management plan does not contain the network diagram or duration estimates and therefore would not be used to simulate the schedule.

6. a.   PMBOK° Guide: Section 11.4.2.2

Y   a. The cost estimates are needed to perform a cost risk analysis.

N   b. We need a schedule network diagram to show path conformance and path divergence as well as the activity duration estimates to simulate the schedule.

N   c. The schedule management plan does not contain the cost estimates and therefore would not be used to perform a cost risk analysis.

N   d. The cost management plan does not contain the cost estimates and therefore would not be used to perform a cost risk analysis.

Plan Risk Responses

☑ **Exam Tip:** Review Figure 11-19 of the PMBOK® Guide.

In this process we develop our responses to particular risks, both threats and opportunities.

INPUTs of plan risk responses

Risk management plan- This plan includes a description of how to plan risk responses.

Risk register- All the information we have so far on the project risks are in the risk register.

TOOLs and TECHNIQUEs of plan risk responses

Make sure you understand the strategies for threats and how they are different from the strategies for opportunities.

Strategies for threats	Strategies for opportunities
Avoid- changing plan so that either the risk will not occur or the risk will not affect the project. Ex. Changing schedule, reducing scope, cancelling project	Exploit- changing the plan to ensure the risk will occur and affect the project. Ex. Assigning the most talented resources to the project
Transfer- changing plan by moving ownership (partially or fully) to another party. Ex. Insurance, subcontractor	Share- changing plan by sharing ownership with an outside party Ex. Partnerships, teams, joint ventures
Mitigate- changing plan to reduce probability or impact or both Ex. Designing redundancy	Enhance- change plan to increase probability or impact or both Ex. Adding more resources
Accept- don't change plan. Passive acceptance- do nothing. Active acceptance– set-up a contingency reserve.	Accept- don't change plan. Passive acceptance- do nothing. Active acceptance- set-up contingency reserve.

Contingent responses strategies- these are risk responses we use only if a particular trigger occurs.

☑ **EXAM TIP**: Contingency plans are associated with active acceptance, and only active acceptance.

OUTPUTs to plan risk responses

Risk register that includes planned responses

Risk category	Risk Name	Priority	Probability	Impact	Potential responses	Owner	Comments
Technology	Late delivery of computer systems	1	95%	1 week to schedule	Mitigate- Proactively work with supplier on delivery dates	Nick	
Resources	Terry moved off project- need replacement	2	45%	4 weeks to schedule	Mitigate- have engineer working with Terry who can take over if Terry moved off	Alex	

Project document updates- multiple documents may be updated based on this process.

Some key words in risk:

Trigger- event that may trigger a response

Contingency plan- plan in place in case an accepted risk occurs

Back-up plan (sometimes called a fallback plan)- plan in place in case your first contingency plan does not work

Residual risk- accepted risks and risks that are expected to still remain after plans have been activated

Secondary risk (sometimes called an emerging risk)- risk that arises out of implementing a response

© January 2016 AME Group, Inc. author Aileen Ellis, PMP, PgMP
aileen@amegroupinc.com 719-659-3658

PLAN RISK RESPONSES - Sample Questions

1. A contingency reserve is set-up for what types of risks?
a. risks that have been passively accepted
b. risks that have been actively accepted
c. as part of a mitigation strategy
d. as part of an avoidance strategy

2. The use of insurance is what type of strategy:
a. avoid
b. transfer
c. mitigate
d. accept

3. When we transfer a risk:
a. the risk is eliminated
b. the risk liability moves to another party
c. the risk is actively accepted
d. the risk is passively accepted

4. Passive acceptance requires:
a. transferring risk to another party
b. setting up a contingency reserve
c. documenting the decision
d. putting redundancy in place to deal with the risk

5. All of the following are strategies for opportunities except:
a. transfer
b. accept
c. exploit
d. enhance

6. A risk that develops because we implemented a risk response is called:
a. a secondary risk
b. a residual risk
c. a fallback
d. a risk trigger

PLAN RISK RESPONSES - Solutions

1. b.   PMBOK® Guide: Section 11.5.2.1

Y   b. A contingency reserve is set-up for risks that have been actively accepted.

N   a. If a risk is passively accepted, it means we do nothing, including not setting up a reserve.

N   c. Mitigation means we change our plan to either lower the probability of the risk or lower the impact of the risk or both. With mitigation we do not set-up contingency reserves.

N   d. Avoidance means we do something so either the risk does not occur or if it does occur it does not affect the project. With avoidance we do not set-up contingency reserves.

2. b.   PMBOK® Guide: Section 11.5.2.1

Y   b. Insurance is an example of a transfer technique.

N   a. Cancelling the project is an extreme avoidance technique.

N   c. Designing redundancy into our system is an example of a mitigation technique. The redundancy may reduce the impact if the risk does occur.

N   d. Doing nothing but documenting the risk, without changing the project plan is an example of passive acceptance.

3. b.   PMBOK® Guide: Section 11.5.2.1

Y   b. When we transfer the risk the risk liability, or at least part of the liability moves to the other party. Buying insurance is a good example of this.

N   a. When we transfer a risk, the risk still exists, but the liability for the risk is now owned, or partially owned by the other party.

N   c. Active acceptance means we do not change our plan because of the risk, but we put a contingency in place. With transfer, we are changing the plan.

N   d. Passive acceptance means we do not change our plan because of the risk and we put no contingency in place. With transfer, we are changing the plan.

4. c.   PMBOK® Guide: Section 11.5.2.1

Y   c. Doing nothing but documenting the risk, without changing the project plan is an example of passive acceptance.

N   a. Transfer means we move the liability for the risk, or at least part of the liability to another party.

N   b. Active acceptance means we do not change our plan because of the risk, but we put a contingency in place.

N   d. Designing redundancy into our system is an example of a mitigation technique. The redundancy may reduce the impact if the risk does occur.

5. a.   PMBOK® Guide: Section 11.5.2.2

Y   a. Transfer is a technique for threats.

N   b., c., and d. Accept, exploit, and enhance are all examples of techniques for opportunities.

6. a.   PMBOK® Guide: Section 11.5.3.2

Y   a. A secondary risk is a risk that develops because of a risk response that was implemented. Example: Because of the snow storm there is a risk that my car may slide off of the road. I decided to walk to work instead of driving so as to avoid the risk of my car sliding off the road. A new risk, called a secondary risk, of me falling on the ice, has now emerged.

N   b. A residual risk is a risk that remains even after we execute planned responses. Also, risks that have been accepted are called residual risks because they remain risks because of our acceptance.

N   c. A fallback plan is the plan you have in place in case your first response does not fully work.

N   d. A risk trigger condition is a situation that leads us to utilize a risk response strategy.

Plan Procurements

In plan procurements we think about what we need on our project and does it make sense to have the work performed inside of the project team or outside. If we feel it makes sense to have an outside organization perform the work we start to think about what contract type we should use, writing a procurement statement of work for the potential supplier, developing a request for proposal, invitation for bid, etc., and also coming up with criteria to help us decide from whom to buy.

INPUTs to plan procurements

Project management plan- there are many things to review inside the project management plan. The three that are most important at this time are the project scope statement, the WBS, and the WBS dictionary. We review these documents to really understand the project work and to help us make good decisions on what work can best be performed by the team and what work can best be performed by an outside organization.

Requirement documentation- this documentation is really the basis for developing the project scope statement, the WBS, and the WBS dictionary. As we decide what work can best be performed by the team and what work can best be performed by an outside organization we need to think if there are any legal implications in the requirements. As an example: intellectual property rights. If we have a seller perform some of the technical work on the project, we need to think about and plan for ownership of intellectual property rights.

Risk register- based on the work of plan risk responses, we may have already decided to utilize contracts. As an example, we may have decided to purchase insurance as a risk transfer technique.

Activity resource requirements- these requirements tell us what type and how much we have estimated for resources (people, equipment, materials, supplies). These estimates need to be considered as we consider using an outside party to perform some of the work of the project.

Project schedule- we need to consider when we planned to have work complete versus when a supplier could have work complete. Also, we may need to consider lead time on equipment orders.

Activity cost estimates- if we request bids, quotes, or proposals from potential suppliers, we may compare their pricing to any estimates we have already developed.

Stakeholder register- we may use this register to understand the impact and interests on the project and how utilizing suppliers may affect other stakeholders.

© January 2016 AME Group, Inc. author Aileen Ellis, PMP, PgMP
aileen@amegroupinc.com 719-659-3658

Enterprise environmental factors - again, there may be several factors to consider. The most important at this point is really understanding our marketplace. Are the products or services we need available on the market at an acceptable price and in an acceptable time frame? How does marketplace pricing compare to our internal pricing?

Organizational assets - there may be several factors to consider. Contract types are of great importance.

Fixed Price Contracts	Seller obligated to deliver Statement of Work (SOW)- very clear Buyer risk lower Seller risk higher
	Firm Fixed Price- most common and most simple.
	Fixed Price Incentive Fee Contract- more flexible. Final price paid based on seller's performance in specific areas such as cost, schedule, or technical. Price ceiling is set to protect buyer. PTA-Point of total assumption- this is the point when the seller assumes all financial risk. EXAM TIP: know this equation for the exam. PTA= target cost + ((ceiling price-target price)/buyer share ratio)
	Fixed Price with Economic Price Adjustment- usually used on contracts that span multiple years. The final price of the contract is adjusted based on changing conditions such as inflation, cost increases, cost decreases, etc. Designed to protect both buyer and seller.

Cost Reimbursable Contracts	Seller obligated to put forth their best effort. Statement of work (SOW)- flexible in case it needs to change or cannot be clearly defined upfront. Seller reimbursed for legitimate actual costs plus a fee (profit). Buyer risk higher. Seller risk lower.
	Cost Plus Fixed Fee- seller reimbursed for all legitimate costs plus paid a fee (profit) that is a percentage of the estimated costs. The fee is **not** a percentage of the actual costs.
	Cost Plus Incentive Fee Contract- more flexible. Final price paid based on seller's performance. No price ceiling is set.

	Cost Plus Award Fee Contract- seller reimbursed for all legitimate actual costs. Fee (profit) based on subjective criteria and awarded at buyer's discretion. Used to help align the seller's objectives to the buyer's objectives.

Time and Materials Contract	Seller paid a fixed price by the hour or day and reimbursed at cost (or cost plus a handling fee) for material. Buyer has more risk since they are paying by the hour or day (and not for finished deliverables). Seller has lower risk since they are being paid for time... not deliverables.
	Considered hybrid type. Fixed price is on labor (fixed price per hour or day). Cost reimbursable since the total contract price is unknown at the beginning.
	Key words to look for: services, emergency, short term, staff augmentation
	Statement of work (SOW)- often a clear, well defined SOW cannot be created. These contracts can be set-up (and cancelled) very quickly.

☑ **EXAM TIP:** On Contract types- for the exam make sure you know for each category:
- Is seller paid based on delivery, effort, or time?
- Who has more risk on the contract?
- Details on type of statement of work.

TOOLs and TECHNIQUEs of plan procurement management

Make-or-buy analysis
- general management technique
- deciding if we should perform the work internally or externally
- if we decide to go external may need to further decide to buy or lease
- while comparing internal and external costs must look at all costs

Market research- important at this point is to really understand our marketplace. Are the products or services we need available on the market at an acceptable price and in an acceptable time frame? How does marketplace pricing compare to our internal pricing? Is there new technology in development that we may want to leverage, and accept the risk associated with it?

Meetings- at this point we may hold meetings with potential bidders. At times, our potential bidders may hold more of an expertise in a certain area than we possess. Working with these bidders early may have very positive long term results on the project.

OUTPUTs of plan procurement management

Procurement management plan- this plan is a subset of the project plan. It is very specific to one procurement and will describe the decisions we have made so far related to the procurement plus outline the other procurement processes.

Procurement statement of work- this is the narrative description of the item (product, service, result) we want to purchase. The statement of work needs to be clear enough and complete enough that the potential bidder can fully understand our needs and summit a reasonable pricing offer.

☑ **EXAM TIP:** Do not confuse this with the project statement of work.
- Project statement of work- comes from our customer or sponsor describing the item they want to purchase (obtain) from us.
- Procurement statement of work- from us to our potential bidder describing the item we want to purchase (obtain) from them.

Procurement documents- these are the documents we use when we are ready to ask the seller to submit an offer to sell.

Request for Information	Used when we want information from our potential bidder but do not want them to make an offer to sell at this time. Often used before the other two below.
Invitation for bid, Request for quote, tender notice	Used when the decision is likely to be made to the low price technically acceptable offer (LPTA).
Request for proposal	Used when the decision will be based on more than just low price. Other items that may influence the decision are: • Technical approach • Reputation and past performance

Source selection criteria- even before we see any bids, quotes, or proposals we should be clear on the criteria we are going to use to select the winning bidder. This criteria will vary greatly from industry to industry and even inside of an industry from product to product.
If we are purchasing an item that is easily available on the market, then price may be the primary criteria. For other items the list of criteria may be objective or subjective.
Examples include:
- Technical approach
- Quality of materials
- Reputation

- Past performance
- Many others

Make or buy decisions- if we decide to make the item in house (and not use an outside source) we will continue with the other project management processes.

If we decide to purchase the item, we then continue with the three other processes from the procurement management knowledge area.

Change requests- we have stated that change requests are an output of many executing processes and all monitoring and controlling processes. This is the only planning process with change requests as an output. The decision to purchase may affect many aspects of the project plan as well as other project documents.

☑ **EXAM TIP:** Remember that this is the only planning process with change requests as an output. No initiating processes have change requests as an output. No closing processes have change requests as an output.

☑ **EXAM TIP:**
- A contract is a legal document.
- A project plan is not a legal document.

OTHER IDEAS-
- **COMPETITIVE AND NON-CONPETITIVE CONTRACTING-** in general we want to use competitive contracting methods in order to find the supplier who can provide the best product and relationship to match our needs.

- **NON-COMPETITIVE FORMS OF CONTRACTING**
  - **SOLE SOURCE-** we (the buying organization) believe there is only one qualified source and therefore if we want to buy we will need to buy from that one source.
  - **SINGLE SOURCE-** we (the buyer) believe there are multiple qualified sources but we have some compelling reasons to only work with one of them. Example- we have other products from this same supplier and want to continue with them because our maintenance people are used to working on their equipment.
  -

For 50 more sample questions and solutions related to contract math please see Aileen's book: *How to get Every Contract Math Question right on the PMP Exam.* The book is available in both print and e-book format on Amazon.

© January 2016 AME Group, Inc. author Aileen Ellis, PMP, PgMP
aileen@amegroupinc.com 719-659-3658

PLAN PROCUREMENT MANAGEMENT- Sample Questions

1. The customer is reviewing the deliverables to determine how the seller has satisfied certain broad subjective performance criteria that was incorporated into the contract. The seller is most likely working under what contract type:
a. firm fixed price
b. fixed price with economic price adjustment
c. cost plus award fee
d. time and materials

2. The general management technique we use in plan procurements to determine what work should be performed by the project team and what work should be performed externally is:
a. make-or-buy analysis
b. contract types
c. proposal evaluation techniques
d. procurement negotiations

3. You are experiencing an emergency on your project and need to bring on a consultant with technical expertise very quickly though it is unclear the exact work he will perform. Most likely you will use what contract type?
a. firm fixed price
b. cost plus fixed fee
c. cost plus award fee
d. time and materials

4. Under this contract type, the seller is required to complete the work. Financial incentives are included that are related to cost, schedule, or technical performance. All costs above the price ceiling are the responsibility of the seller. This contract type is called:
a. firm fixed price
b. fixed price incentive fee
c. fixed price with economic price adjustment
d. cost plus incentive fee

5. We want to ensure that our seller is legally obligated to deliver under a new contract. We most likely will set-up what contract type:
a. firm fixed price
b. time and materials
c. cost plus fixed fee
d. cost plus incentive fee

6. The contract type with the least financial risk for the buyer is:
a. firm fixed price
b. cost plus fixed fee
c. cost plus incentive fee
d. time and materials

7. **The contract type with the most financial risk for the seller is:**
a. firm fixed price
b. time and materials
c. cost plus fixed fee
d. cost plus incentive fee

8. Acquisition of experts is often handled under what contract type?
a. fixed price with economic price adjustments
b. time and materials
c. cost plus fixed fee
d. cost plus incentive fee

9. The contract type that often spans multiple years and allows for final adjustments to the total price due to changed conditions is:
a. fixed price with economic price adjustments
b. time and materials
c. cost plus fixed fee
d. cost plus incentive fee

10. If the buyer is likely to make their final selection on a vendor based on technical capability and not just low price they are most likely to send out a(n):
a. request for quote
b. invitation for bid
c. tender notice
d. request for proposal

11. You are working under a Fixed Price Incentive Contract. The pricing is:
target cost: $100,000
target profit: $ 10,000
target price: $110,000
share ratio: 70/30
Price ceiling: $125,000.
You complete the work for a cost of $120,000. The final contract price is?
a. $ 120,000
b. $ 124,000
c. $ 125,000
d. $ 126,000

12.   You are managing the design/build of a small office building. With your customer, you have signed a Cost Plus Incentive Contract. The negotiated pricing for the contract is:
target cost: $100,000 and the target fee: $ 8,000
max fee $ 12,000 and the min fee is $ 4,000
share ratio   60/40
You complete the work for $105,000. What is the total price the buyer will pay?
a. $105,000
b. $109,000
c. $111,000
d. $113, 000

© January 2016 AME Group, Inc. author Aileen Ellis, PMP, PgMP
aileen@amegroupinc.com 719-659-3658

13. You are working under a Fixed Price Incentive Contract. The pricing is:
target cost: $100,000
target profit: $ 10,000
target price: $110,000
share ratio: 70/30 and a Price ceiling: $125, 000.
If you complete the job for a cost of $131,429 what is the PTA (point of total assumption) ?
a. $ 120,000
b. $ 121,429
c. $ 125,000
d. $ 131,429

14. All the following statements about time and materials contracts are true except:
a. they are a hybrid type of arrangement that contain aspects of both cost-reimbursable and fixed-price arrangements
b. the seller receives a profit in addition to being reimbursed for allowable costs
c. the full value of the agreement is not defined at contract award
d. the exact quantity of items to be delivered is not defined at contract award

PLAN PROCUREMENT MANAGEMENT- Solutions

1. c. PMBOK° Guide: Section 12.1.1.9

Y   c. The key word in the question is "subjective". The award criteria in a cost plus award fee contract is subjective.

N   a. and b. With these contracts the criteria for acceptance should be extremely clear.

N   d. In time and materials, the supplier is paid based on time worked. Therefore, we do not see broad subjective performance criteria.

2. a. PMBOK° Guide: Section 12.1.2.1

Y   a. Make or buy analysis is a general management technique used in plan procurements to determine what work should be performed internally and what work should be performed externally.

N   b. Contract types is an input under the category of organizational process assets.

N   c. Proposal evaluation techniques are used in conduct procurements, not plan procurements. To use these techniques we need to already have the proposals. In general we would not have proposals when we are deciding what work to perform internally and what work to perform externally.

N   d. Procurement negotiations are used in conduct procurements, not plan procurements. If we are using this technique we have already decided the work will be performed externally.

3. d. PMBOK° Guide: Section 12.1.1.9

Y   d. The key word in the question is "emergency". If we need to bring in a consultant quickly and cannot clearly define the work, we most likely will use a time and materials contract.

N   a. If we cannot clearly define the work we will not be able to set-up a firm fixed price contract.

N   b. and c. In general, cost contracts are not used for this type of situation. They often take time to set-up, too much time if you are in an emergency situation.

4. b. PMBOK° Guide: Section 12.1.1.9

Y   b. There are several key words and phrases in the question. The phrase "required to complete the work" tells you that we are in the fixed price category. The word "incentives" brings us to the incentive fee contract.

N   a. This cannot be the correct answer because the question references financial incentives.

N   c. There is no mention in the question of economic price adjustment.

N   d. No cost contract can be the correct answer because of the phrase "required to complete the work." In a cost contract, the supplier has to make their best effort, regardless of if they are able to complete the work.

5. a. PMBOK° Guide: Section 12.1.1.9

Y   a. With a firm fixed price contract the seller is legally obligated to deliver.

N   b. With a time and materials contract, the seller is paid by the hour or day. They are obligated to make their best effort to deliver.

N   c. and d. With cost contracts, sellers are obligated to make their best effort to deliver.

6. a. PMBOK° Guide: Section 12.1.1.9

Y   a. The firm fixed price contract has the least financial risk for the buyer and the most financial risk for the seller. The buyer only pays if the seller is able to deliver.

N   b. and c. Cost contracts carry more financial risk for the buyer and less for the seller.

© January 2016 AME Group, Inc. author Aileen Ellis, PMP, PgMP
aileen@amegroupinc.com 719-659-3658

N   d. Time and materials contracts carry more financial risk for the buyer than fixed price contracts. In a time and materials contract the seller is paid by the hour or day, not the deliverable.

7. a. PMBOK® Guide: Section 12.1.1.9
Y   a. The firm fixed price contract has the least financial risk for the buyer and the most financial risk for the seller. The buyer only pays if the seller is able to deliver.

N   b. and c. Cost contracts carry more financial risk for the buyer and less for the seller.

N   d. Time and materials contracts carry less financial risk for the seller than fixed price contracts. In a time and materials contract the seller is paid by the hour or day, not the deliverable.

8. b. PMBOK® Guide: Section 12.1.1.9
Y   b. We often use time and materials contracts for the acquisition of experts.

N   a. The fixed price with economic price adjustment contract is often used on contracts that span many years and there is a strong potential for changing conditions. Examples include the price of commodities.

N   c.   and d. Cost contracts are usually not used for the acquisition of experts since these contracts can be very complex to set-up and monitor.

9. a. PMBOK® Guide: Section 12.1.1.9
Y   a. The fixed price with economic price adjustment contract is often used on contracts that span many years and there is a strong potential for changing conditions. Examples include the price of commodities.

N   b. Time and materials contracts are usually set-up for much shorter time periods than fixed price with economic price adjustment contracts.

N   c. and d. The final price of a cost contract is tied very much to the legitimate actual costs of the seller, not to changing conditions.

10. d. PMBOK® Guide: Section 12.1.3.3
Y   d. A request for proposal is often used when the buyer hopes to make the final decision based on criteria other than or in addition to low price.

N   a., b., and c. The terms request for quote, invitation for bid, and tender notice are often used when the buyer plans to make the final decision based on a low price acceptable offer.

11. b. Garrett World Class Contracting

Contract type	Fixed Price Incentive
Do we have an overrun or under run? How much?	Overrun of $20,000
Will the seller's profit be increased or decreased for an overrun?	Decreased by the seller's % of the overrun. (go to share ratio, take 2nd %)
Decreased by how much? (Seller's % *overrun)	30% of $20,000= $6,000
Seller profit=target profit-adjustment	Seller profit= $10,000-$6,000 Seller profit= $4,000
Actual price= actual cost + actual profit	Price= $120,000 + $4, 000 Price= $124,000
Is actual price less than the ceiling price?	Yes, Therefore, the actual price is $124,000 and profit is $4,000.

12. c. Garrett World Class Contracting

Contract type	Cost Plus Incentive
Overrun or under run? How much?	Overrun of $5,000
Will the seller's fee be increased or decreased for an overrun?	Decreased by the seller's % of the overrun. (go to share ratio-take 2nd %)
Decreased by how much?	40% of $5,000= $2,000
Seller fee=target fee-adjustment	Seller fee= $8,000-$2,000 Seller fee= $6,000
Is fee between max and min fee?	Yes, so Seller fee=$6,000
Actual price= actual cost + actual fee	Actual price= $105,000+6,000= $111,000

13. b. Garrett World Class Contracting

PTA= target cost+ (ceiling price-target price)/buyer share ratio

PTA= 100,000 + (125,000-110,000)/.7

PTA= 100,000 + (15,00)/.7

PTA= 100,000 + 21,429

PTA= 121,429

14. b. PMBOK® Guide: Section 12.1.1.9

Y   b. This question has the word except in it; therefore, we are looking for the answer that does not belong or is not true. This statement is the definition of a cost-reimbursable contract, not a time and materials contract.

N   a., c., and d. These are all true statements and thus not the correct answer. T&M contracts resemble cost reimbursable type arrangements in that they are open-ended. They resemble fixed price from the standpoint that the price per hour or per day is fixed. Neither the full value of the agreement nor the exact quantity of items to be delivered are defined.

© January 2016 AME Group, Inc. author Aileen Ellis, PMP, PgMP
aileen@amegroupinc.com 719-659-3658

Plan Stakeholder Management

☑ **Exam Tip:** Review Figure 13-6 of the PMBOK® Guide.

Once we have identified our stakeholders we now need to plan how to engage them. The stakeholder management plan should be very specific on how we are going to engage different stakeholders in the best interest of the project.

INPUTs to plan stakeholder management (not all listed)

Project management plan- there are elements of the project plan that may help define the stakeholder management plan. Examples include the project life cycle, the change management plan, etc.

Stakeholder register- the register lists and organizes everything we know so far about the stakeholders. The register also lets us know which stakeholders require the most engagement. This is critical as we plan stakeholder management.

TOOLs and TECHNIQUEs of plan stakeholder management

Analytical techniques- with our most critical stakeholders we want to assess the current engagement compared to the desired engagement for a successful project. See PMBOK® Guide for definitions.

The table below is a stakeholder engagement assessment matrix.

Stakeholder A- we need to engage more to move them from neutral to leading
Stakeholder B- we need to engage enough so they do not slip from supportive to neutral or worse
Stakeholder C- we need to engage more (or differently) to move them from resistant to supportive

	Unaware	Resistant	Neutral	Supportive	Leading
Stakeholder A			C		D
Stakeholder B				C, D	
Stakeholder C		C		D	

C- current engagement D- desired engagement

OUTPUTs of plan stakeholder management

Stakeholder management plan- the stakeholder management plan may take on many forms. At a minimum it should be specific in our strategy to engage our key stakeholders. The stakeholder engagement assessment matrix may be part of the plan as well as a table like the one below that lists the stakeholder, and the strategy to engage the stakeholder as well as the owner.

	Current Engagement Level	Desired Engagement Level	What do we need from them?	Strategy	Owner
Stakeholder A	Neutral	Leading	Provide key staff members	Engage them on project steering committee	Project Manager
Stakeholder B	Supportive	Supportive	Input into requirements	Engage in facilitated workshop	Lead Engineer
Stakeholder C	Resistant	Supportive	Provide mentoring for key members	Engage in planning sessions, have sponsor interact one-on-one	Sponsor

☑ **EXAM TIP:** Not engaging the stakeholders, or the right stakeholders, early and often on a project may lead to more change requests than usual and more expensive change requests. Ignoring negative stakeholders is often found after the fact as a key reason of project failure.

© January 2016 AME Group, Inc. author Aileen Ellis, PMP, PgMP
aileen@amegroupinc.com 719-659-3658

PLAN STAKEHOLDER MANAGEMENT – Sample Questions

1. The stakeholder management plan is used to:
a. increase stakeholder support and decrease their negative impact
b. identify all project stakeholders
c. prioritize project stakeholders
d. assess how stakeholders will react to various scenarios

2. Which of the following represents how the project manager should share the stakeholder management strategies:
a. shared openly
b. use his best judgment when sharing
c. share openly inside the organization but not outside
d. share openly with the project team but not the rest of the organization

3. Your biggest frustration managing your current project is interacting with one of your key stakeholders Mr. Grant. It seems no matter how much planning is conducted, Mr. Grant is always requesting more changes. To help alleviate this situation you should:
a. Interact with Mr. Thompson, who is Mr. Grant's immediate supervisor
b. Get Mr. Grant more involved with your planning activities
c. Ensure that Mr. Grant is not invited to key meetings so that he will not have the opportunity to request changes
d. Move to a different project with less frustrating stakeholders

4. You are only 30 percent through your current project and you have experienced more change requests than any project in your 20 year career. You are using a project management methodology that has been tested out across many groups in your organization. The current project has 200 stakeholders from 20 different countries. The most likely reason for the problems on this project is:
a. technology has progressed
b. communication is more complex
c. a key stakeholder may have been overlooked
d. this project was not planned as well as previous projects

PLAN STAKEHOLDER MANAGEMENT – Solutions

1. a. PMBOK® Guide: Section 13.2.3.1
Y   a. The stakeholder plan is used to increase stakeholder support and decrease their negative impact.

N   b., c., and d. The stakeholder register is used to identify, analyze, prioritize, and assess our stakeholders and their potential reactions to various scenarios.

2. b. PMBOK® Guide: Section 13.2.3.1
Y   b. The project manager should realize there may be sensitive information in the stakeholder management plan and use his best judgment when sharing.

3. b. PMBOK® Guide: Section 13.2 (Implied in materials though not explicit)
Y   b. The more we can get Mr. Grant involved in planning, the more he will become part of the solution, not part of the problem.

N   a. and c. Going around Mr. Grant or leaving him out of meetings will likely only cause more frustration on the part of Mr. Grant and will not help solve the problem.

N   d. Moving to a different project will not solve the problem described in the question.

4. c. PMBOK® Guide: Section 13.2 (Implied in materials though not explicit)
Y   c. If we find that we are experiencing many more change requests than expected we should ask if we have identified and are actively working with our key stakeholders. Often overlooking a key stakeholder will lead to many requested changes that could have been avoided.

N   a. and b. There is no reason to assume that advancing technology or complex communication will be the driver of more change requests than expected.

N   d. The question states that you are using a tested project management methodology. There is nothing in the question to tell us that this project is not as well planned as others.

© January 2016 AME Group, Inc. author Aileen Ellis, PMP, PgMP
aileen@amegroupinc.com 719-659-3658

PLANNING- other ideas

These ideas are based on information in *the PMP® Exam Content Outline* published by PMI® on June 2015 for inclusion on the PMP® Exam beginning January 12, 2016.   For the exam you do not need to know which tasks or which knowledge and skills have been added. The information in the tasks and knowledge and skills may be on your PMP® exam.

Planning Task 13: *develop the stakeholder management plan by analyzing needs, interests, and potential impact in order to effectively manage stakeholders' expectations and engage them in project decisions.*

While this is a new task in the exam content outline this task has been part of this study guide and the PMBOK Guide 5th Edition for years.

Planning Knowledge and Skills

Change management planning:

During the process Develop Project Management Plan the project team should develop both a change management plan and a configuration management plan. Both of these plans are subsets of the project management plan. Change management is a normal part of running a project. We should plan proactively for change. When change requests occur, mostly from the executing and the monitoring and controlling processes, we should have a change management system in place.

Efficiency principles:

Efficiency is creating output with the minimum amount of input (resources and time). Efficiency is being able to produce an input with the minimum amount of waste (recourses and time).
Efficiency is often confused with effectiveness.
Effectiveness is doing the right things. Efficiency is doing things in the right manor.

In project management we think about efficiency in many areas. As an example in earned value management we often use SPI (schedule performance index) and CPI (cost performance index). Both if these indexes are efficiency measures.

Lean principles:

Lean is focused on the pursuit of perfection through the systematic, continual identification and elimination of waste.

Five principles of lean thinking:
1. Identify customers and specify value- define value from end customers point of view and target removal of all non-value activities
2. Identify and map the value stream- the value stream is the entire process that delivers value to the customer
3. Create flow by eliminating waste –eliminate elements of the value stream that do not add value to the customer
4. Respond to customer pull – understand the customer demand and create a process that fulfills this demand
5. Pursue perfection-work towards the point when every asset and every action adds value to the end customer

Lean project management principles

Lean project management is the creation of customer value with the least waste of resources in the shortest amount of time.

Seven principles of lean project management:

1. Eliminate waste- there are many types of waste such as wasted time and effort at handoffs between team members
2. Empowerment, respect and integrity – ex. Functional managers empower team members to represent function
3. Decide later- make decisions as late as possible. Ex. Groom the backlog as late as possible
4. Deliver fast- break into series of small achievable interconnected projects so as to deliver value earlier. Perform active pipeline management.
5. Amplify learning- plan for training. Communicate often, get feedback and learn.
6. Optimize the whole- see the whole project as more than the sum of the project parts. Determine how the project aligns with the whole organization.
7. Build quality in- ensure quality throughout the life of the project and not just at the end. Ex. Refactoring- restructuring existing code to improve readability and reduce complexity.

Regulatory impacts assessment planning:

Regulatory actions may affect project objectives and deliverables. In the *PMBOK® Guide* Regulatory agency regulations are included under government standards as enterprise environmental factors. These items should be planned for over the life of the project. Often regulatory compliance may lead to the need to produce a tremendous amount of documentation. Documentation takes time, money and resources to produce. In the project plan we should plan for regulatory impacts assessment.

Environmental impacts assessment planning:

The project team should assess the impacts the environment may have on the project and the project may have on the environment. Projects may have social, economic and environmental impacts that long outlive the life of the project. Again the project team should assess these impacts as part of their project planning.

Scope backlog:

In the SCRUM model of agile there are two types of backlogs.

1. The product backlog- this is a prioritized list of all the work that needs to happen to deliver the product. The list is a living document and may be continuously updated. Some important terms:
    a. Backlog refinement (sometimes called grooming the backlog)
        i.   Deleting non-relevant user stories
        ii. Adding or splitting user stories
        iii. Refining estimates
        iv. Etc.
    b. The product owner usually has authority to update the product backlog
2. The sprint backlog-this is a subset of the product backlog. It lists all the work expected to be completed in the current sprint.
    a. The sprint backlog should be very visible
    b. The team has authority to update the sprint backlog

© January 2016 AME Group, Inc. author Aileen Ellis, PMP, PgMP
aileen@amegroupinc.com 719-659-3658

MINI-TEST after PLANNING: Questions

Strong suggestion: Do not write on these questions so you can attempt them again later. Realize these questions are coming from all areas of the PMP® Exam and many are coming from outside of the PMBOK® Guide.

1. **Decomposition is a tool and technique of what process(es)?**
a. create WBS
b. create WBS and define activities
c. define activities and develop schedule
d. develop schedule

2. **Product analysis is a tool and technique of what process(es)?**
a. collect requirements
b. define scope
c. collect requirements and define scope
d. define activities

3. **Stakeholder analysis is a tool and technique of what process?**
a. develop project charter
b. identify stakeholders
c. develop schedule
d. collect requirements

4. **Critical path method is a tool and technique of what process?**
a. define activities
b. sequence activities
c. develop schedule
d. estimate activity durations

5. **Another name for hard logic is:**
a. mandatory dependency
b. discretionary dependency
c. external dependency
d. soft logic

6. **Resource leveling is a tool and technique of what process?**
a. define activities
b. sequence activities
c. develop schedule
d. estimate activity durations

7. **Affinity diagrams are a tool and technique of what process(es)?**
a. collect requirements
b. define scope
c. collect requirements and define scope
d. define activities

8. **Facilitated workshops are a tool and technique of what process(es)?**
a. collect requirements
b. define scope
c. collect requirements and define scope
d. define activities

9. **Leads and lags are a tool and technique of what process(es)?**
a. estimate activity durations and sequence activities
b. sequence activities and develop schedule
c. develop schedule and estimate activity resources
d. estimate activity resources and estimate activity durations

10. **Prototypes are a tool and technique of what process(es)?**
a. collect requirements
b. define scope
c. collect requirements and define scope
d. define activities

11. **Rolling wave planning is a tool and technique of what process(es)?**
a. collect requirements
b. define scope
c. collect requirements and define scope
d. define activities

12. **Alternatives generation is a tool and technique of what process(es)?**
a. collect requirements
b. define scope
c. collect requirements and define scope
d. define activities

13. **Alternative analysis is a tool and technique of what process?**
a. define activities
b. sequence activities
c. develop schedule
d. estimate activity resources

14. **Resource optimization is a tool and technique of what process?**
a. define activities
b. sequence activities
c. develop schedule
d. estimate activity resources

15. **Reserve analysis is a tool and technique of what process?**
a. define activities
b. sequence activities
c. develop schedule
d. estimate activity durations

16. **Crashing and fast-tracking are examples of what tool and technique?**
a. critical path method
b. resource optimization
c. schedule compression
d. modeling techniques

17. **The critical path method assumes:**
a. no resource limitations
b. that resource optimization has already occurred
c. resource limitations
d. all start and finish dates are fixed

© January 2016 AME Group, Inc. author Aileen Ellis, PMP, PgMP
aileen@amegroupinc.com 719-659-3658

18. When using rolling wave planning:
a. all work is planning in detail
b. near term work is planning in detail and future work is planned at a higher level
c. near term work is planning at a higher level and long term work is planning in detail
d. all work is planned at a high level

19. Another name for soft logic is:
a. mandatory dependency
b. discretionary dependency
c. external dependency
d. hard logic

20. Affinity diagrams:
a. sort ideas into logical groups
b. vote on ideas so as to make a decision
c. generate ideas
d. prioritize ideas for action

21. Your project team has a very consistent number of resources. Moving around activities to fully utilize these resources is called:
a. critical path method
b. critical chain method
c. resource leveling
d. crashing

22. Based on changing market demands you have been notified to pull in your project schedule by several weeks. Tentatively, you and your team discuss fast tracking the schedule. To fast track, you hope which of the following statements is true:
a. you have extra money in your budget
b. the project is considered high risk
c. the activities have preferential dependencies
d. you have resources available to add to the critical path

23. You need to present to your management on the project. Most likely you will use:
a. a milestone chart
b. a network diagram
c. a project schedule with logical relationships
d. a schedule management plan

24. At this point we have defined the logical relationships between activities and estimated project resources and durations. Now we are determining early and late start and finish dates for project activities. This information tells us:
a. the exact project end date
b. the amount of schedule flexibility we have
c. the dates the project activities will start and finish
d. the critical chain for the project

25. As we control our schedule we like to illustrate project progress. This is best visualized through:
a. a milestone chart
b. a bar chart
c. a project schedule with logical relationships
d. a schedule management plan

26. We are trying to determine where to add feeding buffers and project buffers. The most likely tool and technique we will use is:
a. critical path method
b. what-if analysis
c. resource leveling
d. critical chain method

27. You are struggling as a young and inexperienced project manager. Your mentor suggests that you place less focus on organizational policy and procedures and most focus on understanding organizational culture. Which of the following is not usually considered one of the common experiences that shape organizational culture?
a. operating environments
b. motivation and reward systems
c. shared vision, mission, values and beliefs
d. multiple geographic locations

28. The bridge design and construction project is being initiated. The core team is in disagreement on what should and should not be in the project charter. Which of the following should be part of the project charter:
a. the key deliverables
b. the project schedule
c. the project requirements
d. the change management plan

29. Deliverables are an important output of projects. During initiating we should identify:
a. all the project deliverables
b. the project deliverables that will be outputs of the initiating and planning processes
c. only those deliverables going to the project customer
d. the key deliverables

30. A benefit provides no value until the benefit is:
a. received
b. approved
c. utilized
d. accepted

31. Project Estimating is usually applied to:
a. costs
b. communications
c. organizational budgeting
d. vendor bid and analysis

© January 2016 AME Group, Inc. author Aileen Ellis, PMP, PgMP
aileen@amegroupinc.com 719-659-3658

32. Based on history the project manager knows that a major challenge on projects is having the right resources available. The human resource plan, if well-developed should help us acquire and manage project resources. Another plan that may also help us do this is the:
a. stakeholder management plan
b. schedule management plan
c. procurement management plan
d. communications management plan

33. The project to improve water delivery in your community has been progressing on plan. A critical task, though, performed by your technician, Gamze, is not progressing well. You have approached Gamze and now her manager to try to understand the delay and to offer help. Based on comments from both Gamze and her manager is seems that Gamze can do the task on time but refuses to do so. At this is point you may need to recommend:
a. training
b. mentoring
c. coaching
d. counseling

34. A typical knowledge transfer life cycle has five steps. Of the five steps, which step is often the one least likely to be in place in an organization:
a. identifying the knowledge that is relevant and valuable
b. capturing and retaining that knowledge
c. sharing that knowledge with others
d. assessing the benefits of the transferred knowledge

35. You have been named the project manager over a project to design, build and set up a customer call center. It was determined that this call center was vital to drive the organization's strategy forward. Setting up the call center may be viewed as a(n):
a. key performance indicator (KPI)
b. key success factor (KSF)
c. cost performance index (CPI)
d. organizational process asset (OPA)

36. Your project is to implement a standard customer management system throughout your organization. The sales team manager is your primary customer. You and the sales manager are often in conflict. It was suggested to you to try active listening the next time this manager complains to you about the progress of your project. From what you have learned active listening includes all of the following except:
a. providing feed back to the speaker on your ideas on the topic
b. making eye contact with the speaker
c. watching the body language of the speaker
d. asking questions of the speaker to further your understanding

37. You began your career fifteen years ago as a project engineer. After several successful years as an engineer you moved into a junior and now a senior project manager role. Your mentor is suggesting that you read your company literature including the annual report and the strategic plan. After this he is suggesting you begin to study the competitors of the company and understand where the company fits in the overall marketplace. He says it is critical that you learn when to speak in technical terms and when to eliminate technical words in your conversation. Your mentor is really recommending that you develop skills in:
a. project management
b. strategic planning
c. program management
d. business acumen

38. You have just been assigned as the project manager on a very large project that involves people from many cultures. Although you projects have been cross-cultural in nature before, this project brings opportunity to work with people from many cultures new to you. While it is often important to consider cultures on projects, one of the most important areas for cultural consideration is when:
a. determining rewards and recognition
b. assigning reporting relationships
c. deciding on promotions
d. tasking team members to complete work packages

39. An important aspect of configuration management is configuration identification. Which item(s) below are often kept under configuration control?
a. stakeholder analysis
b. bottom-up estimating
c. parametric estimating
d. quality plan

40. As a project manager you face many decisions on a daily basis. Some of the decisions are small and others have many long-term implications. At this point you are trying to decide between using in-house labor or an outside consultant for a critical design aspect of your product. You are rating the pros and cons of the two alternatives. What phase of your decision making model are you in:
a. solution action planning
b. problem definition
c. ideas to action
d. problem solution generation

41. You have taken over a project in a matrix environment that has not been performing well. Many of the stakeholders are resistant and cannot agree on the path to move forward. The best approach you may take to resolve this issue is:
a. suggest each stakeholder write a detailed description of his or her ideas and use your authority to decide on which method is best
b. request each stakeholder write a detailed description of his or her ideas and then merge all the ideas together in one document
c. bring in a facilitator and have a face to face meeting with the critical stakeholders to develop a strategy to move forward
d. utilize your past experience to develop a strategy. Once the stakeholders see small wins they will be onboard with your ideas.

© January 2016 AME Group, Inc. author Aileen Ellis, PMP, PgMP
aileen@amegroupinc.com 719-659-3658

MINI TEST after PLANNING - Solutions

1. b.   PMBOK® Guide: Section 5.4.2.1 and 6.2.2.1
Y   b. Decomposition is a tool and technique of both create WBS and define activities.
N   a. This answer is good but look for a better one.
N   c. and d. Decomposition is not a tool and technique of develop schedule.

2. b.   PMBOK® Guide: Section 5.3.2.2
Y   b. Product analysis is a tool and technique of define scope.
N   a. and c. Product analysis is not a tool and technique of collect requirements. We need to have the requirements before we can analyze what the product should be.
N   d. By the time we define activities we should already have a good understanding of the product.

3. b.   PMBOK® Guide: Section 13.1.2.1
Y   b. We need to analyze the stakeholders as we identify them so we may classify them.
N   a. Develop project charter is too early to analyze stakeholders.
N   c. Develop schedule is all about the schedule. We should have already analyzed the stakeholders.
N   d. As we collect requirements we use the output of identify stakeholders to help us. The stakeholders were analyzed as part of identify stakeholders.

4. c.   PMBOK® Guide: Section 6.6.2.2
Y   c. Critical path method is used when we develop the schedule.
N   a. To use the critical path method we need to have a network diagram, activity resource requirements, activity duration estimates, etc. We would not have these items as we define the activities.
N   b. To use the critical path method we need to have a network diagram, activity resource requirements, activity duration estimates, etc. We would not have these items as we sequence activities. It is during sequence activities that we produce the network diagram that would need to be an input to using the critical path method.
N   d. To use the critical path method we need to have a network diagram, activity resource requirements, activity duration estimates, etc. We would not have some of these items as we estimate activity durations. It is during the process of estimate activity durations that we produce the activity durations that are needed as an input to the critical path method.

5. a.   PMBOK® Guide: Section 6.3.2.2
Y   a. Hard logic is another name for mandatory logic.
N   b. and d. Discretionary dependency and soft logic mean the same thing as each other and therefore neither can be a correct answer. Both of these answers are for dependencies based on good practices, not mandatory dependencies.
N   c. External dependencies could be hard or soft logic. An external dependency is a link between a project and a non-project activity.

6. c.   PMBOK® Guide: Section 6.6.2.4
Y   c. To resource level we need to have already used the critical path method. Therefore, we are in the develop schedule process.
N   a., b., and d. Define activities, sequence activities, and estimate activity durations are all too early to have resource leveling as a tool and technique.

7. a.   PMBOK® Guide: Section 5.2.2.4

Y   a. Affinity diagrams group like ideas together. They are a tool and technique of collect requirements.

N   b. and c. Affinity diagrams group like ideas together. They are not a tool and technique of define scope.

N   d. Affinity diagrams group like ideas together. They are not a tool and technique of define activities.

8. c. PMBOK° Guide: Section 5.2.2.3 and 5.3.2.4

Y   c. Facilitated workshops are used in both collect requirements and define scope.

N   a. This is a true answer but look for a better answer.

N   b. This is a true answer but look for a better answer.

N   d. Facilitated workshops are not a tool and technique of define activities.

9. b. PMBOK° Guide: Section 6.3.2.3 and 6.6.2.6

Y   b. Leads and lags are a tool and technique of both sequence activities and develop schedule.

N   a. Leads and lags would not be a useful tool and technique of estimate activity durations.

N   c. Leads and lags would not be a useful tool and technique of estimate activity resources.

N   d. Leads and lags would not be a useful tool and technique of estimate activity durations or of estimate activity resources.

10. a. PMBOK° Guide: Section 5.2.2.8

Y   a. Prototypes are a tool of collect requirements. A prototype is a mock-up of a product that lets the customer see something tangible to help define or clarify requirements.

N   b. and c. Prototypes are not a tool and technique of define scope.

N   d. Prototypes are not a tool and technique of define activities. Prototypes are related to requirements, not activities.

11. d. PMBOK° Guide: Section 6.2.2.2

Y   d. Rolling wave planning is planning near term activities in detail and work that is further out in less or no detail. It is a tool and technique of define activities.

N   a. Rolling wave planning is not a tool and technique of collect requirements.

N   b. Rolling wave planning is not a tool and technique of define scope.

N   c. Rolling wave planning is not a tool and technique of collect requirements or define scope.

12. b. PMBOK° Guide: Section 5.3.2.3

Y   b. We use alternative generation to come up with different alternatives to meet the requirements. It is a tool and technique of define scope.

N   a. and c. We use alternative generation to come up with different alternatives to meet the requirements. We must already have the requirements and therefore it is not a tool and technique of collect requirements.

N   d. We use alternative generation to come up with different alternatives to meet the requirements. It helps us define the product and the project scope. It is not about the activities.

13. d. PMBOK° Guide: Section 6.4.2.2

Y   d. We use alternative analysis to analyze how different combinations or types of resources may accomplish the same activity. It is a tool and technique of estimate activity resources.

N   a. We use alternative analysis to analyze how different combinations or types of resources may accomplish the same activity, not to define the activities.

N b. We use alternative analysis to analyze how different combinations or types of resources may accomplish the same activity, not to sequence the activities.

N c. We use alternative analysis to analyze how different combinations or types of resources may accomplish the same activity, not to develop the schedule.

14. c. PMBOK® Guide: Section 6.6.2.4

Y c. Resource optimization is used to match the available resources with the need for resources. It is a tool and technique of develop schedule.

N a. Define activities is too early for resource optimization. At this point we would not have even defined required resources. To optimize resources we need to have already used the critical path method to build an initial schedule.

N b. Sequence activities is too early for resource optimization. To optimize resources we need to have already used the critical path method to build an initial schedule.

N d. Estimate activities resources is too early for resource optimization. To optimize resources we need to have already used the critical path method to build an initial schedule.

15. d. PMBOK® Guide: Section 6.5.2.6

Y d. As we estimate activity durations we may include schedule reserves.

N a. Define activities is too early for reserve analysis. Reserve analysis is used to estimate durations, estimate costs, and determine budgets.

N b. Sequence activities is too early for reserve analysis. Reserve analysis is used to estimate durations, estimate costs, and determine budgets.

N c. The PMBOK® Guide does not list reserve analysis as a tool and technique of develop schedule. It is listed as part of estimate durations in the time knowledge area.

16. c. PMBOK® Guide: Section 6.6.2.7

Y c. Crashing and fast tracking are examples of schedule compression. They are both used with the goal of shortening the schedule.

N a. The goal of critical path method is to estimate the project duration, determine float, etc. This is different than the goal of crashing and fast tracking which is to compress the schedule.

N b. The goal of resource optimization is to match the available number of resources with the required number. This is different than the goal of crashing and fast tracking which is to compress the schedule.

N d. Crashing and fast tracking are not modeling techniques. What-if scenario analysis and simulations are modeling techniques.

17. a. PMBOK® Guide: Section 6.6.2.2

Y a. The critical path method assumes unlimited resources.

N b. Resource optimization occurs after the critical path method.

N c. The critical chain method, not critical path method, assumes resource constraints.

N d. The critical path method assumes theoretical of start and finish dates for each activity. These ranges are what we call the early and late start and finishes.

18. b. PMBOK® Guide: Section 6.2.2.2

Y b. When using rolling wave planning near term work is planning in detail and future work is planned at a higher level.

N a. Be careful of answers with the word "all" in them. Only near term work is planned in detail with rolling wave planning.

N c. This answer is reversed.

N d. Be careful of answers with the word "all" in them. Only work in the long term is planned at a high level with rolling wave planning.

19. b. PMBOK° Guide: Section 6.3.2.2

Y   b. Another name for soft logic is discretionary logic.

N   a. and d. Hard and mandatory logic mean the same thing as each other. Therefore, neither can be the right answer.

N   c. External dependencies could be hard or soft logic. An external dependency is a link between a project and a non-project activity.

20. a. PMBOK° Guide: Section 5.2.2.4

Y   a. Affinity diagrams sort like ideas together.

N   b. Nominal group technique votes on ideas.

N   c. Brainstorming generates ideas.

N   d. Nominal group technique may be used to prioritize ideas.

21. c. PMBOK° Guide: Section 6.6.2.4

Y   c. Resource leveling is used to ensure we have a flat use of resources.

22. c. PMBOK° Guide: Section 6.6.2.7

Y   c. Fast tracking is a process in which we take activities that we would prefer to be completed in series and force them to overlap or to be completed in parallel. If our activities have preferential (and not mandatory) relationships, it is easier to fast track.

23. a. PMBOK° Guide: Section 6.6.3.2

Y   a. A milestone chart is often used for management presentations. It provides enough information without risking that management will get too deep into the details found in other schedule types.

24. b. PMBOK° Guide: Section 6.6.2.2

Y   b. The critical path method helps us determine early start, early finish, late start, and late finish dates for each of the project activities. These dates represent the range of dates when activities may occur. The bigger the range the more flexibility we have on the project.

25. b. PMBOK° Guide: Section 6.6.3.2

Y   b. A bar chart can best visualize the project schedule (the plan) and the actual dates when activities occur.

26. d. PMBOK° Guide: Section 6.6.2.3

Y   d. Feeding buffers and project buffers are used in the critical chain method.

27. d. *PMBOK® Guide Section 2.1.1*

Y   d. Organizational culture is shaped by common experiences. From this list I would select multiple geographic locations as the exception. If we have people working in multiple geographic locations it is less likely they will be shaped by common experiences.

N   a., b. and c. All of these may lead to shared experiences and thus shape organizational culture.

28. a. *PMP® Exam content outline Initiating-Task 2- June 2015*

Y   a. The key deliverables should be included in the project charter.

N   b., c. and d are all too detailed to be included in the project charter.

29. d.   *PMP® Exam content outline Initiating-Task 2- June 2015*

Y   d. Key deliverables should be identified as part of initiating.

30. c.

© January 2016 AME Group, Inc. author Aileen Ellis, PMP, PgMP
aileen@amegroupinc.com 719-659-3658

Y   c. Benefits provide value when they are utilized.

31. a. *PMI® Practice Standard for Project Estimating 2011*
Y   a. Project estimating is usually applied to cost, resources, effort and durations.

32. c. PMBOK Guide 12.1.3.1
Y   c.   Resources are acquired in the Human Resource knowledge area and the Procurement knowledge area. Therefore the procurement management plan may be used to help us acquire and manage resources acquired through procurement.
N   a.   The stakeholder management plan describes our strategy to engage our stakeholders. It does not describe how we will acquire and manage resources.

33. d.
Y   d. Counseling may be required when a person is able to complete a task on time but refuses to do so.

34. d.
Y   d. Based on PMI® research less than one third of organizations have processes in place to assess the benefits of transferred knowledge.

35. b.
Y   b. A Key success factor is what the organization must do to be successful.
N   a. KPIs measure the success of an organization or project.

36. a.
Y   a.   Active listening does not involve sharing our ideas on the topic being discussed. While sharing our ideas may be a good practice, it is not part of active listening.

37. d.
Y   d. Learning about your organization, the competition and the marketplace are all examples of business acumen.

38. a. *PMBOK® Guide 9.3.2.6*
Y   a. Different cultures will have a different view of rewards and recognition. Therefore we should consider culture when determining rewards and recognition.

39. d. *PMI Practice Standard for Project Configuration Management*
Y   d. Often we keep physical items, documents, forms and records under configuration control. The quality plan is an example of a document that most likely would be under configuration control.
N   a., b. and c. These answers are not documents. These answers are tools and techniques. Therefore they are not kept under configuration control.

40. c. *PMBOK® Guide X3.6*
Y   c. During the ideas to action phase we define the evaluation criteria, rate pros and cons of alternatives and select the best solution.

41. c.
Y   c.   On most problems like this the best solution is to hold a meeting with our stakeholders to determine a solution.
N   a., b. and d. It is not likely we will receive stakeholder buy-in with these ideas. Therefore it is less likely that these ideas will lead to a successful outcome.

EXECUTING PROCESSES

There are 8 Executing process of project management. These processes are performed to complete the work defined in the project management plan. A large majority of the project budget is spent during the executing processes. Along with completing the work defined in the project management plan we also have a strong emphasis on acquiring, developing and managing the team. Stakeholder engagement is a large part of executing and often a key factor in determining the success or failure of the project.

Based on the PMP Examination Content outline published in June of 2015 by PMI there are seven (7) tasks of Executing. These processes represent 31% of your exam content. Key phrases associated with each task are:

Task	Key Words
Task 1	Acquire and manage project resources
Task 2	Manage task execution based on the project management plan
Task 3	Implement the quality management plan
Task 4	Implement approved changes and corrective action
Task 5	Implement approved actions by following the risk management plan
Task 6	Manage the flow of information by following the communication management plan
Task 7	Maintain stakeholder relationships by following the stakeholder management plan

The last table lists the key words for the tasks of the Executing Process Group. These tasks are not listed in the PMBOK® Guide. These tasks come from the PMP® Exam Content Outline. You do not need to memorize these tasks for the exam. It is good though for you to review them from time to time because truly these 7 tasks are the basis for the questions on Executing on the PMP® Exam. In the next few pages we cover the 8 processes of the Executing Process Group based on the PMBOK® Guide. If you try you can see how the tasks relate well to the processes. Do not concern yourself with sequencing during Executing. Assume most of these processes occur at the same time.

© Jan 2016 AME Group, Inc. author Aileen Ellis, PMP, PgMP
aileen@amegroupinc.com 719-659-3658

Direct and Manage Project Work

> ☑ **Exam Tip:** Review Figure4-7 of the PMBOK° Guide.

In this process, we complete the activities described in the project management plan. The project manager with help from the project management team ensures that all the work, and only the work that is defined in the project management plan, is performed.

> ☑ **EXAM TIP:** Much of the project budget is spent during direct and manage project work.

INPUTs of direct and manage project work

Project management plan - when you, the project manager, direct and manage the project work, it is important to ensure that the project team only does the work described in the project plan. If work was left out of the project management plan, then the plan needs to be updated.

Approved change requests - when we first enter direct and manage project work there are no approved changes. As the project progresses, change requests are fed into perform integrated change control and if approved become an input to direct and management project work for implementation. The changes may take the form of:
- Corrective action- changes to get your project back on plan
- Preventative action- changes to make sure your project does not get off plan
- Defect repair- rework of a product or part of a product

Enterprise environmental factors - ex. Personnel administration- think how guidelines for hiring and firing may affect how you direct and manage project work.

Organizational process assets - ex. Think how documentation from previous projects including lessons learned may help you as you implement your current project.

TOOLs and TECHNIQUEs of direct and manage project work

Expert judgment - go out and seek expertise to help you with your work on projects. Experts can be anyone and everyone who has knowledge that may help you.

Project management information system (PMIS) - this system provides access to other systems that you will use to implement the project management plan. Also, you may want to use this system to collect data on our KPIs (key performance indicators).

☑ **EXAM TIP:** The PMIS is a tool and technique of some processes and an input (as a subset of environmental factors) for other processes.

☑ **EXAM TIP: Work authorization system-** this system is a subset of the PMIS. The work authorization system ensures that work is performed at the appropriate time, in the appropriate sequence, and by the appropriate organization. Do you have a system that helps you do this?

Meetings- this is a tool and technique of many processes
- there are three types of meetings
  - Information exchange- to give updates to other parties
  - Brainstorming, etc.- to generate ideas
  - Decision-making- to come to a decision.
- Some general guidelines for meetings
  - Be clear on the type of meeting
  - Only call a meeting when a meeting is required
  - Have an agenda, follow an agenda
  - Make sure people know the items to be discussed before the meeting occurs
  - Collect action items- distribute action items in a timely manner
  - Have meeting rules (one person speaks at a time, etc.)
- Face-to-face versus Virtual
  - Face-to-face is most effective – may not be practical
  - Virtual meetings- take more effort to achieve, same result as face-to-face

OUTPUTs of Direct and Manage Project Work

Deliverables- this is the most important output of all the processes. Some people will call project management: deliverable management. These deliverables will become inputs to the control quality process where they are measured for correctness and then inputs of the validate scope process where the customer will inspect them for acceptance. During the close project or phase process, the ownership of the deliverables will transfer to the customer or the operations group.

Work performance data- we discussed this in chapter 3. This is the raw data collected as you implement your project. This data will become an input to several controlling processes for analysis. KPIs (key performance indicators) are an example of this data.

Change requests- as you direct and manage the work of your project you may find a need for changes. Change requests address many aspects of the project. All change requests become inputs to perform integrated change control.

Project plan updates and project documents updates- elements of the plan or other documents may need updating as part of this process.

© January 2016 AME Group, Inc. author Aileen Ellis, PMP, PgMP
aileen@amegroupinc.com 719-659-3658

DIRECT AND MANAGE PROJECT WORK - Sample Questions

1. As the project manager, you are experienced in managing a small team of people. Now your team includes over 500 members located in 4 different countries. It looks like communication is a problem. As an example, Hiram was running late finishing the development of the product. Ravi did not know this and started testing before the product was ready. What may have helped prevent this situation:
a. a change control system
b. a work authorization system
c. a more detailed communication plan
d. a more defined human resource plan

2. The primary output of direct and manage project work is:
a. deliverables
b. work performance reports
c. approved change requests
d. denied change requests

3. Which of the following is a tool and technique of direct and manage project work?
a. change control plan
b. configuration management plan
c. project management information system
d. organizational process assets

4. The project management information system (PMIS) is:
a. part of the organizational process assets
b. part of the enterprise environmental factors
c. a subset of the configuration management system
d. a subset of the change management system

5. Which of the following is an output of direct and manage project work?
a. work performance reports
b. work performance data
c. organizational process assets
d. enterprise environmental factors

6. It seems like we have been planning the project forever. The baselines are now approved and the team is excited to begin the real work. Frustration has set in already related to not only the number of meetings but the way the meetings are being handled. It seems some people come to the meeting expecting to share all their accomplishments. Others are hoping for a lively exchange of ideas with their new teammates. A few just want to come in, make the needed decisions, and get back to the real work. At most meetings, we address all three of these needs. What meeting guideline needs to be reinforced:
a. have an agenda and follow the agenda
b. publish meeting minutes based on the guidelines in the project plan
c. have meetings face-to-face to be most effective
d. do not mix meeting types

DIRECT AND MANAGE PROJECT WORK - Solutions

1. b. PMBOK° Guide: Section 4.3.2.2
Y   b. A work authorization system is a tool that ensures the work is done by the right team member, at the right time, and in the proper sequence.

N   a. There is nothing in the question to tell us that there is an issue with change control.

N   c. and d. The question uses the word communication and the word team. Be careful not to get distracted by these words. The real issue in the example is that Ravi started work without authorization. We need a work authorization system.

2. a. PMBOK° Guide: Figure 4-6
Y   a. Project management is really about deliverable management. Deliverables are the primary output of direct and manage project work.

N   b. Work performance reports are an output of monitor and control project work.

N   c. Approved change requests are an output of perform integrated change control.

N   d. Denied change requests are not noted as an output of any process. In theory, they would be an output of perform integrated change control.

3. c. PMBOK° Guide: Figure 4-6
Y   c. The PMIS is a tool and technique of both direct and manage project work and monitor and control project work.

N   a., b., and d. Plans and organizational process assets are always inputs or outputs and never tools and techniques.

4. b. PMBOK° Guide: Section 4.3.2.2
Y   b. Since this is a system it is likely an enterprise environmental factor.

N   a. Since this is a system it is likely not an organizational process asset.

N   c. The configuration management system is a subset of the PMIS.

N   d. The change management system is a subset of the configuration management system.

5. b. PMBOK° Guide: Figure 4-6
Y   b. As we perform the work of the project (direct and manage project work) data is collected.

N   a. Work performance reports are an output of monitor and control project work.

N   c. and d. OPA and EEF are both inputs to direct and manage project work.

6. d. PMBOK° Guide: Section 4.3.2.3
Y   d. There are basically three meeting types: information exchange, brainstorming and decision-making. The question states that most meetings are a combination of all three. This is the problem that should be addressed.

N   a., b., and c. All three of these ideas are good but none of them address the real issue. The real issue is that we are mixing meeting types and this is causing frustration.

Perform Quality Assurance

☑ **Exam Tip:** Review Figure 8-9 of the PMBOK® Guide.

Understand the difference between perform quality assurance and control quality.

Perform Quality Assurance	Control Quality
Improving our processes	Measuring our products
More managerial	More technical
More big picture	More detailed
Input-quality control measurements (provide input on what processes need improvement)	Output-quality control measurements

INPUTs of Perform quality assurance

Quality management plan- describes how the process of quality assurance will be performed.

Process improvement plan- describes how process improvements will occur on the project.

Quality metrics- lists and details the attributes that will be measured and how they will be measured.

Quality control measurements- these measures help us understand what processes need improving.

TOOLs and TECHNIQUEs of perform quality assurance (see PMBOK® Guide: Figure 8-10)

All tools from Plan Quality and from Control Quality may have a place in quality assurance.

The next seven tools listed are often known as the seven management and planning tools.

Affinity diagrams- used to visually group similar ideas together. Sometimes, we organize our WBSs based on the affinity diagram idea. We may want to group similar ideas together in the WBS.

Process decision program charts (PDPC)- is a technique designed to help prepare contingency plans. The emphasis of the PDPC is to identify the consequential impact of failure on activity plans, and create appropriate contingency plans to limit risks. Process diagrams and planning tree diagrams are extended by a couple of levels when the PDPC is applied to the bottom level tasks on those diagrams

Interrelationship digraphs- This tool displays all the interrelated cause-and-effect relationships and factors involved in a complex problem and describes desired outcomes. The process of creating an interrelationship digraph helps a group analyze the natural links between different aspects of a complex situation.

Tree Diagram- this tool is used to breakdown broad categories into finer and finer levels of detail. It can map levels of details of tasks that are required to accomplish a goal or task. Developing the tree diagram helps one move their thinking from generalities to specifics. Examples of its use in project management include: WBS (work breakdown structure), OBS (organizational breakdown structure), RBS (risk breakdown structure), RBS (resource breakdown structure), etc. In this figure we have a horizontal view but we may also use a vertical view.

Matrix Diagram- This tool shows the relationship between items. At each intersection a relationship is either absent or present. It then gives information about the relationship, such as its strength, and the roles played by various individuals or measurements.

Activity Network Diagrams- we have already discussed these to some extent in the sequence activities process. Different examples include: activity on node diagrams (this is the precedence diagram we already discussed), and activity on arrow diagrams (similar to an activity on node, except the activities sit on the arrows and not on the boxes). In the time knowledge area these diagrams are used with PERT (program evaluation review technique), critical path method (CPM), and precedence diagramming methods (PDM). We have already discussed all three of these ideas.

Prioritization matrix- this is often a combination of a tree diagram feeding into a matrix diagram. Often a pair-wise comparison is used to prioritize items and describe them in terms of weighted criteria. Pairwise comparison generally refers to any process of comparing entities in pairs to judge which of each entity is preferred.

Quality audits- this is a review by someone outside the team to see how we are doing from a quality standpoint and to correct any negatives.

☑ **EXAM TIP:** Audits in general refer to processes while inspections in general refer to deliverables or products. Therefore, we are more likely to:
- Audit a process (and not a deliverable).
- Inspect a deliverable (and not a process).

Process analysis- we use the process improvement plan to analyze our processes and discover the root cause of issues.

OUTPUTs to Perform Quality assurance (not all listed)

Change requests- most monitoring and controlling processes have change requests as an output. All change requests go to perform integrated change control for approval or rejection.

© January 2016 AME Group, Inc. author Aileen Ellis, PMP, PgMP
aileen@amegroupinc.com 719-659-3658

PERFORM QUALITY ASSURANCE – Sample Questions

1. Perform quality assurance includes:
a. the improvement of quality processes
b. identifying which quality standards are relevant and determining how to satisfy them
c. monitoring specific project results to determine if they comply with relevant quality standards and identifying ways to eliminate causes of unsatisfactory performance
d. all the activities of the performing organization that determine quality policies, objectives, and responsibilities so that the project will satisfy the needs for which it was undertaken

2. Which of the following is an input into perform quality assurance:
a. deliverables
b. quality audits
c. quality control measurements
d. change requests

3. Which of the following is a tool and technique of plan quality management:
a. benchmarking
b. project management information system
c. sensitivity analysis
d. organizational theory

4. Which of the following is a tool and technique of perform quality assurance:
a. process analysis
b. product analysis
c. variance analysis
d. reserve analysis

5. A structured, independent review to determine if activities comply with policies, processes, and procedures is known as:
a. quality audit
b. process analysis
c. affinity diagrams
d. product analysis

6. A diagram used to generate ideas that can be grouped to form patterns is:
a. affinity diagram
b. activity network diagram
c. matrix diagram
d. interrelationship diagram

7. What diagram is used to visualize the parent-to-child relationship in a decomposition hierarchy?
a. tree diagram
b. activity network diagram
c. matrix diagram
d. affinity diagram

8. What diagrams are also known as activity on node and activity on arrow diagrams?
a. tree diagram
b. activity network diagram
c. process decision program charts
d. affinity diagram

9. The tool used to understand a goal in relation to the steps for getting to the goal is:
a. tree diagram
b. activity network diagram
c. process decision program charts
d. affinity diagram

10. Perform Quality Assurance is a(n):
a. planning process
b. executing process
c. monitoring and controlling process
d. closing process

© January 2016 AME Group, Inc. author Aileen Ellis, PMP, PgMP
aileen@amegroupinc.com 719-659-3658

PERFORM QUALITY ASSURANCE - Solutions

1. a.   PMBOK° Guide: Section 8.2
Y   a. One of the aspects of quality assurance is process improvement.
N   b. This is a definition of plan quality.
N   c. This is a definition of control quality.
N   d. This is a definition of quality management (the entire knowledge area).

2. c.   PMBOK° Guide: Section 8.2.1.3
Y   c. During quality assurance we may use the quality control measurements to give us insight into which processes need improving and which do not.
N   a. Deliverables are an input to control quality.
N   b. Quality audits are a tool and technique of perform quality assurance.
N   d. Change requests are an output of perform quality assurance.

> ☑ **EXAM TIP:** Audits are always tools and techniques and never inputs or outputs.

> ☑ **EXAM TIP:** Change requests are always inputs or outputs and never tools and techniques.

> ☑ **EXAM TIP:** Change requests are only an input to perform integrated change control and no other process.

3. a.   PMBOK° Guide: Section 8.1.2.4
Y   a. Benchmarking is a tool and technique of plan quality management.
N   b. The PMIS is a tool and technique of direct and manage project work and of monitor and control project work and of no other process.
N   c. Sensitivity analysis is a tool and technique of perform quantitative risk analysis.
N   d. Organizational theory is a tool and technique of plan HR management.

4. a.   PMBOK° Guide: Section 8.2.2.3
Y   a. Quality assurance is the process in which we analyze our processes so as to improve them. Therefore, it makes sense that process analysis is a tool and technique.
N   b. Product analysis is a tool and technique of define scope. We have no product yet in define scope, we are analyzing what the product should be to meet the requirements.
N   c. Variance analysis is a tool and technique of control scope and control cost.
N   d. Reserve analysis is a tool and technique of five processes but not perform quality assurance.

5. a.   PMBOK° Guide: Section 8.2.2.2
Y   a. This is the definition of a quality audit.
N   b. With this tool and technique we look at our processes so as to improve them.
N   c. With this tool and technique we look at how the actual work and results are varying from the project plan.
N   d. Product analysis is a tool and technique of define scope. We have no product yet in define scope, we are analyzing what the product should be to meet the requirements.

☑ **EXAM TIP:** Audits are related to processes. Inspections are related to deliverables and products.

6. a. PMBOK® Guide: Section 8.2.2.1

Y   a. An affinity diagram is used to group like ideas together.

N   b. An activity network diagram is used to show the logical (predecessor and successor) relationships between project activities.

N   c. A matrix diagram looks like a table with items listed across the top and down the side. It provides information about the relationship (or lack of relationship) between the different items.

N   d. An interrelationship diagram visually shows the relationship between various items. It is often used in problem solving.

7. a. PMBOK® Guide: Section 8.2.2.1

Y   a. A tree diagram shows the parent–child relationship. A WBS is a great example. Tree diagram may be vertical or horizontal.

N   b. An activity network diagram is used to show the logical (predecessor and successor) relationships between project activities.

N   c. A matrix diagram looks like a table with items listed across the top and down the side. It provides information about the relationship (or lack of relationship) between the different items.

N   d. An affinity diagram is used to group like ideas together.

8. b. PMBOK® Guide: Section 8.2.2.1

Y   b. An activity network diagram is used to show the logical (predecessor and successor) relationships between project activities. It may be set-up as activity on node (AON) diagram or an activity on arrow (AOA) diagram. Go to sequence activities for more information.

N   a. A tree diagram shows the parent–child relationship. A WBS is a great example. A Tree diagram may be vertical or horizontal.

N   c. These charts are used to help us breakdown the steps to achieve a goal. They often include information on risks that may get in the way of goal achievement and ways to deal with these risks.

N   d. An affinity diagram is used to group like ideas together.

9. c. PMBOK® Guide: Section 8.2.2.1

Y   c. These charts are used to help us breakdown the steps to achieve a goal. They often include information on risks that may get in the way of goal achievement and ways to deal with these risks.

N   a. A tree diagram shows the parent –child relationship. A WBS is a great example. Tree diagram may be vertical or horizontal.

N   b. An activity network diagram is used to show the logical (predecessor and successor) relationships between project activities.

N   d. An affinity diagram is used to group like ideas together.

10. b. PMBOK® Guide: Section 8.2

Y   b. Perform quality assurance is an executing process. The executing processes are more pro-active.

N   a. Plan quality management is a planning process.

N   c. Control quality is a monitoring and controlling process. The monitoring and controlling processes are more reactive.

N   d. There are no quality processes in closing.

© January 2016 AME Group, Inc. author Aileen Ellis, PMP, PgMP
aileen@amegroupinc.com 719-659-3658

Acquire Project Team

☑ **Exam Tip:** Review Figure 9-8 of the PMBOK° Guide.

In this process we work to acquire the people we need to make the project successful. At times the project manager and the project management team have some control over who gets selected (or assigned) to the project team and at other times they do not. Sometimes the skill sets required are not available, or even if they are available are not assigned to the project team. Project managers need to ensure that the project plan is updated based on the actual people assigned to the project team.

INPUTs of Acquire Project Team (not all listed)

Human resource plan- this document, as a subset of the project management plan, describes how we will acquire the team including information on roles and responsibilities, reporting relationships (org chart), and timing for acquiring and releasing project team members (staffing management plan).

TOOLs and TECHNIQUEs of Acquire project team

Pre-assignment- at times we do not get to select some of our team members. Ex. The most likely example of this- sometimes our organization will submit a proposal to a potential customer. The proposal may include resumes of the people who will hold key positions on our team if we were to win the work. If we do win, these people are pre-assigned.

Negotiation- the project management team will need to negotiate with other teams, functional managers, and external organizations to obtain the skill sets required to make the project successful. The ability to negotiate and influence will affect the success of the project.

Acquisition- this sounds like a procurement term and it is. The project management team may need to go outside of the organization if the skill sets are not available internally. This could mean hiring a consultant or using a vendor to do some of the project work.

☑ **EXAM TIP:** Be careful on the exam with the tool and technique called acquisition. Remember it is part of human resources and not procurement.

Virtual teams- a virtual team is a team that is made up of individuals who do not normally meet face-to-face. Some of the negatives that may need to be overcome when using a virtual team include:
- Issues with communications
- Members feeling alone or isolated
- More money needed to be spent on technology related to communications
- Etc.

Some of the positives virtual teams many bring include:
- Considering projects that may be would not have been considered because of geography, etc.

- Ability to obtain very skilled resources that would not have been available locally
- Lower costs associated with office space, relocation of individuals
- Etc.

Multi-criteria decision analysis- often when selecting team members multiple factors may be considered (ex. availability, experience, desire to be on the team, cost, etc.). A decision-making tool may be used that will weigh the different criteria based on the needs of the team and the position. This can make the decision process clearer and less time consuming.

OUTPUTs from acquire project team

Project staff assignments- at this point we should know who will hold what positions on the team. Remember this does not happen all at once. People will join the team as others leave the team based on the current skill sets required.

Resource calendars- for the people assigned to the team a reliable calendar should be created to show when they are available to work on the project and when they are not available. They may not be available 100% of the time due to other commitments such as supporting other projects, vacation time, etc.

Project management plan updates- many sections of the project plan may be updated as human resources are acquired. Example- the project schedule may need to be updated if we were unable to secure the experience we expected and will be using less experienced resources. This may lead to the planned schedule becoming longer.

ACQUIRE PROJECT TEAM - Sample Questions

1. Which plan is an input to acquire project team?
a. communications management plan
b. human resource plan
c. procurement management plan
d. stakeholder management plan

2. One of the positives of utilizing virtual teams is:
a. feelings of isolation
b. difficulty in communicating
c. expense of technology
d. new possibilities when acquiring team members

3. Having to use the resources promised as part of a proposal is an example of:
a. negotiation
b. acquisition
c. pre-assignment
d. virtual teams

4. If the project manager is unable to acquire the required resources to complete the project he should:
a. try to move to a better project
b. be clear that management is responsible for project failure
c. cut corners on the work and hope no one notices
d. request management support to get the required resources

5. Organizational structure is an example of:
a. organizational process asset
b. enterprise environmental factor
c. negotiation
d. acquisition

6. Hiring consultants or subcontracting work to an outside organization is an example of?
a. organizational process asset
b. enterprise environmental factor
c. negotiation
d. acquisition

7. Multi-Criteria decision analysis involves:
a. hiring individual consultants
b. negotiating with functional managers
c. forming teams whose members live in widespread geographic areas
d. using criteria to rate potential team members

8. Resource calendars document:
a. who is responsible for what deliverables
b. the time periods that each team member can work on the project
c. the reporting relationships of project team members
d. the successors of each activity

9. Communication planning is very important with:
a. pre-assignment
b. acquisition
c. virtual teams
d. multi-criteria decision analysis

10. The impact of the unavailability of resources must be:
a. kept quiet unless someone asks
b. reflected in key documents
c. used to blame senior management for project failure
d. not allowed to affect the project

© January 2016 AME Group, Inc. author Aileen Ellis, PMP, PgMP
aileen@amegroupinc.com 719-659-3658

ACQUIRE PROJECT TEAM – Solutions

1. b. PMBOK® Guide: Section 9.2.1.1
Y b. The human resource plan is all about the team and therefore would be an input of acquire project team.
N a. The communications management plan is about communications and not about the team. It would be an input of manage communications.
N c. The procurement management plan would describe the processes of procurement. It would be an input of conduct procurements.
N d. The stakeholder management plan is about the stakeholders. The team is a subset of the stakeholders but there is a plan just about the team. The stakeholder management plan would be an input of manage stakeholder engagement.

2. d. PMBOK® Guide: Section 9.2.2.4
Y d. If we have the opportunity to use virtual teams, we may be able to bring human resources to the team from any place in the world. This may allow us to recruit the best talent.
N a., b., and c. Feelings of isolation, difficulty in communicating, and expense of technology are examples of negatives we may encounter when utilizing virtual teams.

3. c. PMBOK® Guide: Section 9.2.2.1
Y c. Pre-assignment of resources may limit our flexibility when acquiring team members. As an example, specific human resources may have been promised in a proposal.
N a. Negotiation with other project managers, functional managers, etc. may be used to help us acquire the people we need.
N b. Acquisition may be used to help us acquire resources from outside the organization for the team.
N d. One of the positives of virtual teams is we may be able to recruit the best talent if the whole world can be viewed as a potential labor pool.

4. d. PMBOK® Guide: Chapter 9 - Introduction (implied)
Y d. As the project manager we are responsible to achieve the project objectives. If we cannot get the human resources we need, we may need to request management support.
N a. We have a responsibility to do the best job possible for our organization. When we run into issues we cannot just give up and try to move to another project.
N b. As the project manager we are responsible to achieve the project objectives.
N c. We should never cut corners. We need to request support when we need support.

5. b. PMBOK® Guide: Section 9.2.1.2
Y b. Organizational structure is an example of an enterprise environmental factor that may affect how we acquire team members.
N a. Hiring policies is an example of an organizational process asset that may affect how we acquire team members.
N c. Negotiation with other project managers, functional managers, etc. may be used to help us acquire the people we need.
N d. Acquisition may be used to help us acquire resources from outside the organization for the team.

6. d. PMBOK® Guide: Section 9.2.2.3
Y d. Acquisition may be used to help us acquire resources from outside the organization for the team or to subcontract out a certain portion of project work.

N a. Hiring policies is an example of an organizational process asset that may affect how we acquire team members.

N b. Organizational structure is an example of an enterprise environmental factor that may affect how we acquire team members.

N c. Negotiation with other project managers, functional managers, etc. may be used to help us acquire the people we need.

7. d. PMBOK® Guide: Section 9.2.2.5

Y d. Using criteria to rate potential team members is an example of multi-criteria decision analysis.

N a. Hiring individual consultants is an example of the tool and technique acquisition.

N b. Negotiation with other project managers, functional managers, etc. may be used to help us acquire the people we need.

N c. One of the positives of virtual teams is we may be able to recruit the best talent if the whole world can be viewed as a potential labor pool. Our team may be very geographically diverse.

8. b. PMBOK® Guide: Section 9.2.3.2

Y b. If we want to know the time periods that each team member is available for the project we should review the resource calendars.

N a. A resource assignment matrix shows who is responsible for what deliverables (or activities).

N c. The project organizational chart shows the reporting relationships for the project team members.

N d. The project network diagram shows predecessors and successors for activities.

9. c. PMBOK® Guide: Section 9.2.2.4

Y c. Communication planning is important for all teams but even more critical with virtual teams.

N a., b., and d. While any of these answers may look good, there is another answer that is much more associated with the question.

10. b. PMBOK® Guide: Section 9.2

Y b. If key resources are not available for the project, this information must be shared and the stakeholders informed.

N a. We do not want to hide this type of information on the project.

N c. No one should be blamed for project failure. That being said, if the project does fail, we want to collect lessons learned, not to cast blame, but to ensure we have a better chance of success on future projects.

N d. If key resources are not available, this may have an effect on the project. Senior management should be informed to see if they are able to help get the resources we need to ensure project success.

© January 2016 AME Group, Inc. author Aileen Ellis, PMP, PgMP
aileen@amegroupinc.com 719-659-3658

Develop Project Team

☑ **Exam Tip:** Review Figure 9-10 of the PMBOK® Guide.

There are two parts to develop the project team. One part is developing the competencies of the individual team members. The other part of this process is to develop the individuals into a working team. Both of these ideas together should lead to improved project performance.

Building **trust** is a big part of building a successful team. And building a highly effective working team is a big part of being a project manager. As a project manager, we often have team members representing many different cultures. Learning to work with these other cultures and even using the different cultures to the advantage of the team is critical to team success.

INPUTs of develop project team

Human resource plan- this plan, as a subset of the project plan, provides guidance on how to develop the competences of the individual team members and also how to develop these individuals into a team.

Project staff assignments- to develop the team we need to know who is on the team.

Resource calendars- the calendars show when team members are joining and leaving the teams. They may also show when members are available for different team activities, including training and team building.

TOOLs and TECHNIQUEs of develop project team

Interpersonal skills- these are those soft skills that help us get things accomplished, especially accomplished through other people. Empathy is an example. Empathy means to put ourselves in someone else's shoes to try to understand what they are experiencing.

Training- is about improving the competency of an individual team member.

☑ **EXAM TIP:** An interesting question is who pays for the training of a project team member. If the training is specific to project needs often the project budget will cover the cost. If the training will be useful on other projects, then often the organization will cover the cost.

Team building activities- team building should start early on the project and continue for the life of the project. The goal is to improve relationships so as to improve the performance on the projects. Some organizations believe in professionally facilitated team building activities. While this is great, day-to-day activities may have just as much of a positive effect.

Most teams progress through team development in various **stages**. One such model was developed by Tuckman. He first developed a four stage model and then later added a fifth stage. Most teams progress through this model sequentially. Teams need to be careful to not get STUCK in a stage or even move backwards. If new people join the team or current people leave the team, the team will often go back to stage one- Forming. The five states of Tuckman's model are:

- Forming- this is when team members first meet and learn about the project and each other. Individuals often are on their best behavior and work independently.
- Storming- at this stage different ideas and ways of progressing are often discussed, conflict may arise. Some teams get STUCK here, while others are more collaborative and move through this stage quicker.
- Norming- at this stage the team members often agree to a common goal and a common approach to achieve the goal. Members begin to put team goals ahead of individual goals.
- Performing- often at this point team members are motivated and begin to achieve results. Positive results lead to more positive results. Not all teams reach a performing stage.
- Adjourning- at this stage the work of the project is complete and the team members go their separate ways.

☑ **EXAM TIP:** Know the name Tuckman as the originator of this model (sometimes called the Tuckman ladder). Also know that some teams get STUCK in a stage and some teams even move backwards. **Expect 5 or 6 questions on this model.**

Ground rules- helps to set expectations on behaviors. The team together should develop the rules and also enforce the rules. Examples of ground rules include:

- All team members attend required meetings or communicate in advance why they will not be there
- All team members take responsibility for the completion of their own work
- All team members bring up issues before they become personal
- Action items from team meetings are distributed within 2 hours of meeting completion

Colocation- this means that most if not all of the project teams members are physically located together for a period of time. The goal of colocation is to improve project performance. Examples include:

- Kickoff meeting that may span several days with most team members present
- War room for team meetings, etc.

While colocation may be very beneficial there are also some benefits of using virtual teams. The two ideas need to be evaluated to determine which, or a combination of both, is optimal for team performance.

☑ **EXAM TIP:** Another name for colocation is a tight matrix. A "tight matrix" has nothing to do with a weak or a strong matrix though the phrase "tight matrix" may show up on the exam as a wrong answer if the right answer is weak matrix, strong matrix, or balanced

© January 2016 AME Group, Inc. author Aileen Ellis, PMP, PgMP
aileen@amegroupinc.com 719-659-3658

matrix. The term colocation is often associated with a projectized team though a team may be projectized and not collocated.

Recognition and Rewards- some guidelines for recognition and rewards: Only reward desirable behavior- you can laugh but we have all witnessed undesirable behavior being rewarded.

- The reward must be something the person wants (values), not something you want for them
- Think about cultural differences when deciding on rewards
- Recognize the team throughout the project, not just at the end
- Tangible reward- money
- Intangible rewards- may be even more valuable than money. Examples include:
  - Recognition privately or in front of others
  - Access to new technology
  - Ability to grow skills, meet new people, etc.

Personnel Assessment tools- these are tools we use to help us really understand our team members including their strengths and weaknesses. Examples include:

- The Myers-Briggs Type Indicator (MBTI)
- The Everything DISC Profile

OUTPUTs of develop project team

Team Performance Assessments- both formally and informally the project manager will want to assess the effectiveness of the team. The expectation is that a focus on team building will lead to increased performance in many areas. Items that the project manager will evaluate:

- Performance against requirements
- Performance against schedule baseline
- Performance against cost baseline

DEVELOP PROJECT TEAM - Sample Questions

1. **Which plan is an input of develop project team?**
a. communications management plan
b. human resource plan
c. procurement management plan
d. stakeholder management plan

2. **Communication skills, emotional intelligence, and conflict resolution are proficiencies also known as:**
a. project management skills
b. general management skills
c. interpersonal skills
d. overrated skills

3. **The five stage model used for team development was developed by whom?**
a. Tuckman
b. Shewhart
c. Deming
d. Ishikawa

4. **One of the purposes of team building activities is to:**
a. help build trust and good working relationships
b. enhance the competencies of the team members
c. establish acceptable behavior expectations
d. place most of all of the team members in one location

5. **In the five stages of team development, all of the following often occur except:**
a. the stages occur in order
b. teams may get stuck in a stage
c. teams may slide back into a previous stage
d. teams skip a stage going forward

6. **A tight matrix is another name for:**
a. a team where the project manager has more authority than the functional manager
b. a team where the functional manager has more authority than the project manager
c. a team that has members geographically dispersed
d. a team that is co-located

7. **Intangible rewards:**
a. should never be used if money is available
b. include money
c. may be equally or even more effective than money
d. should be the same for everyone, to ensure fairness

8. **Colocation may bring benefits such as:**
a. lower costs
b. access to more skilled labor
c. lower relocation expenses
d. sense of community

© January 2016 AME Group, Inc. author Aileen Ellis, PMP, PgMP
aileen@amegroupinc.com 719-659-3658

9. Which input to develop project team has the purpose to identify the people who are on the team:
a. human resource plan
b. staffing management plan
c. project staff assignments
d. resource calendars

10. Training:
a. is used to increase the competencies of the individual team members
b. should always be billed to the performing organization and not the project
c. has the objective to help team members work together
d. follows the five stages of team development

DEVELOP PROJECT TEAM – Solutions

1. b. PMBOK® Guide: Section 9.3.1.1
Y   b. The human resource plan is all about the team and therefore would be an input of develop project team.
N   a. The communications management plan is about communications and not about the team. It would be an input of manage communications.
N   c. The procurement management plan would describe the processes of procurement. It would be an input of conduct procurements.
N   d. The stakeholder management plan is about the stakeholders. The stakeholder management plan would be an input of manage stakeholder engagement.

2. c. PMBOK® Guide: Section 9.3.2.1
Y   c. Communication skills, etc. are examples of interpersonal skills.
N   a. Project management skills include skills such as identifying requirements, building a schedule, etc.
N   b. General management skills would include skills in accounting, finance, etc.
N   d. An answer like overrated skills is not likely to be a good answer for this exam.

3. a. PMBOK® Guide: Section 9.3.2.3
Y   a. Tuckman developed the five stages of team development.
N   b. Shewhart defined the plan-do-check-act cycle that is often associated with quality.
N   c. Deming modified the plan-do-check-act cycle that is often associated with quality.
N   d. Ishikawa is best known for the fishbone diagram.

4. a. PMBOK® Guide: Section 9.3.2.3
Y   a. One of the main purposes of team building is to build trust among team members.
N   b. Training is used to enhance the competencies of the team members.
N   c. Ground rules establish acceptable behaviors for team members.
N   d. Colocation is placing most if not all of the team members in one physical location.

5. d. PMBOK® Guide: Section 9.3.2.3
Y   d. In general, teams do not skip stages of team development going forward.
N   a. In general, the stages of team development occur in the same sequence.
N   b. In general, teams may get stuck in a stage.
N   c. In general, teams may slide back a stage.

6. d. PMBOK® Guide: Section 9.3.2.5
Y   d. Another name for colocation is tight matrix.
N   a. We call a team a strong matrix when the project manager has more authority than the functional manager.
N   b. We call a team a weak matrix when the functional manager has more authority than the project manager.
N   c. We call a team virtual when it has some of its members geographically dispersed.

7. c. PMBOK® Guide: Section 9.3.2.6
Y   c. Intangible rewards, such as an opportunity to develop or test a new skill set may be as effective or even more effective than money.

© January 2016 AME Group, Inc. author Aileen Ellis, PMP, PgMP
aileen@amegroupinc.com 719-659-3658

N   a. Because intangible rewards may be as effective or even more effective than money they should be used even if money is available.

N   b. Money is a tangible, not an intangible reward.

N   d. Different people may value intangible rewards differently. Not everyone needs to receive the same one.

8. d.   PMBOK° Guide: Section 9.3.2.5

Y   d. Location may bring a sense of community that is harder to develop with a virtual team.

N   a., b., and c. Some benefits often achieved with a virtual team include lower relocation costs, access to more skilled labor, lower costs overall, etc.

9. c.   PMBOK° Guide: Section 9.3.1.2

Y   c. Project staff assignments tell us who is on the team and in what role.

N   a. The human resource plan includes the organizational chart for the project, the staffing management plan, etc.

N   b. The staffing management plan describes training needs, staff acquisition plan, staff release plan, etc.

N   d. Resource calendars show when each team member is available for the project.

10. a.   PMBOK° Guide: Section 9.3.2.2

Y   a. Training focuses on improving the competencies of the individual team members.

N   b. Training may or may not be billed to the performing organization. It depends on how much will the organization or the project benefit from the training.

N   c. Team building, not training, has the focus of helping individuals work as a team.

N   d. Team building, not training, follows the five stages of team development.

Manage Project Team

> ☑ **Exam Tip:** Review Figure 9-12 of the PMBOK® Guide.

In this process we interact with our team members on a day-to-day basis to work on improving project performance. This may involve dealing with issues and conflicts, etc. Regardless of the tools that we use, the goal is always improved performance for the project. This is the process in which the project manager really must utilize his management skills to not only provide appropriate feedback but also provide assignments that help the team members grow as individuals and as a team.

INPUTs to manage project team

Human resource plan- this plan, as a subset of the project plan, provides guidance on how to manage the project team.

> ☑ **EXAM TIP**: Since we are in the H.R. chapter it is a good guess that the HR plan and not another plan is an input.

Project staff assignments- to manage the team we need a current list of members. This may seem simple but on a big project the team may change very quickly based on the current work.

Team Performance assessments- these assessments, along with other inputs, drive improvements in team communication and interaction, as well as issue and conflict resolution.

> ☑ **EXAM TIP**: Team performance assessments (how the team is performing against the project objectives) are often confused on the exam with project performance appraisals (appraisals of individual team members against their performance goals).

Issue Logs- these logs are an output of manage stakeholder engagement. Issue logs should be utilized to ensure that all project issues are resolved and closed.

Issue #	Description	Priority	Owner	Target Resolution Date	Status	Date Resolved	Resolution and Comments
001	Late delivery of computer systems	High	Nick	Aug 20, 2013	In progress		
002	Terry moved off project- need replacement	Medium	Alex	April 14, 2013	Complete	April 1, 2013	Jose brought on a team to replace Terry

© January 2016 AME Group, Inc. author Aileen Ellis, PMP, PgMP
aileen@amegroupinc.com 719-659-3658

Work Performance Reports- these reports are an output of monitor and control project work. These reports tell us the status or progress of the project against the project plan and include forecasts. This information can guide future requirements related to the team.

TOOLs and TECHNIQUEs of manage project team

Observation and conversation- some people call this manage by walking around. Think of this as interacting with our team members one-on-one on an on-going basis. This can be done face-to-face or virtually through instant messaging, etc.

Project performance appraisals- the title of this tool may be confusing. Think of this as the yearly performance reviews that managers perform on their workers. On some projects, the project manager owns these appraisals on their team members. On other projects, the functional manager owns these appraisals and the project manager provides input. Either way, the goal of the appraisals is to improve performance through communication, feedback, etc.

Conflict Management- Historically, there has been a negative connotation with the word conflict. Not anymore. If conflict is managed in a healthy way it may lead to innovations that could not be achieved without conflict. There are many sources of conflict on a project:
1. Schedules
2. Project priorities
3. Resources

☑ **EXAM TIP:** Notice this list has numbers (1,2,3). Almost all the other lists in this book are just bullets. For the exam, know the top 3 sources of conflict in order.

When project team members initially run into conflict, they should try to resolve it themselves. Only if they cannot resolve it on their own should the project manager get involved. The success of a project, the project manager, and the project team is very much determined by how well they can overcome negative conflict and use healthy conflict to foster innovation and higher productivity.

For the exam know these five (5) conflict resolution techniques and when you would use each one:
- **Withdrawal (avoid)**- in this technique we walk away from a conflict. If we walk away with the idea to never address the conflict, this is very bad. If we walk away to calm down, or be better prepared with facts then a temporary withdrawal can be a good thing.
- **Smooth (accommodate)**- in this technique we often give in to the other's wishes for the sake of maintaining a positive relationship. We agree on what we can agree on and then often give in on areas where we do not have agreement. If the issue is more important to the other party than to you, smoothing may have merit.
- **Compromise (reconcile)**- in this technique both parties try to meet half way. This may result in a lose-lose situation. On the positive side, if the conflict is not that important or if a quick resolution is necessary this technique may have merit.

- **Force (direct)**- in this technique one person pushes their viewpoint at the expense of another. This will lead to a win-lose solution. This technique may be the best technique in an emergency, especially an emergency that deals with people's safety or security.
- **Collaborate (problem solving)**- in this technique we work with the other party to find a win-win. While this method may take more time than the others, it often leads to a more beneficial result for both parties. For this method to work, a high level of trust in each other and commitment to resolving the conflict needs to be present.

☑ **EXAM TIP:** Notice each technique has two names listed. On the exam if you see a question with answer (a) being withdrawal and answer (b) being avoid, both answers need to be wrong since the two words mean the same thing and you cannot have two answers that are right.

☑ **EXAM TIP:** Collaborate is the method most likely to lead to a win-win. The negative of collaborate is that it may take some time and you may not have time available. That being said, collaborate is not always the best method. The most likely example is during an emergency we most likely do not want to collaborate, we may want the person with the most knowledge and experience to force the solution.

Interpersonal skills- these are those soft skills that help us get things accomplished, especially accomplished through other people. Several specific skills to consider for the project manager include:

Leadership- inspiring others to meet their goals and commitments.

Influencing- often the project manager is not the manager, in the official reporting structure, over his team members. Therefore, the project manager cannot use positional power to influence the team members. He may need to rely on his ability to influence, without power, to get the work of the project accomplished in a timely manner. Great communication skills, including listening skills will help.

Effective decision-making- there are several decision-making processes available to project managers. The appropriate process should be selected for the situation.

OUTPUTs of Manage project team (not all listed)

Change requests- Changes related to people may have a huge effect on the project plan and other project documents.

A few (many) additional ideas- there will be many questions on the exam related to teams where the information is not in the *PMBOK® Guide*.

Motivational theories

© January 2016 AME Group, Inc. author Aileen Ellis, PMP, PgMP
aileen@amegroupinc.com 719-659-3658

MASLOW's Hierarchy of Needs:

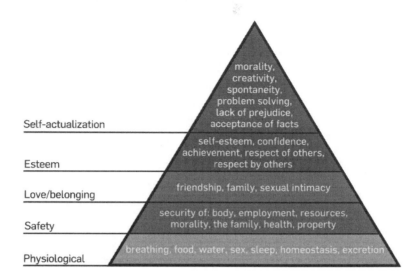

McGregor 's Theory X and Theory Y- perceptions that managers have of their workers.

- Theory X view is that workers are generally lazy and will avoid work.
- Theory Y view is that workers may be willing and eager to work and may be self-motivated.
- An important idea is that McGregor's theories may be self-fulfilling. If the manage treats the workers as lazy (theory X) the workers may become lazy. If a manager treats the workers as self-motivated (theory Y) the workers may become self-motivated.

Ouchi's Theory Z- focused on increasing employee loyalty to the company by providing a job for life with a strong focus on the well-being of the employee, both on and off the job. According to Ouchi, Theory Z management tends to promote stable employment, high productivity, and high employee morale and satisfaction.

McClelland's Need Theory- created by a psychologist, David McClelland, it is a motivational model that attempts to explain how...

- the need for achievement
- the need for power
- the need for affiliation

...affects the actions of people from a managerial context.

Herzberg's Two Factor Theory- distinguishes between:

Motivators (e.g. challenging work, recognition, responsibility) that give positive satisfaction, arising from intrinsic conditions of the job itself, such as recognition, achievement, or personal growth, and

Hygiene factors (e.g. status, job security, salary, fringe benefits, work conditions) that do not give positive satisfaction, though dissatisfaction results from their absence. These are extrinsic to the work itself, and include aspects such as company policies, supervisory practices, or wages/salary.

Essentially, hygiene factors are needed to ensure an employee is not dissatisfied. Motivation factors are needed to motivate an employee to higher performance.

Vroom- Expectancy Theory - states in very simplistic terms that a person will be motivated based on the combination of 3 factors:

- The person's effort will lead to success
- The person will be rewarded
- The reward is something the person values

Power Sources: A project manager may have five types of power available

- Formal- positional power
- Reward- the power to give positive consequences
- Penalty- the power to give negative consequences
- Expert- earned through a recognized level of knowledge
- Referent- power gained from knowledge/relationship with an individual or group

The first three listed (formal, reward, and penalty) come from a person's position. Expert and referent powers come from a person's knowledge or relationships.

Leadership Styles:

Autocratic: traditional view of a management- a boss who makes decisions without asking for input, valuable for quick decisions

Laissez-faire: hands off view of management, valuable when creativity is required

Democratic: manager involves team members in decisions

- Participative- decisions made jointly
- Consultative- manager asks for input but makes decisions alone

MANAGE PROJECT TEAM – Sample Questions

1. The technique used to manage conflict when a project situation is too important to be compromised and involves incorporating multiple ideas and viewpoints from people with different perspectives:
a. smoothing
b. collaborating
c. withdrawing
d. forcing

2. Which plan is an input to manage project team?
a. communications management plan
b. human resource plan
c. procurement management plan
d. stakeholder management plan

3. To clarify roles and responsibilities on the project, what tool and technique of manage project team is often used?
a. team performance assessments
b. issue logs
c. work performance reports
d. project performance appraisals

4. During a fire drill, the safety manager mandates his point of view. This conflict resolution technique is known as:
a. problem solve
b. force
c. compromise
d. smooth

5. Conflict should be:
a. addressed early and usually in private
b. addressed early and publicly
c. avoided
d. viewed as an individual and not a team issue

6. Observation and conversation is a tool and technique of:
a. plan human resource management
b. acquire project team
c. develop project team
d. manage project team

7. Another name for the collaborate technique to resolve conflict is:
a. problem solve
b. force
c. compromise
d. smooth

8. Issue logs are an input of manage project team. They are an output of what process:
a. plan human resource management
b. manage stakeholder engagement
c. develop project team
d. acquire project team

9. Project performance appraisals is a tool and technique of:
a. plan human resource management
b. acquire project team
c. develop project team
d. manage project team

10. Team performance assessments are an output of:
a. plan human resource management
b. acquire project team
c. develop project team
d. manage project team

11. Which of the following represents the true Theory Y manager:
a. workers are inherently lazy
b. workers need to be constantly monitored
c. a hierarchy is the best way to manage workers
d. satisfaction of a job well done is a strong motivator

12. Which of the following sources of power is earned, regardless of a person's position in an organization:
a. formal
b. reward
c. penalty
d. expert

13. There are multiple motivational theories today. Who created the theory that is related to the management's view of workers and not the way workers behave:
a. Vroom
b. Maslow
c. McGregor
d. McClelland

14. The theory most associated with gaining long term loyalty from workers is:
a. McGregor's Theory X
b. McGregor's Theory Y
c. Maslow's Hierarchy
d. Ouchi Theory Z

© January 2016 AME Group, Inc. author Aileen Ellis, PMP, PgMP
aileen@amegroupinc.com 719-659-3658

MANAGE PROJECT TEAM – Solutions

1. b. PMBOK® Guide: Section 9.4.2.3

Y   b. Collaborating is the conflict resolution technique that incorporates multiple viewpoints in order to get to a better solution.

N   a. Smoothing is the conflict resolution technique in which we agree on what we agree on and often do not resolve the disagreement.

N   c. Withdrawing is the conflict resolution technique in which one party pulls back, either on a temporary or permanent basis.

N   d. Forcing is the conflict resolution technique in which one party makes the other party accept the forcer's solution. It is often used as a last resort. This technique may be appropriate in a safety or security situation. The outcome is win-lose.

2. b. PMBOK® Guide: Section 9.4.1.1

Y   b. The human resource plan is a likely input as this plan addresses the team.

N   a. The communications plan is a more likely input to communication processes, not team processes.

N   c. The procurement plan is a more likely input to procurement processes, not team processes.

N   d. The stakeholder plan is a more likely input to stakeholder processes, not team processes.

3. d. PMBOK® Guide: Section 9.4.2.2

Y   d. Project performance appraisals are really appraisals of the individual team member's performance. These appraisals help clarify roles and responsibilities.

N   a. The team performance assessment is an input, not a tool and technique of manage team.

N   b. Issue logs are an input, not a tool and technique of manage team.

N   c. Work performance reports are an input, not a tool and technique of manage team.

> ☑ **EXAM TIP:** "Logs" are never tools and techniques.

> ☑ **EXAM TIP:** "Reports" are never tools and techniques.

4. b. PMBOK® Guide: Section 9.4.2.3

Y   b. Forcing is the conflict resolution technique in which one party makes the other party accept the forcer's solution. It is often used as a last resort. This technique may be appropriate in a safety or security situation. The outcome is win-lose.

N   a. Problem solving, another name for collaborating, is the conflict resolution technique that incorporates multiple viewpoints in order to get to a better solution.

N   c. Compromise is the conflict resolution technique in which both parties give in to the other so as to reach a partial solution.

N   d. Smoothing is the conflict resolution technique in which we agree on what we agree on and often do not resolve the disagreement.

5. a. PMBOK® Guide: Section 9.4.2.3

Y   a. We want to address conflict early before people become locked into their positions.

N   b. Conflict should be addressed in private.

N   c. If conflict is managed in a healthy way it may lead to innovations that we could not achieve without conflict.

N   d. Conflict may be a team issue. It is critical that the project manager knows how to address conflict.

6. d. PMBOK® Guide: Section 9.4.2.1

Y   d. Observation and conversation, sometimes called management by walking around, is a tool and technique of manage project team. We need to have a team to use this tool and technique.

N   a. Plan human resource management is too early for the tool, observation, and conversation. We need to have a team to use this tool and technique.

N   b. Develop project team is too early for the tool, observation, and conversation. We need to have a team to use this tool and technique.

N   c. The focus on develop project team is to develop the individuals as individuals and develop the individuals as a team. This is a little early for the tool and technique of observation and conversation.

7. a. PMBOK® Guide: Section 9.4.2.3

Y   a. Problem solving, another name for collaborating, is the conflict resolution technique that incorporates multiple viewpoints in order to get to a better solution.

N   b. Forcing is the conflict resolution technique in which one party makes the other party accept the forcer's solution. It is often used as a last resort. This technique may be appropriate in a safety or security situation. The outcome is win-lose.

N   c. Compromise is the conflict resolution technique in which both parties give in to the other so as to reach a partial solution.

N   d. Smoothing is the conflict resolution technique in which we agree on what we agree on and often do not resolve the disagreement.

8. b. PMBOK® Guide: Figure 9-2

Y   b. Issue logs are an output of manage stakeholder engagement and an input to manage project team, control communications, and control stakeholder engagement.

N   a. The human resource plan is the output of develop human resource plan.

N   c. Team performance assessments are one of the outputs of develop project team.

N   d. The project staff assignments are one of the outputs of acquire project team.

9. d. PMBOK® Guide: Section 9.4.2.2

Y   d. The project performance appraisals are a tool and technique of manage the project team. These are appraisals on individual team members.

N   a. Plan human resource management is too early for project performance appraisals. You need to have team members to use this tool and technique.

N   b. Acquire project team is too early for project performance appraisals. You need to have team members to use this tool and technique.

N   c. Develop project team is too early for project performance appraisals. The purpose of this process is to develop the team members, not appraise their performance.

10. c. PMBOK® Guide: Section 9.3.3.1

Y   c. The team performance assessment is the output of develop project team. This assessment helps us understand if the tools we are using to develop the team are improving project performance.

N   a. Plan human resource management is too early for team performance assessment. This assessment helps us understand if the tools we are using to develop the team are improving project performance.

N   b. Acquire project team is too early for team performance assessment. This assessment helps us understand if the tools we are using to develop the team are improving project performance.

N   d. The team performance assessment is an input to manage project team. This assessment helps us understand if the tools we are using to develop the team are improving project performance.

11. d. Wikipedia search Theory X and Theory Y

Y   d. Theory Y states that management has a positive view of workers and that workers can be self-motivated.

N   a., b., and c. There statements could all be associated with Theory X not Theory Y.

12. d. Wikipedia search power (social and political)

Y   d. Expert power can be developed by anyone, regardless of position.

N   a., b., and c. Formal, reward, and penalty power all come from a person's position in the organization.

13. c. Wikipedia search Theory X and Theory Y

Y   c. McGregor's Theory X and Y are related to the management's view of workers and not the way the worker actually behaves.

14. d. Wikipedia search Theory Z

Y   d. Ouchi's Theory Z, simplistically states that for an organization to achieve loyalty from its workers the organization must first be loyal to its workers. One way to do this is to provide long term stable employment.

Manage Communication

In this process we follow the communications plan which includes all the details related to project communications including creating the information, sharing the information, and finally disposition of the information. Most people think this process is just about sharing information with the stakeholders. There is a lot more to it than that. We need to ensure that the appropriate information is created and put into a format that adds value. We need to think about the communication methods (push, pull, interactive) to ensure the best method is picked for the situation.

INPUTs of manage communications (not all listed)

Communications management plan- all information about what, when, and how to communicate with stakeholders should be in this plan.

☑ **EXAM TIP:** If you get a question asking who you will be providing specific information to, the best answer is usually: follow the communications plan.

Work performance reports- these are an output of monitor and control project work. These reports are the physical (hard copy or electronic) representation of work performance information.

TOOLs and TECHNIQUEs of manage communications

Communication technology- many factors affect the type of technology used for project communication. The project manager should select the technology that best fits the needs of the stakeholders based on certain factors:
- What technology is available to different stakeholders
- What level of knowledge, experience, and comfort do the stakeholders possess on the different technologies
- How quickly do stakeholders require information
- What is the project environment- do people meet face-to-face, is the team virtual, are people working on different shifts in different time zones, etc.

Communication methods- it is important to choose the appropriate communication methods based on the needs of the stakeholders, the project, and the particular type of communication.

© January 2016 AME Group, Inc. author Aileen Ellis, PMP, PgMP
aileen@amegroupinc.com 719-659-3658

Interactive	Most efficient way to ensure a common understanding	Meetings, phone calls, video conferences, etc.
Push	Sent to specific recipients, does not ensure receipt or understanding	Letters, memos, reports, e-mails, faxes, voice mails, press releases, etc.
Pull	Used for large volumes of info and/or large audiences. People may decide to access or not access information	Intranet sites, e-learning, knowledge repositories, etc.

Information management systems- as a project manager we want standardized ways to collect and distribute information. Information may be distributed in several ways:
- Hard-copy document management- while this may be appropriate for some communications, much of project communications is moving away from this distribution method
- Electronic communications management- these are the basic electronic methods we would see regardless of whether we are involved in project management or not
- Electronic project management tools- these are electronic tools specific to managing projects. Ex. project management software tools

Performance reporting- this is specific to performance information. It is the collection and distribution of that information. Often, it is reported in a form that compares actual performance with planned performance (as documented in the scope, schedule, and cost baselines).

OUTPUTs of manage communications (not all listed)

Project communications- these are the actual artifacts (reports, etc.) related to communications. These artifacts will vary greatly from project to project based on the stakeholder needs, project environment, etc.

Performance measurement baseline (PMB)- at a minimum this is the integration of our scope, schedule, and cost baselines though it may contain other baselines as well.

☑ **EXAM TIP:** Make certain you are very clear that every project should have three (3) baselines:
- Scope baseline—made up of three components
  - Scope statement
  - WBS
  - WBS Dictionary
- Schedule baseline
- Cost baseline

MANAGE COMMUNICATIONS - Sample Questions

1. Which plan is an input to manage communications?
a. communications management plan
b. human resource plan
c. procurement management plan
d. project management plan

2. Which of the following is an input of manage communications?
a. work performance data
b. work performance information
c. work performance reports
d. project communications

3. Which of the following in an output of manage communications?
a. work performance data
b. work performance information
c. work performance reports
d. project communications

4. Awareness of the impact of body language is an example of:
a. meeting management technique
b. presentation technique
c. facilitation technique
d. listening technique

5. The performance measurement baseline typically integrates:
a. scope, schedule, and cost
b. schedule, cost, and risk
c. cost, risk, and procurement
d. risk, procurement, and scope

6. Building consensus and overcoming obstacles are examples of:
a. meeting management techniques
b. presentation techniques
c. facilitation techniques
d. listening techniques

7. The project management information system is an example of:
a. meeting management techniques
b. enterprise environmental factors
c. facilitation techniques
d. organizational process assets

© January 2016 AME Group, Inc. author Aileen Ellis, PMP, PgMP
aileen@amegroupinc.com 719-659-3658

MANAGE COMMUNICATIONS - Solutions

1. a. PMBOK° Guide: Section 10.2.1.1
Y   a. The communications plan is an input to manage communications.
N   b. The human resource plan would be associated with processes in the human resource area, not the communication area.
N   c. The procurement plan would be associated with processes in the procurement area, not the communications area.
N   d. The project management plan is an input to both plan communications management and control communications.

2. c. PMBOK° Guide: Section 10.2.1.2
Y   c. Work performance reports, which are an output of monitor and control work, become an input of manage communications.
N   a. Work performance data is not an input of manage communications.
N   b. Work performance information is not an input of manage communications.
N   d. Project communications are an output of, not an input of, manage communications.

3. d. PMBOK° Guide: Section 10.2.3.1
Y   d. Project communications are an output of manage communications.
N   a. and b. Work performance data and work performance information are both not outputs of manage communications. If the work performance reports are an input, the data or information certainly would not be an output.
N   c. Work performance reports, which are an output of monitor and control work, become an input of manage communications.

4. b. PMBOK° Guide: Section 10.2
Y   b. Presentation techniques include awareness of our own body language and its impact as well as awareness of the body language of our audience members.
N   a. Having an agenda, using the agenda, collecting action items, etc. are all examples of meeting management techniques.
N   c. Facilitation techniques such as encouraging and balancing help a group reach an agreement.
N   d. Listening techniques such as restating or paraphrasing help with effective communication.

5. a. PMBOK° Guide: Section 10.2.3.2
Y   a. The performance measurement baseline typically integrates the triple constraint of project management: scope, schedule, and cost.
N   b. Risk is not one of the three primary elements integrated in the performance measurement baseline.
N   c. and d. Risk and procurement are not included as two of the three primary elements integrated in the performance measurement baseline.

6. c. PMBOK° Guide: Section 10.2
Y   c. Facilitation techniques often help us build consensus and overcome obstacles.
N   a. Having an agenda, using the agenda, collecting action items, etc. are all examples of meeting management techniques.
N   b. How we set-up our visual aids is an example of a presentation technique.
N   d. Listening techniques such as restating or paraphrasing help with effective communication.

7. b. PMBOK® Guide: Section 10.2.1.3

Y   b. The PMIS is an example of an enterprise environmental factor.

N   a. Having and using the agenda, collecting action items, etc. are meeting management techniques.

N   c. Facilitation techniques such as encouraging and balancing help a group reach an agreement.

N   d. Lessons learned would be an example of an organizational process asset that may be used in manage communications.

© January 2016 AME Group, Inc. author Aileen Ellis, PMP, PgMP
aileen@amegroupinc.com 719-659-3658

Conduct Procurements

☑ **Exam Tip:** Review Figure 12-5 of the PMBOK® Guide.

In the process conduct procurements we follow the procurement management plan. We send out our procurement documents, decide who (which supplier) we are going to buy from, and award a contract to them. If we are purchasing an off the shelf item, the process of conduct procurements may be very simple. For a larger, more complicated purchase, the process may require much more work. On very large purchases we often will go through two rounds. In round one we eliminate all the bidders who are not technically qualified based on preliminary proposals. At this point we short list those bidders who are technically qualified. Then with the short list we go through a more detailed approach.

The timing of the details of this process are worth reviewing.
1. In general, we (the buyer) send out the request for proposal.
2. We (the buyer) may hold a bidder conference.
3. The bidder (seller) then submits his proposal.
4. We (the buyer) evaluate the proposal (see tools and techniques).
5. We (the buyer) decide who we will buy from and award the contract to the selected seller.

INPUTs of conduct procurements

Some of the inputs we just covered as outputs in the last process.
- Procurement management plan
- Procurement documents
  - Request for information
  - Invitation for bid
  - Request for quote
  - Tender notice
  - Request for proposal
- Source selection criteria
- Make or buy decisions
- Procurement statement of work

Sellers' proposals - the term proposal here is used to represent bids, quotes, and proposals.
The timing of this input is interesting. In general, we (the buyer) send out the request for proposal. We may hold a bidder conference. The bidder (seller) then submits their proposal. (This is the input we are discussing). At that point we evaluate the proposal (see tools and techniques). Then we decide who we will buy from and award the contract.

Project documents - there are several project documents we may review at this point. An important one is the updated risk register that may include any contract related decisions made during plan risk responses. An example we used already: We may have made the decision to purchase insurance so as to transfer a risk to the insurance company.

TOOLs and TECHNIQUEs of conduct procurements

Bidder conference- this is a meeting we hold with potential bidders. At this point the bidders already have received our procurement document (request for bid, etc.) including our procurement statement of work. The bidders often will submit questions in writing to the buyer before the meeting. At the meeting we answer all their questions. All the bidders hear all the answers, even the answers to questions submitted by other bidders (their competition). If the project is a construction type project there may be a walkthrough of the construction site.

We (the buyer) want to be sure we are being fair to all the bidders and also that we are giving off the perception (a true perception) that we are being fair. The objective is to ensure the bidders have the information they need to submit a good response to our request. The bidders are often required to submit their bid (or proposal) within a certain number of days after the bidder conference.

Proposal evaluation technique- often as buyers we will weigh our selection criteria. As an example:
- 30% of decision based on price
- 20% of decision based on past performance
- 50% of decision based on advanced technical ideas

A committee may be used to evaluate the proposals against the criteria and then a recommendation is made to management for the final selection.

Independent estimates- with some procurements the organization will have a third party prepare an independent estimate. The reason is to ensure that when the proposals are received, we (the buyer) know if the prices proposed truly reflect the market. There are several reasons we could receive prices that are very different from the prepared independent estimate:
- the bidder(s) did not understand our needs
- our procurement documents were not clear
- a bidder is buying-in (this term is sometimes used to describe a bidder who bids low with the hope of winning). Some unethical bidders will do this with the hope of making up the difference with change orders once they win the work

☑ **EXAM TIP:** A most likely question... when are we more likely to want an independent estimate, when we receive a few proposals back or when we receive many proposals? The answer is just a few. The fewer the number of proposals the less likely we are to really know a fair price.

Advertising- the primary reason to advertise is to let others know we are planning to make a purchase. By advertising we hope to get more and higher quality responses to our request for bid (or proposal). Some government agencies are required to advertise.

Analytical techniques- many different analytical techniques may be used to help select a seller. The goal is to make sure we select a seller who can meet our needs including technical, cost, and schedule needs.

© January 2016 AME Group, Inc. author Aileen Ellis, PMP, PgMP
aileen@amegroupinc.com 719-659-3658

Procurement negotiations - on complex procurements often the contract cannot be signed right after the bidder is selected. Most people will assume negotiations are all about price, and that is true to some degree. Many other items may need to be negotiated to provide clarity. Often one of the biggest items is centered around responsibility. What will the buying organization be responsible for and what will the selling organization be responsible for. For simple procurements the terms and conditions may be standard and not require much if any negotiation.

OUTPUTs of conduct procurements (not all listed)

Selected seller(s) - these are the sellers from whom we plan to purchase the procurement item.

Agreements - this is the document that clearly describes the responsibilities of the buying organization and the selling organization. Other names include: contract, sub-contract, understanding, or purchase order.
- A purchase order is often a simple contract. Most purchase orders are set-up to be firm fixed price.
- A contract is a legal document between two separate legal entities with remedies in the courts. It is important that our team members understand the legal implications of their actions when we have a contract in place. We stated earlier that in a contract the buyer must provide some sort of compensation (this does not have to be money) and a seller must provide a product, service, or result of value.

Resource calendars - these calendars tell us when contracted personal or resources will be available.

Other Ideas:

CENTRALIZED CONTRACTING	DE-CENTRALIZED CONTRACTING
The procurement group is a corporate group.	There is a procurement person sitting on your project team.
Advantages: Volume discounts Better able to specialize	Advantages: More loyalty to team and project Quicker response to project requests

The five (5) elements of a contract – For a contract to be legal there needs to be:
1. An offer
2. An acceptance
3. Competent parties- needs to be two separate legal entities
4. Legality of purpose- the contract cannot be to buy or sell something that is illegal to buy or sell
5. Consideration- something of value needs to be exchanged though it need not be money

Contract terminology

Force majeure- translated as "a major force", often translated as an act of God or an act of nature. A party of the contract may be temporarily relieved of contract commitments if a force majeure clause is in the contract and the force majeure occurs.
Typical force majeure includes: an epidemic, an earthquake, etc.
Typical items not considered force majeure include: an employee getting sick, the organization running out of money, etc.

Negotiating techniques- Fait accompli- stating during a negotiation that an item has already been negotiated and cannot be reopened for more negotiation

Other documents:
A letter of intent is not a contract. It states that if the buyer decides to buy they most likely will buy from the seller (who receives the letter). A letter of intent is not a commitment. It is not a contract.

☑ **EXAM TIP:** The contract should reflect what both parties are doing and what both parties are doing should match the contract.
- If something is in the contract then it needs to be accomplished (or the contract adjusted).
- If something is not in the contract then it should not be accomplished (or the contract should be adjusted).

© January 2016 AME Group, Inc. author Aileen Ellis, PMP, PgMP
aileen@amegroupinc.com 719-659-3658

CONDUCT PROCUREMENTS - Sample Questions

1. Purchase orders are usually set-up in what form:
a. firm fixed price
b. cost plus fixed fee
c. cost plus award fee
d. fixed price economic price adjustment

2. Bidder conferences:
a. are used to ensure that all sellers have a clear understanding of the requirement
b. are held after the proposals have been submitted
c. are a meeting between the buyer and the winning seller(s)
d. are used by the buyer to select the winning seller(s)

3. Some government jurisdictions require what tool and technique of conduct procurements:
a. advertising
b. seller proposals
c. procurement statement of work
d. make-or-buy decisions

4. Independent estimates:
a. serve as a standard... what should the work cost?
b. are always prepared internally
c. are always prepared externally
d. are prepared by the potential sellers who are bidding on the work

5. If sellers deviate greatly from the independent estimate we need to ask all of the following questions except:
a. was the procurement statement of work clear
b. is there a misunderstanding
c. is there a seller who failed to respond fully
d. did the negotiations take too long

CONDUCT PROCUREMENTS - Solutions

1. a. PMBOK° Guide: Section12.2.3.2 (this idea is not explicit in the book)
Y   a. Purchase orders are usually simple contracts set-up as firm fixed price.

2. a. PMBOK° Guide: Section 12.2.2.1
Y   a. The bidder conference is a meeting in which the buyer invites all the potential sellers. The sellers are allowed to ask questions, though in general the questions are submitted in writing before the conference. The primary goal is to ensure that all potential sellers truly understand the needs of the buyer.
N   b. The bidder conference is held before the proposals are submitted. Often sellers need to have questions answered at the bidder conference to write the proposals.
N   c. All the potential sellers are invited to the bidder conference.
N   d. The bidder conference is not about selecting the winning seller. The meeting is to ensure that all potential sellers understand the needs of the buyer.

3. a. PMBOK° Guide: Section 12.2.2.5
Y   a. Some government jurisdictions require that certain government procurements be advertised.
N   b., c., and d. While these answers are all good ideas, the question is getting at a legal requirement.

4. a. PMBOK° Guide: Section 12.2.2.3
Y   a. Independent estimates tell us how much "should" the work cost.
N   b. and c. Be careful of the word always. Independent estimates may be developed internally or externally.
N   d. Independent estimates are independent. They are not developed by the potential sellers.

5. d. PMBOK° Guide: Section 12.2.2.3
Y   d. Negotiations occur after the proposals are submitted. Therefore, they do not affect the proposal price.
N   a. If the procurement statement of work was not clear, the sellers may propose prices different from the independent estimates.
N   b. If there is a misunderstanding, especially regarding requirements, the sellers may propose prices different from the independent estimates.
N   c. If there is a seller who fails to respond fully, the seller's proposed price may be different from the independent estimates.

© January 2016 AME Group, Inc. author Aileen Ellis, PMP, PgMP
aileen@amegroupinc.com 719-659-3658

Manage Stakeholder Engagement

In this process we follow the stakeholder management plan to actively engage with our stakeholders to increase the likelihood of success.

INPUTs to Manage stakeholder engagement (not all listed)

Stakeholder management plan- this plan tells us very specifically how to engage our key stakeholders to increase the chance of project success.

Communication management plan- this plan tells us what communication goes to what stakeholders at what time, in what format, etc.

Change log- stakeholders request changes on the project. Regardless of whether they were the stakeholder who requested the change, stakeholders want to be informed of what changes were approved and what ones were rejected and the status of the approved changes.

TOOLs and TECHNIQUEs of manage stakeholder engagement

Communication methods- it is important to choose the appropriate communication methods based on the needs of the stakeholders, the project, and the particular type of communication.

Interactive	Most efficient way to ensure a common understanding	Meetings, phone calls, video conferences, etc.
Push	Sent to specific recipients. Does not ensure receipt or understanding	Letters, memos, reports, e-mails, faxes, voice mails, press releases, etc.
Pull	Used for large volumes of info and/or large audiences. People may decide to access or not access the information.	Intranet sites, e-learning, knowledge repositories, etc.

OUTPUTs of manage stakeholder engagement (not all listed)

Issue logs- these logs are an output of manage stakeholder engagement. Issue logs should be utilized to ensure that all project issues are resolved and closed. They also are a great communication tool as they let our stakeholders know that their issues are important to us, that owners have been assigned and resolution will occur.

Issue #	Description	Priority	Owner	Target Resolution Date	Status	Date Resolved	Resolution and Comments
001	Late delivery of computer systems	High	Nick	Aug 20, 2013	In progress		
002	Terry moved off project- need replacement	Medium	Alex	April 14, 2013	Complete	April 1, 2013	Jose brought on team to replace Terry

Change requests- many executing processes and all monitoring and controlling processes have change requests as an output.

© January 2016 AME Group, Inc. author Aileen Ellis, PMP, PgMP
aileen@amegroupinc.com 719-659-3658

MANAGE STAKEHOLDER ENGAGEMENT – Sample Questions

1. **The ability of the stakeholders to influence the project is:**
   a. lowest at the start and gets progressively higher as the project progresses
   b. flat throughout the life of the project
   c. highest at the start and gets progressively lower as the project progresses
   d. lowest at the start, peaks during execution, and gets lower throughout closure

2. **How is the change log related to manage stakeholder engagement?**
   a. an input
   b. a tool and technique
   c. an output
   d. not related

3. **Issue logs are an input to what processes?**
   a. manage project team, control communications, and control stakeholder engagement
   b. manage stakeholder engagement and manage project team
   c. control communications and manage stakeholder engagement
   d. control communications and perform integrated change control

4. **Interpersonal skills include:**
   a. presentation skills
   b. negotiating
   c. writing skills
   d. building trust

5. **The change log is an output of what process?**
   a. manage stakeholder engagement
   b. monitor and control project work
   c. perform integrated change control
   d. control stakeholder engagement

MANAGE STAKEHOLDER ENGAGEMENT – Solutions

1. c. PMBOK® Guide: Section 13.3

Y   c. The ability of any stakeholder to influence the project is highest at the start and gets lower throughout the project.

N   a. In general the cost of changes is lowest at the start and get progressively higher.

N   b. Hard to imagine anything that stays flat throughout the project life cycle.

N   d. Often our cost and staffing levels are lowest at the start, peak during an implementation type phase, and drops off during closure.

2. a. PMBOK® Guide: Section 13.3.1.3

Y   a. The change log is an input to manage stakeholder expectations. The stakeholders want to know the status of their change requests.

N   b. Logs are never tools and techniques.

N   c. The issue log is an output of manage stakeholder expectations.

3. a. PMBOK® Guide: Figure 13-9

Y   a. Issue logs are an input to manage project team, control communications, and control stakeholder engagement.

4. d. PMBOK® Guide: Section 13.3.2.2

Y   d. Interpersonal skills include building trust.

N   a. and c. These are great skills to have but would not be considered interpersonal skills.

N   b. Negotiating is a management skill, not an interpersonal skill.

5. c. PMBOK® Guide: Figure 13-9

Y   c. The change log is an output of perform integrated change control and an input to manage stakeholder expectations. All change requests are either approved or rejected as part of perform integrated change control.

© January 2016 AME Group, Inc. author Aileen Ellis, PMP, PgMP
aileen@amegroupinc.com 719-659-3658

EXECUTING- other ideas

These ideas are based on information in the *PMP® Exam Content Outline* published by PMI® on June 2015 for inclusion on the PMP® Exam beginning January 12, 2016. For the exam you do not need to know which tasks or which knowledge and skills have been added. The information in the tasks and knowledge and skills may be on your PMP® exam.

Task 6: Manage the flow of information by following the communication plan in order to keep stakeholders engaged and informed.

While this is a new task for the exam content outline this task has been part of this study guide and the PMBOK® Guide 5th Edition for years. We plan for communication in the process Plan Communications Management. The output of this process is the communications management plan. In the process Manage Communications we follow the communications management plan. In the process Control Communications we ask if the communications management plan is working and we may recommend changes. Please see more information earlier in this chapter in the process Manage Communications.

Task 7: maintain stakeholder relationships by following the stakeholder management plan in order to receive continued support and manage expectations.

While this is a new task in the exam content outline this task has been part of this study guide and the PMBOK® Guide 5th Edition for years. We plan for stakeholder engagement in the process Plan Stakeholder Management. The output of this process is the stakeholder engagement plan. In the process Manage Stakeholder Engagement we follow the stakeholder management plan. In the process Control Stakeholder Engagement we ask if the stakeholder management plan is working and we may recommend changes. Please see more information earlier in this chapter in the process Manage Stakeholder Engagement.

Executing Knowledge and skills

Interdependencies among project elements:

The project management plan is a central document that integrates the outputs of the other planning processes. There is a tremendous amount of interdependencies among the many project elements. It is the role of the project manager to understand and manage these interdependencies. The PMIS (project management information system) is a tool and technique of both Direct and Manage Project Work as well as Monitor and Control Project Work. The PMIS provides access to many project tools.

MINI-TEST after EXECUTING PROCESSES – Questions

Strong suggestion: Do not write on these questions so you can attempt them again later. Realize these questions are coming from all areas of the PMP® Exam and many are coming from outside of the PMBOK® Guide.

1. Your manager has just returned from a two-hour executive briefing on project management. He has the *PMBOK® Guide* in hand and is very excited to teach you everything he has learned. What should be your response when he explains the importance of following the *PMBOK® Guide* processes on all your projects?
a. the project manager, along with the project management team should determine which *PMBOK® Guide* processes are appropriate as well as the appropriate degree of rigor
b. the *PMBOK® Guide* processes should all be applied uniformly to every project
c. the probability of project success increases based on the number of *PMBOK® Guide* processes applied to the project
d. the *PMBOK® Guide* is a methodology. It should either be applied completely or not at all on projects

2. The system upgrade project is almost ready to enter into the planning processes. What is often the last task in Initiating before moving to planning?
a. perform a project assessment
b. conduct benefit analysis
c. inform stakeholders of the approved charter
d. propose an implementation strategy

3. Most successful organizations today have a strategic plan. A key element of the plan is the organization's mission. One definition of a mission is:
a. why the organization exists and what it plans to achieve
b. what the future state of the organization will look like
c. how the organization will evaluate necessary trade-offs and balance the decisions to be made
d. what benefits the project is expected to deliver

4. The project manager should participate in the development of the project charter and inform stakeholders of the approved project charter. The charter should include:
a. the strategy to engage project stakeholders
b. key deliverables
c. the project exclusions
d. the project schedule baseline

5. All of the following are considered characteristics of a good estimate except:
a. clear identification of task
b. narrow participation in preparing the estimate
c. recognition of inflation
d. recognition of excluded costs

6. Currently you are overseeing the planning for a large software upgrade project. Your team is in the process of deconstructing the scope. A likely tool and technique they may use is:
a. scope backlog
b. precedence diagraming method
c. cause and effect diagram
d. dependency determination

© January 2016 AME Group, Inc. author Aileen Ellis, PMP, PgMP
aileen@amegroupinc.com 719-659-3658

7. After an exhaustive search on best practices related to knowledge management it was concluded that one person or organization should own responsibility for knowledge management on projects. As the head of your organization's PMO you have been also named chief knowledge officer.   The research also tells you that people place a strong value on:
a. capturing all the knowledge of an organization
b. identifying critical knowledge in the organization
c. focusing on knowledge outside not inside of the organization
d. limiting sharing of knowledge inside of divisions and not sharing across boundaries such as research, development and operations

8. Leadership is important throughout the life of the project. Effective leadership is most important:
a. early in the project to communicate the vision
b. during project planning to obtain a detailed project plan
c. late in the project as the plan is being executing and the team is getting off track
d. at the end of the project as we are obtaining final acceptance

9. As a project manager you are hearing multiple "unofficial" complaints about the safety of the work site. In fact, some suppliers now are hesitant to have people support your project. What should you do first?
a. have the site inspected for safety and then follow up with any required actions
b. remind your suppliers that they are under contract and must perform
c. find out who is making the complaints and discuss the situation with them so they feel better
d. do nothing. If there was really a problem your safety manager would have brought it to your attention.

10. Geert Hofstede's cultural dimension of long term orientation refers to:
a. virtues such as perseverance and thrift
b. minimizing unstructured situations
c. our obligation to others
d. unequal distribution of power is a basic fact of life

11. Most of your project team is struggling with Jeff, the lead developer on the team. Jeff has trouble managing relationships to move people in the desired direction. Based on Daniel Goleman's mixed model for emotional intelligence Jeff needs to work more on:
a. self-awareness
b. self-regulation
c. social skills
d. empathy

12. Your current web upgrade project is at an impasse.   The current platform the team is using is working well. A new platform is being proposed. There are pros and cons to switching. At this point you realize that acceptance and buy in to the decision are more important than the actual decision. The most likely decision making model you will use is:
a. command
b. consultation
c. consensus
d. coin flip

© January 2016 AME Group, Inc. author Aileen Ellis, PMP, PgMP
aileen@amegroupinc.com 719-659-3658

13. Early on in the project you are working with the critical stakeholders to determine requirements. You have many years of experience as a technologist and now as a project manager on this type of work. Stakeholders want to meet with you separately to share their unique point of view. At this point you should:

a. request each stakeholder write a detailed description of his or her ideas and then merge all the ideas together

b. write a detailed list of requirements based on your past experience for stakeholder approval

c. set up focus groups and have a facilitator walk the stakeholders through an interactive discussion on requirements

d. demand that stakeholders agree with your ideas on requirements since you are the most qualified person from a technical standpoint to determine requirements

14. Historically, your organization has struggled with cost management. While running projects it is often confusing to the team how much money has been allocated for each activity. Even more confusing is how to collect actual cost data. Therefore, you have decided on your current project to put a much stronger focus on cost management. At an early team meeting the members of the core team are arguing as to what is really the first thing to do to address this issue. You tell them we must focus first on:

a. developing a cost management plan

b. using specific levels of accuracy to estimate costs

c. tracking every cost on the project regardless of the size of the cost

d. gaining management approval for the project budget

15. General financial management techniques such as return on investment are considered part of project cost management:

a. for every project

b. for all projects with large budgets

c. for capital facilities projects

d. never for projects

16. Often spending less money on the project than we should leads to:

a. a higher quality product

b. more detailed requirements

c. spending less money to maintain the project's product long term

d. spending more money to maintain the project's product long term

17. A general management technique sometimes used in cost management is:

a. make or buy analysis

b. discounted cash flow

c. leading teams

d. organizational theory

18. The cost baseline is developed as part of which process?

a. plan cost management

b. estimate costs

c. determine budget

d. control costs

© January 2016 AME Group, Inc. author Aileen Ellis, PMP, PgMP
aileen@amegroupinc.com 719-659-3658

19. The amount of cost variance allowed on a project usually:
a. increases over the life of the project
b. decreases over the life of the project
c. remains the same over the life of the project
d. starts low, gets much higher in the intermediate phases, and drops off during the final phase

20. It is easier to have a large influence on project cost:
a. late in the project
b. early in the project
c. after the scope has been defined
d. throughout the project life cycle

21. Historically, your organization has struggled with quality management. In fact if you asked most team members about quality on projects their response may be - what quality? Therefore, you have decided on your current project to put a much stronger focus on quality management. At an early team meeting the members of the core team are arguing as to what is really the first thing to do to address this issue. You tell them we must focus first on:
a. analyzing the quality processes
b. assesses current performance
c. recommending changes
d. developing a quality management plan

22. Shewhart and Deming are famous for what cycle?
a. concept-development-execution-closeout
b. plan-do-check-act
c. forming-storming-norming-performing
d. initiating-planning-executing-monitoring, and controlling-closing

23. The monitoring and controlling process group corresponds to what component of the plan-do-check-act cycle?
a. do-check
b. check-act
c. act-plan
d. plan-do

24. Conformance to requirements means:
a. the product or service needs to satisfy the real needs
b. category for products having same use but different characteristics
c. fitness for use
d. the project produces what it was created to produce

25. Fitness for use means:
a. the product or service needs to satisfy the real needs
b. category for products having same use but different characteristics
c. conformance to requirements
d. the project produces what it was created to produce

26. Accuracy is:
a. the product or service needs to satisfy the real needs
b. an assessment of correctness
c. conformance to requirements
d. a measure of exactness

27. Precision is:
a. the product or service needs to satisfy the real needs
b. an assessment of correctness
c. conformance to requirements
d. a measure of exactness

28. Which of the following statements is true related to prevention and inspection:
a. quality management believes in inspection over prevention
b. prevention and inspection result in the same costs
c. prevention and inspection mean the same thing
d. quality management believes in prevention over inspection

29. Modern quality management wants to:
a. minimize variation
b. focus on inspection over prevention
c. increase grade on all products
d. increase the cost of quality

30. The process of auditing the results of quality control measurements is called:
a. plan quality management
b. project quality management
c. perform quality assurance
d. control quality

31. Quality management plans:
a. should be created for all projects
b. should be created for all large projects
c. should be created for all projects with complex products
d. should be created only for software projects

32. The basis for quality improvement is:
a. Monte Carlo analysis
b. plan-do-check-act
c. configuration management
d. change control system

33. Which of the following statements is true related to quality and grade?
a. low quality may not always be a problem
b. we should always deliver high grade
c. quality and grade are basically the same thing
d. low grade may not always be a problem

34. Grade is:
a. category for products having the same use but different characteristics
b. conformance to requirements
c. fitness for use
d. a measure of exactness

35. At the end of your last project your team spent a good amount of time collecting lessons learned. The biggest lessons were related to the project team itself. It seems that many team members did not understand their responsibilities let along understand the responsibilities of other members of the project team. Most senior members did not understand the reporting structure or when and how to acquire and release other team members. You have decided to put a strong focus on human resource management on your current project. You believe the first thing to do is:
a. hire more experienced team members for senior positions
b. monitor more closely how senior team members interact with junior team members
c. be more involved with the acquisition and release of each team member
d. create a human resource management plan

36. The project management team is another name for:
a. the project team
b. the project stakeholders
c. the core, executive, or leadership team
d. the program managers

37. Conflict management is a tool and technique of:
a. plan human resource management
b. acquire project team
c. develop project team
d. manage project team

38. The process of improving the overall team environment is called:
a. plan human resource management
b. acquire project team
c. develop project team
d. manage project team

39. Team performance assessments are an output of:
a. plan human resource management
b. acquire project team
c. develop project team
d. manage project team

40. Project performance appraisals are a tool and technique of:
a. plan human resource management
b. acquire project team
c. develop project team
d. manage project team

41. Matters such as funding are often the responsibility of the:
a. project team
b. project management team
c. project manager
d. project sponsor

MINI-TEST after EXECUTING PROCESSES – Solutions

1. a. *PMBOK® Guide Section 1.1*
Y   a. The project manager and project management team must determine what information from the *PMBOK® Guide* will benefit the project.
N   b., c. and d. The *PMBOK® Guide* is not a methodology. It should not be applied uniformly. Not all processes may be required or be beneficial on all projects.

2. c. *PMP® Exam content outline Initiating-Task 8- June 2015*
Y   c. Based on the Exam content outline, the last task of Initiating is to inform stakeholders of the approved charter.

3. a. Web search on Vision, Mission, Values
Y   a. The mission of an organization is why it exists.
N   b. The desired future state of an organization is the organization's vision.
N   c. Organizations often look at their values to help evaluate necessary trade-offs and make decisions.
N   d. The benefits register should list the expected benefits from a project or program.

4. b. *PMP® Exam content outline Initiating-Task 2- June 2015*
Y   b. The key deliverables should be included in the project charter.
N   a. The stakeholder management (engagement) plan should describe the strategy to engage the stakeholders.
N   c. The project exclusions should be included in the scope statement.
N   d. The project schedule baseline should be included in the project plan.

5. b. *PMI® Practice Standard for Project Estimating 2011*
Y   b. A best practice with project estimating is wide participation in preparing the estimate. Multiple people may be involved in preparing estimates.

6.   a. *PMP Exam Content Outline June 2015*
Y   a. There are multiple tools that may be used to deconstruct the scope including the scope backlog.
N   b. and d. These tools are related to time and not scope.
N   c. The cause and effect diagram is often associated with quality though it could be used in many other areas.

7.   b.
Y   b. The key word in the answer is "critical".
N   a. I would eliminate this answer because of the word "all".
N   c. Knowledge may be captured both inside and outside the organization.
N   d. An important idea of knowledge sharing is the sharing across boundaries.

8.   a.   *PMBOK® Guide Section X3.1*
Y   a. Leadership is important throughout the project but most important early on when we communicating the vision.

9.   a.
Y   a. If people are concerned about safety we must investigate and take corrective action as required.
N   b. We should not force our contractors into situations that they feel are unsafe.
N   c. The last part of this statement makes it wrong. We need to address the safety concern, not just make people feel better.

N   d. We are the project manager and must take responsibility for the project, including safety.

10.   a.   _Wikipedia- Hofstede's cultural dimensions theory_
Y   a.   In Hofstede's cultural dimension of long-term orientation we value the future and therefore think of perseverance and thrift as virtues.
N   b. A society with strong uncertainty avoidance will try to minimize unstructured situations.
N   c. A society with a collective view will focus on our obligations to others.
N   d. A society that believes in a large power difference may see unequal distribution of power as a basic fact of life.

11.   c.   _Wikipedia-Emotional Intelligence_
Y   c. Jeff is struggling with social skills. Social skills help us manage relationships to move people in the desired direction.

12.   c.   _PMBOK® Guide X3.6_
Y   c. If buy-in is more important than the decision itself we most likely will use the consensus decision making style.

13. c. _PMBOK® Guide Section 5.2.2.2_
Y   c. In general when we have an issue with stakeholders or stakeholders have an issue with each other we want to have a meeting to resolve.

14. a. PMBOK° Guide: Chapter 7 - Introduction
Y   a. The cost management plan defines all the other cost processes.
N   b., c., and d. The cost management plan defines how to do each of these activities. Therefore, we must have the cost management plan first.

15. c. PMBOK° Guide: Chapter 7 - Introduction
Y   c. Capital facility projects often have Return on Investment (ROI) as part of cost management.
N   a., b., and d. Be careful of the word "every", the word "all", and the word "never". ROI is not considered part of project cost management on "every" project.

16. d. PMBOK° Guide: Chapter 7 - Introduction
Y   d. We need to balance spending decisions on the project as they relate to long term costs of the project. Often by spending less on the project, we end up spending more maintaining the product long term. If we use cheap material to build a product, it may cost more long term to maintain the product.
N   a. Often spending less on the project leads to a lower quality product.
N   b. Often spending less on the project means we spend less on developing good requirements.
N   c. Often when we spend less on the project we end up spending more, not less, maintaining the product long term.

17. b. PMBOK° Guide: Chapter 7 - Introduction
Y   b. Discounted cash flow is a general management technique sometimes used in project cost management. Discounted cash flow is a way of estimating the value of a project by using the idea of the time value of money.
N   a. Make or buy analysis is a general management tool and technique sometimes used in project procurement management.
N   c. Leading teams is an idea used in project human resource management.
N   d. Organizational theory is a tool and technique of plan human resource management.

18. c. PMBOK® Guide: Chapter 7 - Introduction

Y   c. The cost baseline is an output of determine budget.

N   a. Plan cost management is the process that develops the cost management plan not the cost baseline.

N   b. The output of estimate costs is the cost estimates, not the cost baseline.

N   d. The input, not the output of control costs is the cost baseline.

19. b. PMBOK® Guide: 7.1.3.1 (control thresholds)

Y   b. The closer we get to completion the less cost variance we often will allow. This is not clearly defined in the book.

N   a. This statement is just the opposite of what is true.

N   c. and d. At the beginning of a project we usually will allow a wide cost variance. As we get closer to completion, the amount of cost variance allowed tends to get smaller and smaller.

20. b. PMBOK® Guide: Figure 2-9 and Chapter 7 - Introduction (implied)

Y   b. The earlier we are in a project the easier it is to influence cost.

N   a. The later we are in a project the harder it is to influence cost.

N   c. and d. It is easier to influence costs the earlier we are in the project.

21. d. PMBOK® Guide: Project Quality Management - Introduction

Y   d. The quality management plan will tell us how to perform these other activities. Therefore, the quality management plan must come first.

N   a., b., and c. The quality management plan will tell us how to inspect deliverables, access performance, and recommend changes.

22. b. PMBOK® Guide: Project Quality Management - Introduction

Y   b. Shewhart and Deming are famous for the plan-do-check-act cycle.

N   a. For some organizations these may be the phases of their project life cycle.

N   c. These are four of the five phases of Tuchman's ladder.

N   d. These are the five process groups.

23. b. PMBOK® Guide: Figure 8-2

Y   b. Monitoring and controlling corresponds to check-act.

N   a., c., and d. Planning corresponds to plan. Executing corresponds to do.

24. d. PMBOK® Guide: Project Quality Management - Introduction

Y   d. Conformance to requirements, and idea of Crosby, means the project produces what it was created to produce.

N   a. and c. Fitness for use, an idea of Juran, means the product or service needs to satisfy real needs.

N   b. Grade is a category for products having the same use but different characteristics.

25. a. PMBOK® Guide: Project Quality Management - Introduction

Y   a. Fitness for use, an idea of Juran, means the product or service needs to satisfy real needs.

N   b. Grade is a category for products having the same use but different characteristics.

N   c. and d. Conformance to requirements, and idea of Crosby, means the project produces what it was created to produce.

26. b. PMBOK® Guide: Project Quality Management - Introduction

Y   b. Accuracy is a measure of how close a measurement is to its true value; it is a measure of correctness.

N   a. Fitness for use means the product or service needs to satisfy real needs.

N   c. Conformance to requirements means the project produces what it was created to produce.
N   d. Precision is the degree that repeated measures show the same results. It is a measure of exactness.

27. d. PMBOK® Guide: Project Quality Management - Introduction
Y   d. Precision is the degree that repeated measures show the same results. It is a measure of exactness.
N   a. Fitness for use, an idea of Juran, means the product or service needs to satisfy real needs.
N   b. Accuracy is a measure of how close a measurement is to its true value; it is a measure of correctness.
N   c. Conformance to requirements means the project produces what it was created to produce.

28. d. PMBOK® Guide: Project Quality Management - Introduction
Y   d. This is a true statement.
N   a. This statement is reversed.
N   b. It is usually less expensive to prevent than to inspect and correct mistakes.
N   c. Prevention is proactive. Inspection is reactive.

29. a. PMBOK® Guide: Project Quality Management - Introduction
Y   a. Reducing variation in our processes is a goal of quality management.
N   b. This answer is reversed.
N   c. We should not increase grade on all products. We should produce the grade that is required by the customer.
N   d. We want to decrease the cost of quality while maintaining the same (or higher) quality standards.

30. c. PMBOK® Guide: Project Quality Management - Introduction
Y   c. Auditing quality control measurements is part of perform quality assurance.
N   a. Plan quality management is determining our quality standards and developing a plan to achieve these standards.
N   b. Project quality management is a knowledge area, not a process.
N   d. Control quality is the process of measuring our deliverables (or products) for correctness.

31. a. PMBOK® Guide: Project Quality Management - Introduction
Y   a. Quality management plans should be created for all projects. NOTE- we want to be careful of answers with the word "all" in the answer. Here is an example where the answer with the word "all" is the best answer.
N   b. and c. These answers are true. Is there a better answer though?
N   d. Be careful of answers with the word "only". Quality management plans should be created for all projects.

32. b. PMBOK® Guide: Project Quality Management - Introduction
Y   b. Plan-do-check–act is the basis for quality improvement.
N   a. Monte Carlo analysis is a simulation tool.
N   c. Configuration management is a system for establishing control of products (and services).
N   d. A change control system helps maintain the scope on a project.

33. d. PMBOK® Guide: Project Quality Introduction
Y   d. Low grade may not always be a problem. Low grade is acceptable if the customer only needs low grade.

N   a. Quality products should always be delivered. Quality is the degree to which a set of inherent characteristics fulfills requirements.

N   b. We should deliver the grade the customer needs—no more, no less.

N   c. Quality and grade are very different. Quality is the degree to which a set of inherent characteristics fulfill requirements. Grade is a category assigned to a product or service having the same functional use but different technical characteristics.

34. a. PMBOK® Guide: Project Quality Management - Introduction
Y   a. Grade is a category for products having the same use but different characteristics.

N   b. Crosby defined quality as conformance to requirements.

N   c. Joseph Juran defined quality as fitness for use.

N   d. Precision sometimes is defined as a measure of exactness. It is a measure of repeatability.

35. d. PMBOK® Guide: Chapter 9 - Introduction
Y   d. The human resource plan will describe the roles and responsibilities of each position on the team. It will also include an organizational chart to show reporting relationships.

N   a. The question does not tell us if our senior team members lacked experience.

N   b. The question does not tell us if there are issues between the senior and junior team members that need to be monitored more closely.

N   c. It may not be a good use of our time to be involved in the acquisition and release of each team member.

36. c. PMBOK® Guide: Chapter 9 - Introduction
Y   c. The project management team are the members of the project team that help with the project management work. They are sometimes also called the core, executive, or leadership team.

N   a. The project management team is a subset of the project team. On an example project the project management team might have 10 members while the project team has 1,000 members.

N   b. The project management team is a subset of the project team. The project team is a subset of the stakeholders. The team does the work of the project. The stakeholders are anyone and everyone who could affect or be effected by the project.

N   d. The program managers manage the programs, not the projects.

37. d. PMBOK® Guide: Figure 9-1
Y   d. Manage the project team is what we do day-by-day with our team, including managing conflict.

N   a. Organizational theory is a tool and technique of plan human resource management.

N   b. Pre-assignment is an example of a tool and technique of acquire project team.

N   c. Training and team building are examples of tools and techniques of develop project team.

38. c. PMBOK® Guide: Chapter 9 - Introduction
Y   c. During the process of develop project team we want to improve the environment so as to improve project performance.

N   a. During the process of plan human resource development we want to develop our human resource plan including the organizational chart, staffing management plan, etc.

N   b. During the process of acquire project team we get the people we need for the project team. Realize that most likely we will not get the whole team at once, but in stages, based on when we need of particular skill sets.

N   d. During the process of manage project team we interact with our team members in a way to help them perform their work on the project. This may include conflict management, etc.

39. c. PMBOK® Guide: Figure 9-1
Y   c. As we develop the project team we will want to create team performance assessments to measure how the team and the project are performing against the project objectives.
N   a. It is too early to assess team performance during plan human resource management because we have not acquired the project team.
N   b. It is too early to assess team performance during acquire project team because our focus at this point is on acquiring the team members, not measuring performance.
N   d. Manage project team is really about interacting with our team members and measuring their individual performance. It is not about measuring how the team is performing against project objectives.

40. d. PMBOK® Guide: Figure 9-1
Y   d. The title of this tool and technique may be misleading to many of us, including me. The tool project performance appraisals is used to measure the performance of individual team members. It is used during manage project team.
N   a. The tool project performance appraisals is used to measure the performance of individual team members. Plan human resource management would be too early.
N   b. The tool project performance appraisals is used to measure the performance of individual team members. Acquire project team would be too early.
N   c. The tool project performance appraisals is used to measure the performance of individual team members. We use this tool during manage project team.

EXAM TIP: Do not confuse the phrase "team performance assessment" with the phrase "project performance appraisals."

41. d. PMBOK® Guide: Chapter 9 - Introduction
Y   d. The sponsor is at a high enough level to secure funding for the project.
N   a., b., and c. The project team, the project management team, and the project manager are usually not high enough in an organization to secure funding.

MONITORING AND CONTROLLING

There are 11 processes of Monitoring and Controlling. There are several important aspects to the monitoring and controlling process group:
- Monitoring includes those activities when we ask how work is progressing on the project
- Controlling includes recommending corrective action to get us back on plan and preventative action to keep us on plan
- During the monitoring and controlling process group the project manager should be very proactive regarding change control. Change management includes:
  - Ensuring that all approved changes are implemented
  - Ensuring that only approved changes are implemented

Based on the *PMP Examination Content* outline published in June of 2015 by PMI there are seven (7) tasks of Monitoring and Controlling. These processes represent 25% of your exam content. Key phrases associated with each task are:

Task	Key Words
Task 1	Measure project performance
Task 2	Manage changes to the project
Task 3	Verify that the project deliverables conform to the quality standards
Task 4	Monitor and access risks
Task 5	Review the issue log, update if necessary and determine correct actions
Task 6	Capture, analyze, and manage lessons learned
Task 7	Monitor procurement activities

The last table lists the key words for the tasks of the Monitoring and Controlling Process Group. These tasks are not listed in the PMBOK® Guide. These tasks come from the PMP® Exam Content Outline. You do not need to memorize these tasks for the exam. It is good though for you to review them from time to time because these 7 tasks are the basis for the questions on Monitoring and Controlling on the PMP® Exam. This Content Outline is absolutely an outline and therefore not robust enough to guide our studying in depth. In the next few pages we cover the 11 processes of the Monitoring and controlling Process Group based on the PMBOK® Guide. If you try you can see how the tasks relate well to the processes.

© Jan 2016 AME Group, Inc. author Aileen Ellis, PMP, PgMP
aileen@amegroupinc.com 719-659-3658

Monitor and Control Project Work

> ☑ **Exam Tip:** Review Figure 4-9 of the PMBOK® Guide.

Monitor project work is what we do day by day to track, review, and report on how we are progressing against the project plan. This process is important because the project reports are created to keep the stakeholders informed of project status and forecasts.

Monitoring and Controlling:

Monitoring- this should be continuous over the life of the project. It gives you and your project management team insight into how the project is going.
Controlling- determining what corrective action is needed to get us back on plan and what preventative action is needed to make sure we don't get off of the plan and following up.

> ☑ **EXAM TIP:** The process "monitor and control project work" can easily be confused with the process group "monitoring and controlling." Be very careful to read the questions when you see these terms to know if they are referring to just the one process or the entire process group.

INPUTs of monitor and control project work

Project management plan:
- the baselines of the project plan are used to help you see how your project is progressing against the plan
- The management plans are used to help you control the project

Schedule forecasts- these forecasts come from the control schedule process. They help you understand how your project is progressing against your schedule baseline and if you need to request changes.

Cost forecasts- these forecasts come from the control cost process. They help you understand how your project is performing against the cost baseline and if you need to request changes.

Validated Changes- these come from the control quality process. Validated means the change was implemented correctly. This information is required for the work performance reports.

Work performance information- this information comes from several controlling processes. This information, based on work performance data, may be used for decision-making.

Enterprise environment factors- this is your project environment. The PMIS (project management information system) is an environmental factor.

Organizational process assets- Example –Organizational communication requirements- knowing these requirements may help you as you create work performance reports from the work performance information.

TOOLs and TECHNIQUEs of monitor and control project work

Expert judgment- go out and seek experts to help monitor (see how your project is doing) and control (determining what corrective or preventative action is required) the project work

Analytical techniques- these techniques are used to forecast potential future events on the project

Project management information system (PMIS)- this system provides access to other systems to help with monitoring and controlling

☑ **EXAM TIP: Work authorization system-** This system is a subset of the PMIS. The work authorization system ensures that work is performed at the appropriate time, in the appropriate sequence, and by the appropriate organization. Do you have a system that helps you do this?

Meetings- used to help you monitor and control project work. Remember the types of meetings and rules for meetings?

OUTPUTs of monitor and control project work

Change requests- these requests will be outputs of many processes. Change requests become an input to integrated change control for approval (or rejection).

☑ **EXAM TIP:** All monitoring and controlling processes and many of the executing processes have change requests as an output.

Work performance reports- reports are the physical or electronic versions of work performance information. Reports are required to keep the stakeholders informed.

Project management plan updates- after change requests are approved through perform integrated change control they may lead to project management plan updates.

Project documentation updates- after change requests are approved through perform integrated change control they may lead to project documentation updates. Note: work performance reports are an example of project documentation.

MONITOR AND CONTROL PROJECT WORK -Sample Questions

1. Approved change requests are an input to which process:
a. monitor and control project work
b. perform integrated change control
c. develop project management plan
d. direct and manage project work

2. The enterprise environmental factor that ensures activities start at the right time and in the right sequence is:
a. work authorization system
b. lessons learned database
c. process measurement database
d. financial control procedures

3. The project management plan has many elements including:
a. forecasts
b. issue log
c. performance reports
d. scope baseline

4. The project management information system (PMIS) is:
a. considered work performance information
b. considered an organizational process asset
c. a tool and technique of monitor and control project work
d. a tool and technique of integrated change control

5. Which of the following statements is true about change requests:
a. most monitoring and controlling processes have change requests as output
b. all executing processes have change requests as output
c. all planning processes have change requests as output
d. all initiating processes have change requests as output

6. It has been determined that several of the deliverables due today do not meet the technical specifications. A change request has been generated and approved. The defects are repaired. Defect repair is really another name for:
a. corrective action
b. preventive action
c. rework
d. scope updates

7. It seems that project activities never follow the sequence of the project plan. What system may help address this problem?
a. the configuration management system
b. the change control system
c. the information distribution system
d. the work authorization system

MONITOR AND CONTROL PROJECT WORK - Solutions

1. d. PMBOK® Guide: Figure 4-7
Y   d. The project plan and the approved changes are inputs to direct and manage project work.
N   a. Change requests are an output of monitor and control project work.
N   b. Approved changes are an output, not input, of perform integrated change control.
N   c. Approved changes are not an input or output of develop project management plan.

2. a. PMBOK® Guide: Section 4.4.1.6 and 4.5.1.4
Y   a. In general systems are EEFs.
N   b., c., and d. Databases, though not commercial databases, and procedures are normally organizational process assets (OPAs).

3. d. PMBOK® Guide: Section 4.5.1.1
Y   d. The project plan has at least three (3) baselines: scope, schedule, and cost.
N   a., b., and c. These are examples of project documents, not elements of the project plan.

4. c. PMBOK® Guide: Section 4.4.2.3
Y   c. PMIS is a tool and technique of direct and manage project work and monitor and control project work.
N   a. This answer is not related. Work performance information comes from work performance data.
N   b. Systems are usually considered EEFs not OPAs.
N   d. PMIS is not a tool of perform integrated change control.

5. a. PMBOK® Guide: Section 4.5.1.3 and Figure 4-9
Y   a. Most monitoring and controlling processes have change requests as output.
N   b. Many executing processes have change requests as output.
N   c. Only one planning process has change requests as output.
N   d. No initiating processes has change requests as an output.

6. c. PMBOK® Guide: Section 4.3.3.3
Y   c. Rework is another name for defect repair.

7. d. PMBOK® Guide: Glossary
Y   d. The work authorization system ensures that work is performed at the appropriate time, in the appropriate sequence, and by the appropriation organization.

Perform Integrated Change Control

> ☑ **Exam Tip:** Review Figure 4-11 of the PMBOK® Guide.

Perform integrated change control is the process where change requests are evaluated and either approved or rejected. Notice Figure 4-11 in the PMBOK® Guide. On the left hand side of this Figure, we can see that change requests come from many processes (most of the monitoring and controlling processes and many of the executing processes).

It is important to ensure that only approved changes make it into the documents.
A few important ideas about perform integrated change control
  • Change requests may come from any stakeholder
  • Change requests should always be put in writing
  • When a change request is initiated:
     a. Evaluate the change request to see how each of the six constraints may be affected.
     b. Determine options along with a recommendation
        i. One recommendation may be to not accept the change request
        ii. Another recommendation may be to accept the change request but add X amount of money to the budget and Y amount of time to the schedule
     c. Get change approved through the change control board (CCB)
     d. If the customer is not on CCB, get change approved through customer
  • This is a high level way to think about integrated change control.

> ☑ **EXAM TIP:** On the exam you may get questions that say such things as: "You have received a change request. It will have no effect on the project schedule. What should be done next?" This is tricky. What you want to do next is see if the change request will have an effect on any of the other project constraints. You want to do this first before you determine options.

A few important ideas about configuration control:
  • Focused on the specification of deliverables and processes
  • Change control is a subset of configuration management
  • Configuration management is a subset of the PMIS (project management information system)
  • The PMIS is a subset of the EEF (enterprise environmental factors)

INPUTs of perform integrated change control

Project management plan- this plan contains information that will help us with change control.
  • Change management plan
  • Configuration management plan
  • Scope baseline- scope changes may drive changes to other baselines

Work performance reports- ex. Earned value reports help us understand how the project is performing from an integrated scope, time, and cost standpoint against the plan.

Change requests- this is the only process where change requests are an input. Remember that all change requests are processed for approval or rejection through integrated change control.

> ☑ **EXAM TIP:** Corrective action and preventative action affect performance against the baselines, not the baselines themselves.

Enterprise environmental factors: ex. PMIS (project management information system). The PMIS includes configuration management. Change management is a subset of configuration management.

Organizational process assets: ex. Change control procedures: steps to modify documents

TOOLs and TECHNIQUEs of perform integrated change control

Expert judgment- bring in experts from inside the team. Also utilize the stakeholders to help evaluate change requests and approve or reject changes.

Meetings: the change control board (or boards) will have meetings to evaluate change requests and approve or reject changes.

Change control tools- may help streamline:
- Managing the change requests
- Managing the decision process
- Communicating with stakeholders
- Distribution of decisions

OUTPUTs of perform integrated change control

Approved change requests- change requests are either approved or rejected. Approved change requests become an input for direct and manage project execution. Requested changes may be fully rejected or rejected temporarily until more information is available.

Change log- this log documents all change requests and the decisions to approve or reject changes. The change log becomes an input into manage stakeholder expectations.

© January 2016 AME Group, Inc. author Aileen Ellis, PMP, PgMP
aileen@amegroupinc.com 719-659-3658

Question- You have just been handed a change request. Your team member tells you that the change will lead to a three week delay in project completion. What should you do next:

a. recommend options to your management
b. make the change as soon as possible so as to shorten the three week delay
c. reject the change since it will delay the project
d. evaluate the change request

Solution- Answer d is the best answer. I know you are thinking that we already did this and we know the project will be delayed three weeks. Even if we know this, we still need to see how the proposed change may affect the cost, risk, etc. on the project. Just because we know the schedule impact does not mean we know the other impacts.

PERFORM INTEGRATED CHANGE CONTROL - Sample Questions

1. Change requests are approved or rejected in which process:
a. monitor and control project work
b. perform integrated change control
c. develop project management plan
d. direct and manage project work

2. Corrective action and preventative action normally affect the:
a. scope baseline
b. schedule baseline
c. cost baseline
d. performance against the baselines

3. Every change request related to the project, regardless of where they originate, are inputs into which process:
a. monitor and control project work
b. perform integrated change control
c. develop project management plan
d. direct and manage project work

4. Who may request changes on a project:
a. the customer
b. the sponsor
c. the project team members
d. any stakeholder involved with the project

5. Which of the following statements is true about configuration management and change control:
a. configuration management is focused on the specification while change control is focused on baselines
b. change management is focused on the specification while configuration control is focused on baselines
c. a configuration management knowledge base and change control procedures are considered enterprise environmental factors
d. a configuration management knowledge base is considered an organizational process asset while change control procedures are considered enterprise environmental factors

6. The change log is a(n):
a. subset of the project plan
b. project document
c. subset of the work authorization system
d. enterprise environmental factor

7. History tells you that projects in your organization have been troubled by the lack of a system to submit, track, and validate changes. A configuration management system is certainly what is needed. The configuration management system is considered a subset of the:
a. organizational process assets
b. project management information system
c. change control system
d. expert judgment

© January 2016 AME Group, Inc. author Aileen Ellis, PMP, PgMP
aileen@amegroupinc.com 719-659-3658

8. You are managing a highway reconstruction project. The project includes several miles of highway that have been damaged because of a recent flood. The local government has created a new regulation that may affect your project. The goal of the new regulation is to reduce the need for rescue and relief efforts associated with flooding. A change request has been initiated. What should you do first in regard to this request?
a. meet with your management to discuss the potential change
b. meet with the project sponsor to discuss the potential change
c. evaluate the change request
d. make the change since it is government mandated

9. A major fire occurred in your community six months ago. A final report was developed that included many recommendations going forward. Your project is to ensure that all the approved recommendations occur in a timely fashion. Now another recommendation has been suggested. You realize that if approved this change will increase the project cost by $80,000. At this point you should:
a. reject the change
b. make the change as soon as possible since it related to human and environmental safety
c. get the change approved internally first
d. see how the change effects the other project constraints

10. The customer has requested another change to your public safety project. The requested change is for public safety volunteers to act as scribes at geographically diverse locations during safety incidents. This requested change sounds like a great idea to you but you realize this idea was discussed before the project charter was signed and the sponsor decided to reject the idea. At this point you should:
a. reject the change
b. make the change as soon as possible since the customer has requested it
c. get the change approved internally first
d. see how the change effects the other project constraints

PERFORM INTEGRATED CHANGE CONTROL - Solutions

1. b. PMBOK® Guide: Section 4.5

Y   b. The primary purpose of perform integrated change control is to approve or reject change requests.

N   a. and d. Change requests are an output of direct and manage project work and of monitor and control project work and therefore cannot be approved or rejected in these processes.

N   c. Change requests are not an input to develop a project management plan and therefore cannot be approved or rejected in this process.

2. d. PMBOK® Guide: Section 4.5.1.3

Y   d. Corrective and preventative action are the actions we take to stay on baseline or to get back on the baseline. They normally do not change the baselines.

3. b. PMBOK® Guide: Figure 4-11

Y   b. All project change requests are an input into perform integrated change control.

4. d. PMBOK® Guide: Section 4.5

Y   d. Any stakeholder may request a change.

N   a., b., and c. While all these answers are true answer d best answers the question.

5. a. PMBOK® Guide: Section 4.5

Y   a. This answer is true.

N   b. This answer is reversed.

N   c. and d. Knowledge bases and procedures are normally considered OPAs.

6. b. PMBOK® Guide: Table 4-1

Y   b. Change logs, issue logs, etc. are project documents; not part of the project plan.

7. b. PMBOK® Guide: Section 4.5.1.4

Y   b. The configuration management system is a subsystem of the PMIS which is a subset of the enterprise environmental factors (EEFs).

N   a. Systems are not organizational process assets (OPAs).

N   c. The change control system is a subset of the configuration management system.

N   d. Expert judgment is not related to this question.

8. c. PMBOK® Guide: 4.5

Y   c. Evaluate the change request is the first thing we do when a change request comes to us, regardless from whom the change request came.

N   a. and b. We don't want to meet with our management or sponsor until we have information about the impact of the requested change and are able to recommend alternatives.

N   d. Every change request must be evaluated, even if it is mandated by the government. We may decide to cancel the project instead of making the change.

9. d. PMBOK® Guide: 4.5

Y   d. Evaluate the change request is the first thing we do.

10. a. PMBOK® Guide: 4.5

Y   a. Since this idea was already discussed and the sponsor has already rejected it, we should reject it again. The question tells us nothing to make us believe that it would be considered now.

© January 2016 AME Group, Inc. author Aileen Ellis, PMP, PgMP
aileen@amegroupinc.com 719-659-3658

Control Scope

☑ **Exam Tip:** Review Figure 5-17 of the PMBOK® Guide.

CONTROL SCOPE, CONTROL SCHEDULE, and CONTROL COST are similar to each other. Seeing trends in processes may make the processes easier to understand and remember. We will look at these three processes one after the other in this book.

As we review the definitions we can see similarities.

CONTROL SCOPE	CONTROL SCHEDULE	CONTROL COST
Monitoring how the project is performing from a scope standpoint	Monitoring how the project is performing from a schedule standpoint	Monitoring how the project is performing from a cost standpoint
Managing changes to the scope baseline	Managing changes to the schedule baseline	Managing changes to the cost baseline

☑ **EXAM TIP:** Control scope is only about scope. Control schedule is only about schedule. Control costs is only about costs.

Scope creep- uncontrolled changes to the project scope. We do NOT want there to be scope creep on our project.

INPUTs of control scope

Project management plan- contains multiple documents that we may use now.

- Scope baseline- made up of three documents:
    - the scope statement
    - the WBS
    - the WBS dictionary
- Other plans inside the project management plan:
    - Scope management plan- describes how to develop and manage scope
    - Change management plan- defines how we make changes
    - Configuration management plan- defines items that fall under the configuration management system and how to make changes to those items
    - Requirements management plan- describes how to manage requirements

Requirements documentation and the requirements traceability matrix- notice how we often see these two documents together.
We use these to monitor how we are doing as far as scope.

Organizational process assets – related to scope

Work performance data– related to scope

TOOLs and TECHNIQUEs of control scope

Variance analysis- this is a tool and technique of many monitoring and controlling processes. In this process, we are asking: How are we varying from the scope baseline?

OUTPUTs of control scope

Project plan updates – specifically, the scope baseline updates correspond to the input of scope baseline, yet now the scope baseline may be updated.

Project documentation updates- corresponds to the inputs of requirements documentation and the requirements traceability matrix but now they may be updated.

Organizational process assets updates- corresponds to the input of organizational process assets, yet now there may be updates.

Work performance information- this corresponds to the input of work performance data. Think of the data as raw data points. The work performance information shows a comparison of the data with the scope baseline.

Change requests- every monitoring and controlling process has change requests as an output. They all go to perform integrated change control for approval or rejection.

© January 2016 AME Group, Inc. author Aileen Ellis, PMP, PgMP
aileen@amegroupinc.com 719-659-3658

CONTROL SCOPE – Sample Questions

1. Which of the following is an input of control scope?
a. cost baseline
b. schedule baseline
c. scope baseline
d. performance measurement baseline

2. The change requests that are an output of validate scope become an input of which process?
a. develop project management plan
b. monitor and control project work
c. perform integrated change control
d. close project or phase

3. Variance analysis is a tool and technique of which process?
a. plan scope management
b. define scope
c. validate scope
d. control scope

4. Work performance information is an input to which process?
a. develop project management plan
b. monitor and control project work
c. perform integrated change control
d. close project or phase

5. Scope creep is another name for:
a. uncontrolled expansion of project scope
b. small changes that are processed through the change control system
c. changes that are rejected during the change control process
d. changes sent to integrated change control for processing

6. Project management plan updates become an input to which process?
a. develop project management plan
b. monitor and control project work
c. perform integrated change control
d. close project or phase

7. Work performance data is an input to control scope. This data comes from what process?
a. develop project management plan
b. monitor and control project work
c. perform integrated change control
d. direct and manage project work

8. You are trying to introduce project management to your organization. The other project managers see no reason to use standard project management practices including no reason to use work breakdown structures. You explain that work breakdown structures:
a. show the dependencies between project activities
b. describe the project objectives
c. list the project exclusions
d. help with project communications

9. You have completed 90 percent of your project deliverables. The customer has been involved on a regular basis and to this point, has seemed very pleased with your on schedule and on budget performance. The customer informs you that they were expecting several additional deliverables that are not part of your plan. What process may have prevented this situation?
a. define scope
b. control scope
c. control costs
d. perform quality control

10. The project team seems overwhelmed with the number of documents required for the project. Which of the following documents should be created first?
a. scope statement
b. work breakdown structure
c. requirements documentation
d. scope baseline

11. Define scope is the process of:
a. creating the project scope management plan
b. creating the project scope statement
c. creating the work breakdown structure
d. creating the project management plan

12. The change management plan is an output of what process?
a. develop project management plan
b. integrated change control
c. monitor and control project work
d. plan communications

© January 2016 AME Group, Inc. author Aileen Ellis, PMP, PgMP
aileen@amegroupinc.com 719-659-3658

CONTROL SCOPE – Solutions

1. c. PMBOK® Guide: Section 5.6.1.1
Y   c. Since the process is about scope, the input will be the scope baseline.
N   a. The cost baseline is an input of control cost.
N   b. The schedule baseline is an input of control schedule.
N   d. The performance measurement baseline integrates scope, schedule, and cost.

2. c. PMBOK® Guide: Figure 5-17
Y   c. All change requests become an input of perform integrated change control.
N   a. Change requests are neither an input of nor an output of develop project management plan.
N   b. Change requests are an output of, not an input of, monitor and control project work.
N   d. Change requests are neither an input of nor an output of close project or phase.

3. d. PMBOK® Guide: Section 5.6.2.1
Y   d. Variance analysis is a tool and technique of both control scope and control cost.
N   a. and b. Variance analysis would not be a tool and technique of any planning process.
N   c. Inspections and group decision-making techniques are tools and techniques of validate scope.

4. b. PMBOK® Guide: Figure 5-15
Y   b. All work performance information is an input of monitor and control project work and only monitor and control project work.
N   a., c., and d. Work performance information is only an input of monitor and control project work.

5. a. PMBOK® Guide: Section 5.6
Y   a. Scope creep in another name for uncontrolled changes to the project scope. We do not want scope creep on our projects.
N   b. and d. We want all change requests to be processed through integrated change control.
N   c. Changes that are rejected are called rejected changes.

6. a. PMBOK® Guide: Figure 5-17
Y   a. This is a tricky question. If you look, outputs from other processes is an input to develop project management plan. If you look at the details you see that project plan updates is an example of an output from other processes.
N   b. The project plan is an input of monitor and control project work.
N   c. The project plan is an input of perform integrated change control.
N   d. The project plan is an input of close project or phase.

7. d. PMBOK® Guide: Figure 5-17
Y   d. All work performance data come from (is an output of) direct and manage project work.
N   a., b., and c. All work performance data come from (is an output of) direct and manage project work and only from direct and manage project work.

8. d. PMBOK Guide: Section 5.4
Y   d. The WBS does help with communication. Mostly though, I know this is the right answer because I know the other three answers are wrong.
N   a. The schedule or the network diagram show the dependencies between activities.
N   b. The project charter describes the project objectives.

N   c. The scope statement lists the project exclusions.

9. a. PMBOK Guide: Section 5.3
Y   a. Define scope helps us communicate what work we will be performing and what work we will provide, and what work will be excluded.

N   b., c., and d. Control scope, Control costs, and perform quality control are all processes of the monitoring and controlling column. They are reactive not proactive processes and therefore most likely would not prevent this situation.

10. c. PMBOK Guide: Figure 3-1
Y   c. From the list the order would be: requirements documentation, scope statement, WBS, and finally the scope baseline (much later).

11. b. PMBOK® Guide: Section 5.3.3.1
Y   b. Creating the project scope statement is the purpose of the define scope process.

N   a. The scope management plan is created during the develop project management process.

N   c. Creating the work breakdown structure is the purpose of create WBS.

N   d. Creating the project management plan is the purpose of develop project management plan.

12. a. PMBOK® Guide: Section 4.2.3.1
Y   a. The change management plan is a subset of the project plan. Therefore, it is an output of develop project management plan.

© January 2016 AME Group, Inc. author Aileen Ellis, PMP, PgMP
aileen@amegroupinc.com 719-659-3658

Control Schedule

☑ **Exam Tip:** Review Figure 6-23 of the PMBOK° Guide.

Control scope, control schedule, and control cost are similar to each other. Seeing trends in processes may make the processes easier to understand and remember.

CONTROL SCOPE	CONTROL SCHEDULE	CONTROL COST
Monitoring how the project is performing from a scope standpoint	Monitoring how the project is performing from a schedule standpoint	Monitoring how the project is performing from a cost standpoint
Managing changes to the scope baseline	Managing changes to the schedule baseline	Managing changes to the cost baseline

☑ **EXAM TIP:** Control scope is only about scope. Control schedule is only about schedule. Control cost in only about costs.

☑ **EXAM TIP:** Notice how some of the inputs have matching outputs. As an example: the scope baseline is an input and the scope baseline updates are an output.

INPUTs of control schedule

Project management plan- contains multiple documents that we may use now.
- Schedule baseline- we review how the project is progressing against the baseline
- Another plan inside the project management plan:
  - Schedule management plan – describes how to develop and manage the schedule

Other documents related to the schedule
Project schedule- this is the working schedule
Project calendars- shows work periods for the project, etc.
Schedule data- data related to the planning of the schedule. Ex. Milestones

Work performance data- data (actuals) on what is occurring related to the schedule

Organizational process assets- related to the schedule

TOOLs and TECHNIQUEs of control schedule

Performance reviews- review of how the project is performing against the schedule baseline.

- **Trend analysis**- collects data to see if project performance is getting better or worse against the schedule baseline.
- **Critical path method**- looks at how the project is performing on the critical path.
- **Critical chain method**- looks at how the project is performing on the critical chain. Specifically asks if we have enough buffer left to protect the project end date.
- **Earned value method**- earned value looks at schedule performance based on what work should be complete (from the schedule baseline) to what work is complete. Much more on this when we get to control costs.

Other tools and techniques from develop schedule- in simplistic terms, the same tools and techniques we use to develop the schedule we will use to control the schedule. Examples include:

- Project management software
- Resource optimization techniques
- Modeling techniques
- Leads and lags
- Schedule compression
- Scheduling tool

OUTPUTs of control schedule

Work performance information- this corresponds to the input of work performance data. Think of the data as raw data points. The work performance information shows a comparison of the data with the schedule baseline.

Schedule forecasts- based on actual performance. Now that we know how the project is performing against the schedule baseline we can forecast future performance. (more on this in control costs in earned value discussion).

Change requests- most monitoring and controlling processes have change requests as an output. Change requests all go to perform integrated change control for approval or rejection.

Project plan updates- specifically the schedule baseline updates corresponds to the input of schedule baseline.

Project documentation updates- correspond to the input- the project schedule.

Organizational process assets updates- corresponds to the input of Organizational process assets.

NOTE- See sample questions after control costs

© January 2016 AME Group, Inc. author Aileen Ellis, PMP, PgMP
aileen@amegroupinc.com 719-659-3658

Control Costs

☑ **Exam Tip:** Review Figure 7-11 of the PMBOK° Guide.

Control Scope, Control Schedule, and Control Costs are similar to each other. Seeing trends in processes may make the processes easier to understand and remember.

CONTROL SCOPE	CONTROL SCHEDULE	CONTROL COST
Monitoring how the project is performing from a scope standpoint	Monitoring how the project is performing from a schedule standpoint	Monitoring how the project is performing from a cost standpoint
Managing changes to the scope baseline	Managing changes to the schedule baseline	Managing changes to the cost baseline

We already reviewed Control scope and Control schedule. Now, do you see how control cost is similar?

☑**EXAM TIP:** Notice how some of the inputs have matching outputs.
As an example: the cost baseline is an input and the cost baseline updates are the outputs.

INPUTs of control costs

Project management plan- contains multiple documents that we may use now.
- Cost baseline
- Cost management plan – describes how to develop and manage the costs

Other documents related to the schedule:

Project funding requirements- this is what funding is required for the project

Work performance data- data (actuals) on what is occurring related to the costs

Organizational process assets- related to costs

TOOLs and TECHNIQUES of control costs

Earned Value Management
Forecasting (EAC and ETC)
To-Complete Performance Index (TCPI)

Performance reviews
- **Variance analysis**- looks at how the project is varying from the cost baseline.
- **Trend analysis**- collects data to see if project performance is getting better or worse against the cost baseline.
- **Earned value performance**- earned value looks at cost performance based on what work is complete, what we should have spent on that work that is complete, and what we did spend on the work that is complete. Much more on this shortly.

Project Management Software
Reserve Analysis

OUTPUTs of control costs

Work performance information- this corresponds to the input of work performance data. Think of the data as raw data points. The work performance information shows a comparison of the data with the cost baseline.

Cost forecasts- based on actual performance. Now that we know how the project is performing against the cost baseline we can forecast future performance.

Change requests- every monitoring and controlling process has change requests as an output. All change requests go to perform integrated change control for approval or rejection.

☑ **EXAM TIP:** It would be difficult to memorize all the inputs, tools, and techniques, and outputs of the 47 processes. When you see a summary statement like "every ..." above, that is a good way to cover a lot of outputs with just one statement.

Project plan updates– specifically the cost baseline updates corresponding to the input of cost baseline.

Project documentation updates- corresponds to the inputs related to the cost estimates.

Organizational process assets updates- corresponds to the input of Organizational process assets.

☑ **EXAM TIP:** At this point we have talked about all three (3) baselines. Make sure you know when each baseline is created and when each is updated.

© January 2016 AME Group, Inc. author Aileen Ellis, PMP, PgMP
aileen@amegroupinc.com 719-659-3658

BASELINES	When created	When updated
Scope baseline (scope statement, WBS, and WBS Dictionary)	Create WBS	Control scope
Schedule baseline	Develop schedule	Control schedule
Cost baseline	Determine budget	Control costs

Earned Value Management

Critical terms for earned value:

Budget at completion (BAC)- the total budget for the project.

Planned Value (PV)- a measure of how much work should be completed as of today.

Earned Value (EV)- a measure of how much work is completed as of today.

Actual Cost (AC)- how much we have spent as of today.

Now let's walk through an Earned Value example.

We will use the following scenario to help us understand earned value:

You are building a fence for your horses. The fence will have four sides, all exactly the same. Your budget for the project is $400, or $100 per side. The schedule for the project is four days, one side per day. You started the project on Monday morning. It is now the end of the day on Tuesday. You have 25% of the total work complete. You have spent $400 for the work that is complete.

Planned Value
Example 1. What is the planned value as of today?
a. $ 100
b. $ 200
c. $ 400
d. $ 1600
Read PMBOK° Guide page 218, the top paragraph on planned value. PV (planned value) is the budgeted cost of the work scheduled. The scenario states, "You started the project on Monday. It is now the end of the day on Tuesday." Therefore, two days of work should be complete. The schedule is one side per day. Therefore, we should have two sides completed. The budget for each side is $100; therefore, $200 worth of work should be completed. Therefore, PV= $200. Answer b.

Actual Cost
Example 3. What is the actual cost for the project?
a. $ 100
b. $ 200
c. $ 400
d. $ 1600
Read PMBOK° Guide page 218, the paragraph on actual cost. AC (actual cost) is the amount of money spent for the work completed. The question states, "You have spent $400 for the work that is complete." Therefore, AC= $400. Answer c.

Schedule Variance
Example 4. The project schedule variance is:
a. -$ 300
b. -$ 200
c. -$ 100
d. $ 0
Read PMBOK° Guide page 218, the paragraph on schedule variance.
Schedule variance = (EV – PV) = ($100 - $200) = -$100. The project is running behind schedule. It took two days to complete one day's worth of work (one side). You are behind by one day's worth of work (one side). A negative schedule variance means you are behind schedule. Answer c.
NOTE- a positive schedule variance means you are ahead of schedule (a good thing).
A zero schedule variance means that you are on schedule.

Cost Variance
Example 5. The project cost variance is:
a. -$ 300
b. -$ 200
c. -$ 100
d. $ 0
Read PMBOK° Guide page 218, the paragraph on cost variance. Cost variance = (EV-AC)
=   ($100 -$400) = -$300. The project is running over budget. You spent $400 to complete one side ($100 worth of work). A negative cost variance means you are running over budget. Answer a.
NOTE- a positive cost variance means you are under budget (a good thing).
A zero cost variance means that you are on budget.

Schedule Performance Index (SPI)
Example 6. The schedule performance index for the scenario is:
a. 0.5
b. 1
c. 0.25
d. 1.5
Read PMBOK° Guide page 219, the paragraph on schedule performance index. SPI=EV/PV= 100/200= ½= 0.5. Answer a. Since the SPI is less than one, the project is running behind schedule. What this really means is that the project is progressing at ½ the rate expected. We expected to have two sides complete as of today and we only have one side complete.
NOTE- if the SPI=1 the project is running on schedule.
If the SPI is greater than one the project is running ahead of schedule (a good thing).

Cost Performance Index (CPI)
Example 7. The cost performance index for the scenario is:
a. 0.5
b. 1
c. 0.25
d. 1.5
Read PMBOK° Guide page 219, the paragraph on cost performance index. CPI= EV/AC= 100/400=1/4= .25. Answer c. Since the CPI is less than one the project is running over budget. What this really means is that only ¼ of the expected work is being completed for

the money spent. We have spent $400. According to the project we should have 4 sides complete for $400 but we only have one side complete.
NOTE- if the CPI=1 the project is running on budget.
If the CPI is greater than one the project is running under budget (a good thing).

Forecasting EAC- most likely for the exam

Example 8. If the workers continue to spend at the same rate as they have so far, what do you forecast the entire project will cost?
a. $ 700
b. $ 2800
c. $ 400
d. $ 1600
Read PMBOK° Guide page 220, the bottom bullet point. For the assumption described in the question:
EAC = (BAC/CPI) = $400/(.25)= $1600. We now expect the entire project to cost $1600. Answer d. We spent $400 for the first side. If we continue to spend at the same rate each side will cost $400. Since there are four sides the estimate for the total project is 4 sides* $400/side = $1600.

To-complete performance index

Read PMBOK° Guide: Section 7.4.2.3
Example 9. Assuming that you are given no more money for the project, what is your TCPI?
EAC= (BAC-EV)/(BAC-AC)= (400-100)/ (400-400)= 300/0. Ask if this makes sense for this project. We have already spent all of the budget. Is there any index possible that would allow us to finish the job with the money that is left? No... since there is no money left.

To-complete performance index

Example 10. Assuming that you are given the EAC of $1600, what is the TCPI (to-complete performance index)?
a. .25
b. 1.00
c. 1.25
d. 1.50
If the BAC is no longer a viable number then the TCPI= (BAC-EV)/(EAC-AC).
TCPI= (400-100)/(1600-400)= .25. The TCPI is the calculated projection of cost performance that must be achieved on the remaining budget to meet a specified management goal.

VAC- variance at completion

Example 11: Based on the above scenario what is the VAC (variance at completion) for the project?
a. $1200
b. -$1200
c. $1600

© January 2016 AME Group, Inc. author Aileen Ellis, PMP, PgMP
aileen@amegroupinc.com 719-659-3658

d. -$1600

VAC is how much we expect to vary from the budget. Since the budget was $400 (this is our BAC) and our estimate to complete the whole project is $1600 (this is our EAC) then our VAC is -$1200. The answer is a negative number because we expect to overrun the project budget. If you like equations: VAC= BAC-EAC= 400-1600= -1200.

VARIANCES	POSITIVE NUMBER	ZERO	NEGATIVE NUMBER
SCHEDULE	Ahead of schedule	On schedule	Behind schedule
COST	Under budget	On budget	Over budget

Trick- negative variances are bad, positive variances are good

INDEXES	GREATER THAN ONE	ONE	LESS THAN ONE
SCHEDULE	Ahead of schedule	On schedule	Behind schedule
COST	Under budget	On budget	Over budget

Trick- indexes greater than one are good, less than one are bad.

Earned Value Measurement Methods- there are multiple methods to measure earned value. We will discuss four here.

Fixed formula- a specific percentage of the PV (planned value) is assigned to the start of a work package (or activity) and the remaining percentage is assigned to the completion. Often used for smaller work packages.
0/100 rule. The activity obtains 0% credit when the activity begins and 100% credit when the activity is completed. The 0/100 rule is often used for material delivery.
20/80 rule. The activity obtains 20% credit when the activity begins and 80% credit when the activity is completed.
50/50 rule. The activity obtains 50% credit when the activity begins and 50% credit when the activity is completed.

Weighted milestone- this method breaks the work package into milestones. A weighted value is assigned to the completion (not partial completion) of each milestone. Often used for longer work packages with tangible outputs.

Percent complete- at the end of each time period the percent complete of the work package is multiplied by the BAC of the work package to calculate the earned value (EV). For this method to have real meaning, the measurement of percent complete should be as objective as possible.
Ex. The value (BAC) of the work package is $1000. 75% of the work is complete and therefore the EV (earned value) for the work package is 75% of $1000= $750.

Physical measurement- relates very much to the amount of work completed.
Ex. 1000 feet of cable should be laid on the construction project. 600 feet of cable have been laid and therefore the EV (earned value) is $600.

☑ **EXAM TIP:** If a question provides you quantitative information (ex. Your CPI is .98 and qualitative information (you are two weeks behind schedule), focus on the quantitative information. See example below.

Question- Your project assistant just informed you that the project has 320 stakeholders in 35 countries. You are now managing over 75 team members. The project has a CPI =.98 and is eight weeks behind schedule. What should you focus on first?
a. cost
b. schedule
c. stakeholders
d. human resources

Solution- answer (a) is the best answer to this question. CPI (cost performance index) is a quantitative measurement. .98 is less than 1.0 and therefore the project is running over budget. Put your focus here. I know, you are saying but we are eight weeks behind schedule. This is not quantitative from the standpoint that we do not know how long the schedule is. Therefore, we want to look at SPI (schedule performance index). The question does not say anything about issues with stakeholders or team members.

For 50 more sample questions and solutions related to Earned Value Management please see Aileen's book: ***How to get Every Earned Value Management question right on the PMP Exam.*** The book is available in both print and e-book format on Amazon. This book is often a best seller in the PMP Exam Prep Category.

© January 2016 AME Group, Inc. author Aileen Ellis, PMP, PgMP
aileen@amegroupinc.com 719-659-3658

CONTROL SCHEDULE AND CONTROL COSTS - Sample Questions

1. **The scope baseline is an input to which process:**
a. control scope
b. control schedule
c. control costs
d. develop schedule

2. **The cost baseline is an input to which process:**
a. control scope
b. control schedule
c. control costs
d. determine budget

3. **The schedule baseline is an input to which process:**
a. control scope
b. control schedule
c. control costs
d. develop schedule

4. **Control scope, control schedule, and control costs all have what input in common:**
a. work performance data
b. work performance information
c. work performance reports
d. variance analysis

5. **Control scope, control schedule, and control costs all have what output in common:**
a. work performance measurements
b. work performance information
c. work performance data
d. variance analysis

6. **Earned value management is a tool and technique of which process:**
a. plan cost management
b. estimate costs
c. control costs
d. determine budget

7. **Schedule compression is a tool and technique of which process(es):**
a. control scope and create WBS
b. control schedule and develop schedule
c. control costs and development schedule
d. determine budget and develop schedule

8. **Project funding requirements are an:**
a. input of control costs
b. input of plan cost management
c. input of estimate costs
d. input of determine budget

9. Project funding requirements are an:
a. output of control costs
b. output of plan cost management
c. output of estimate costs
d. output of determine budget

10. Which of the following is an example of a cost estimate?
a. schedule variance (SV)
b. budget at completion (BAC)
c. cost performance index (CPI)
d. Estimate at completion (EAC)

11. The project CPI= .8 and your SPI= 1.1. This means:
a. over budget, behind schedule
b. over budget, ahead of schedule
c. under budget, behind schedule
d. under budget, ahead of schedule

12. The project SPI = .92. This means:
a. the project is ahead of schedule
b. the project is over budget
c. the project is progressing at 92% of the rate expected
d. you have completed 92% of the work on the project

13. The project CPI= 1.2. This means:
a. the project costs are 20% higher than planned
b. for every dollar spent on the project the earned value is $1.20
c. it is costing $1.20 to complete $1.00 worth of work
d. you are likely to run out of money on the project

14. The planned value (PV) is $200. The actual cost (AC) is $400. The earned value (EV) is $300. The schedule variance is equal to:
a. $200
b. -$100
c. -$200
d. $100

15. The total project budget is $1,000. 80% of the total work should be complete as of today. 60% of the total work is complete. You have spent 50% of the project budget. At this point, your cost variance is:
a. $100
b. $200
c. $300
d. $400

16. You are leading a team on a very large product development project. Your CPI is .90. You are running two weeks behind schedule and you have over 30 stakeholders in 10 different countries. Where should you increase your focus?
a. schedule
b. cost
c. stakeholder management
d. conflict management

© January 2016 AME Group, Inc. author Aileen Ellis, PMP, PgMP
aileen@amegroupinc.com 719-659-3658

17. Your organization will be using earned value for the first time. You realize that different types of work packages should utilize different earned value measurement methods. Work packages associated with equipment deliveries often use:
a. the 0/100 rule
b. the 20/80 rule
c. the 50/50 rule
d. the 100/0 rule

18. An example of a cost usually considered direct is:
a. cost for a subcontractor working on the project
b. cost for health insurance
c. cost for utilities in your office area
d. cost of office space

CONTROL SCHEDULE AND CONTROL COSTS - Solutions

1. a. PMBOK® Guide: Section 5.6.1.1
Y   a. The scope baseline is an input of control scope.
N   b. The schedule baseline is an input of control schedule.
N   c. The cost baseline is an input of controls costs.
N   d. The scope baseline would not be an input of a schedule process.

2. c. PMBOK® Guide: Section 7.4.1.1
Y   c. The cost baseline is an input of controls costs.
N   a. The scope baseline is an input of control scope.
N   b. The schedule baseline is an input of control schedule.
N   d. The cost baseline is an output, not an input of determine budget.

3. b. PMBOK® Guide: Section 6.7.1.1
Y   b. The schedule baseline is an input of control schedule.
N   a. The scope baseline is an input of control scope.
N   c. The cost baseline is an input of controls costs.
N   d. The schedule baseline is an output of not an input of develop schedule.

4. a. PMBOK® Guide: Sections A1.7.4, A1.7.5, and A1.7.6
Y   a. Work performance data is an input of control scope, control schedule, and control costs.
N   b. Work performance information is an output of control scope, control schedule, and control costs.
N   c. Work performance reports is an output of monitor and control project work.
N   d. Variance analysis is a tool and technique of control costs and control scope.

5. b. PMBOK® Guide: Sections A1.7.4, A1.7.5, and A1.7.6
Y   b. Work performance information is an output of control scope, control schedule, and control costs.
N   a. Work performance reports is an output of monitor and control project work.
N   c. Work performance data is an input of control scope, control schedule, and control costs.
N   d. Variance analysis is a tool and technique of control costs and control scope.

6. c. PMBOK® Guide: Figure 7-1
Y   c. Earned value management is a tool and technique of control costs.
N   a., b., and d. Earned value management is not a tool of any planning processes.

7. b. PMBOK® Guide: Figure 6-1
Y   b. Schedule compression is a tool and technique of control schedule and develop schedule.
N   a. Schedule compression would not be a tool and technique of scope processes.
N   c. and d. Schedule compression would not be a tool and technique of a cost process.

8. a. PMBOK® Guide: Section 7.4.1.2
Y   a. Project funding requirements are an input to control costs. We need these to monitor cost performance as part of control costs.
N   b., c. and d. Project funding requirements are an output of determine budget.

9. d. PMBOK® Guide: Figure 7-1
Y   d. Project funding requirements are an output of determine budget.

N   a. Project funding requirements are an input to control costs. We need these to monitor cost performance as part of control costs.

N   b. and c. Project funding requirements are an output of determine budget.

10. d. PMBOK® Guide: Section 7.4.2.2

Y   d. Estimate at complete is our estimate on what we believe the entire project will cost.

N   a. Schedule variance is not an estimate. It is the difference between earned value and planned value.

N   b. Budget at completion is the original project budget.

N   c. The cost performance index is the earned value divided by the planned value.

11. b. PMBOK® Guide: Table 7-1

Y   b. If your CPI is less than one you are over budget. If your SPI is greater than one you are ahead of schedule.

12. c. PMBOK® Guide: Table 7-1

Y   c. An SPI of .92 means that the project is progressing at 92% of the rate expected.

13. b. PMBOK® Guide: Table 7-1

Y   b. A CPI greater than 1.0 is a good thing. A CPI= 1.2 means that for every dollar spent on the project the earned value is $1.20.

14. d. PMBOK® Guide: Table 7-1

Y   d.   Schedule variance (SV)= EV - PV= $300-$200 = $100

15. a. PMBOK® Guide: Table 7-1

Y   a.   What we know. The BAC (total project budget) is $1,000. The planned value (a measure of how much work should be complete as of today) is 80% $1,000= $800= PV. The earned value (a measure of how much work is complete) is 60% of $1,000= $600=EV. The actual cost is 50% of $1,000=$500=AC. Cost Variance (CV) = EV-AC=$600-$500=$100.

16. b. PMBOK® Guide: 7.4.2.1 (not explicit)

Y   b. You have a CPI that is less than one. You are therefore running over budget and need to put your focus on cost first.

N   a. The question says you are two weeks behind schedule. This is noise. You do not know if it is a two week or ten year project. You need to know your SPI before deciding to put your focus on schedule.

N   c. There is nothing in the question that states we need to put more focus on stakeholder management. 30 stakeholders is noise.

N   d. There is no information in the question to lead us to believe we need a larger focus on conflict management. 30 stakeholders is noise.

17.   a.   PMBOK® Guide: 7.1.3.1 (not explicit)

Y   a.   Often earned value for equipment deliverables uses the 0/100 rule. The equipment is often useless until it is delivered and therefore all the earned value credit is taken at delivery.

18.   a.   PMBOK® Guide: 7.2 (not explicit)

Y   a. The work of a subcontractor is billed direct to the project as long as their work is 100% associated with the project.

Control Quality and Validate Scope- make sure you understand the terms deliverables, verified deliverables and accepted deliverables.

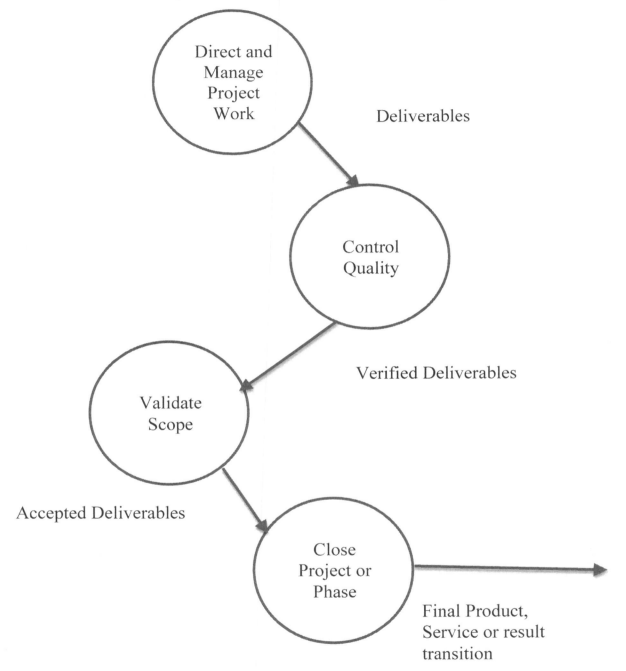

© January 2016 AME Group, Inc. author Aileen Ellis, PMP, PgMP
aileen@amegroupinc.com 719-659-3658

Control Quality

> ☑ **Exam Tip:** Review Figure 8-12 of the PMBOK® Guide.

There are two focuses of control quality:
- Ensuring that the deliverables are correct and forwarding them to validate scope for acceptance.
- Identifying and eliminating causes of poor quality.

Make sure you know the difference between control quality and validate scope. See diagram on the previous page.

CONTROL QUALITY	VALIDATE SCOPE
Measuring deliverables (products)	Measuring deliverables (products)
Performed internally	Performed by the customer
Usually performed before validate scope	Usually performed after control quality
Product may fail control quality and the customer may accept it anyway as part of validate scope	Product may pass control quality and the customer may not accept it as part of validate scope

CONTROL QUALITY

PREVENTION	INSPECTION
Proactive	Reactive
Keeping errors out of the process	Catching errors before the customer does

ATTRIBUTE SAMPLING	VARIABLE SAMPLING
Pass-fail testing	Measuring results along a scale
Example: A person must be 48 inches tall to ride the roller coaster. Your son is 46 inches tall and therefore he is not allowed to ride.	Example: You are 65 inches tall. Your son is 46 inches tall.

TOLERANCES	CONTROL LIMITS
Set by the customer	Set by the process
Represents what the customer will accept	Represents how well we control the process
We want the customer's tolerances to be wider (bigger) than our control limits.	

INPUTs of Control quality

Project management plan- the quality plan as part of the project plan describes how the control quality process will be performed.

Quality metrics- measures of different aspects of the project or product.

Work performance data- this is the raw data related to elements of the project. It is an output of direct and manage project work.

Approved change requests- these are outputs of integrated change control where requested changes are approved or rejected. In control quality we verify that approved changes have been implemented.

Deliverables- this is a very important input. The deliverables are an output of direct and manage project work. They come to quality control to be measured for correctness. After they are measured and deemed correct, we call them verified deliverables and send them to validate scope for the customer to inspect and accept them.

TOOLs and TECHNIQUEs of control quality

Seven basic quality tools- at this point you should recognize what tools make-up this list.
- Cause and effect diagrams
- Flowcharts
- Checksheets
- Pareto diagrams
- Histograms
- Control charts
- Scatter diagrams

☑ **EXAM TIP:** Understand why you would use one of these tools instead of another.

Statistical sampling- with this tool we want to select a sample of the population that is representative of the entire population. The two primary reasons for testing a sample instead of an entire population is that it is quicker and less expensive. A third reason may be that the testing you want to do is destructive so you can only test a sample if you want any product left.

Inspection- we often measure work products to ensure they are correct.

© January 2016 AME Group, Inc. author Aileen Ellis, PMP, PgMP
aileen@amegroupinc.com 719-659-3658

☑ **EXAM TIP:** Audits in general refer to processes while inspections refer to deliverables and products. Therefore, we are more likely to:
- Audit a process (and not a deliverable).
- Inspect a deliverable (and not a process).

This little tip may help you get multiple questions on the exam correct.

Approved change request review- as part of control quality we want to review the approved change requests to ensure that all of them were implemented correctly.

OUTPUTs of control quality

Quality control measurements- these are the physical representations of the measurements taken. They become an input to perform quality assurance where they are used to help determine which processes need improvements.

Validated changes- we are validating that all approved change requests have been implemented correctly.

Verified deliverables- we want to ensure that all deliverables were built correctly. After they are measured and deemed correct we call them verified deliverables and send them to validate scope for the customer to inspect them.

Work performance information- the work performance data (raw data) is processed in control quality and used to develop work performance information.

Change requests: every monitoring and controlling process has change requests as an output.

CONTROL QUALITY - Sample Questions

1. Accepted deliverables are:
a. an input of control quality
b. an output of control quality
c. an input of validate scope
d. an output of validate scope

2. Deliverables are an input to control quality. These deliverables come from which process:
a. validate scope
b. control quality
c. perform quality assurance
d. direct and manage project work

3. Verified deliverables are:
a. an input of control quality
b. an output of control quality
c. an input of direct and manage project work
d. an output of validate scope

4. Verified deliverables are:
a. an input of validate scope
b. an input of control quality
c. an input of direct and manage project work
d. an output of validate scope

5. Quality control measurements are:
a. an input of control quality
b. an input of perform quality assurance
c. an input of validate scope
d. an input of direct and manage project work

6. Another name for an Isikawa diagram is:
a. fishbone diagrams
b. Pareto chart
c. control chart
d. scatter diagram

7. The requirements documentation and traceability matrix are:
a. inputs of validate scope
b. outputs of validate scope
c. inputs of control quality
d. outputs of control quality

8. Quality metrics are:
a. inputs of validate scope
b. outputs of validate scope
c. inputs of control quality
d. outputs of control quality

9. Control quality is related to validate scope in that:

a.   control quality is about acceptance, whereas validate scope is about meeting requirements

b. control quality is normally performed after validate scope

c. control quality is about building the products correctly, whereas validate scope is about the customer accepting the products

d. control quality and validate scope are always performed in parallel

10. Control quality is:

a. applying the planned, systematic quality activities to ensure that the project employs all processes needed to meet requirements

b. identifying which quality standards are relevant to the project and determining how to satisfy them

c. monitoring specific project results to determine if they comply with relevant quality standards and identifying ways to eliminate causes of unsatisfactory performance

d.   all the activities of the performing organization that determine quality policies, objectives, and responsibilities so that the project will satisfy the needs for which it was undertaken.

CONTROL QUALITY - Solutions

1. d.   PMBOK° Guide: Section 5.5.3.1
Y   d. Accepted deliverables are an output of validate scope.
N   a. Deliverables are an input of control quality.
N   b. Verified deliverables are an output of control quality.
N   c. Verified deliverables are an input of validate scope.

2. d.   PMBOK° Guide: Figure 8-12
Y   d. Deliverables are created as an output of direct and manage project work.
N   a. "Accepted" deliverables are an output of validate scope.
N   b. "Verified" deliverables are an output of control quality.
N   c. Deliverables in any form are not an input or output of perform quality assurance.

3. b.   PMBOK° Guide: Section 5.5.1.4
Y   b. Verified deliverables are an output of control quality.
N   a. Deliverables are an input of control quality.
N   c. There are no type of deliverables that are an input of direct and manage project work.
N   d. Accepted deliverables are an output of validate scope.

4. a.   PMBOK° Guide: Section 5.5.1.4
Y   a. Verified deliverables are an input of validate scope.
N   b. Deliverables are an input of control quality.
N   c. There are no type of deliverables that are an input of direct and manage project work.
N   d. Accepted deliverables are an output of validate scope.

5. b.   PMBOK° Guide: Section 8.2.1.4
Y   b. Quality measurements are an output of control quality and an input of perform quality assurance. During quality assurance we may use the quality control measurements to give us insight into which processes need improving and which do not.
N   a., c., and d. Quality measurements are an output of control quality and an input of perform quality assurance. We see them as inputs and outputs to no other processes.

6. a.   PMBOK° Guide: Section 8.1.2.3
Y   a. The name fishbone, cause and effect, and Isikawa diagram may all be used interchangeably.
N   b. Pareto diagrams help us set priority.
N   c. Control charts help us understand if our process is running under control and is stable.
N   d. Scatter diagrams show data for two variables using an X and Y plot.

7. a.   PMBOK° Guide: Section 5.5.1.2 and 5.5.1.3
Y   a. We need both the requirements documentation and the traceability matrix of validate scope.
N   b. Accepted deliverables are an output of validate scope.
N   c. Deliverables and the quality metrics are inputs of control quality.
N   d. Verified deliverables are an output of control quality.

8. c.   PMBOK° Guide: Section 8.3.1.2

© January 2016 AME Group, Inc. author Aileen Ellis, PMP, PgMP
aileen@amegroupinc.com 719-659-3658

Y   c. Quality metrics are an output of plan quality and an input of control quality and also perform quality assurance.

N   a. and b. Quality metrics are not an input or an output of validate scope.

N   d. Verified deliverables are an output of control quality.

9. c. PMBOK° Guide: Section 5.5

Y   c. This is the only true answer.

N   a. Think control quality- correctness and validate scope- acceptance.

N   b. This answer is reversed.

N   d. Be careful of the word "all". Control quality is normally performed before validate scope.

10. c. PMBOK° Guide: Section 8.3

Y   c. This is the definition of control quality. The word "monitoring" is the key word.

N   a. This is the definition of perform quality assurance. The word "processes" is the key word.

N   b. This is the definition of plan quality. The word "identifying" is the key word.

N   d. This is the definition of quality management.

Validate Scope

The process validate scope is often confused with the process of control quality. Here is a table to get at the high level differences.

CONTROL QUALITY	VALIDATE SCOPE
Measures deliverables (products)	Measures deliverables (products)
Performed internally	Performed by the customer
About building deliverables correctly	About acceptance
Usually performed before validate scope	Usually performed after control quality
Product may fail quality control and the customer may accept the product anyway as part of validate scope	Product may pass quality control and the customer may not accept the product as part of validate scope
Input of control quality is: deliverables (from direct and manage project work) Output of control quality is: verified (meaning correct) deliverables	Input of validate scope is verified deliverables (from control quality) Output of validate scope is: accepted deliverables

INPUTs of validate scope (not all listed)

Project plan- the plan includes two documents that we will use at the point:
- **Scope management plan-** since we are in the scope knowledge area I hope it makes sense now that the scope management plan tells us the processes for obtaining acceptance of the completed scope from our customer.

Scope baseline- contains 3 documents that are used to ensure we are delivering everything we said we would deliver. The 3 documents of the scope baseline include: Scope statement, WBS, and WBS Dictionary.

☑ **EXAM TIP:** Make sure you are clear what three documents make-up the scope baseline. The scope management plan is not part of the scope baseline since there is no scope listed in the scope management plan. The scope management plan provides a description of the processes to define and manage scope.

Requirements documentation and the requirements traceability matrix- the verified deliverables will be measured against these requirements.

Verified deliverables- these have already been inspected internally as part of control quality for correctness. Now the team sends the verified deliverables to the customer (or sponsor) for acceptance.

TOOLs and TECHNIQUEs of validate scope

Inspections- the customer (or sponsor on internal projects) inspects the deliverable to determine if the deliverables meet the requirements.

Group decision-making techniques- used to determine whether the customer (or sponsor) will accept the deliverables.

OUTPUTs of validate scope (not all listed)

Accepted deliverables- the customer or sponsor may accept or reject the deliverables. Accepted deliverables and the documentation become inputs to close project/phase.

VALIDATE SCOPE – Sample Questions

1. Accepted deliverables are:
a. an input of control quality
b. an output of control quality
c. an input of validate scope
d. an output of validate scope

2. The requirements traceability matrix used in validate scope comes from what process?
a. define scope
b. collect requirements
c. develop project management plan
d. control quality

3. Verified deliverables are:
a. an input of control quality
b. an output of control quality
c. an input of direct and manage project work
d. an output of validate scope

4. Verified deliverables are:
a. an input of validate scope
b. an input of control quality
c. an input of direct and manage project work
d. an output of validate scope

5. Verified deliverables:
a. have passed the validate scope process
b. have passed the control quality process
c. are an output of direct and manage project work
d. are an output of close project or phase process

6. Which of the following is an input into validate scope?
a. work performance data
b. work performance information
c. work performance reports
d. quality metrics

7. The requirements documentation and traceability matrix are:
a. inputs of validate scope
b. outputs of validate scope
c. inputs of control quality
d. outputs of control quality

© January 2016 AME Group, Inc. author Aileen Ellis, PMP, PgMP
aileen@amegroupinc.com 719-659-3658

VALIDATE SCOPE - Solutions

1. d. PMBOK° Guide: Section 5.5.3.1
Y   d. Accepted deliverables are an output of validate scope.
N   a. Deliverables are an input of control quality.
N   b. Verified deliverables are an output of control quality.
N   c. Verified deliverables are an input of validate scope.

2. b. PMBOK° Guide: Section Figure 5-15
Y   b. The traceability matrix is an output of collect requirements.
N   a. The scope statement is an output of define scope.
N   c. The project management plan is an output of develop project management plan.
N   d. The verified deliverables are an output of control quality.

3. b. PMBOK° Guide: Section 5.5.1.4
Y   b. Verified deliverables are an output of control quality.
N   a. Deliverables are an input of control quality.
N   c. There are no type of deliverables that are an input of direct and manage project work.
N   d. Accepted deliverables are an output of validate scope.

4. a. PMBOK° Guide: Section 5.5.1.4
Y   a. Verified deliverables are an input of validate scope.
N   b. Deliverables are an input of control quality.
N   c. There are no deliverables that are an input of direct and manage project work.
N   d. Accepted deliverables are an output of validate scope.

5. b. PMBOK° Guide: Section 5.5.1.4
Y   b. Verified deliverables have passed the control quality process and are viewed as correct.
N   a. Accepted deliverables have passed the validate scope process and are accepted.
N   c. Deliverables are an output of direct and manage project work.
N   d. The transition of ownership of the product is an output of close product or phase.

6. a. PMBOK° Guide: Section 5.5.1.5
Y   a. Work performance data (raw data) is an input of validate scope.
N   b. Work performance information is an output of validate scope.
N   c. Work performance reports are an output of monitor and control project work.
N   d. Quality metrics are an input of control quality.

7. a. PMBOK° Guide: Section 5.5.1.2 and 5.5.1.3
Y   a. We need both the requirements documentation and the traceability matrix to validate scope.
N   b. Accepted deliverables are an output of validate scope.
N   c. Deliverables and the quality metrics are inputs of control quality.
N   d. Verified deliverables are an output of control quality.

Control Communication

☑ **Exam Tip:** Review Figure 10-8 of the PMBOK® Guide.

Control communications is the day-to-day work we do to ensure that the communications processes are working and stakeholders are receiving the information they need for their role on the project.

Manage Communications	Control Communications
In this process we follow the communications plan.	In this process we ask if the communications plan is working and we may recommend changes to the plan.

INPUTs of control communications (not all listed)

Project management plan- this plan, and more specifically the communications plan describe the process for controlling communication.

Project communication- this is the actual information being communicated.

Issue logs – these logs are an output of manage stakeholder engagement. Issue logs should be utilized to ensure that all project issues are resolved and closed. They also are a great communication tool as they let our stakeholders know that their issues are important to us, that owners have been assigned, and resolution will occur.

Issue #	Description	Priority	Owner	Target Resolution Date	Status	Date Resolved	Resolution and Comments
001	Late delivery of computer systems	High	Nick	Aug 20, 2013	In progress		
002	Terry moved off project - need replacement	Medium	Alex	April 14, 2013	Complete	April 1, 2013	Jose brought on team to replace Terry

Work performance data- this data is an output from the process, direct and manage project work. This is the data that we may want to share with our stakeholders.

TOOLs and TECHNIQUEs of control communications

Information management systems- as a project manager we want standardized ways to collect and distribute information. Information may be distributed in several ways:

- Hard-copy document management- while this may be appropriate for some communications, much of project communications is moving away from this distribution method
- Electronic communications management- these are the basic electronic methods we would see regardless of whether we are involved in project management
- Electronic project management tools- these are electronic tools specific to managing projects. Ex. Project management software tools

Meetings- this is a tool and technique of many processes. There are three types of meetings.

- Information exchange- to give updates to other parties
- Brainstorming, etc.- to generate ideas
- Decision-making- to come to a decision

OUTPUTs of control communications (not all listed)

Work performance information- work performance data from the direct and manage project work process is examined in context and turned into information.

Example:

Work performance data: The utility bill is $250 for the month of October.

Work performance information: The October utility bill is 7% higher than the average utility bill for October for the last ten October billings.

CONTROL COMMUNICATIONS - Sample Questions

1. Issue logs are an input of control communications. They are an output of what process:
a. direct and manage project work
b. manage stakeholder engagement
c. manage communications
d. plan communications management

2. Work performance information is an output of control communications. It is an input of what process:
a. direct and manage project work
b. manage stakeholder engagement
c. manage communications
d. monitor and control project work

3. Control communications is really about:
a. everything to do with project information
b. developing a strategy to ensure stakeholders have the information they need
c. following the communications plan
d. ensuring the stakeholders' information needs are being met

4. The tool and technique that allows the project manager to capture, store, and distribute information is:
a. information management system
b. issue log
c. communications requirements analysis
d. communications model

5. Work performance data is an input of control communications. It is an output of what process:
a. direct and manage project work
b. manage stakeholder engagement
c. manage communications
d. plan communications management

© January 2016 AME Group, Inc. author Aileen Ellis, PMP, PgMP
aileen@amegroupinc.com 719-659-3658

CONTROL COMMUNICATIONS - Solutions

1. b. PMBOK® Guide: Figure 10-8
Y   b. Issue logs are an output of manage stakeholder engagement.
N   a. Work performance data is an output of direct and manage project work.
N   c. Project communications is an output of manage communications.
N   d. The communications plan is the output of plan communications management.

2. d. PMBOK® Guide: Figure 10-8
Y   d. Work performance information is an input of monitor and control project work.
N   a. Work performance data is an output of direct and manage project work.
N   b. Work performance data, information, and reports are not inputs or outputs to manage stakeholder engagement.
N   c. Work performance reports are an input to manage communications.

3. d. PMBOK® Guide: Chapter 10 - Introduction
Y   d. Control communications is about making sure the stakeholders information needs are being met.
N   a. The knowledge area of communications is all about project information.
N   b. The process plan communications manageent is developing a strategy to ensure that the stakeholders have the information they require on the project.
N   c. Manage communications is the process in which we the team follow the communications plan.

4. a. PMBOK® Guide: Section 10.3.2.1
Y   a. The information management system is used to capture, store, and share information.
N   b. The issue log is not a tool and technique.
N   c. Communications requirements analysis is the tool and technique in which we analyze the information needs of the project stakeholders.
N   d. The communications model helps us visualize the importance of encoding, decoding, choosing a communication method, noise, and the feedback loop in communicating.

5. a. PMBOK® Guide: Figure 10-8
Y   a. Work performance data is an output of only one process: direct and manage project work.
N   b. Issue logs are an output of only one process: manage stakeholder engagement.
N   c. Project communications are an output of manage communications.
N   d. The communications plan is an output of plan communications management.

Control Risks

☑ **Exam Tip:** Review Figure 11.6 of the PMBOK® Guide.

This process is the day-to-day work we do to control risks.

INPUTs of perform control risk

Project management plan- Contains the risk management plan that includes a description of the process to control risks.

Risk register- all the information we have so far on the project risks are in the risk register.

Work performance data- this is raw data from the direct and manage project work process. We will review this data to check for new risks, etc.

Work performance reports- these are the reports that compare what is actually occurring on the project to our project plan. We will review these reports to check for new risks, etc.

TOOLs and TECHNIQUEs of plan risk responses

☑ **EXAM TIP:** Know the difference between a risk reassessment and a risk audit

Risk reassessment	Risk audit
Identification of new risks	Evaluation of effectiveness of risk processes
Reassessment of current risks	Evaluation of effectiveness of risk responses on risk and their root causes
Closing of outdated risks	

Variance and trend analysis- we want to review project variances (cost variance, schedule variance, etc.) as well as trends (cost performance index, schedule performance index, etc.) to review risks in the variances and trends.

Technical performance measurement- we want to review these measurements (ex. Number of product returns) to review risks.

Reserve analysis- we want to ensure that we have enough reserve (both cost and schedule) to cover the amount of risk that is still present.

OUTPUTs of control risks (not all listed)

© January 2016 AME Group, Inc. author Aileen Ellis, PMP, PgMP
aileen@amegroupinc.com 719-659-3658

Work performance information- if we have work performance data coming into a monitoring and controlling process we should assume that the data will be turned into work performance information (useful information... not just raw data).

Tricky question on contingency:

Your software development project is going very well. At your review it is reported that you have closed out several risks that did not occur as expected. There is contingency reserve associated with these risks. In general we should:

a. keep the contingency reserve on the project in case other risks occur unexpectedly

b. return the contingency reserve back to the organization to free up resources for other projects and operations

c. move the contingency reserve into a category called workaround funds for the project

d. hide the contingency reserve in case we planned poorly and need it later

Solution- Hopefully, you were able to see that this unused contingency should be returned to free up resources for other projects and/or operations. If we require it later for a new risk we would need to request it and be able to justify that request.

CONTROL RISKS - Sample Questions

1. Risk audits look at:
a. identification of new risks
b. Reassessment of current risks
c. closing of outdated risks
d. effectiveness of the risk management processes

2. Risk reassessment looks at all of the following except:
a. identification of new risk
b. Reassessment of current risks
c. closing of outdated risks
d. effectiveness of the risk responses

3. Risk management should be:
a. a topic at periodic status meetings
b. only discussed if there is extra time
c. only discussed at review meetings with the customer
d. a topic at risk management meetings only

4. The purpose of reserve analysis as part of control project risks is to ask:
a. are new risks emerging
b. what risks require responses
c. how much risk do we have left compared to how much reserve we have left
d. are the risk management processes working

5. Sensitivity analysis, expected monetary value analysis and modeling and simulation are all tools and techniques of which process:
a. identify risk
b. control risk
c. perform qualitative risk analysis
d. perform quantitative risk analysis

6. You are deeply involved in the monitoring and control of your design/build project. Several risk events have occurred unexpectedly and you do not have risk response plans in place. Therefore, you are most likely to go to a:
a. contingency plan
b. fallback plan
c. backup plan
d. workaround

7. Project risks are:
a. always negative
b. always positive
c. may be positive or negative
d. may begin positive but always turn negative

8. Workarounds are:
a. unplanned before the risk event occurs
b. developed to aid in risk avoidance
c. associated with risk mitigation
d. the same as contingency plans

© January 2016 AME Group, Inc. author Aileen Ellis, PMP, PgMP
aileen@amegroupinc.com 719-659-3658

CONTROL RISKS - Solutions

1. d. PMBOK® Guide: Section 11.6.2.2
Y   d. The key word in the question is the word audit. Audits are usually associated with our processes. During a risk audit we examine how well our risk processes are working as well as how well are the risk responses working.
N   a., b., and c. During the risk reassessment we identify new risks, reassess the current risks, and close out the outdated risks.

2. d. PMBOK® Guide: Section 11.6.2.1
Y   d. During the risk audit we look at the effectiveness of the risk responses.
N   a., b., and c. During the risk reassessment we identify new risks, reassess the current risks and close out the outdated risks.

3. a. PMBOK® Guide: Section 11.6.2.6
Y   a. Risk management should be a topic at all of our project status meetings. Risk is so important, we want to keep it high visibility.
N   b., c., and d. Be careful of the word "only". We should be reviewing risk regularly.

4. c. PMBOK® Guide: Section 11.6.2.5
Y   c. As we perform reserve analysis as part of control risks we should ask: How much risk is left compared to how much reserve is left? We do not want to run out of reserve.
N   a. and b. As part of risk reassessment we ask questions such as: Are new risks emerging? What risks require responses, etc.?
N   d. As part of the risk audit we ask: Are the risk management processes working?

5. d. PMBOK® Guide: Section 11.4.2.2
Y   d. These tools and techniques listed are all part of perform quantitative risk analysis.
N   a. Documentation reviews and assumption analysis are examples of tools and techniques of identify risks.
N   b. Risk reassessment, risk audit, and reserve analysis are examples of tools and techniques of control risks.
N   c. Risk probability and impact assessment and the probability and impact matrix are examples of tools and techniques of perform qualitative risk analysis.

6. d. PMBOK® Guide: Section 11.6.3.2
Y   d. Workarounds are unplanned responses to risk events.
N   a. Contingency plans are set-up proactively. The question states that you have no risk plans in place.
N   b. and c. Fallback and backup plans are two names for the same idea. They represent your second contingency and would be set-up proactively. The question states that you have no risk plans in place.

7. c. PMBOK® Guide: Chapter 11 - Introduction
Y   c. Risks are uncertain events that may have either a positive or negative effect on at least one project objective.
N   a., b., and d. Risks can have either a positive or negative effect. (these lines need moving up)

8. a. PMBOK® Guide: Section 11.6.3.2
Y   a. Workarounds are unplanned responses to emerging risks.

N   b. Clarifying requirements, obtaining information, improving communication, and acquiring expertise are examples of changing the project management plan to aid in risk avoidance.

N   c. Designing redundancy is associated with risk mitigation.

N   d. Contingency plans are planned responses associated with active acceptance.

Control Procurements

In the process control procurements we are ensuring that the contracted supplier is meeting all their obligations under the contract and that we (the buyer organization) are meeting all of our obligations.

Due to the legal implications of actions and decisions, often the contract administrator for both the buying and the selling organization reports into an organization separate from the project organization.

Financial elements- as the buying organization we hold the responsibility to ensure the seller is receiving payments in a fair and timely manner. On most procurements we try to tie payment to work accomplished and not just to time or activity. From the other perspective if the seller is not performing we need to document it and take corrective action. This documentation may be required later in the case of early termination.

INPUTs to control procurements

A few of the inputs are the outputs of the last two processes:
* Project management plan- specifically the procurement management plan describes the process of control procurements
* Procurement documents- this may include our RFP (request for proposal) of other such documents, the procurement statement of work (describes the items we are purchasing from the supplier), and documents related to contract award
* Agreements- documents the obligations of both parties (buyer and seller)

Other inputs include:

Approved change requests- these are the approved change requests specific to the contract relationship. They are implemented in the control procurement process.

Work performance reports- these are the reports from the seller on their work performance. We may take these reports and make them part of our work performance reports on the project.

Work performance data- this is the raw data collected. This data will be turned into work performance information and then later the information will be documented in the work performance reports.

TOOLs and TECHNIQUEs of control procurements

Contract change control system- this system defines the processes to make changes on the procurement. Since the procurement has legal implications this system needs to be very clear with information on required documentation. In some organizations this system is linked to the integrated change control system on the project.

Procurement performance reviews- this is a review of the seller's ability to meet the requirements of the contract. Requirements may include technical, schedule, cost, quality, and others.

Inspections and audits- the buyer will inspect the deliverables of the seller to ensure these deliverables meet the requirements of the contract. The buyer will audit the seller's processes to ensure these processes meet the requirements of the contract.

☑ **EXAM TIP:** Keep in mind the difference between an inspection and an audit.
- We inspect deliverables (or products).
- We audit processes.

Performance reporting- the seller supplies work performance data and reports (see inputs) to us (the buyer). We evaluate this information against the contract requirements to see how the seller is performing and also to report to our management on that performance.

Payment systems- systems should be in place to ensure the seller is paid in a fair and timely manner. As an example:
1. Seller completes deliverable (or group of deliverables)
2. Seller submits invoice to buyer (may be someone in procurement)
3. Invoice is forwarded to designated member of project team for approval or non-approval
4. If approved, the invoice (with approval) is forwarded to accounts payable
5. Accounts payable makes payment to the seller

The key idea is that the seller should be paid, if possible, based on completed deliverables and not based on time or effort. Different contract types will allow for different rules regarding payment.

Claims administration- contracts are relationships and often disagreements arise. A system should be in place to deal with these claims, disputes, and appeals. If possible, work should continue as claims and disputes are processed. Below is a list, in order of preference in dealing with claims, etc.
- Negotiations- both parties negotiate and work out disagreements (preferred method)
- Mediation- a third party mediator is brought in to help parties work out their disagreements
- Arbitration- a third party arbitrator is brought in to make a decision
- Litigation- the disagreement goes to court and a decision is made (least desirable method due to time, cost, and potential loss of reputation)

Records management system- contract documentation, including correspondence, is archived in a records management system. Due to the legal nature of contracts it is important to archive appropriate information in a system where that information can be retrieved later.

OUTPUTs of control procurements (not all listed)

© January 2016 AME Group, Inc. author Aileen Ellis, PMP, PgMP
aileen@amegroupinc.com 719-659-3658

Work performance information- this information relates to the performance of the supplier. It is closely tied to the work performance data that is an input to this process. This information is necessary for several reasons:
- In case of later claims or disputes
- To aid in future procurements
- To help us better plan based on historical records

Change requests- since this is a monitoring and controlling process we should expect change requests as an output. As we monitor we often request changes.

Other Ideas:

Privity of Contract- privity is the legal relationship between two parties of a contract.
- Buyer A buys from Seller B who then subcontracts to Subcontractor C.
- Buyer A has privity with Seller B but not with Subcontractor C. In simplistic terms, Buyer A should not be giving direction to Subcontractor C.

CONTROL PROCUREMENTS - Sample Questions

1. As part of control procurements the project manager should focus on all the following except:
a. managing the relationships with our suppliers
b. making sure both parties are living up to the contract (us and our supplier)
c. monitoring payments to the seller
d. writing requests for proposals

2 . Which of the following statements are true about inspections and audits:
a. inspections focus more on the product while audits focus more on the processes
b. inspections focus more on the processes while audits focus more on the products
c. the customer performs inspections while internally we perform audits
d. we perform inspections while the customer performs audits

3. The preferred method for settling claims and disputes is:
a. litigation
b. arbitration
c. mediation
d. negotiation

4. During the control procurement process, the project team should be focusing on:
a. the bidder conference
b. the weighting factors
c. the make-or-buy analysis
d. the procurement performance reviews

5. When making payments to the seller we hope to establish a close relationship between:
a. payments to work accomplished
b. payments to work periods
c. payments to work attempted
d. payments to work promised

© January 2016 AME Group, Inc. author Aileen Ellis, PMP, PgMP
aileen@amegroupinc.com 719-659-3658

CONTROL PROCUREMENTS - Solutions

1. d. PMBOK° Guide: Section 12.3.2
Y   d. During control procurements, we are past the point of writing requests for proposals. The seller has already been selected and is under contract.
N   a. During control procurements, the buyer's project manager should be managing the relationship with the sellers.
N   b. During control procurements, the buyer's project manager should be ensuring that both parties are living up to the obligations of the contract.
N   c. During control procurements, the buyer's project manager should be ensuring that deliverables are being received and accepted (or rejected) and payments being made appropriately.

2. a. PMBOK° Guide: Section 12.3.2.3
Y   a. Inspections focus more on the product while audits focus more on the processes. As an example, during a quality audit the processes are reviewed and process improvements recommended.
N   b. This statement is reversed.
N   c. and d. Either we or the customer may perform inspections or audits. At times, audits are defined as independent reviews, meaning they are performed by someone outside of the team, though not necessarily the customer.

3. d. PMBOK° Guide: Section 12.3.2.6
Y   d. Negotiation is the preferred method. If possible we want to try to resolve issues in a timely manner and dispassionately.
N   a. Litigation is often the least preferred method because of the time, the cost, and the risk to our reputation.
N   b. Mediation means bringing in a third party to help us work out the issue. If we cannot work things out between ourselves and the supplier through negotiation, then mediation may be a good fallback option.
N   c. Arbitration means bringing in a third party to hear both sides and make a decision on the issue. If we cannot work things out between ourselves and the supplier through negotiation, then mediation or arbitration may be good fallback options.

4. d. PMBOK° Guide: Section 12.3.2.2
Y   d. During the control procurement process we should be focused on the procurement performance reviews as well as other items.
N   a. The bidder conference is used during the conduct procurement process.
N   b. Weighting factors may be used during the conduct procurement process to select the seller.
N   c. The make-or-buy analysis is a tool and technique of the plan procurement process.

5. a. PMBOK° Guide: Section 12.3
Y   a. In general we should try to tie payments to work performance.
N   b. At times we may need to tie payments to work periods but when it makes sense we want to try to tie payments to work accomplished.
N   c. The word "attempted" makes this a wrong answer.
N   d. The word "promised" makes this a wrong answer.

Control Stakeholder Engagement

☑ **Exam Tip:** Review Figure 13-11 of the PMBOK® Guide.

In this process we interact with our stakeholders. The primary question to ask: Is the stakeholder engagement strategy working? Stakeholder engagement strategies, as found in the stakeholder management plan, may need to be adjusted.

Manage Stakeholder Engagement	Control Stakeholder Engagement
In this process we follow the stakeholder management plan.	In this process we ask if the stakeholder management plan is working and we may recommend changes to the plan.

INPUTS to control stakeholder engagement

Project management plan - This plan contains the stakeholder management plan. Both ideas from the overall project plan and the stakeholder management plan are used to guide us in this process.

Issue logs - these logs are an output of manage stakeholder engagement. Issue logs should be utilized to ensure that all project issues are resolved and closed. They also are a great communication tool as they let our stakeholders know that their issues are important to us, that owners have been assigned, and resolution will occur.

Issue #	Description	Priority	Owner	Target Resolution Date	Status	Date Resolved	Resolution and Comments
001	Late delivery of computer systems	High	Nick	Aug 20, 2013	In progress		
002	Terry moved off project - need replacement	Medium	Alex	April 14, 2013	Complete	April 1, 2013	Jose brought on team to replace Terry

Work performance data - this is the raw data as collected during direct and manage project work.

☑ **EXAM TIP**: If work performance data is an input, you should be able to guess one of the outputs- yes... it is work performance information.

Project Documents - multiple documents outside of the project plan may aid in this process. An example includes the change log. Stakeholders will want to know the status of their change requests.

TOOLs and TECHNIQUEs for control stakeholder engagement (not all listed)

Information management systems- these systems allow the project manager to consolidate information from several systems so as to provide the stakeholders the information they need in a format that works for them.

OUTPUTs from control stakeholder engagement (not all listed)

Work performance information- this information is really the work performance data that now has been correlated and contextualized.

☑ **EXAM TIP:** If work performance information is an output, we should be able to guess one of the inputs- yes ... work performance data is one of the inputs.

Change requests- as we work with our stakeholders we may request changes on the project.

☑ **EXAM TIP:** At this point we should be able to guess that change requests would be an output. Why? Because change requests are an output of most monitoring and controlling processes.

CONTROL STAKEHOLDER ENGAGEMENT – Sample Questions

1. The process of communicating and working with stakeholders is:
a. identify stakeholders
b. plan stakeholder management
c. manage stakeholder engagement
d. control stakeholder engagement

2. The process of monitoring overall project stakeholder relationships is:
a. identify stakeholders
b. plan stakeholder management
c. manage stakeholder engagement
d. control stakeholder engagement

3. The work performance data that is an input to control stakeholder engagement comes from:
a. direct and manage project work
b. monitor and control project work
c. integrated change control
d. validate scope

4. The change management plan is a subset of:
a. project documents
b. work performance data
c. project management plan
d. work performance information

5. The issue log and the change log are subsets of:
a. project documents
b. work performance data
c. project management plan
d. work performance information

6. Stakeholder analysis is a tool and technique of what process?
a. develop project charter
b. identify stakeholders
c. develop schedule
d. collect requirements

CONTROL STAKEHOLDER ENGAGEMENT – Solutions

1. c. PMBOK° Guide: Section 13.3

Y   c. The process of actively communicating and working with our stakeholders is called manage stakeholder engagement.

N   a. Identify stakeholders is the process of determining who are the project stakeholders and setting priority.

N   b. Plan stakeholder management is the process of coming up with a strategy to actively engage our stakeholders.

N   d. Control stakeholder engagement is the process of reviewing our stakeholder engagement practices and making changes as needed.

2. d. PMBOK° Guide: Section 13.4

Y   d. Control stakeholder engagement is the process of reviewing our stakeholder engagement practices and making changes as needed.

N   a. Identify stakeholders is the process of determining who are the project stakeholders and setting priority.

N   b. Plan stakeholder management is the process of coming up with a strategy to actively engage our stakeholders.

N   c. The process of actively communicating and working with our stakeholders is called manage stakeholder engagement.

3. a. PMBOK° Guide: Figure 13-11

Y   a. All work performance data comes as an output of direct and manage project work.

4. c. PMBOK° Guide: Section 13.4.1.1

Y   c. The change management plan and the configuration management plan are both subsets of the project management plan.

5. a. PMBOK° Guide: 13.4.1.4

Y   a. Issue logs, change logs, the risk register, etc. are all a subset of the project documents.

6. b. PMBOK° Guide: 13.1.2.1

Y   b. Stakeholder analysis is a tool and technique of identify stakeholders.

MONITORING and CONTROLLING-other ideas

These ideas are based on information in the *PMP® Exam Content Outline* published by PMI® on June 2015 for inclusion on the PMP® Exam beginning January 12, 2016. For the exam you do not need to know which tasks or which knowledge and skills have been added. The information in the tasks and knowledge and skills may be on your PMP® exam.

Task 6- *Capture, analyze, and manage lessons learned, using lessons learned management techniques in order to enable continuous improvement.*
While this is a new task in the exam content outline this task has been part of this study guide and the *PMBOK® Guide 5th Edition* for years.

Task 7- *Monitor procurement activities according to the procurement plan in order to verify compliance and project objectives.*
While this is a new task in the exam content outline this task has been part of this study guide and the *PMBOK® Guide 5th Edition* for years.

Monitoring and controlling Knowledge and skills

Trend analysis:
Trend analysis is a mathematical technique that uses history to predict the future. Often with trend analysis we compare data against a baseline such as scope, schedule or cost to predict future variance.

Process analysis techniques:
LEAN is a system in which we maximize customer value while minimizing waste.
LEAN- Examples of lean project management may include:
- 6 sigma DMAIC (define, measure, analyze, improve and control)
- Deming cycle (called A3)
  - Statement of the problem
  - The current situation
  - The root cause of the problem
  - Suggest alternative solutions
  - Suggest a recommended solution
  - Have a cost-benefit analysis

Kanban *is* a pull system that provides a focused sustainable pace and regular delivery.
Why use it-
- It ensures a sustainable (manageable) pace of work for your team members
- It ensures faster delivery to your customers
- It supports small continuous improvements

Kanban is based on four foundational principles
- Start with your existing process
- Respect the current process, roles and responsibilities, job titles
- Agree to pursue incremental evolutional improvements
- Encourage acts of leadership at all levels

Kanban is based on core practices
- Visualize your work flow
- Limit work in progress (WIP)

© January 2016 AME Group, Inc. author Aileen Ellis, PMP, PgMP
aileen@amegroupinc.com 719-659-3658

- Manage flow
- Make process policies explicit
- Improve collaboratively

Kanban is a pull system, not a push system. When a team completes an item of work, this completion triggers a pull to bring in the next item.

Six Sigma is a set of tools and techniques for process improvement. Six Sigma seeks to improve the quality of the output of a process by identifying and removing the causes of defects and minimizing variability.

Project quality best practices and standards- there are many organizations that produce standards related to quality best practices. An example of a few are:

ISO -International Organization for Standards. ISO 9001 is often associated with project management and covers documentation, design, development, production, testing, installation, servicing, and other processes.

BS- British Standards are standards produced by the BSI Group. The BSI Group produces British Standards.

CMMI- the capability maturity model was developed by the Software Engineering Institute. The model has five levels of organizational maturity related to software development.

Level one- characterized by chaos, periodic panics, and heroic efforts required by individuals to successfully complete projects. Few if any processes in place; successes may not be repeatable.

Level two – software project tracking, requirements management, realistic planning, and configuration management processes are in place; successful practices can be repeated.

Level three – standard software development and maintenance processes are integrated throughout an organization; a Software Engineering Process Group is in place to oversee software processes, and training programs are used to ensure understanding and compliance.

Level four – metrics are used to track productivity, processes, and products. Project performance is predictable, and quality is consistently high.

Level five – the focus is on continuous process improvement. The impact of new processes and technologies can be predicted and effectively implemented when required.

Quality validation and verification techniques:

CMMI (see previous section) helps us understand the terms verification and validation by:

Verification addresses the question: Are we building the product correctly? This process looks at specifications, standards and guidelines.

In the PMBOK® Guide we associate the process Quality Control with Verification. You may remember that verified deliverables are an output of Quality Control .

Validation addresses the questions: Are we building the correct product? If we place the deliverable (or product) in the proper environment does it fulfill the needs of the end user as expressed in the requirements?

In the PMBOK® Guide we associate the process Validate scope with validation.. The customer is testing the deliverable (or product) to determine if the customer will accept the deliverable. The requirements along with the verified deliverables are inputs into validate scope.

MINI-TEST after MONITOR and CONTROL PROCESS GROUP – Questions

Strong suggestion: Do not write on these questions so you can attempt them again later.

1. Your project is constantly plagued by the right activities starting at the wrong time or not starting at all. What tool and technique most likely can help you resolve this issue?
a. the Responsibility Assignment Matrix (RAM)
b. the work authorization system
c. the human resource management plan
d. the stakeholder management plan

2. While initiating the project the project manager along with relevant stakeholders conducts benefit analysis. The primary reason to perform benefit analysis at this point is to:
a. formalize the authority of the project manager
b. validate project alignment with organizational strategy and expected business value
c. gain commitment and acceptance of the project
d. ensure a common understanding of the key deliverables, milestones and stakeholder roles and responsibilities

3. Typical financial analysis techniques used to establish the project feasibility include all of the following except:
a. return on investment (ROI)
b. internal rate of return (IRR)
c. net present value (NPV)
d. earned value analysis

4. Business value is the sum of all tangible and intangible elements. Benefit analysis is conducted in part to validate project alignment with business value. An example of an intangible element of business value is:
a. trademarks
b. monetary assets
c. stockholder equity
d. utility

5. In general an important person who should be involved in creating the estimate for a given activity is the:
a. project manager
b. person who will perform the activity
c. person who will audit the activity
d. risk manager

6. Your organization is starting to implement a product backlog on your software upgrade project. A critical rule concerning this backlog is:
a. the backlog should be set as a baseline as early as possible on the project
b. the items in the backlog should be prioritized
c. the product backlog should be a subset of the sprint backlog
d. only the development team may update the product backlog

© January 2016 AME Group, Inc. author Aileen Ellis, PMP, PgMP
aileen@amegroupinc.com 719-659-3658

7. High performing organizations are likely to focus on a number of foundational practices including knowledge transfer. A typical knowledge transfer life cycle includes:
a. forming, storming, norming, performing, and adjourning
b. initiating, planning, executing, monitoring and controlling, closing
c. plan, do, check, act
d. identifying, capturing, sharing, applying, assessing

8. Your organization is using both LEAN and Six Sigma as process analysis techniques. While these two techniques complement each other there is often disagreements between the LEAN people and the Six Sigma people. One of the tenants of Six sigma is the reduction of:
a. extra processes
b. extra features
c. wait time
d. variation and defects

9. Several of your team members have the task to collect the requirements for the project. They have brainstormed and believe they have too many ideas related to requirements. The suggestion is to vote on their ideas. What group creatively idea is being suggested:
a. multi-criteria decision analysis
b. affinity diagrams
c. idea/mind mapping
d. nominal group technique

10. An organization scoring high on Geert Hofstede's power distance index believes:
a. power is distributed equally in their organization
b. many highly powerful people in their organization have expert power as their primary power source
c. unequal distribution of power is a basic fact of the organization
d. there are many opportunities to move up in the organization based on knowledge and skills

11. Goleman's model of emotional intelligence includes:
a. forming, storming, norming, performing and adjourning
b. self-awareness, self-regulation, social skill, empathy and motivation
c. withdraw, smooth, compromise, force and collaborate
d. formal, reward, punishment, expert and referent

12. Change management can be a long and tedious process. In your organization often the last step of change management is overlooked. From the list below which item would you perform last?
a. submit change request
b. establish or adjust work packages
c. implement change if approved
d. approved change request review

13. Your project is to plan and host the largest soccer competition in the history of your country. One of the most important early decisions is the location of the event. There are many items to consider including stadium size, infrastructure and security. You recommend that clear evaluation criteria be defined as an input into decision-making. Most likely you are in what decision making phase:
a. solution action planning
b. problem definition
c. ideas to action
d. problem solution generation

14. Your organization is struggling with the perceived attitudes and lack of experience of your younger workers. Many of the older and more experienced workers seem to not value the enthusiasm of these newer employees. One proactive way to bridge the gap is through:
a. training sessions for the more experienced workers on the value of our new hires
b. reverse mentoring
c. ensuring that teams do not have mixed generations so that the more experience workers will not be frustrated by these younger workers
d. limiting the number of new hires

15. At the end of your last project your team spent a good amount of time collecting lessons learned. The biggest lessons were related to the project communications. It seems that many team members did not understand who should get what information and in what format. Many stakeholders complained that they felt they did not have visibility into the project. Others stated that they struggled to make good decisions based on the lack of information. Interestingly, some stakeholders stated that they were in information overload and therefore looked at little of the information supplied to them. You have decided to put a strong focus on communications management. You believe the first thing to do is:
a. distribute every project report to every stakeholder. Therefore, no stakeholder can complain they were not informed of the project status
b. post all project communications using an electronic knowledge repository. Therefore, each stakeholder can find the information and only the information they require
c. develop a communications plan that describes who should get what information, etc.
d. develop a stakeholder register to ensure every stakeholder receives the information they require

16. Body language is an example of what dimension of communication?
a. written
b. oral
c. verbal
d. nonverbal

17. Communication with peers is considered:
a. vertical
b. horizontal
c. up
d. down

18. The annual report is an example of what dimension of communication?
a. official
b. unofficial
c. verbal
d. nonverbal

© January 2016 AME Group, Inc. author Aileen Ellis, PMP, PgMP
aileen@amegroupinc.com 719-659-3658

19. Voice inflections are an example of what dimension of communication?
a. written
b. oral
c. verbal
d. nonverbal

20. Reports are an example of what type of communication?
a. formal written
b. formal oral
c. informal written
d. informal oral

21. At the end of your last project your team spent a good amount of time collecting lessons learned. The biggest lessons were related to the risk management. Most team members felt that there was a lot of talk about risk management but very little risk management actually occurring. The project experienced multiple delays and overruns. Some team members think if the team had been more proactive in relation to risk these delays and overruns would not have occurred. You have decided to put a strong focus on risk management. You believe the first thing to do is:
a. have more risk experts involved when identifying project risks
b. perform quantitate risk analysis and not just qualitative risk analysis
c. incorporate the risk response technique of avoid into your risk plans
d. develop a risk management plan

22. A risk that may have a positive result is called:
a. an opportunity
b. a threat
c. there is no such thing as a positive risk
d. an issue

23. The amount of risk that an organization is willing to accept is called the organization's:
a. risk appetite
b. risk tolerance
c. risk threshold
d. risk probability

24. A risk that may lead to a negative result is called:
a. an opportunity
b. a threat
c. all risks are negative
d. an issue

25. Overall project risk is:
a. the sum of all individual risks on a project
b. the effect of uncertainty on a project
c. the sum of all negative risks on a project
d. the sum of all positive risks on a project

26. What is the difference between a risk and an issue?
a. a risk is an issue that has occurred
b. an issue is a negative risk that has occurred
c. issues and risks are the same thing
d. there is no relationship between risks and issues

27. At the end of your last project your team spent a good amount of time collecting lessons learned. The biggest lessons were related to the procurement management. Most team members felt that it was unclear what work would be performed in house and what work would be performed by an outside supplier. If it was clear that an outside supplier would be used it was still unclear how long lead items would be handled, etc. Because of this the project experienced multiple delays and overruns. Some team members think if the team had been more proactive in relation to procurement these delays and overruns would not have occurred. You have decided to put a strong focus on procurement management on your current project. You believe the first thing to do is:

a. write more detailed procurement statements of work for the suppliers
b. use letters of intent to get suppliers working while we put official contracts in place
c. put strong penalties in contracts for late deliveries of critical items
d. develop procurement management plans

28. A contract may also be called a:
a. purchase order
b. request for proposal
c. request for quote
d. request for information

29. Before the seller is called the selected source they are often referred to as:
a. contracted vendor
b. contracted supplier
c. bidder
d. client

30. The process of awarding contracts is called:
a. plan procurement management
b. conduct procurements
c. control procurements
d. close procurements

31. Make or buy analysis is a tool and technique of what process:
a. plan procurement management
b. conduct procurements
c. control procurements
d. close procurements

32. A contract obligates the buyer to provide:
a. monetary compensation
b. nothing
c. monetary or other valuable compensation
d. product, service, or result

© January 2016 AME Group, Inc. author Aileen Ellis, PMP, PgMP
aileen@amegroupinc.com 719-659-3658

MINI-TEST after MONITORING and CONTROLLING- Solutions

1. b. *PMBOK Guide Section 4.3.2.2*
Y   b. The work authorization system is used to ensure the right organization or person is doing the right work at the right time and in the right sequence.
N   a. There is no time element associated with the RAM.
N   c. and d. Plans are documents. Plans are not tools and techniques.

2. b. *PMP® Exam content outline Initiating-Task 7- June 2015*
Y   b. We conduct benefit analysis with relevant stakeholders in order to validate project alignment with organizational strategy and expected business value.

3. d. *PMBOK Guide Sections 4.1.1.2 and 7.4.2.1*
Y   d. Earned value analysis is used to access project performance and predict future performance. Earned value analysis is often an important input into project decisions.
N   a. ROI, IRR and NPV may all be contained in the business case.

4. a. *PMBOK® Guide Section 1.6*
Y   a. Trademarks as well as good will would be considered intangible elements of business value.
N   b., c and d. Monetary assets, stockholder equity and utility are all examples of tangible elements of business value.

5. b.
    Y   b. Multiple people may be involved in creating an estimate. It is important to include the person who will be performing the activity in the estimate if reasonable.

6. b.
Y   b. It is important to prioritize the items in the product backlog.

7.   d.
Y   d. A typical knowledge transfer life cycle includes identifying, capturing, sharing, applying and assessing.
N   a. These are the five stages of team development.
N   b. These are the five process groups.
N   c. This life cycle is the basis for quality improvement.

8.   d.
Y   d. Six sigma means reducing variation and defects on any product.
N   a., b. and c.   LEAN focuses on waste. Extra processes, extra features, and wait time may be examples of waste.

9.   d.   *PMBOK® Guide 5.2.2.4*
Y   d. Nominal group technique is often used after brainstorming. It is a voting technique.

10.   c.   *Wikipedia- Hofstede's cultural dimensions theory*
Y   c.   An organization scoring high on Hofstede's power distance index believes that an unequal distribution of power is a basic fact of the organization.
N   a., b. and d. An organization scoring low on Hofstede's power distance index may believe these ideas.

11. b. *Wikipedia-Emotional Intelligence*

Y   b. Based on Goleman's mixed model, the five main emotional intelligence constructs are: self-awareness, self-regulation, social skill, empathy and motivation.

N   a. These are the five stages of team development.

N   c. These are five methods for conflict resolution.

N   d. These are five sources of power.

12. d. *PMBOK® Guide section 8.3.2.3*
Y   d. As part of control quality we need to ensure that the approved change request was implemented as approved.

13. c. *PMBOK® Guide X3.6*
Y   c. During the ideas to action phase we define the evaluation criteria, rate pros and cones of alternatives and select the best solution.

14. b.
Y   b. Reverse mentoring is often a very proactive method to bridge the generation gap. It allows people of different generations to get to know each other, to learn from each other and to value each other.

15. c. PMBOK® Guide: Chapter 10 - Introduction
Y   c. The communications plan tells us who gets what information, etc. It also tells us how to manage and control communications.

N   a. and b. Be careful of the word "all" and the word "every".

N   d. The stakeholder register helps us list and prioritize our stakeholders. It does not tell us who should receive what communication.

16. d. PMBOK® Guide: Chapter 10 - Introduction
Y   d. Body language is an example of nonverbal communication.

N   a. Reports are an example of written communication.

N   b. Speeches are an example of oral communication.

N   c. Voice inflections are an example of verbal communication.

17. b. PMBOK® Guide: Chapter 10 - Introduction
Y   b. Communications with peers is considered horizontal.

N   a. Communication with your management or your team members is considered vertical.

N   c. Communication with your management is considered up communications.

N   d. Communication with your team members is considered down communications.

18. a. PMBOK® Guide: Chapter 10 - Introduction
Y   a. The annual report would be considered official communication.

N   b. Off the record comments would be considered unofficial communication.

N   c. Voice inflections are an example of verbal communication.

N   d. Body language is an example of nonverbal communication.

19. c. PMBOK® Guide: Chapter 10 - Introduction
Y   c. Voice inflections are an example of verbal communication.

N   a. The annual report would be considered written communication.

N   b. Speeches are an example of oral communication.

N   d. Body language is an example of nonverbal communication.

20. a. PMBOK® Guide: Chapter 10 - Introduction
Y   a. Reports are an example of formal written communication.

N   b. Speeches are an example of formal oral communication.

N   c. E-mails are an example of informal written communication.

N   d. Hallway conversations are an example of informal oral communication.

21. d. PMBOK® Guide: Chapter 11 - Introduction

Y   d. Developing a risk management plan is the first thing we should do in risk management. This plan will tell us how to perform the other risk processes.

N   a. The risk management plan will us who should be involved in identifying risks.

N   b. The risk management plan will help us understand if it makes sense to perform quantitative risk analysis. There are many factors to consider.

N   c. At this point we do not know if avoid will be a good risk response technique or not for our project. There are many factors to consider.

22. a. PMBOK® Guide: Chapter 11 - Introduction

Y   a. An opportunity is a risk that has the potential for a positive outcome.

N   b. A threat is a risk that has the potential for a negative outcome.

N   c. An opportunity is a risk that has the potential for a positive outcome. Many organizations only use the term risk in association with possible negative outcomes. Be careful on the exam. Risk is a neutral word.

N   d. An issue is a negative risk that has occurred.

23. b. PMBOK® Guide: Chapter 11 - Introduction

Y   b. The risk tolerance is the amount of risk an organization is willing to take.

N   a. The risk appetite is how much risk an entity will take in anticipation for a certain reward.

N   c. The risk threshold is used to determine which risks require responses.

N   d. The risk probability is the chance of a risk occurring.

24. b. PMBOK® Guide: Chapter 11 - Introduction

Y   b. A threat is a risk that may lead to a negative outcome.

N   a. An opportunity is a risk that has the potential for a positive outcome.

N   c. An opportunity is a risk that has the potential for a positive outcome. Many organizations only use the term risk in association with possible negative outcomes. Be careful on the exam. Risk is a neutral word.

N   d. An issue is a negative risk that has occurred.

25. b. PMBOK® Guide: Chapter 11 - Introduction

Y   b. The overall project risk is the total effect of uncertainty on a project.

N   a. Adding up the value of the individual risks does not give us the overall risk on the project. Overall project risk looks at the project as a whole and not just individual elements added together.

N   c. Adding up the value of the negative individual risks does not give us the overall risk on the project.

N   d. Adding up the value of the positive individual risks does not give us the overall risk on the project.

26. b. PMBOK® Guide: Chapter 11 - Introduction

Y   b. An issue is a negative risk that has occurred.

N   a. This statement is reversed.

N   c. Issue and risks are not the same thing. Issues are negative risks that have occurred.

N   d. There is a strong relationship between risks and issues. An issue is a negative risk that has occurred.

27. d. PMBOK® Guide: Chapter 12 - Introduction

Y   d. A procurement management plan (or plans) would make it clear what items will be purchased from outside suppliers. Also these plans should address long lead items.

N   a. The question states nothing about issues with procurement SOWs.

N   b. and c. The procurement management plans will tell us if we should use letters of intent and penalties with our suppliers.

28. a. PMBOK° Guide: Chapter 12 - Introduction

Y   a. A purchase order is often considered a simple contract.

N   b. and c. A request for proposal and a request for quote are documents that are requesting the seller to make an offer to sell. These documents themselves are not contracts though they may be referenced in the final contract.

N   d. A request for information is a document that requests potential sellers to provide information. This document is not a contract though it may be referenced in the final contract.

29. c. PMBOK° Guide: Chapter 12 - Introduction

Y   c. Sellers are often referred to as the bidder before they are selected.

N   a. and b. Sellers are often referred to as the contracted vendor or contracted supplier once they are under contract to the buyer.

N   d. The customer is sometimes referred to as the client.

30. b. PMBOK° Guide: Chapter 12 - Introduction

Y   b. The process of awarding the contract is called conduct procurements.

N   a. The process of coming up with a plan for the procurement is called plan procurement management.

N   c. The process of overseeing the day-to-day work of the contracted supplier, including making payments, is called control procurements.

N   d. The process of ending the contract relationship with the contracted supplier is called close procurements.

31. a. PMBOK° Guide: Chapter 12 - Introduction

Y   a. Make or buy analysis is a general management technique used in plan procurements.

N   b. A bidder conference is an example of a tool and technique used in conduct procurements.

N   c. A contract change control system is an example of a tool and technique used in control procurements.

N   d. The procurement audit is an example of a tool and technique used in close procurements.

32. c. PMBOK° Guide: Chapter 12 - Introduction

Y   c. In a contract both the buyer and the seller have obligations. At a minimum the buyer has the obligation to provide monetary or other valuable compensation.

N   a. The buyer has an obligation but it does not always need to be in the form of money. The buyer may have an obligation to write a review of the seller's work.

N   b. The buyer and the seller both have obligations under a contract.

N   d. The seller has the obligation to provide a product, service, or result.

© January 2016 AME Group, Inc. author Aileen Ellis, PMP, PgMP
aileen@amegroupinc.com 719-659-3658

CLOSING PROCESS

There are 2 processes of closing. These processes ensure that all processes across all process groups are finished so as to close out the phase, project or contractual obligation.

Closing may occur when all the work is completed or may occur prematurely. An example of a premature close would be a terminated contract with a supplier.

Normally we would close out all procurements on a project before we would state that the project is officially closed. Also releasing final resources is often the final activity on a project.

Based on *the PMP Examination Content outline* published in June of 2015 by PMI there are seven (7) tasks of Closing. These processes represent 7% of your exam content. Key phrases associated with each task are:

Task	Key Words
Task 1	Obtain final acceptance of the project deliverables
Task 2	Transfer the ownership of the project deliverables
Task 3	Obtain financial, legal and administrative closure
Task 4	Prepare and share the final project report
Task 5	Collate lessons learned
Task 6	Archive project documents
Task 7	Obtain feedback from relevant stakeholders

The last table lists the key words for the tasks of the Closing Process Group. These tasks are not listed in the PMBOK® Guide. These tasks come from the PMP® Exam Content Outline. You do not need to memorize these tasks for the exam. It is good though for you to review them from time to time because these 7 tasks are the basis for the questions on Closing on the PMP® Exam. This Content Outline is absolutely an outline and therefore not robust enough to guide our studying in depth. Therefore almost everyone, if not everyone uses the PMBOK® Guide as their main reference when studying. The PMBOK® Guide includes processes not tasks. In the next few pages we cover the 2 processes of the Closing Process Group based on the PMBOK® Guide. If you try you can see how the tasks relate well to the processes. Both of the closing processes may occur at the same time though the close project or phase process would finish last.

© Jan 2016 AME Group, Inc. author Aileen Ellis, PMP, PgMP
aileen@amegroupinc.com 719-659-3658

Close Procurements

> ☑ **Exam Tip:** Review Figure 12-9 of the PMBOK° Guide.

In the process close procurements we take the steps necessary to close-out each procurement. This may include many administrative items (administrative close-out) such as:
- Dealing with claims and disputes
- Managing records

Some procurements close even before all the deliverables are complete. We call this early termination. There are three (3) types of early termination:

Termination for default	The contract ends because one party believes the other party is not living up to its obligations.
Termination for mutual agreement	Both parties agree it is in their mutual best interest to end the contract even though there are still open obligations.
Termination for convenience	The contract may stipulate that the buyer has the right to terminate the contract at any time without a reason other than "it is convenient." In some countries the government of the country sets up all their purchases this way. In reality, the seller could also have this right stipulated in the contract though the focus here is on the buyer having the right.

INPUTs to close procurements

Project management plan - the procurement management plan, as a subset of the project management plan, provides guidance on the process of close procurements.

Procurement documents - appropriate documents associated with the procurement should be collected and archived. The documentation may be used in the future to help plan new procurements and even to help select seller.

TOOLs and TECHNIQUEs of close procurements

Procurement audit - during close procurements we may audit all the procurement processes to collect lessons learned.

> ☑ **EXAM TIP:** Remember the word audit is associated with processes not deliverables. We are auditing the procurement processes, not inspecting the deliverables from the supplier.

Procurement negotiations - as our contract with our supplier ends we want to reach a fair settlement. As stated earlier, below is a list in order of preference of methods to help us reach a fair settlement, etc.

© January 2016 AME Group, Inc. author Aileen Ellis, PMP, PgMP
aileen@amegroupinc.com 719-659-3658

- Negotiations- both parties negotiate and work out disagreements (preferred method)
- Mediation- a third party mediator is brought in to help parties work out their disagreements
- Arbitration- a third party arbitrator is brought in to make a decision
- Litigation- the disagreement goes to court and a decision is made (least desirable method due to time, cost, and potential loss of reputation)

Records management system- hopefully we were archiving our documents related to this procurement throughout the control procurements process. At the end we want to archive the final documents.

OUTPUTs from close procurements (not all listed)

Closed procurements- after the final deliverable has been accepted and the final invoice submitted and paid, the buyer, through its procurement administrator should give the seller formal written notice that the contract is closed out.

CLOSE PROCUREMENTS - Sample Questions

1. Which of the following is the most desirable option to deal with disagreements on contracts:
a. negotiation
b. mediation
c. arbitration
d. litigation

2. Administrative items that are part of close procurements include all of the following except:
a. finalizing open claims
b. updating records
c. archiving information
d. responding to request for proposals

3. All of the following are types of early termination except:
a. termination for default
b. termination for completion
c. termination by mutual consent
d. termination for convenience

4. A procurement audit is:
a. a review of the procurement processes
b. a review of the accepted procurement product
c. a review of the rejected procurement product
d. a review of the contract for missed requirements

5. Which of the following is the least desirable option to deal with disagreements on contracts:
a. negotiation
b. mediation
c. arbitration
d. litigation

6. Reserve analysis as a tool and technique of risk monitoring and control looks at:
a. plan versus actual on cost performance
b. plan versus actual on schedule performance
c. the amount of contingency reserve remaining versus the amount of risk remaining
d. the amount of money remaining versus the amount of work remaining

© January 2016 AME Group, Inc. author Aileen Ellis, PMP, PgMP
aileen@amegroupinc.com 719-659-3658

CLOSE PROCUREMENTS - Solutions

1. a. PMBOK® Guide: Section 12.4.2.2
Y   a. Negotiation is the preferred method. If possible we want to try to resolve issues in a timely manner and dispassionately.

N   b. Mediation means bringing in a third party to help us work out the issue. If we cannot work things out between ourselves and the supplier through negotiation, then mediation may be a good fallback option.

N   c. Arbitration means bringing in a third party to hear both sides and make a decision on the issue. If we cannot work things out between ourselves and the supplier through negotiation, then mediation or arbitration may be good fallback options.

N   d. Litigation is often the least preferred method because of the time, the cost, and the risk to our reputation.

2. d. PMBOK® Guide: Section 12.4
Y   d. Responding to requests for proposal is an action the seller would take during the conduct procurements process, not the close procurements process.

N   a. During close procurements we may have open claims that need to be closed.

N   b. During close procurements we may have records that need to be updated.

N   c. During close procurements we may have information that needs to be achieved.

3. b. PMBOK® Guide: Section 12.4
Y   b. There is no such phrase as termination for completion. The word termination implies ending something before it is completed.

N   a. Termination for default is the premature end of a contract because one (or more) of the parties is not meeting its obligations.

N   c. Termination by mutual agreement is the premature end of a contract with all parties in agreement even though there are open obligations.

N   d. Termination for convenience must be defined in the contract. It is the premature end of a contract because one party, usually the buyer, feels it is in their best interest to end the contract and the contract gives them the right to do this.

4. a. PMBOK® Guide: Section 12.4.2.1
Y   a. A procurement audit is the review of the procurement processes.

N   b. and c. Audits usually are associated with processes not products.

N   d. The procurement audit is performed at the end of the contract life. This would be too late to look for missing requirements.

> ☑ **EXAM TIP:** Remember the word audit is associated with processes not deliverables. We are auditing the procurement processes, not inspecting the deliverables from the supplier.

5. d. PMBOK® Guide: Section 12.4.2.2
Y   d. Litigation is often the least preferred method because of the time, the cost, and the risk to our reputation.

N   a. Negotiation is the preferred method. If possible we want to try to resolve issues in a timely manner and dispassionately.

N   b. Mediation means bringing in a third party to help us work out the issue. If we cannot work things out between ourselves and the supplier through negotiation, then mediation may be a good fallback option. Mediation is preferred over litigation.

N   c. Arbitration means bringing in a third party to hear both sides and make a decision on the issue. If we cannot work things out between ourselves and the supplier through negotiation, then mediation or arbitration may be good fallback options. Arbitration is preferred over litigation.

6. c.   PMBOK® Guide 11.6.2.1

Y   c. Reserve analysis as part of risk monitoring and control compares the amount of contingency reserve remaining versus the amount of risk remaining.

N   a. Earned value analysis compares plan versus actual on cost performance through the CPI.

N   b. Earned value analysis compares plan versus actual on schedule performance through the SPI.

N   d. Earned value analysis compares the amount of money remaining versus the amount of work remaining through the TCPI (to complete performance index).

☑ **EXAM TIP:** The last question has nothing to do with close procurements. Every time you read a question ask yourself- What knowledge area am I in? What process group am I in? Do I know what process I am in? These answers may give you clues to the right answers.

© January 2016 AME Group, Inc. author Aileen Ellis, PMP, PgMP
aileen@amegroupinc.com 719-659-3658

Close Project or Phase

☑ **Exam Tip:** Review Figure 4-13 of the PMBOK® Guide.

Close project or phase is the process of completing all work for the project or the phase. Closure is measured against the scope baseline.

A big element of close project or phase is administrative closure. Administrative closure includes actions to:
- meet exit criteria
- transition of ownership of product
- manage project records
- release final resources
- etc.

INPUTs of close project or phase

Project management plan- completion of the project is measured against the project and specifically the scope baseline.

Accepted deliverables- these accepted deliverables are an output of validate scope. The customer has already accepted the deliverables as part of validate scope and now are going to receive ownership.

Organizational process assets- ex. Closure guidelines

TOOLs and TECHNIQUEs of close project or phase

Expert judgment- bring in experts to ensure all closure standards are met.

Analytical techniques- these techniques are used to measure project metrics.

Meetings- multiple meetings may be needed at the end of the project or phase. Ex. Lessons learned session.

OUTPUTs of close project or phase

Final product or service or result transition- the customer has already accepted the individual project deliverables. At this point we want to turn over ownership of the product(s) in total.

☑ **EXAM TIP:** The exam may ask multiple questions about closing the project. We have to make sure:

- Completion of the project is measured against the project management plan. We must make sure we have completed the work of the project.

- Completing the work of the project is not enough. We must achieve acceptance from the customer.

- Records must be managed and lessons learned collected.

The final "event" is to release the final resources.

CLOSE PROJECT OR PHASE - Sample Questions

1. The project has entered the close project or phase process. Along with the organizational process assets updates another critical output is:
a. verified deliverables
b. final product, service, or result transition
c. accepted deliverables
d. procurement documents

2. Accepted deliverables come into the close project or phase process from:
a. validate scope
b. control quality
c. perform quality assurance
d. direct and manage project work

3. All of the following are considered elements of the close project or phase process except:
a. finalizing all activities for the phase or the project
b. ensuring the project work is complete and project has met its objectives
c. finalizing open claims with our vendors
d. completing other administrative closure activities

4. The project has entered the close project or phase process. Along with the project management plan and the organizational process assets another critical input is:
a. verified deliverables
b. final product, service, or result transition
c. accepted deliverables
d. issue logs

5. Your project has finally reached the close project or phase process. There is a lot to do and you and your few remaining team members are very busy. All of the following are examples of close project or phase activities except:
a. customer acceptance of completed deliverables
b. satisfaction of exit criteria
c. collection of final project or phase records
d. audit of project success or failure

6. Your organization has been producing snack foods for over 50 years. Your current project is an extension of a very successful product line of highly processed chips. With the current interest in healthy food, your project has suddenly been terminated. There is a lot to do when a project is terminated. What is most important to focus on first?
a. archiving all phase/project records
b. releasing resources
c. reviewing work packages to understand current status
d. working with subcontractors to end all open contracts

CLOSE PROJECT OR PHASE - Solutions

1. b. PMBOK° Guide: Section 4.6.3.1
Y   b. At the close of a phase or a project, ownership of the deliverables is transferred to the sponsor or the customer.
N   a. Verified deliverables are an output of control quality. Verified means the deliverables are correct.
N   c. Accepted deliverables are an output of validate scope and an input to close project/phase.
N   d. Procurement documents are not related to this process.

2. a. PMBOK° Guide: Figure 4-13
Y   a. Accepted deliverables are an output of validate scope.
N   b. Verified deliverables are an output of control quality. Verified deliverables are an input to validate scope, not close project or phase.
N   c. Deliverables are not inputs or outputs of perform quality assurance.
N   d. Deliverables, not verified, not accepted, are an output of direct and manage project work.

3. c. PMBOK° Guide: Sections 4.6 and 12.4.2.2
Y   c. Finalizing open claims with our vendors is part of close procurements not close project/phase.
N   a., b., and d. All of these ideas are part of close project or phase. Completing administrative elements during this process is sometimes called administrative closure.

4. c. PMBOK° Guide: Section 4.6.1.2
Y   c. Accepted deliverables, as an output of validate scope, become an input to close project/phase.
N   a. Verified deliverables, meaning the deliverables are correct, are an output of control quality and an input of validate scope.
N   b. The final product, service, or result transition is an output of close project/phase.
N   d. Issue logs are not an input or an output of close project/phase.

5. a. PMBOK° Guide: Section 4.6 and 5.5
Y   a. Each of the deliverables should be accepted by the customer in the validate scope process not the close project or phase process.
N   b., c., and d. These activities are all part of close project or phase.

6. c. PMBOK° Guide: Section 4.6.1.2
Y   c. We need to understand the status of the work packages for multiple reasons. It is important to know if any of the work on the project to date is salvageable. From a different standpoint we need to review the status of the work packages to collect lessons learned.
N   b., c., and d. While we should do all of these activities, we first want to review the status of the work packages. We may need resources, including subcontractor resources to do this.

© January 2016 AME Group, Inc. author Aileen Ellis, PMP, PgMP
aileen@amegroupinc.com 719-659-3658

CLOSING- Other ideas

These ideas are based on information in the PMP® Exam Content Outline published by PMI® on June 2015 for inclusion on the PMP® Exam beginning January 12, 2016.   For the exam you do not need to know which tasks or which knowledge and skills have been added. The information in the tasks and knowledge and skills may be on your PMP® exam.

Closing knowledge and skills:

Performance measurement techniques (KPI and key success factors):

Based on business objectives organizations determine their key success factors (KSFs). Many organizations will use the terms critical success factors (CSF) and key success factors (KSF) interchangeably.   Key performance indicators (KPIs) are set up to track the key success factors. In other words KSFs are what we must do to be successful while the KPIs are what measures we are successful.

Key Performance Indicators (KPIs) are the performance measures an organization uses to determine if the project (or the organization) is successful. Deciding on KPIs requires a good understanding of what is important for the project to be successful. Some organizations use a balanced scorecard as a management framework to help them choose and measure their KPIs. In general we apply to SMART technique to KPIs. KPIs should be specific, measurable, attainable, realistic and time-based.

An important idea with KPIs is that of a leading indicator versus a lagging indicator. A lagging indicator is a measure of output produced. Lagging indicators are often easier to measure but harder to influence. A leading indicator is a measure of inputs. Leading indicators are sometimes harder to measure.

Here is an example. A big part of my business is selling project management workshops to individuals. A lagging indicator would be how many participants attend my workshops each month. A leading indicator would be how many potential participants call or email me to ask questions about attending a potential workshop.

Example of project KPIs:
- estimate to completion (ETC)
- Planned delivery date versus actual delivery date
- Return on Investment
- Number of open issues
- Current scope backlog

The PMIS (project management information system) may be used to gather and report on KPIs as well as other key success factors.

MINI-TEST after CLOSING- Questions

Strong suggestion: Do not write on these questions so you can attempt them again later.

1. The project manager has been working with the sponsor as well as other key stakeholders on the project charter. The project charter has been approved and it is time to inform the stakeholders. One of the primary reasons we want to inform the stakeholders of charter approval is:
a. formalize the authority of the project manager
b. validate project alignment with organizational strategy and expected business value
c. support the evaluation of the feasibility of new products or services
d. ensure a common understanding of the key deliverables, milestones and stakeholder roles and responsibilities

2. While initiating a project a project manager may often perform a project assessment based upon available information, lessons learned from previous projects, and meetings with relevant stakeholders in order to:
a. validate project alignment with organizational strategy and expected business value
b. support the feasibility of new products or services within the given assumptions and constraints
c. ensure a common understanding of the key deliverables, milestones and stakeholder roles and responsibilities
d. ensure stakeholders are in agreement with the project charter

3. Most successful organizations today have a strategic plan. The strategic plan must fit within the organizations values. One view of organizational values is:
a. why the organization exists and what it plans to achieve
b. what the future state of the organization will look like
c. how the organization will evaluate necessary tradeoffs and balance the decisions to be made
d. what benefits the program is expected to deliver

4. Value is delivered when:
a. the beneficiaries receive the project deliverables
b. the beneficiaries utilize the project benefits
c. the beneficiaries accept the verified deliverables
d. the beneficiaries accept the project benefits

5. The estimating technique that most likely will result in a transparent and structured estimate that can be tracked and managed is:
a. analogous estimating
b. top-down estimating
c. parametric estimating
d. bottom-up estimating

6. We are in the process of determining if the product deliverables are being built correctly. Often we use our organization's quality standards to help with this determination. These quality standards are included in the:
a. enterprise environmental factors
b. organizational process assets
c. work performance data
d. quality management plan

© January 2016 AME Group, Inc. author Aileen Ellis, PMP, PgMP
aileen@amegroupinc.com 719-659-3658

7. An important part of knowledge management is determining what knowledge is valuable and what knowledge is not as valuable. All of the following are ways organizations may determine what knowledge is valuable except:
a. project managers specify critical knowledge
b. reviewing what knowledge is required for regulatory compliance
c. realizing that all knowledge is valuable
d. utilizing industry practices and benchmarks to determine critical knowledge

8. Organizations often struggle to get the learning expected from KPIs. A typical mistake many organizations make when setting up KPIs is:
a. the organization makes KPIs too simple and easy to understand
b. the organization relates KPIs to corporate and project goals
c. the organization creates too many KPIs
d. the organization includes leading indicators of performance

9. All of the following are elements of active listening except:
a. watching the body language of the speaker
b. paraphrasing what the speaker has said
c. stating agreement or disagreement with the ideas of the speaker
d. making eye contact

10. It has been decided that we want individuals to brainstorm ideas related to requirements. Once these ideas have been generated they will be consolidated in a visual way to reflect commonality and differences in understanding and to generate new ideas. What group creativity idea is being used:
a. multi-criteria decision analysis
b. affinity diagrams
c. idea/mind mapping
d. nominal group technique

11. An organization scoring high on Geert Hofstede's uncertainty avoidance index:
a. likes uncertainty and can deal with it easily
b. has a positive attitude town change
c. prefers a competitive climate
d. has a low tolerance for deviate behavior

12. Emotional Intelligence is the capacity to be aware of, control, and express one's emotions, and to handle interpersonal relationships judiciously and empathetically. The term gained prominence in 1995 when which prominent psychologist published a book on the topic?
a. Goleman
b. Goldratt
c. McGregor
d. Maslow

13. Most unsuccessful projects are impacted by poor decision-making. Many successful organizations improve decision making by all of the following except:
a. elevating most project decisions to the project sponsor
b. embedding a culture that enables an effective decision-making process and supports the people making the decisions
c. providing the right support and information to the people making project and program decisions
d. establishing and following a transparent process to support decision making

14. In your providence there is currently one major road connecting the east and west. There are many problems with this road. The most pressing problem is that the road is closed on multiple days each year because of weather. It has been proposed to design and build a tunnel through a mountain pass that is the current site of the road closures. The government has approved the proposal and you have been named the project manager. An important step at this point is to get the project stakeholders to accept and commit to the tunnel project. Most likely what phase of the decision making model is the project in:
 a. solution action planning
 b. problem definition
 c. ideas to action
 d. problem solution generation

15. The project is at a critical go/no-decision point. Based on history you realize this is a good time to collect lessons learned. Lessons learned should be:
a. followed as long as they support the strategic vision of the organization
b. published on the corporate website so that others may benefit from your knowledge
c. discussed with the current relevant parties but otherwise remain private
d. documented as part of the historical database for both the project and the performing organization

16. Historically, your organization has struggled with stakeholder management. In fact the term stakeholder management is new to your organization and most people do not understand what it really means. Your projects experience a tremendous number of change requests and many of these requests occur late in the project causing schedule delays and cost overruns. You believe the root cause of these requests is the lack of stakeholder engagement. Therefore, you have decided on your current project to put a much stronger focus on stakeholder management. At an early team meeting the members of the core team are arguing as to what is really the first thing to do to address this issue. You tell them we must focus first on:
a. identifying and prioritizing our project stakeholders
b. developing a stakeholder management plan to help us engage our stakeholders
c. actively engaging with all stakeholders the same way so no stakeholder feels left out
d. actively engaging with the most important stakeholders

17. Work performance information is an output of what process?
a. identify stakeholders
b. plan stakeholder management
c. manage stakeholder engagement
d. control stakeholder engagement

18. Stakeholder analysis is a tool and technique of what process?
a. identify stakeholders
b. plan stakeholder management
c. manage stakeholder engagement
d. control stakeholder engagement

19. Information management systems is a tool and technique of what process?
a. identify stakeholders
b. plan stakeholder management
c. manage stakeholder engagement
d. control stakeholder engagement

© January 2016 AME Group, Inc. author Aileen Ellis, PMP, PgMP
aileen@amegroupinc.com 719-659-3658

20. What plans are inputs of manage stakeholder engagement?
a. stakeholder management plan and communications management plan
b. stakeholder management plan and human resource plan
c. human resource plan and communications management plan
d. human resource plan and configuration management plan

21. Issue logs are an output of what process?
a. identify stakeholders
b. plan stakeholder management
c. manage stakeholder engagement
d. control stakeholder engagement

22. The five project management process groups include:
a. initiating, planning, executing, monitoring and controlling
b. integration, scope, time, cost, and quality
c. initiating, planning, executing, monitoring and controlling, and closing
d. concept, planning, execution, controlling, and closeout

23. Verified deliverables are an output of which process?
a. validate scope
b. control quality
c. close project or phase
d. direct and manage project work

24. Accepted deliverables are an output of:
a. validate scope
b. control quality
c. close project or phase
d. direct and manage project work

25. Large projects are often separated into distinct phases. The process groups are:
a. the same as these project phases
b. normally repeated in each of these phases
c. related to the product and, therefore, not related to the project phases
d. related to project management and, therefore, not related to the project phases

26. Some of the work of which process group are normally performed external to the project's boundary?
a. initiating
b. planning
c. executing
d. monitoring and controlling

27. In multi-phase projects, the initiating processes occur:
a. only during the concept phase
b. in every phase
c. only in the early phases
d. only when the sponsor requests them

28. The project becomes officially authorized through the:
a. approval of the concept phase gate
b. approval of the project charter
c. approval of the WBS
d. approval of the scope statement

29. The document that describes in detail the project's deliverables and the work required to create those deliverables is:
a. project charter
b. scope statement
c. scope management plan
d. WBS

30. The process group that must provide feedback to implement corrective or preventive action is:
a. planning
b. executing
c. monitoring and controlling
d. implementation

31. The project scope statement is the primary output of:
a. define scope
b. collect requirements
c. develop project management plan
d. create WBS

32. The scope baseline is an output of:
a. create WBS
b. collect requirements
c. define scope
d. define activities

33. The schedule baseline is an output of:
a. define activities
b. develop project management plan
c. develop schedule
d. estimate activity durations

34. The cost baseline is an output of:
a. estimate costs
b. determine budget
c. control costs
d. develop schedule

35. The procurement statement of work is an output of:
a. collect requirements
b. plan procurement management
c. develop project management plan
d. define scope

36. The cost management plan is an output of which process?
a. estimate costs
b. determine budget
c. plan cost management
d. estimate activity resources

© January 2016 AME Group, Inc. author Aileen Ellis, PMP, PgMP
aileen@amegroupinc.com 719-659-3658

MINI-TEST after CLOSING- Solutions

1. d. *PMP® Exam content outline- June 2015*
Y   d. We want to inform the stakeholders of charter approval in order to ensure a common understanding of the key deliverables, milestones and stakeholder roles and responsibilities.
N   a. We want to obtain charter approval in order to formalize the authority of the project manager.
N   b. We want to conduct benefit analysis in order to validate project alignment with organizational strategy and expected business value.
N   c. We want to perform a project assessment in order to support the evaluation of the feasibility of new products or services.

2. b. *PMP® Exam content outline Initiating-Task 1- June 2015*
Y   *b.* We perform a project assessment based on available information, lessons learned from previous projects, and meetings with relevant stakeholders in order to support the feasibility of new products or services within the given assumptions and constraints.

3. c.
Y   c. Organizations often look at their values to help evaluate necessary trade-offs and make decisions.
N   a. The mission of an organization is why it exists.
N   b. The desired future state of an organization is the organization's vision.
N   d. The benefits register should list the expected benefits from a project or program.

4. b.
Y   Value is delivered when the beneficiaries (often called the customer or end users) utilize the project benefits.

5. d. *PMBOK® Guide Section 6.4.2.4*
Y   d. Bottom-up estimates provide a transparent means of tracking and managing an estimate.

6. b. *PMBOK® Guide Section 8.3.1.8*
Y   b. Organizational standards are contained in the organizational process assets.

7. c.
Y   c. This answer is the exception because of the word "all". All is an extreme word.

8. c.
Y   c. If we have too many KPIs we become lost in the detail and managing KPIs becomes a project of its own.

9. c. *Wikipedia on Active Listening*
Y   c. Active listening is about listening. While stating agreement or disagreement with the speaker's ideas may be a good practice at times it is not considered part of active listening.

10. c. *PMBOK® Guide Section 5.2.2.4*
Y   c. Idea/mind maps are a way to plot ideas on a visual map to see commonality as well as differences and to generate new ideas.

11. d. *Wikipedia Hofstede's cultural dimensions theory*

Y   d. The Uncertainty Avoidance Index is defined as " a society's tolerance for ambiguity." An organization that scores high has a strong uncertainty avoidance index and therefore has a low tolerance for deviate behavior.

N   a., b. and c. An organization that scores low on the uncertainty avoidance index likes uncertainty, has a positive attitude toward change and often prefers a competitive climate.

12.   a.   *Wikipedia- Emotional Intelligence*

Y   a.   The term emotional intelligence gained prominence in 1995 when Daniel Goleman published a book by that title.

13. a.

Y   a. Elevating most project decisions to the project sponsor turns the sponsor into the project manager. Most projects sponsors do not have time or interest in being the project manager.

14. a. *PMBOK® Guide Section X3.6*

Y   a. During solution action planning our goal is to involve key stakeholders so as to gain acceptance and commitment to making the solution work.

15.   d.   *PMBOK® Guide Section 8.3.3.8*

Y   d. Lessons learned sound become part of the historical database for both the project and the organization.

16. a. PMBOK® Guide: Figure 13-1

Y   a. Did you get tricked by this question? Many people will pick answer b. The best answer though is answer a. We must first identify the stakeholders before we can plan how to engage them.

N   b., c., and d. We must first identify stakeholders before we can plan how to engage with them. The stakeholder management plan will tell us how to engage with stakeholders. Most likely we will not engage with each stakeholder the same way since each stakeholder is different. Some are more interested in the project than others. Some are more powerful than others. Etc.

17. d. PMBOK® Guide: Figure 13-1

Y   d. Work performance information is an output of control stakeholder engagement.

EXAM TIP: Remember work performance information is only an output of control processes.

18. a. PMBOK® Guide: Figure 13-1

Y   a. Stakeholder analysis is a tool and technique of identify stakeholders.

19. d. PMBOK® Guide: Figure 13-1

Y   d. Information management systems is a tool and technique of control stakeholder engagement.

20. a. PMBOK® Guide: Figure 13-1

Y   a. Manage stakeholder engagement has two plans as inputs: the stakeholder management plan and the communications management plan.

N   b., c., and d. The human resource plan is associated with the team, and not the stakeholders. It would only be an input to processes related to the team.

21. c. PMBOK® Guide: Figure 13-1

Y   c. Issue logs are an output of manage stakeholder engagement.

22. c. PMBOK° Guide: Chapter 3 - Introduction
Y   c. The five process groups are: initiating, planning, executing, monitoring and controlling, and closing.

23. b. PMBOK® Guide: A1.7.7
Y   b. Verified deliverables are an output of control quality.

24. a. PMBOK° Guide: A1.7.2
Y   a. Accepted deliverables are an output of validate scope.

25. b. PMBOK° Guide: A1.3
Y   b. The five process groups are repeated in each of the project phases.

26. a. PMBOK° Guide: A1.4
Y   a. The develop project charter process on the initiating process group is performed before the project begins (external to the project's boundary).

27. b. PMBOK° Guide: A1.4
Y   b. In multi-phase projects the initiating processes occur in every phase.

28. b. PMBOK° Guide: A1.4
Y   b. The project charter is the document that officially authorizes the project.

29. b. PMBOK° Guide: A1.5.4
Y   b. The scope statement describes the project deliverables and the work required to create those deliverables.

30. c. PMBOK° Guide: A1.7
Y   c. The monitoring and controlling process group provides feedback to implement corrective and preventative action.

31. a. PMBOK° Guide: A1.5.4
Y   a. The scope statement is an output of the process define scope.

32. a. PMBOK° Guide: A1.5.5
Y   a. The scope baseline is an output of the process create WBS.

33. c. PMBOK° Guide: A1.5.11
Y   c. The schedule baseline is an output of the process develop schedule.

34. b. PMBOK° Guide: A1.5.14
Y   b. The cost baseline is an output of determine budget.

35. b. PMBOK° Guide: A1.5.23
Y   b. The procurement statement of work is an output of plan procurement management.

36. c. PMBOK° Guide: A1.5.12
Y   c. The cost management plan is an output of plan cost management.

Cross-Cutting Knowledge and Skills

These ideas are based on information in the PMP® Exam Content Outline published by PMI® on June 2015 for inclusion on the PMP® Exam beginning January 12, 2016.   For the exam you do not need to know which tasks or which knowledge and skills have been added. The information in the tasks and knowledge and skills may be on your PMP® exam.   Many of these ideas have been covered elsewhere in this book.   Therefore not all new cross-cutting knowledge areas and skills are listed here.

Active Listening
Active listening is a communication technique in which the listener feeds back to the speaker what the listener has heard in his own words. The goal of active listening is for the speaker to confirm what he has heard and more importantly to confirm an understanding between both parties. An understanding does not imply an agreement.

Applicable Laws and Regulations:
In order to sit for the PMP® Exam we need to have agreed to follow the *Project Management Institute Code of Ethics and Professional Conduct.* It carries the obligation to comply with laws, regulations, and organizational and professional policies.   Another place on the exam we might see a reference to laws and regulations is with regards to collect requirements. As we collect requirements we should perform a document analysis. Laws may help us elicit requirements.

Brainstorming techniques
Brainstorming is a group creativity technique use to generate multiple ideas on a single topic. There are several guidelines (some people would say rules) on brainstorming. In no particular order:
- We want lots of ideas. Quantity may lead to quality
- Every idea is a good idea. Do not critique ideas while brainstorming
- Welcome crazy ideas
- Allow and encourage the combination or add-on effect of ideas

There are many variations and/or other methods related to brainstorming:
- Nominal group technique- this is a voting technique usually used after brainstorming
- Group passing technique- People sit in a circle. Each person writes down one idea and then passes the paper to the next person. It continues until each person gets his or her original idea back. The original ideas most often will have been greatly elaborated by this point.
- Team idea mapping method- each person brainstorms one idea separately. Ideas are then added to an idea map. As the map is developed commonalities may be visible and new ideas emerge due to association.
- Question brainstorming- sometimes called Questorming.   The questions are brainstormed.   Therefore everyone should be able to participant. Often the questions are prioritized before determining solutions.
- Affinity diagrams- group similar ideas together

Business Acumen
Business acumen is keenness and quickness in understanding and dealing with a business situation in a manner that is likely to lead to a good outcome.[The term "business acumen" can be broken down literally as a composite of its two component words: Business literacy is defined in SHRM's Business Literacy Glossary as "the knowledge and understanding of the financial, accounting, marketing and operational functions of an organization." The Oxford English Dictionary defines acumen as "the ability to make good judgments and quick

decisions. Another ideas I would add to this is that business acumen includes using appropriate business terms when communicating with others in the organization.

We need to understand how our project, the work we do and the decisions we make affect the others in the organization and the organization itself.

Coaching, mentoring, training and motivational techniques

Coaching: Example- we coach a team member on how to write better requirements
- Means to develop the project team to higher levels of competency and performance
- Often a shorter term relationship with more specific and measurable outcomes when contrasted with mentoring
- Also used to address poor performance
- Not the same as counseling
  - Coaching- helps the person move from "can't do" to "can do"
  - Counseling- helps the person move from "won't do" to "will do"

Mentoring: Example- we mentor a team member on how to be a more inspiring leader
- Often a more long term relationship than coaching
- The mentor guides the mentee

Training-See the process Develop Project Team for information on Training.

Motivation: creating a project environment where individuals can achieve maximum satisfaction based on what they value. Examples of what they value may include:
- a sense accomplishment related to performance
- a sense of belonging based on work relationships
- a sense of growth and learning
- rewards, recognition, etc.

See the process Manage Project Team for information on Motivation.

Configuration management (CM)

Configuration management are the processes, activities, etc. used to manage certain items during the life of the project. Items to be managed under configuration control often include physical items, documents, forms and records. CM provides visibility and control over an items performance as well as functional and physical attributes.

Decision making: (*Pulse of the Profession®: Capturing the Value of Project Management Through Decision Making 6 August 2015 PMI and PMBOK® Guide 5th Edition*)

There are four basic decision styles used by project managers:
- Command- the project manager makes the decision. This may be appropriate provided that the project manager has the required knowledge and experience. We would only use this style if quality is more important than acceptance.
- Consultation- the project manager asks his team members for their opinions before he goes away and makes the decision. Often a project manager would use this style when the project manager is willing to admit, at least to himself, that he does not know everything. We would use this style when quality and acceptance are both important.
- Consensus –the team members are involved and reach agreement. We would use this style when acceptance is more important than quality.
- Coin flip (random)

There are four major factors that affect the decision style:
- Time constraints
- Trust
- Quality
- Acceptance

There are multiple decision-making models or processes. One six-phase model is:
1. Problem definition- fully explore, clarify, and define the problem
2. Problem solution generation- brainstorming multiple solutions and discouraging premature decisions
3. Ideas to action- define evaluation criteria, rate pros and cons of alternatives, select best solution
4. Solution action planning- involve key participants to gain acceptance and commitment
5. Solution evaluation planning- perform post-implementation analysis, evaluation and lessons learned
6. Evaluation of the outcome and process-evaluate how well the problem was solved or project goals obtained (extension of previous phase)

Diversity and cultural sensitivity:
Hofstede studies five cultural dimensions.

1.   **Power distance index**- measures to what extent the less powerful members of a group accept and expect that power is distributed unequally.
High power distance countries believe an unequal distribution of power is a basic fact of life. Power often comes from coercive or referent power. Low power distance countries believe in a more equal distribution of power. Power often comes from expect or legitimate power.

2.   **Individualism versus collectivism**- Individualism is about your separateness as a person while collectivism is about your obligation to others.

3.   **Masculinity versus feminism (stereotypes for each word)**- Masculine traits include assertiveness, self-centeredness, power, and a focus individual achievements and material success. Feminine traits would be more modest and caring.

4.   **Uncertainty avoidance index**- This index measures the extent in which people feel uncomfortable with uncertainty. High uncertainty avoidance countries try to minimize unstructured situations through laws and rules as well as safety and security measures.
Low uncertainty avoidance countries will try to make their citizens feel comfortable in unstructured and different situations.

5.   **Long term orientation versus short term orientation**-Long term orientation stands for the fostering of virtues oriented toward future rewards, in particular perseverance and thrift. Short term orientation stands for the fostering of virtues related to the past and present. An emphasis on quick results as well as the idea that leisure time is important would be traits of a short term orientation.

Emotional Intelligence:
Emotional Intelligence is the capacity to be aware of, control, and express one's emotions, and to handle interpersonal relationships judiciously and empathetically. Many believe that emotional intelligence may have a strong effect on both personal as well as professional success.

Facilitation :
In the *PMBOK®* Guide four types of facilitation techniques are listed. *They include:* Brainstorming , conflict resolution, problem solving and meeting management.. Please see more in previous sections on these ideas.

Generational sensitivity and Diversity:
Each generation has their own strengths and weaknesses. Understanding and respecting these differences in important to building a successful multigenerational workforce. Embracing the fact that young workers have knowledge to share can help to bridge the generation gap.

© January 2016 AME Group, Inc. author Aileen Ellis, PMP, PgMP
aileen@amegroupinc.com 719-659-3658

Example: Reverse mentoring- having a younger worker mentor an older more experienced worker in a new technology can help build and strength relationships. The long-term result is often that both parties learn from each other.

Knowledge management (*Pulse of the Profession®: Capturing the Value of Project Management Through Knowledge Transfer* by PMI 6 March 2015):

Knowledge transfer is the methodical replication of the expertise, wisdom, insight, and tacit knowledge of key professionals into the heads and hands of their coworkers.

Steps of the Knowledge Transfer Life Cycle:
1. Identifying- Determine what knowledge needs to be transferred
2. Capturing- Accumulate the essential knowledge that needs to be transferred
3. Sharing- Establish methods for transferring the knowledge
4. Applying- Use the knowledge that is transferred
5. Assessing- Evaluate the benefits of the knowledge that is transferred

Lessons learned:

Lessons learned are the knowledge collected throughout the project. We want to understand what we did, why we did it and what we may want to do differently in the future so as to improve performance. It is important to remember we should be collecting lessons learned throughout the project and not just at the end of the project. Also we want to be using the knowledge acquired through the lessons learned throughout the project and not just on the next project.

Influencing techniques:

Many projects occur in a matrix environment. Often the project manager has less authority than desired in this structure. Therefore the project manager may need to rely heavily on his/her ability to influence.

Organizational awareness:

Organizational awareness is a level of understanding and knowledge of our organization including culture, structure and governance. Understanding how things get done, through both official and un-official channels is an element of organizational awareness.

Peer-review processes:

A peer-review is the evaluation of scientific, academic, or professional works by others in the same field. In project management it often means having other project managers review your project in order to identify:
- Things you are doing well
- Things you could be doing better
- Things you are not doing that you should be doing
- Things you are doing that you should not be doing.

There are many benefits to a peer review. Often as the project manager we are to close to the project to identify the items listed above. A peer, with experience in project may be able to point out things we cannot see. We may later be asked to provide a peer review for someone else's project.

Situational awareness:

In simplistic terms situational awareness is knowing what is going on around you. It is understanding the environment in order to make critical decisions.

Quick Review - Sample Questions

1. Communication methods is a tool and technique of what process?
a. plan human resource management
b. plan communication management
c. identify stakeholders
d. plan quality

2. Avoid is a tool and technique of what process?
a. plan risk responses
b. plan human resource management
c. plan communications management
d. identify stakeholders

3. The cost of quality is a tool and technique of what process(es)?
a. perform quality assurance and control quality
b. estimate costs and plan quality
c. plan quality and determine budget
d. perform quality assurance and determine budget

4. Cost-benefit analysis is a tool and technique of what process?
a. estimate costs
b. determine budgets
c. control costs
d. plan quality

5. The people famous for Plan-Do-Check-Act are:
a. Juran and Crosby
b. Isikawa and Pareto
c. Tuckman and Isikawa
d. Shewhart and Deming

6. The change management plan is an output of what process?
a. develop project management plan
b. integrated change control
c. monitor and control project work
d. plan communications

7. The configuration management plan is an output of what process?
a. develop project management plan
b. integrated change control
c. monitor and control project work
d. plan communications

8. Sensitivity analysis is a tool and technique of what process?
a. plan human resource management
b. plan communications
c. identify stakeholders
d. perform quantitative risk analysis

© January 2016 AME Group, Inc. author Aileen Ellis, PMP, PgMP
aileen@amegroupinc.com 719-659-3658

9. Fixed price contracts and cost-reimbursable contracts are inputs to:
a. plan procurements
b. plan risk responses
c. plan communications
d. plan human resource management

10. Funding limit reconciliation is a tool and technique of what process?
a. estimate costs
b. determine budget
c. develop project management plan
d. plan quality

11. Overlapping activities or running them in parallel when we would prefer to run them in sequence is called:
a. crashing
b. resource leveling
c. fast tracking
d. critical chain

12. Benchmarking is a tool and technique of what process?
a. plan quality
b. plan communications
c. plan human resource management
d. plan procurements

13. Organizational theory is a tool and technique of what process?
a. plan quality
b. plan communications
c. plan human resource management
d. plan procurements

14. The document that describes how the project scope will be defined, documented, validated, managed, and controlled is called?
a. scope baseline
b. scope statement
c. scope management plan
d. WBS dictionary

15. The document that sets the criteria for planning and controlling project costs is called?
a. cost baseline
b. project budget
c. project funding
d. cost management plan

16. The document that describes the scheduling methodology, format, etc. is called?
a. project schedule
b. schedule baseline
c. network diagram
d. schedule management plan

17. Make or buy analysis is a general management technique used in?
a. plan procurements
b. plan communications
c. conduct procurements
d. control procurements

18. Roles and responsibilities and the project organization chart are subsets of what plan?
a. staffing management plan
b. communications plan
c. human resource plan
d. communications plan

19. Looking at other organizations to set quality standards and learn best practices is called?
a. cost-benefit analysis
b. benchmarking
c. flowcharting
d. affinity diagrams

20. The document that shows the planned start and finish dates for each project activity is called?
a. the project plan
b. the work breakdown structure
c. the project schedule
d. the activity list

21. A bidder conference is a tool and technique of what process?
a. conduct procurements
b. plan procurements
c. control procurements
d. plan human resource management

22. Buying insurance is an example of what risk response technique?
a. sharing
b. transfer
c. mitigate
d. avoid

23. Ground rules are a tool and technique of what process?
a. plan human resource management
b. acquire project team
c. develop project team
d. manage project team

24. Advertising is a tool and technique of what process?
a. conduct procurements
b. plan procurements
c. plan communications
d. plan human resource management

© January 2016 AME Group, Inc. author Aileen Ellis, PMP, PgMP
aileen@amegroupinc.com 719-659-3658

25. Teambuilding, used to build trust, is a tool and technique of what process?
a. plan human resource management
b. acquire project team
c. develop project team
d. manage project team

26. Quality audits are a tool and technique of what process?
a. plan quality
b. perform quality assurance
c. control quality
d. integrated change control

27. Deliverables are an output of what process?
a. direct and manage project work
b. perform quality assurance
c. control quality
d. integrated change control

28. Work performance information is an output of what process?
a. direct and manage project work
b. perform quality assurance
c. control quality
d. integrated change control

29. Project performance appraisals are a tool and technique of what process?
a. manage stakeholder engagement
b. manage project team
c. develop project team
d. monitor and control project work

30. Pre-assignment, often as part of a competitive proposal process, is a tool and technique of what process?
a. plan human resource management
b. acquire project team
c. develop project team
d. manage project team

31. The customer accepts the project deliverables during what process?
a. control quality
b. close project
c. validate scope
d. direct and manage project work

32. The deliverables are tested for correctness during what process?
a. control quality
b. close project
c. validate scope
d. direct and manage project work

33. Ensuring that the processes we are using are working is part of what process?
a. control quality
b. perform quality assurance
c. monitor and control project work
d. perform integrated change control

34. Setting priority for future risk work is the objective of what process?
a. plan risk management
b. risk identification
c. qualitative risk analysis
d. plan risk responses

35. Risk reassessment is a tool and technique of what process?
a. control risks
b. identify risks
c. qualitative risk analysis
d. plan risk responses

36. Change requests are an input to what process?
a. monitor and control project work
b. validate scope
c. control quality
d. perform integrated change control

37. Approved change requests are an output of what process?
a. monitor and control project work
b. validate scope
c. control quality
d. perform integrated change control

38. The project management information system is a tool of what process(es)?
a. develop project management plan and direct and manage project work
b. direct and manage project work and perform integrated change control
c. monitor and control project work and perform integrated change control
d. direct and manage project work and monitor and control project work

39. Change control tools are a tool and technique of what process?
a. develop project management plan
b. direct and manage project work
c. monitor and control project work
d. perform integrated change control

40. The document that describes explicitly what is out of scope is called?
a. project charter
b. scope statement
c. scope management plan
d. cost baseline

41. The WBS is:
a. task oriented
b. deliverable oriented
c. both task and deliverable oriented
d. neither task or deliverable oriented

42. The relationship between the scope management plan and the project management plan is described by which of the following?
a. the scope management plan is a subset of the project management plan
b. the project management plan is a subset of the scope management plan
c. the plans are not related
d. the plans are exactly the same

© January 2016 AME Group, Inc. author Aileen Ellis, PMP, PgMP
aileen@amegroupinc.com 719-659-3658

43. Critical path method is a tool and technique of what process?
a. define activities
b. sequence activities
c. develop schedule
d. estimate activity durations

44. All of the following are strategies to deal with risks with potentially positive impacts on project objectives except:
a. mitigate

b. exploit
c. share
d. enhance

45. Pre-assignment, negotiation, acquisition, and virtual teams are tools and techniques of:
a. plan human resource management
b. develop project team
c. acquire project team
d. manage project team

46. One tool and technique to help manage the project team is:
a. recommended corrective actions
b. recommended preventive actions
c. conflict management
d. team building

47. Alternative generation is a tool and technique of what process(es)?
a. collect requirements
b. define scope
c. collect requirements and define scope
d. define activities

48. Ad hoc conversations with our peers are examples of what type of communication?
a. vertical
b. horizontal
c. formal verbal
d. informal written

49. Which statement represents the relationship between precision and accuracy?
a. precise measurements are accurate
b. accurate measurements are precise
c. precision and accuracy are not equivalent
d. a high level of precision and accuracy are always required

50. Virtual teams support all the following except:
a. people on different shifts
b. people who need to co-locate
c. people with mobility handicaps
d. people who must live in widespread areas

51. The risks placed on a watch list for continued monitoring usually include:
a. risks requiring a near-term response
b. risks assessed as important, based on qualitative risk analysis
c. risks assessed as not important, based on qualitative risk analysis
d. risk requiring additional analysis and response

52. The configuration management plan is an output of what process?
a. develop project management plan
b. integrated change control
c. monitor and control project work
d. plan communications

53. The leadership style that has the most risk of "perceived lip service" is:
a. consultative in a group
b. consensus
c. autocratic
d. directing

54. The upper and lower control limits are usually set at:
a. +/- 1 sigma
b. +/- 2 sigma
c. +/- 3 sigma
d. +/- 6 sigma

55. The 50-50 rule of progress reporting states that:
a. an activity gets credit when it is 50% complete and when it is 100% complete
b. an activity gets 50% credit for starting and the other 50% for completing
c. the contractor gets paid when the project is 50% complete and then again when the project is 100% complete
d. the contractor gets paid 50% when the project starts and the other 50% when the project completes

56. Your map making project has been going very well. With great resistance from upper management you have been using the technique of rolling wave planning. You are at the point of planning the closing of the project. The last thing we often do on projects is:
a. deliver the product to the customer
b. conduct lessons learned
c. hold a celebration
d. release resources

57. Project scope creep is another name for:
a. uncontrolled changes
b. influencing the factors that create project scope changes
c. controlling the impact of those changes
d. use of the integrated change control system

© January 2016 AME Group, Inc. author Aileen Ellis, PMP, PgMP
aileen@amegroupinc.com 719-659-3658

58. Your management is going through their quarterly process of project selection. In the past the organization has always used benefit measurement methods to select projects. It seems now they want to use constrained optimization methods. Which method below is your organization most likely to use now?
a. comparative approaches
b. scoring model
c. linear programming algorithm
d. murder board

59. As a project manager in the electronics field, it is clear that your projects are not top priority. After speaking with your management it is clear that the real issue is that your projects are not aligned with the corporate objectives. You convince your organization that one approach to help with alignment is to adopt the Management by Objectives (MBO) concept developed by Peter Drucker. All of the following are ideas associated with the objectives except:
a. focused on activities
b. specific
c. related to time
d. attainable

60. After several months of negotiations your organization is almost ready to sign a contract. The contract will span multiple years and allow for final price adjustments based on changing conditions. The ideal contract type is:
a. firm fixed price
b. fixed price incentive fee
c. fixed price with economic price adjustment
d. time and materials

61. Your organization is in the process of identifying risks for your project. You explain that there are really two types of risks called:
a. pure and insurable
b. pure and business
c. legal liability and personnel-related
d. direct property damage and indirect consequential loss

62. All of the following statements are true about communication blockers *except*:
a. the phrase "this will never work" is an example
b. they can get in the way of communication
c. they should be addressed proactively by the project manager
d. they should be ignored at all costs

63. Maslow's highest level, self-actualization needs, can be met in the workplace through:
a. rest periods, adequate compensation
b. safe working conditions
c. creative work
d. friendly co-workers

64. During control quality it has been determined that several of the deliverables due today do not meet the technical specifications. A change request has been generated and will be approved or rejected in which process?
a. monitor and control project work
b. perform integrated change control
c. validate scope
d. direct and manage project work

65. Colocation is most often associated with the:
a. strong matrix
b. projectized structure
c. weak matrix
d. composite structure

66. A system upgrade project is 60% complete. There are over 250 stakeholders located at hospitals throughout the region. The project is running on budget and slightly ahead of schedule. Risk management has been provided throughout the project. During control project risks several large risks have been closed out since the project is past the point when these threats would occur. Large cost contingencies had been set-up for these threats. The unused contingency should be:
a. moved to other risks on the project but stay as contingency reserve
b. moved to management reserve on this project
c. not moved, in case we need the money later
d. moved off the project and back to the organization

Quick Review – Solutions

1. b. PMBOK® Guide: Figure 10-1
Y   b. Communication methods is a tool and technique of plan communications management, manage communications, and manage stakeholder engagement.

2. a. PMBOK® Guide: Section 11.5.2.1
Y   a. Avoid is a tool and technique of plan risk responses.

3. b. PMBOK® Guide: Figure 7-1 and 8-1
Y   b. The cost of quality is a tool and technique of estimate costs and plan quality management.

4. d. PMBOK® Guide: Figure 8-1
Y   d. Cost-benefit analysis is a tool and technique of plan quality management.

5. d. PMBOK® Guide: Chapter 8 - Introduction
Y   d. Shewhart and Deming are well known for the plan-do-check-act cycle.

6. a. PMBOK® Guide: Section 4.2.3.1
Y   a. The change management plan is a subset of the project management plan. Therefore, it is an output of develop project management plan.

7. a. PMBOK® Guide: Section 4.2.3.1
Y   a. The configuration management plan is a subset of the project management plan. Therefore, it is an output of develop project management plan.

8. d. PMBOK® Guide: Section 11.4.2.2
Y   d. Sensitivity analysis helps us understand what risks the project is most sensitive to. It is a tool and technique of perform quantitative risk analysis.

9. a. PMBOK® Guide: Section 12.1.1.9
Y   a. Fixed price contracts and cost reimbursable contracts are inputs of plan procurements.

10. b. PMBOK® Guide: Figure 7-1
Y   b. Funding limit reconciliation is a tool and technique of determine budget. We use this tool to make sure our planned expenditures are in line with project funding.

11. c. PMBOK® Guide: Section 6.6.2.7
Y   c. Fast tracking is a tool and technique of develop schedule. We use it to compress the schedule by overlapping project phases or activities.

12. a. PMBOK® Guide: Section 8.1.2.4
Y   a. Benchmarking is a tool and technique of plan quality management and collect requirements.

13. c. PMBOK® Guide: Section 9.1.2.3
Y   c. Organizational theory is a tool and technique of plan human resource management.

14. c. PMBOK® Guide: Section 5.1
Y   c. The scope management plan describes the processes in which the scope will be defined, controlled, and validated.

15. d. PMBOK® Guide: Section 7.1

Y   d. The cost management plan describes how costs will be estimated, budgeted, and controlled.

16. d. PMBOK® Guide: Section 6.1

Y   d. The schedule management plan describes the scheduling methodology, format etc., as well as the processes for developing and controlling the project schedule.

17. a. PMBOK® Guide: Figure 12-1

Y   a. Make or buy analysis is a general management technique used in plan procurements.

18. c. PMBOK® Guide: Section 9.1.3.1

Y   c. The human resource plan contains the project organizational chart, the roles and responsibilities of different positions, as well as the staffing management plan.

19. b. PMBOK® Guide: Section 8.1.2.4

Y   b. Benchmarking is a tool and technique in which we look at another organization to help set quality standards or develop ideas on how to meet those standards.

20. c. PMBOK® Guide: Section 6.6.3.2

Y   c. The project schedule shows the planned start and finish dates for project activities.

21. a. PMBOK® Guide: Figure 12-1

Y   a. A bidder conference is a tool and technique of conduct procurements.

22. b. PMBOK® Guide: Section 11.5.2.1

Y   b. Buying insurance is an example of a transfer technique as part of plan risk responses.

23. c. PMBOK® Guide: Section 9.3.2.4

Y   c. Ground rules are a tool and technique of develop project team.

24. a. PMBOK® Guide: Section 12.2.2.5

Y   a. Advertising is a tool and technique of conduct procurements.

25. c. PMBOK® Guide: Section 9.3.2.3

Y   c. Teambuilding is a tool and technique of develop project team.

26. b. PMBOK® Guide: Section 8.2.2.2

Y   b. Quality audits are a tool and technique perform quality assurance.

27. a. PMBOK® Guide: Section 4.3.3.1

Y   a. Deliverables are an output of direct and manage project work.

28. c. PMBOK® Guide: Section 8.3.3.4

Y   c. Work performance information is an output of control quality.

29. b. PMBOK® Guide: Section 9.4.2.2

Y   b. Project performance appraisals are a tool and technique of manage team.

30. b. PMBOK® Guide: Section 9.2.2.1

Y   b. Pre-assignment is a tool and technique of acquire project team.

© January 2016 AME Group, Inc. author Aileen Ellis, PMP, PgMP
aileen@amegroupinc.com 719-659-3658

31. c. PMBOK® Guide: Section 5.5
Y   c. The customer accepts the project's deliverables as part of validate scope.

32. a. PMBOK® Guide: Section 8.3.3.3
Y   a. The deliverables are tested for correctness as part of control quality.

33. b. PMBOK® Guide: Section 8.2
Y   b. During quality assurance we ensure that the processes are working.

34. c. PMBOK® Guide: Section 11.3
Y   c. During qualitative risk analysis we set priority for future risk processes.

35. a. PMBOK® Guide: Section 11.6.2.1
Y   a. Risk reassessment is a tool and technique of control risks.

36. d. PMBOK® Guide: Section 4.5.1.3
Y   d. All change requests are approved or rejected as part of perform integrated change control. Therefore, change requests are an input of this process.

37. d. PMBOK® Guide: Section 4.5.3.1
Y   d. All change requests are approved or rejected as part of perform integrated change control. Therefore, approved changes are an output of this process.

38. d. PMBOK® Guide: Figure 4-1
Y   d. The project management information system (PMIS) is a tool and technique of both direct and manage project work and monitor and control project work.

39. d. PMBOK® Guide: Section 4.5.2.3
Y   d. Change control tools are a tool and technique of integrated change control.

40. b. PMBOK® Guide: Section 5.3.3.1
Y   b. The scope statement describes the product and the project scope. It also lists explicitly what is out of scope.

41. b. PMBOK® Guide: Section 5.4
Y   b. The WBS is deliverable oriented.
N   a., c., and d. The WBS is deliverable oriented only.

42. a. PMBOK® Guide: Section 5.1.3.1
Y   a. The scope management plan is a component of the project management plan.
N   b. The statement is backwards.
N   c. The plans are related. The scope management plan is a subset of the project management plan.
N   d. The plans are not exactly the same. The scope management plan is a subset of the project management plan and only addresses scope.

43. c. PMBOK® Guide: Section 6.6.2.2
Y   c. The critical path method is a tool and technique of the process develop schedule.

44. a. PMBOK® Guide: Section 11.5.2.2
Y   a. Mitigate is a tool to lower the probability and/or lower the negative impact on project objectives, not positive impact. Be careful of the word except.
N   b. Exploit is a tool for risks with a potentially positive impact. Be careful of the word except.

N c. Share is a tool for risks with a potentially positive impact. Be careful of the word except.

N d. Enhance is a tool for risks with a potentially positive impact. Be careful of the word except.

45. c. PMBOK® Guide: Figure 9-1

Y c. The list represents all the tools and techniques of acquire project team.

N a. Examples of tools and techniques of plan human resource management are organizational charts and position description.

N b. An example of a tool and technique of develop project team is team-building.

N d. An example of a tool and technique of manage project team is observation and conversation.

46. c. PMBOK® Guide: Figure 9-1

Y c. Conflict management is a tool and technique for manage project team.

N a and b. Recommended corrective actions and recommended preventive actions are examples of change requests that are outputs not tools of manage project team.

N d. Team building is a tool and technique of develop project team.

47. b. PMBOK® Guide: Section 5.3.2.3

Y b. Alternative generation is a tool and technique of define scope.

48. b. PMBOK® Guide: Chapter 10 - Introduction

Y b. Horizontal communication is communication with your peers.

N a. Vertical communication is either up or down in the organization. An example of vertical up would be communication with your management.

N c. A formal verbal example would be a project presentation. The example in the question is verbal, but not formal.

N d. An informal written would be an e-mail. The example in the question is informal, but not written.

49. c. PMBOK® Guide: Chapter 8- Quality Introduction

☺ c. Precision is consistency that the value of repeated measurements are clustered and have little scatter. Accuracy is correctness that the measured value is very close to the true value. They are not equivalent.

N a. Precise measurements are consistent.

N b. Accurate measurements are correct.

☹ d. The project management team must determine the level of precision and accuracy required. Be careful of answers that contain the word always.

50. b. PMBOK® Guide: Section 9.2.2.4

Y b. Colocation involves placing all of the most active team members in the same physical location. Virtual team members spend little or no time face-to-face.

N a., c., and d. All of these ideas can be supported by the virtual team format.

51. c. PMBOK® Guide: Section 11.3.3.1

Y c. A watchlist is used for risks assessed as not important based on qualitative risk analysis.

N a. Risks requiring a near-term response are usually viewed as important and thus would not be placed on a watchlist.

N b. Risks assessed as important will often be run through quantitative analysis, not placed on a watchlist.

N d. Risks requiring additional analysis will often be run through quantitative analysis, not placed on a watchlist.

© January 2016 AME Group, Inc. author Aileen Ellis, PMP, PgMP
aileen@amegroupinc.com 719-659-3658

52. a.   PMBOK° Guide: Section 4.2.3.1
Y   a. The configuration management plan is a subset of the project plan. Therefore, it is an output of develop project management plan.

53. a.   Verma, *Human Resource Skills for the Project Manager*, page 218
Y   a. Consultative in a group refers to group decision-making where the project manager invites ideas and suggestions of team members in a meeting. If the project manager does not take these ideas into account when making the decisions, though, the PM runs the risk of being perceived as doing "lip service" and not really using the team members input.
N   b. Consensus refers to sharing problems with team members in a group and then reaching a decision by consensus.
N   c. Autocratic style refers to the project manager making a decision without input from others.
N   d. Directing style refers to the project manager telling others what to do.

54. c.   PMBOK° Guide: Section 8.1.2.3
Y   c. Control limits are normally set at +/-3 sigma (standard deviation).
☹   a., b., and d. Control limits are normally set at +/-3 sigma (standard deviation).

55. b.   *Earned Value Management*, Fleming and Koppelaman
Y   b. The 50-50 rule states that an activity will receive 50% of its PV (planned value) as earned value (EV) when it starts and 50% of its PV as earned value when it completes.
N   a. With the 50-50 rule an activity gets credit for starting, not being 50% complete. It gets the rest of the credit when it finishes.
N   c. and d. The 50-50 rule is used at the activity level not the project level.

56. d.   General Knowledge
Y   d. The last thing to do on a project is to release resources. All of the other answers take resources and thus must come before we release those resources.
N   a. It takes resources to deliver the product to the customer, so this would not be the last thing to do.
N   b. It takes resources to conduct lessons learned, so this would not be the last thing to do.
N   c. It takes resources to hold a celebration, so this would not be the last thing to do.

57. a.   PMBOK° Guide: Section 5.6
Y   a. Uncontrolled changes are often called project scope creep.
N   b. Influencing the factors that create project scope changes is a concern of control scope.
N   c. Controlling the impact of scope changes is a concern of control scope.
N   d. All requested changes should be processed through the integrated change control system. Good documentation and use of a change control system decreases the amount of scope creep.

58. c.   Search online- mathematical models for project selection
Y   c. The linear programming algorithm is an example of a constrained optimization method, often called a mathematical model.
N   a., b., and d. Comparative approaches, scoring model, and murder board are all examples of benefit measurement methods.

59. a.   Web Search on Management by Objectives - Peter Drucker
Y   a. Objectives should be focused on results, not on activities.

N   b., c., and d. Objectives should be SMART (specific, measurable, attainable, relevant, time bounded).

60.   c.   PMBOK° Guide: Section 12.1.1.9
Y   c. A fixed price with economic price adjustment contract is often used when the seller's performance period spans a long period of time and special provisions may be needed for changing conditions (such as the price of commodities).
N   a. A firm fixed price contract will not address fluctuations in the price of commodities.
N   b. A fixed price incentive fee contract will not address fluctuations in the price of commodities.
N   d. A time and materials contract is often used when a precise statement of work cannot be developed quickly.

61.   b.   Project Risk - Wideman
Y   b. Pure risks carry only the chance for a loss. Business risks carry a chance for either gain or loss.
N   a. Pure and insurable as they relate to risk mean the same thing. A pure (insurable) risk carries only the chance for a loss. An example would be property damage.
N   c. Legal liability and personnel are both types of insurable risk. Most organizations would buy insurance to deal with these risks.
N   d. Direct property damage and indirect consequential loss are examples of insurable risks. Most organizations would buy insurance to deal with these risks.

62.   d.   Verma, *Human Resource Skills for the Project Manager*, pages 24-25
Y   d. Communication blockers must be dealt with so that they do not interrupt the project.
N   a., b., and c. These statements are all true. The question is asking for the *exception*.

63.   c.   Verma, *Human Resource Skills for the Project Manager*, page 61
Y   c. Creative work is how the workplace can help meet the Maslow's hierarchy of needs for self-actualization.
N   a. Rest periods and adequate compensation can help meet Maslow's physiological needs.
N   b. Safe working conditions can help meet Maslow's safety/security needs.

64.   b.   PMBOK° Guide: Figure 4-1
Y   b. Perform integrated change control has change requests as an input and change requests status updates as an output.
N   a. Change requests are an output of monitor and control project work.
N   c. Validate scope is the process in which the customer inspects the deliverables for acceptance.
N   d. Direct and manage project work is where change requests are implemented (not approved or rejected).

65.   b.   PMBOK° Guide: Section 2.1.3
Y   b. Colocation is a strategy to place team members physically close together to improve communication and productivity. In a projectized organization, the PM often has a lot of independence and authority. Placing the team members in one place makes it easier for the team to work together. One objective of projectizing is to move the loyalty from the functional groups to the project team, which is one benefit of collocation.
N   a. and c. In a matrix the workers are borrowed from the functional groups and support one or more projects. In general the workers are still physically located within their functional groups.
N   d. A composite is made up of all structures, which may allow for some collocation.

66.   d.   PMBOK Guide: Section 7.4.2.6

Y   d. If a risk does not occur, the unused contingency should be removed from the project budget.

N   a., b., and c. This money no longer belongs to the project. The project would need to request the money and show additional risk analysis to justify the money being approved again for the project budget.

Before you take this full sample test we strongly suggest that you review the sample questions at the end of Initiating, planning, executing, monitoring and controlling, and closing one last time. See if you score higher than your first attempt.

FULL SAMPLE TEST

Questions

© Jan 2016 AME Group, Inc. author Aileen Ellis, PMP, PgMP
aileen@amegroupinc.com 719-659-3658

A001. A customer has come to you requesting a major change to the project objectives. You realize that to change the objectives means there needs to be a change to the project charter. History tells you that when the objectives in the project charter change, the projects in your organization are much more likely to fail. You and your sponsor have seen this over and over again and therefore your sponsor is less likely to approve this change even though he strongly agrees with the change. To be successful it is most important to:

a. update the charter as quickly as possible

b. ensure that the project stays aligned to the organization's strategic objectives as changes to the project objectives and the project charter occur

c. always reject changes to the project objectives and charter as you know this raises the risk of failure

d. update the project management plan, including baselines to reflect the new objectives but don't bother to update the charter

A002. You have just taken over a project that involves designing and building a factory. There are numerous stakeholders, including several government agencies. The project is already behind schedule and over budget. Risk management is critical to project success. The rooms that will contain the hazardous chemicals and gases for the factory are considered high risk. Alarm systems are being identified to aid in risk management once the factory is operational. Alarm #1 will sound if there is a gas leak that will require your personnel to put on gas masks while factory operations continue. Alarm #2 will ring to notify factory personnel to evacuate the building and shut down the factory. The ringing of Alarm #2 lets us know we have reached a:

a. risk appetite

b. risk tolerance

c. risk threshold

d. risk workaround

A003. You have been working as an engineer for many years in your organization. Just over a year ago you were promoted to a project management role and assigned a very large project. You have over 400 team members from around the world. Your technical background did not prepare you for the work you are doing today. Most of your team members are virtual. Your focus right now is on negotiating for the team members you need as well as facilitating team building activities for the team members you already have working. In what project management process group are you working?

a. initiating

b. planning

c. executing

d. monitoring and controlling

A004. Your organization has just been awarded the largest contract in its 40 year history. Because of your 10 year history with the organization you have been selected to lead the project. Based on the rumors you have heard, you are expecting the project to last over 5 years with at least 300 stakeholders from dozens of countries. The schedule is critical. At this point you start working on the project charter even though no sponsor has been identified. Your manager tells you there is no time to worry about a charter and to just get working on the project plan. What should you do now?
a. be happy to be named the project manager and begin working on planning
b. develop a project charter on your own but don't worry that you have no sponsor to sign it
c. work on developing the project charter and the project plan concurrently
d. explain to your management the risk of proceeding without a project charter

A005. The construction of a new soccer stadium in your country is finally complete. The first large sporting event is about to be held. Athletes will be arriving over the next few days from several different countries. The tournament is planned to run for five consecutive evenings. There seems to be confusion on basic issues related to transportation and housing for the athletes. What should you do first?
a. Inform your sponsor of the issues.
b. Develop a better plan to collect all transportation and housing requirements for future events.
c. Not worry too much about this. There certainly are enough hotels locally to support the athletes.
d. Determine the impacts of these issues on the current project and resolve.

A006. Variations inside the control limits on a control chart provides us information related to ?
a. special causes
b. common causes
c. assignable causes
d. unnatural pattern

Use the following table to answer questions: A007-A009.

	Predecessor	Successor	Duration
Task A	start	B	5 days
Task B	A	C,D	3 days
Task C	B	E	7 days
Task D	B	E	2 days
Task E	C, D	Finish	9 days

A007. What is the duration of the critical path?
a. 15 days
b. 24 days
c. 26 days
d. 19 days

© January 2016 AME Group, Inc. author Aileen Ellis, PMP, PgMP
aileen@amegroupinc.com 719-659-3658

A008. What is the float of Task D?
a. 0 days
b. 1 days
c. 2 days
d. 5 days

A009. What activities are on the critical path?
a. a-b-e
b. a-b-d-e
c. a-b-c
d. a-b-c-e

A010. Your project is to oversee the design and implementation of a new patient information system for a large chain of hospitals. You have the technical background to accomplish the project and your team is highly qualified. The project seems to be running smoothly except for the issue of the wrong stakeholders getting the wrong information at the wrong time and in the wrong format.   It seems that the stakeholders are being given information that does not interest them and are not receiving the information they need to perform their role on the project. The process that may have prevented this is:
a. control communications
b. control risks
c. manage communications
d. plan communications

A011. You are managing the equipment installation side of a brand new factory. You have over 30 different suppliers who will be working for you over a three year period. The work of each supplier is contingent on the other suppliers meeting their timelines. To meet the schedule end date provided by management, you need a critical supplier, Kirkpatrick and Associates to start work, and incur costs now. Contract negotiations have been going on for months with Kirkpatrick and you expect it will still be several weeks before all the details are worked out and the contract is signed. Your project timeline cannot wait. While negotiations continue you are most likely to send a:
a. purchase order
b. request for proposal
c. purchase agreement
d. letter of intent

A012. The Olympics are coming to your home town. There is excitement as transportation systems are upgraded, venues are built, and the world watches. It has been decided that the schedule is more important than cost at this point. Because we cannot have a delay, we decide to use Monte Carlo to simulate the schedule. Most likely we will run Monte Carlo simulations on a weekly basis to help us account for uncertainty.   Which of the following is used as a model for a schedule risk analysis?
a. work breakdown schedule
b. schedule network diagram and duration estimates
c. project management plan
d. schedule management plan

A013. You have been assigned the project manager to replace an existing bridge on a major road through Colorado Springs. You have managed several similar projects and are excited about having another highly visible project to manage. The project will include working with many organizations, including the city, the county, the police department, and several suppliers.

Your sponsor is very involved and has issued a project charter. He has also helped you navigate the political environment. You have a complete project plan including baselines for scope, time, and cost. As the work progresses you issue status reports and hold progress meetings for all interested stakeholders.

After twelve months the bridge is constructed on budget and on schedule. All requirements have been met. During your final lessons learned meeting, you present that the project experienced 25% more change requests than other comparable projects. The most likely reason for this is:

a. Your sponsor did not fully engage all stakeholders
b. The project plan did not provide enough detail on how to execute the project
c. One or more key stakeholders was not involved early in the project
d. Too many organizations were identified early on as stakeholders

A014. For the first 24 months your project was progressing well and team members were working together successfully. Now the project schedule has been pulled in dramatically to address a changing market window. Meetings are tense and conflict is arising. The biggest issue surrounds accountability. You want to use a tool to make it clear who is the one person accountable for each activity. Most likely you will use a(n):

a. organizational breakdown structure
b. project organization chart
c. responsibility assignment matrix
d. resource calendar

A015. Severe weather has hit your community. Bridges and roads were washed away with the flooding. Your project is to oversee the re-construction of a major highway. There are many stakeholders involved including your friends and neighbors. Everyone has an opinion of what is important to ensure quality construction. Due to time constraints you need a tool that will help you focus on the most critical issues related to quality. Most likely you will use a:

a. cause and effect diagram
b. flowchart
c. check sheet
d. Pareto diagram

A016. Nick is a project manager with 30 years of experience managing the organization's most successful projects. He now works in the PMO developing business cases and providing feasibility studies for future projects. The head of the PMO just rushed into Nick's office and requested that Nick develop a cost estimate for a potential customer project in the next 15 minutes. The organization completed a similar project last year to the one management is now describing. Therefore, Nick is most likely to use what type of cost estimating technique?

a. vendor bid analysis
b. parametric estimating
c. bottom-up estimating
d. analogous estimating

© January 2016 AME Group, Inc. author Aileen Ellis, PMP, PgMP
aileen@amegroupinc.com 719-659-3658

Full Sample Test

A017. A project manager for a large construction company is responsible for the construction of a new football stadium. There are over 100 different vendors involved. The lead scheduler provided the project manager with a integrated schedule. The schedule has taken weeks to develop and needs to be closely managed. There are four critical paths. One critical activity on the schedule is the pouring of the concrete. Once the concrete is poured it will take five to seven days for it to cure. During the curing time many of the team members will take a short vacation since they have been working around the clock. Curing of the concrete is an example of:
a. float
b. free float
c. lead
d. lag

A018. Several of your team members hope to move into project management positions. They will all be taking the CAPM° exam shortly and are busy studying the *PMBOK° Guide*. They come to you and ask for help understanding the difference between plan human resource management and estimate activity resources. Their view is that both processes relate to planning for people and therefore there is duplication in the *PMBOK° Guide*. You explain that:
a. these are two different names for the same process step
b. plan human resource management is related to defining roles, responsibilities, and relationships whereas estimate activity resources is related to determining the type, quantity, and timing of needed resources
c. plan human resources leads to estimate costs, whereas estimate activity resources leads to acquire project team
d. an output of plan human resources is the resource breakdown structure; an output of estimate activity resources is the project organization chart

A019. The project SPI is 1.12 and the CPI is 1.2. The schedule shows an end date four months from today. At your monthly status meeting your customer seems pleased with project progress. Two days later the customer requests that scope be added since there is "extra" time in the schedule and "extra" money in the budget. This is not new as your customer seems to regularly request additional work once they feel the project is ahead of schedule and/or under budget. Requested changes are an output of what process?
a. develop project management plan
b. monitor and control project work
c. perform integrated change control
d. close project or phase

A020. You oversee drug trials for a global pharmaceutical company. In the pharmaceutical industry, project management is the key to addressing the unique regulatory, compliance, and quality related needs of the industry. Change control is a critical component of successful project management for all projects but even more important in your industry. Which of the following is not one of the elements of perform integrated change control?
a. immediately implementing all government mandated changes
b. controlling factors that create changes to make sure those changes are beneficial
c. determining when a change has occurred
d. managing the approved changes

© January 2016 AME Group, Inc. author Aileen Ellis, PMP, PgMP
aileen@amegroupinc.com 719-659-3658
409

A021. The PMO for your organization has just rolled out a project management methodology that has been tested and proven on a very large successful project. You manage multiple small projects and have been instructed to apply this detailed methodology to each of these small projects. The best thing to do is:

a. ask the PMO to review its mandate to use the methodology on all projects as you remind them that the project management's effort should be reflective of the project's size, complexity, and priority

b. follow the methodology explicitly since it has already been tested and proven on a successful project

c. ignore the methodology because you believe it does not make sense for your projects

d. follow the parts of the methodology that make sense for your projects

A022. As a program manager, you have seventeen project managers reporting to you. Some are members of PMI° and some are not. All the junior project managers are CAPM° certified, while all the senior project managers are PMP° certified. A few new project managers have joined your group in the last few months and have submitted their application for PMP° certification. Based on the fact that all of your staff are either certified through PMI° or have submitted applications to be certified, which document must all of your staff adhere to?

a. *PMBOK° Guide:* 5th Edition

b. All PMI° published materials

c. PMI° Code of Ethics and Professional Conduct

d. All PMI° standards

A023. One of your team members asks you who should get a copy of the performance report just completed. You respond:

a. all stakeholders

b. all key stakeholders

c. all project team members

d. follow the communications management plan

A024. You have taken over a project from another project manager. The project seems to be running very smoothly. As the project gets closer to completion several team members feel they are ready to move on to another project. Based on your experience you know that there is often a lot more work involved in close-out than most people realize. From your view there is still much work to be done and conflict is starting to arise about release criteria. Release criteria should have been addressed in what document?

a. the project management plan

b. the staffing management plan

c. the project organizational chart

d. communication management plan

A025. In your lumber company, three standard deviations has been your standard for decades. Your new quality manager wants to adopt a six sigma approach. Which of the following statements is true?
a. six sigma is twice as stringent as three sigma
b. control limits are usually set at plus or minus six sigma
c. with three sigma, defects occur only about 3 times in a thousand and with six sigma defects occur only about 3.3 times in a million
d. six sigma approach means plus or minus three standard deviations on each side of the mean

A026. Your project is running so far over budget that you can no longer provide a realistic basis for performance measurement. Your next step is to:
a. update your cost management plan
b. create a revised project schedule
c. create a revised cost baseline
d. update your WBS

A027. As a project scheduler you are trying to use statistics as part of project scheduling. If Activity A has a pessimistic estimate of 24 days and an optimistic estimate of 12 days, what is the variance of Activity A?
a. 12 days
b. 6 days
c. 4 days
d. 2 days

A028. You have just received your PMP® and are now a mentor for new project managers. They all are arguing that a WBS is really a long list of items to complete. You explain that a WBS is all of the following except:
a. a deliverable oriented hierarchy of the work to be done
b. a document that shows the sequence of work
c. a team building tool
d. an input to many other planning processes

A029. As a project manager for a large international organization, you often run projects in many parts of the world. Business practices are often different, depending on where you are in the world. As a Project Management Professional (PMP®) the PMI® Code of Ethics and Professional Conduct guides your actions. Which of the following is not one of the four core values described in the PMI® Code of Ethics and Professional Conduct?
a. loyalty
b. honesty
c. respect
d. responsibility

A30. It seems that your team does a great job of planning projects but somehow loses insight into the project during executing. Based on this you have decided to put more effort into the monitoring and controlling of the project. You realize that monitoring and controlling involves all of the following except:
a. validate scope
b. control risk
c. manage stakeholder engagement
d. control stakeholder engagement

A031. As the project manager of the equipment installation side of a new factory, you expect to deal repeatedly with Lewis and Associates, a plumbing firm. You don't know the exact quantity or exact products you will buy from this firm, but you expect to be buying from them often over the next 18 months. You are most likely to want to sign a:
a. purchase order
b. request for proposal
c. purchase agreement
d. letter of intent

A032. You have been working all week in Baltimore and plan to fly home late tonight to New York. There is a surprise snow storm in New York and a risk the airport may close. You cancel your flight and rent a car to get home. As you are driving you hear on the radio that the highway is closing 50 miles north of you. The closing of the highway is an example of a:
a. fallback plan
b. contingency plan
c. secondary risk
d. workaround

A033. A project manager developing a global website realizes that stakeholder involvement is key to project success. On past projects he has run into issues where he has delivered on all the requirements but still some stakeholders were not satisfied. He wants a picture that shows not only the current level of stakeholder involvement but also the desired level. He can use this to develop his stakeholder strategy. Most likely the project manager will utilize a:
a. communication management plan
b. stakeholder register
c. stakeholder engagement matrix
d. requirements documentation

A034. It is important on your software development project to accurately estimate the durations of activities. You suggest to management that PERT estimates be completed on each activity. You give them the following example. Your programmer estimates that most likely it will take 100 hours to complete the work. Optimistically, it may only be 80 hours and pessimistically it could take as long as 150 hours. The PERT estimate is:
a. 100 hours
b. 105 hours
c. 110 hours
d. 150 hours

A035. **The project is to design a "future car" that focuses not only on safety but also on comfort and cost. An important part of the design is to determine which combination of suspension and tires will produce the most anticipated ride characteristics at a reasonable price. To determine the best combination the engineers most likely will use a(n):**
a. Pareto chart
b. control chart
c. design of experiment
d. inspection

A036. **Once again you are estimating the cost for your new project. Your team members have expressed frustration in the past that you are unclear about the rounding you want in their estimates. As an example should they round up or down. Really, they are asking you about the required:**
a. precision levels
b. control thresholds
c. earned value rules
d. report formats

A037. **Management is reviewing your schedules and asks why all of the work packages are different sizes. They suggest that you consider the 80 hour rule. The 80 hour rule is an example of:**
a. a heuristic
b. a PMI regulation
c. a constraint
d. ground rules

A038. **The project to build a semiconductor factory is drawing to a close. The operations group has started wafers in the factory that after processing will be the chips we use in our phones and computers. As the wafers pass through each piece of equipment on the factory floor it is important to track performance over time to ensure the processes are stable. Which of the seven basic quality tools are we likely to use :**
a. cause and effect diagrams
b. histograms
c. scatter diagrams
d. control charts

A039. **Based on lessons learned you realize that maintaining the integrity of project baselines has been a real challenge. It seems that some non-approved changes were released for incorporation into the project product and that some approved changes never made it into the project products. To better manage this in the future tighter control will need to occur in:**
a. develop project management plan
b. direct and manage project work
c. monitor and control project work
d. perform integrated change control

A040. You have been working as a project manager for six years and have never really had to manage a project budget before. This is changing now that money has become tighter. Based on your experience and your outside reading, which of the following statements is false?
a. a majority of the project's budget will be spent during the executing process group
b. cost and price always mean the same thing
c. cost estimates should be developed before cost budgets
d. the ability to influence costs is highest early in the project

A041. The project is to upgrade the entire customer engagement system for the organization. The upgrade will occur in thirty (30) hospitals around the country. The project team will utilize fifty (50) different suppliers over a three year time period. With each procurement it is important that there is a clear understanding of the requirement and that no one receive preferential treatment. To ensure this during the conduct procurement process we most likely will utilize:
a. bidder conference
b. proposal evaluation techniques
c. analytical techniques
d. procurement negotiations

A042. Examples of mitigate include all of the following except:
a. establishing a contingency reserve
b. adopting less complex processes
c. conducting more tests
d. choosing a more stable supplier

A043. A project report is an example of what type of communication?
a. formal written
b. informal written
c. formal verbal
d. informal verbal

A044. Zero sum rewards are rewards that:
a. cost no money
b. only a limited number of project team members can receive
c. everyone can receive
d. everyone or no one must receive

A045. You have been studying for the PMP® Exam for the last several months. For you, the best study method is to review many sample questions and learn from each one. To guide and focus your studies you would like to be able to see the frequency that you are missing questions by knowledge area. Most likely you will use a:
a. Pareto diagram
b. cause and effect diagram
c. flow chart
d. scatter diagram

© January 2016 AME Group, Inc. author Aileen Ellis, PMP, PgMP
aileen@amegroupinc.com 719-659-3658

A046. On what contract type does the buyer typically have the lowest risk?
a. Time and materials
b. Cost plus percentage of cost
c. Cost plus fixed fee
d. Fixed price

A047. When you first planned the development of your organization's new medical device, it seems that most of the activities contained float. You met with your team to develop the schedule and explained float to all of the team members. Now you are running with several critical paths with more paths becoming critical each month. This is an example of:
a. Parkinson Theory
b. lazy team members
c. critical chain
d. critical path method

A048. The project is finally over after years of frustration. The customer in the end made payment but it is clear they will never use the product delivered to them. It seems the biggest lesson learned is that we need to be sure that the project team's interpretation of the deliverables matches the customer's interpretation of the deliverables. While the product met the technical requirements it was clear that throughout the project the customer was often surprised by our deliverables. The documented lesson learned is: Different individuals will have different interpretations of the work packages. To decrease the probability of this in the future each project should now include:
a. WBS dictionary
b. detailed WBS
c. work authorization system
d. control accounts

A049. Examples of mathematical models used for project selection include:
a. benefit contribution
b. linear programming algorithms
c. comparative approaches
d. economic models

A050. You have spent months with your team planning your project and it is time to begin the executing work. Executing involves all of the following except:
a. perform integrated change control
b. perform quality assurance
c. acquire project team
d. manage stakeholder engagement

A051. You are the manager of the design/build of a large manufacturing facility. With your customer, you have signed a Fixed Price Incentive Contract. You know that in this type of contract the risk is shared between the buyer and the seller. The time at which your organization picks up all of the financial risk is called:
a. contract award
b. contract breach
c. contract termination
d. point of total assumption

A052. In your product development group, risk management has always been a low priority. Management does not want to talk about risk until the risk event has occurred. You are trying to explain the importance of timing to them. One idea you share is:
a. as we move further into a project the amount at stake goes up
b. as we move further into a project the level of uncertainty increases
c. as we move further into a project the amount at stake goes down
d. as we move further into a project the risk of failing increases

A053. You are the project manager for a logging company. This month you are committed to deliver 10,000 units that are 60 centimeters each. Your upper control limits on your process is 63 centimeters. Your lower control limits on your process is 57 centimeters. Your mean is 60 centimeters. What percentage of your units will fall between 58 and 62 centimeters?
a. 68.3%
b. 75.5 %
c. 95.5%
d. 99.7%

A054. Under McGregor's Theory Y, the management view is that most people:
a. dislike their work and will try to avoid it
b. lack ambition
c. are self-centered
d. are creative, imaginative, and ambitious

A055. The project is to design and build a new website for all 30 schools in the local school district. Many stakeholders want to be included as we collect requirements. It is important to collect early feedback on requirements. It has been strongly suggested that we use storyboards. These storyboards will use mock-ups to show navigation paths through pages, screens, etc. Storyboarding in an example of:
a. prototypes
b. benchmarking
c. facilitated workshops
d. brainstorming

© January 2016 AME Group, Inc. author Aileen Ellis, PMP, PgMP
aileen@amegroupinc.com 719-659-3658

A056. Your project has over 200 stakeholders. The stakeholders are located in 20 different countries and speak too many languages for you to name. In fact, your manager lives in another country and speaks a different language than you. Your SPI is running at .85. Your CPI is running at 1.2. Based on this scenario, what should you be most concerned about?
a. schedule
b. cost
c. stakeholder management
d. your management

A057. You are managing a large ship building project for a government customer. The project has been progressing well from both a schedule and a cost standpoint. Due to world events the customer has requested that you pull in the schedule by several months. No additional resources will be made available. To accomplish this you will:
a. crash
b. fast-track
c. resource level
d. implement the use of project management software

A058. After months of planning, you are at the point of having your baselines approved. All of the following documents are part of the scope baseline except:
a. scope management plan
b. scope statement
c. WBS
d. WBS dictionary

A059. The system that identifies and documents the functional and physical characteristics of a product or component is called:
a. change control system
b. configuration management system
c. change control meetings
d. expert judgment

A60. Project planning has begun with your core team and there is conflict on the sequence of the planning activities. From the list below which sequence is *least* likely to occur?
a. determine budget before estimate costs
b. qualitative risk analysis before quantitative risk analysis
c. plan procurements before conduct procurements
d. collect requirements before define scope

A061. A contract change control system is normally part of what process?
a. plan procurements
b. conduct procurements
c. control procurements
d. close procurements

A062. Your organization has become very good at accessing and evaluating characteristics of individual project risks. Management is now asking you to provide an estimate of the overall effect of risk on the project objectives. Management is really asking you to:
a. perform qualitative risk analysis
b. monitor and control risks
c. plan risk responses
d. perform quantitative risk analysis

A063. When using rolling wave planning:
a. all work is planned in detail
b. near term work is planning in detail and future work is planned at a higher level
c. near term work is planning at a higher level and long term work is planning in detail
d. all work is planned at a high level

A064. The type of power anyone can earn, regardless of their position is:
a. formal power
b. reward power
c. penalty power
d. expert power

A065. Your medical component business is growing at an exponential rate. As far as product testing you are moving to testing samples instead of entire populations. In general, the main reasons to test samples instead of populations include all of the following except:
a. the testing may be destructive
b. the testing is expensive
c. the testing takes a long time
d. the testing is variable related not attribute related

A066. The performance measurement baseline is made up of what categories:
a. distributed and undistributed
b. contingency reserve and management reserve
c. cost and profit
d. planning packages and work packages

A067. Your program manager has just returned for a class on program/project management and is filled with ideas. He seems to be using the terms fast tracking and concurrent engineering interchangeably. You try to explain the high level in the difference by stating:
a. fast tracking is about overlapping activities while concurrent engineering is moving implementers to an earlier phase of the project
b. fast tracking is overlapping activities while concurrent engineering is adding resources to the critical path
c. fast tracking is about moving implementers to an earlier phase of the project while concurrent engineering is about adding resources to the critical path
d. fast tracking is overlapping phases while concurrent engineering is overlapping activities

A068. If a project is performed through a legal relationship, the constraints are defined:
a. by the customer
b. in the contract provisions
c. by the performing organization
d. by the project manager

A069. It is hard to imagine a project without change requests. Change requests on projects may be either rejected or approved. Approved changes are processed through which step for implementation?
a. develop project management plan
b. direct and manage project work
c. monitor and control project work
d. perform integrated change control

A70. You are managing an internal Information Technology (IT) project for your organization. During planning, the WBS, schedule, and cost estimate your team developed were approved and set as the project baselines. You should be able to meet all of your baselines but it seems that your critical resources keep getting pulled to support other projects and programs. Setting priorities across projects and programs is often the responsibility of:
a. the customer
b. the project sponsor
c. senior management
d. the project managers

A071. You are managing the design/build of a small office building. With your customer, you have signed a Cost Plus Incentive Contract. The negotiated pricing for the contract is:
target cost: $100,000
target fee: $ 8,000
max fee: $ 12,000
min fee: $ 4,000
share ratio: 60/40 (buyer/seller)

You complete the work for $105,000. What is the fee you will receive?
a. $8, 000
b. $10,000
c. $4,000
d. $6, 000

A072. While working on a construction project, it is brought to your attention that you need an environmental permit. You are concerned that the permitting agency may take longer than planned to issue the permit. If this occurs, the project will be three weeks late, and may run over budget by $20,000. Quality may also suffer, but you do not know how to quantify the quality degradation. The risk event in the above scenario is:
a. the project will finish three weeks late
b. the uncertainty that the project may run over budget
c. the degradation in quality
d. the permitting agency possibly taking longer than planned to issue the permit

A073. In the communication model, who is responsible to encode the initial message?
a. the sender
b. the sender and the receiver
c. the receiver
d. the sender or the receiver

A074. The technique to manage conflict that involves emphasizing areas of agreement
while avoiding points of disagreement is: (this line needs moving up)
a. smoothing
b. collaborating
c. withdrawing
d. forcing

A075. Common causes of variation are also called:
a. special causes
b. unusual events
c. control limits
d. random causes

A076. Which classification model describes classes of stakeholders based on the power, urgency, and legitimacy?
a. power/interest grid
b. power/influence grid
c. influence/impact grid
d. salience model

A077. You along with your project management team have spent a great amount of time developing the WBS, the schedule, and the cost estimate. Your work has finally been approved and you now have baselines for the triple constraint. What will you do next?
a. celebrate as a team
b. begin recommending preventive action
c. begin recommending corrective action
d. hold a kick-off meeting

A078. Your technology transfer project is wrapping up and you are determining where you stand as far as scope. Completion of project scope is measured against all of the following except:
a. project management plan
b. scope statement
c. WBS
d. product requirements

© January 2016 AME Group, Inc. author Aileen Ellis, PMP, PgMP
aileen@amegroupinc.com 719-659-3658

A079. You are managing a technology transfer project moving technology from a development line into a manufacturing line. The manufacturing manager has requested yet another change. As you evaluate this change it seems to have a major effect on the high-level project objectives. If a decision is made to accept this change, what document must be changed first?
a. project management plan
b. WBS
c. scope statement
d. project charter

A80. The type of organization in which each employee has one clear superior is?
a. strong matrix
b. composite structure
c. weak matrix
d. functional structure

A081. You have been assigned as the project manager for a large technology transfer project. The technology will be developed in Sweden and then transferred to manufacturing facilities in several countries including China. You have approximately 200 people working on your team, including engineers from each of the manufacturing locations. Most team meetings occur through electronic means and there is often much healthy debate.
Your sponsor has been fully engaged throughout the life of the project. You have a signed charter, a full project plan including baselines for scope, cost, and time. Your identified stakeholders have been fully involved throughout the life of the project. Each transfer is occurring on schedule and within budget. All requirements are being met. As you wrap up the final transfer efforts, the operations manager at one of the manufacturing facilities in Ireland informs you that he will not be using the technology being transferred. He states that the technology is already outdated. You do not know this person and are surprised by his comment. One likely cause for this customer not using the product of your project is:
a. your sponsor did not fully engage all stakeholders
b. the project plan did not provide enough detail on how to execute the project
c. your team was too large to manage, especially since it included people from several countries
d. At least one key stakeholder was overlooked when identifying stakeholders

A082. The project manager has been brought in long before initiating the project. Often one of the first tasks performed before we may initiate a project is:
a. develop the project charter
b. identify key deliverables based on business requirements
c. perform a project assessment in order to evaluate the feasibility of the project
d. conduct benefits analysis to validate project alignment

A083. Projects may produce benefits as well as deliverables. For a benefit to have value the benefit must be realized:
a. as early as possible in the project
b. in a timely manner even if this is after project closeout
c. before the end of the project
d. anytime over the life of the project

A084. Benefits analysis should ensure that the project is in alignment with the organizational strategy. Organizational strategy is the result of:
a. reviewing the organizations portfolios and determining strategy based on the anticipated outcomes of these portfolios
b. the strategic planning cycle where the vision and the mission of the organization are translated into a strategic plan
c. a yearly review of the ongoing operations that produce value and the programs and projects that increase value production capability
d. customer-focused programs that determine the organizations strategic plan

A085. You have just been moved onto a project that is well into project implementation. You want to be clear on the priority you should use for stakeholder requests so you search for the stakeholder register. You come to realize that no stakeholder register exists for the project. Since you are new to the organization you want to make sure you use their templates for documents. Therefore you search for a template for a stakeholder register in the:
a. enterprise environmental factors
b. stakeholder management plan
c. organizational process assets
d. current project files

A086. Often on your project deliverables occur at the wrong time. Sometimes customers receive deliverables early, sometime late. Regardless it seems that your customers never receive the deliverable when the deliverable would be most valuable to them. Therefore it was suggested that you invest in just-in-time thinking. Just-in-time is related to what type of system?
a. push system
b. pull system
c. forecast demand system
d. bottleneck system

A087. During the implementation phase of your project many deliverables have been produced on time and on budget. At this point it is important that the deliverables are tested to determine if we are building the product correctly. Most likely we determine this during which process?
a. collect requirements
b. perform quality assurance
c. control quality
d. validate scope

A088. As part of your role as a project manager you are responsible for capturing critical knowledge. You are likely to use all of the following methods for capturing knowledge except:
a. memory of senior team members
b. lessons learned debriefing reports
c. mentoring
d. company intranet

A089. As part of your knowledge transfer life cycle it is important to apply the knowledge that has been transferred. A technology often used to apply the transferred knowledge is:
a. searchable database of lessons learned and success stories
b. project success rates
c. quality of deliverables
d. project efficiency

A090. You have been named the project manager over a project to design, build and set up a customer call center. It was determined that this call center was vital to drive the organization's strategy forward. After the project is complete your organization will track the number of new customers based on the success of the call center. The number of new customers is considered a(n):
a. key performance indicator(KPI)
b. key success factor (KSF)
c. critical success factor (CSF)
d. cost performance index (CPI)

A091. Nicholas is managing a project to integrate multiple customer relationship management systems into one enterprise wide system. The work is very technical in nature and Nicholas was chosen as the project manager due to his strong technical education and experience. As part of managing the project Nicholas needs to interact with multiple business unit leaders throughout the organization to understand how his actions and decisions affect their business units. While Nicholas has strong technical skills he is struggling to use the appropriate terminology when interacting with these other leaders. At this point Nicholas may want to put more focus on:
a. the technical work of the project
b. project management skills
c. business acumen
d. benefits realization

A092. An organization scoring low on Geert Hofstede's dimension for individualism believes in:
a. social mobility
b. direct communication
c. "I" more important than "we"
d. keeping opinions to oneself

A093. Most of your project team is struggling with Rich, the senior designer on the team. Rich has trouble controlling and redirecting his disruptive behaviors and impulses as well as adapting to changing situations. Based on Daniel Goleman's mixed model for emotional intelligence Rich needs to work more on:
a. self-awareness
b. self-regulation
c. social skills
d. empathy

A094. All of the following are examples of items normally placed under configuration control except:
a. physical items
b. documents
c. forms and records
d. tools and techniques

A095. Usually the project decision-making processes are included in the:
a. project management plan
b. project documents
c. project governance framework
d. project charter

A096. Your project is approaching a critical milestone. At this milestone you will need to decide if the project should stay on course or take a major turn in how the work is being performed. It is important that you make a good decision though you are concerned that you do not have all the detailed knowledge required to way options. Therefore you need input from several of your key team members. At this point what decision making style are you most likely to use:
a. command
b. consultation
c. consensus
d. coin flip

A097. You are nearing the end of the project and have begun compiling all of your lessons learned. It is important to collect lessons learned in order to:
a. identify who was accountable for all project errors
b. provide documentation on any perceived late deliveries or cost overruns
c. update your enterprise environmental factors for future projects
d. compare plan to actual so as to improve project estimating on future projects

A098. You project is running with a CPI of 1.2. The EAC is $100,000. What is the BAC?
a. $ 83,333
b. $100,000
c. $120,000
d. $150,000

A099. You are working on a medical device development project. Your organization embraced project management about a year ago and many of your team members now have their PMP°. At this point you are developing your network diagrams. There is a heated discussion about the use of critical path method versus critical chain method. You explain the difference by stating:
a. critical path and critical chain are different names for the same method
b. the critical path is time constrained while the critical chain is resource constrained
c. the critical path assumes limited resources while the critical chain assumes unlimited resources
d. the critical path method is a newer idea while the critical chain idea has been around for many decades

© January 2016 AME Group, Inc. author Aileen Ellis, PMP, PgMP
aileen@amegroupinc.com 719-659-3658

A100. The document that states explicitly what is excluded from the project is the:
a. WBS
b. project scope statement
c. scope management plan
d. project management plan

A101. It has been determined that several of the deliverables due today do not meet the technical specifications. A change request has been generated and approved. The defect is repaired, or so it seems. During what process are changes validated?
a. validate scope
b. control quality
c. direct and manage project work
d. monitor and control project work

A102. Termination may occur for all of the following reasons except:
a. completion
b. cause
c. mutual agreement
d. convenience

A103. We are presently trying to identify potential risks on our project. In our organization, the senior people often dominate a meeting and everyone else goes along with their ideas. One technique to identify risk that keeps one person from having an undue influence on the outcome is:
a. brainstorming
b. SWOT analysis
c. root cause analysis
d. Delphi technique

A104. Your CPI= .8 and your SPI=1.1. How is your project doing?
a. ahead of schedule, under budget
b. ahead of schedule, over budget
c. behind schedule, under budget
d. behind schedule, over budget

A105. Rank ordering of defects is done through:
a. control charts
b. process flowcharts
c. cause and effect diagrams
d. Pareto charts

A106. Parametric estimates are most likely to be accurate when all the following statements are true except:
a. the historical information is accurate
b. the project manager creates the model without inputs from other stakeholders
c. the parameters used in the model are readily quantifiable
d. the model is scalable

A107. Receipt from the customer that the terms of the contract have been met is done during:
a. close project
b. plan procurements
c. validate scope
d. control quality

A108. Organizational cultures are often reflected in all of the following except?
a. regulations
b. shared values, norms, and beliefs
c. policies and procedures
d. work ethics and work hours

A109. An example of horizontal communication is:
a. with your peers
b. with your team
c. with your management
d. with your suppliers

A110. The first four stages of team development in order are:
a. storming, forming, performing, norming
b. forming, storming, performing, norming
c. forming, storming, norming, performing
d. storming, norming, forming, performing

A111. You want to be able to systematically change all of the important factors for a product or process to provide the optimal conditions. Based on this need you are most likely to use:
a. benchmarking
b. control chart
c. design of experiment (DOE)
d. run chart

A112. The BAC (budget at completion) for your project is $100,000. Your EAC is $120,000. What is your CPI?
a. .83
b. 1.0
c. 1.2
d. 1.5

A113. The vast majority of the project budget is spent during which process group?
a. initiating
b. planning
c. executing
d. monitoring and controlling

© January 2016 AME Group, Inc. author Aileen Ellis, PMP, PgMP
aileen@amegroupinc.com 719-659-3658

A114. You work in a large mapmaking organization. Your project is really a new product development. At your first team meeting you are trying to help your team understand the difference between product scope and project scope. All of the following statements are true except:

a. product scope is defined first, then project scope
b. all project deliverables should be related to the product scope
c. the project life cycle is a subset of the product life cycle
d. the configuration management system manages and controls changes to the product scope

A115. After your last status meeting, your customer has come to you with a change request. What should you do first?

a. meet with your management
b. meet with the project sponsor
c. evaluate the change request
d. make the change since it is the customer making the request

A116. As the new business manager for a large construction company, it is important for you to be able to quantify new opportunities. You are looking at a new venture now and have determined that there is a 20% probability of income in year one of $40,000. There is a 30% probability of income in year one of $10,000 and there is a 50% probability of a loss of $20,000 in the first year. What is the expected monetary value of this venture for year one?

a. $30,000
b. $10,000
c. $ 1,000
d. $ 0

A117. If the earned value is higher than the planned value:

a. the project is ahead of schedule
b. the project is behind schedule
c. the project is over budget
d. the project is under budget

A118. Examining project performance over time to determine if performance is improving or deteriorating is called:

a. variance analysis
b. earned value technique
c. trend analysis
d. cost-benefit analysis

A119. When a project terminates early, what process should be followed to document the level and extent of completion?

a. control quality
b. validate scope
c. close procurement
d. control scope

A120. Reserve analysis during control risks looks at:
a. plan versus actual on cost performance
b. plan versus actual on schedule performance
c. the amount of contingency reserve remaining versus the amount of risk remaining
d. the amount of money remaining versus the amount of work remaining

A121. If the actual cost is higher than the earned value:
a. the project is ahead of schedule
b. the project is behind schedule
c. the project is over budget
d. the project is under budget

A122.   Your quality manager comes to you with a list of tools typically used to plan quality. This list is likely to include all the following except:
a. cause and effect diagrams
b. flowcharts
c. Pareto diagrams
d. quality audits

A123. You have been assigned to a project with major cost and schedule overruns, as well as a long list of uncontrolled changes. Uncontrolled changes are also known as:
a. cost growth
b. schedule growth
c. scope creep
d. scope changes

A124. If your project is running on budget, your CPI will be:
a. 0
b. 1
c. greater than 1
d. less than 1

A125. You have been managing a large mapmaking project for the government. Your customer is asking for multiple scope changes. You are looking at these requested changes and trying to determine the true magnitude of these changes. You are most likely to review what document?
a. scope management plan
b. WBS
c. project charter
d. cost management plan

A126. The schedule baseline is an output of:
a. define activities
b. develop project management plan
c. develop schedule
d. estimate activity durations

© January 2016 AME Group, Inc. author Aileen Ellis, PMP, PgMP
aileen@amegroupinc.com 719-659-3658

A127. Your business is building and maintaining the railroad systems for the country. Projects have always been managed using a functional structure and you, as a new project manager, are pushing to move to a projectized structure. What disadvantage of a projectized structure might this functional manager use to support staying in a functional structure:
a. higher potential for conflict
b. more complex to manage
c. extra administration required
d. less efficient use of resources

A128. EAC= (BAC/CPI) is the equation used for estimate at completion when:
a. past performance shows that the original estimating assumptions were fundamentally flawed
b. current variances are seen as atypical
c. conditions have changed
d. current variances are seen as typical of future variances

A129. Based on your success on previous projects you have been asked to manage a project for a different department in your organization. This department has documented processes for most of their work. You realize that you will need to tailor many of their standard processes so they will make sense for your new project. Which organizational process asset may help you the most:
a. personnel administration
b. infrastructure
c. project management information system (PMIS)
d. project plan templates

A130. As a project manager in a global company, you realize that you need not only project management skills but also interpersonal skills. Decision-making is an example of an interpersonal skill. Which of the following is not an element of decision-making?
a. risk management
b. problem definition
c. problem solution generation
d. ideas to action

A131. An emergency has occurred and you need a safety contractor fast to do some consulting work for you. In this circumstance you are most likely to use a:
a. fixed price
b. fixed price incentive
c. cost plus incentive
d. time and materials

A132. The forecasted estimate at completion is also called the:
a. EV
b. EAC
c. BAC
d. PV

A133. You are a project manager who manages the equipment installations in an automobile manufacturing facility. Early in the planning process you are asked to generate ideas for improvement and to provide a basis by which to measure performance. You are most likely to use:
a. control charts
b. Pareto charts
c. scatter diagrams
d. benchmarking

A134. Cost forecasts are an output of what process?
a. plan cost management
b. estimate costs
c. determine budget
d. control costs

A135. It is early on in the software development project and the core team is in the process of collecting requirements. Key inputs the team should review are?
a. the WBS and the project plan
b. the schedule and the risk management plan
c. the project charter and the stakeholder register
d. the requirements management plan and the requirements traceability matrix

A136. You have moved into the project management role on a project to develop the marketing collateral for a major ad campaign. The collateral will be both hard copy and electronic. Thousands of project stakeholders will receive the results of your work. At this point more than 80 percent of the work is complete. The project has 147 team members. Most of the team members have limited experience on the new technology being used to design all the collateral. There seems to have been little work done so far related to risk. You should begin with:
a. risk identification
b. plan risk responses
c. risk qualification
d. risk quantification

A137. If your project is over budget your cost variance (CV) will be:
a. negative
b. positive
c. 0
d. 1

A138. You are walking through the construction site for your project when a fire breaks out and chaos will likely ensue. The site safety manager is most likely to use which conflict resolution technique in this situation to get people off the site quickly?
a. problem solving
b. compromising
c. withdrawal
d. forcing

A139. Your project work is expected to be constant for the six month length of the project. During each month your budget is $200. At the end of month four you have 40% of the total work complete and you have spent 70% of your total budget. The budget at completion for the project is:
a. $ 80
b. $ 140
c. $ 840
d. $1,200

A140. Projects within a given organization have the following in common except:
a. similar project life cycles
b. similar project deliverables
c. the same products
d. the same WBS templates

A141. As a project manager in the software industry, it seems your projects are overridden with requested changes. You try to explain to your customers the effect changes have on the competing project constraints. One simple way to explain the idea is that if one constraint changes:
a. the project cost will increase
b. the project schedule will get longer
c. at least one other factor is likely to be affected
d. all of the other factors will be affected

A142. A procurement audit:
a. identifies any weaknesses in the seller's work processes or deliverables
b. determines whether project activities comply with organizational and project policies, processes, and procedures
c. documents the effectiveness or risk responses in dealing with identified risks and their root causes, as well as the effectiveness of the risk management processes
d. reviews processes from the plan procurement process through the control procurement process

A143. Several of your key engineers are constantly showing up late for work. When they do arrive they are dressed very well, much better than is standard practice in your firm. You are wondering if what you are noticing is really a warning sign that they have been interviewing at other companies. Another name for a warning sign is:
a. risk event
b. risk impact
c. risk score
d. risk trigger

A144. Cost estimates based on project team members' recollection are generally:
a. useless
b. less reliable than documented performance
c. more reliable than documented performance
d. the most reliable form of estimating

A145. You are struggling to get your team members focused on your project. It seems that there are unclear priorities across the projects in the program. Setting priority across projects inside a program is most often handled by:
a. the project manager
b. the project stakeholders
c. senior management
d. the program manager

A146. Due to your great success on your last project you have been assigned to a new project with a very difficult customer. Based on lessons learned from others, you know it is critical that your project has clear acceptance criteria. Which of the following statements is false in regards to acceptance criteria?
a. the criteria includes performance requirements that must be achieved before the project deliverables are accepted
b. the criteria is defined in the project scope statement
c. the deliverables meeting the acceptance criteria signify that customer needs have been satisfied
d. quality control validates that the customer's acceptance criteria has been met

A147. Your project work is expected to be constant for the six month length of the project. During each month your budget is $200. At the end of month four you have 40% of the total work complete and you have spent 70% of your total budget. The planned value for the project is:
a. $ 80
b. $ 140
c. $ 800
d. $1,200

A148. You are involved in the design/build of a large manufacturing facility. The project life cycle is expected to span several years. You are able to do a detailed WBS for the early phases but not for the later phases. Your management though feels all sections of the WBS should be decomposed to the same level at the same time. You need to explain what concept to them?
a. rolling wave planning
b. the use of templates
c. define activities
d. product analysis

A149. The project is to provide clean safe drinking water to an isolated community that has been hit by massive droughts. The CPI is .90. The project is two weeks behind schedule and you have over 30 stakeholders. Where should you increase your focus?
a. schedule
b. cost
c. stakeholder management
d. conflict management

A150. In your organization, the terms projects, programs, and portfolios are often used interchangeably. You explain to management the difference between these words. Which of the following is a true statement?
a. projects and portfolios are often a subset of programs
b. senior management or senior management teams often manage portfolios
c. programs are a group of projects that may or may not be related
d. projects are usually bigger than programs

A151. You are working on your first large-scale project. Your CPI is .90. You are running two weeks behind schedule and you have over 30 stakeholders. Where should you increase your focus?
a. schedule
b. cost
c. stakeholder management
d. conflict management

A152. Project A has an initial investment at the start of the project of $80,000. At the end of year one there is a benefit of $50,000 and at the end of year two there is another benefit of $30,000. There are no other benefits. Use a discount rate (interest rate) of 8%. What is the Net Present Value of Project A?
a. -$7,983.55
b. $0
c. +$72,016.45
d. +$80,000

A153. Your project is to build the first green roof in your island community. Green roofs serve many purposes including absorbing rainfall, providing insulation, and creating a habitat for wildlife. The government has created a new regulation related to the collection of rain water that may affect your project. Based on this government mandate, what should you do first?
a. meet with your management
b. meet with the project sponsor
c. evaluate the change request
d. make the change since it is government mandated

A154. In the past, your organization has done a poor job of "killing" projects. To be more proactive a portfolio steering committee has been formed. The committee is having its first quarterly meeting. One of their primary responsibilities is to review the list of current and future projects and perform project selection. You have been assigned the responsibility to ensure they have all the information they need to make good decisions. When selecting projects the committee should take into account all of the following except:
a. sunk costs
b. opportunity costs
c. net present value
d. payback period

A155. As a member of the quality control department it is your responsibility to teach entry-level courses to all technical personnel. In this course, one of the ideas that must be addressed is tolerances versus control limits. Which statement below is *true*?
a. tolerances should be tighter than control limits
b. a data point may be outside of the control limits but still inside of the tolerances
c. your customer usually sets the control limits
d. your process or equipment usually sets the tolerances

A156. As part of plan purchase and acquisitions you are trying to decide if you should rent or buy a piece of equipment. To rent the equipment will cost $100/week. To purchase the equipment will be $900 plus a usage cost of $10/week. When will the cost to rent equal the cost to buy?
a. 8 weeks
b. 10 weeks
c. 15 weeks
d. 20 weeks

A157. Your project is expected to run for 3 consecutive years. Your organization is introducing earned value management as part of planning and managing this project. Your project assistant does all the earned value calculations for you but has a hard time interpreting the results. The project budget $100,000. The budget is consistent across the 3 years. You are exactly 18 months into the project. 30 percent of the total budget has been spent and 40% of the work is complete. Your project is:
a. ahead of schedule and over budget
b. ahead of schedule and under budget
c. behind schedule and over budget
d. behind schedule and under budget

A158. The portfolio steering committee is having their quarterly project selection meeting. At this point they are considering 4 new projects. The projects are similar in nature. The primary difference is their payment period. Project A has a payback period of 8 months. Project B has a payback period of 10 months. Project C has a payback period of 12 months. Project D has a payback period of 22 months. Based on this limited information, most likely the project that will be selected is:
a. project A
b. project B
c. project C
d. project D

© January 2016 AME Group, Inc. author Aileen Ellis, PMP, PgMP
aileen@amegroupinc.com 719-659-3658

A159. You have been selected to lead the project to move the organization into a leadership role in social media. There are many stakeholders involved from both inside and outside the organization.

Your sponsor issued the charter and the stakeholders have been kept informed throughout the life of the project. Your monthly status meetings are going well and everyone seems pleased. Your project is running on schedule, on budget, and the requirements are being achieved according to plan. As you prepare for your last deliverable you hear that the solution developed has been rejected and the project cancelled. The most likely reason for this is:

a. your sponsor was not at a high enough level in the organization to support your project
b. your timeline was not aggressive enough for the market
c. you did not control your budget to the level required for such a large project
d. a critical stakeholder was not involved or not involved early enough

A160. Your risk manager likes to use expected monetary value to quantify risk. It seems that some of your stakeholders though ignore expected monetary value and base risk decisions on the satisfaction they will obtain from each option. This theory is called:

a. hierarchy of needs
b. hygiene theory
c. utility theory
d. expectancy theory

A161. A new technician has joined your team. He and your sponsor worked together in a previous organization. Whenever you direct the work of the team he brings up what the sponsor would like the team to do. Your team is struggling with who they should be listening to as far as direction. The power being exercised by your new technician is an example of:

a. expert power
b. referent power
c. penalty power
d. formal power

A162. You are conducting lessons learned on your project. The final SPI is 1.01. The final CPI is 1.12. We had 150 geographically dispersed team members. The final product was accepted by the customer but at this point they have decided to shelve it. Where might you have put more focus?

a. managing the schedule
b. managing the budget
c. managing your team members
d. managing the relationship with the project stakeholders

A163. As a project manager in a global company, you realize that you need not only project management skills but also interpersonal skills. Problem solving is an example of an interpersonal skill. Which of the following is *not* an element of problem solving?

a. risk management
b. problem identification
c. alternative identification
d. decision-making

A164. The conflict resolution technique that definitely resolves the conflict quickly but should only be used as a last resort is:
a. compromising
b. forcing
c. confronting
d. withdrawing

A165. Your quality control group has recommended statistical sampling, which is often conducted for all the following reasons *except*:
a. sampling often can reduce costs
b. sampling is often a quicker process
c. testing may be destructive so we need to sample
d. attribute sampling measures the degree of conformance

A166. A project manager should be rewarded on cost elements he can actually influence. Which of the following is hardest for the project manager to influence?
a. direct costs
b. indirect costs
c. variable costs
d. fixed costs

A167. As a project manager in the pharmaceutical industry your projects include running many drug trials. To accurately represent this on your network diagrams you need to include conditional statements. Most likely, what type of network diagramming technique will your project use?
a. arrow diagramming technique
b. precedence diagramming technique
c. graphical evaluation review technique
d. fast tracking technique

A168. The WBS dictionary is developed during:
a. define scope
b. create WBS
c. define activities
d. develop project management plan

A169. Your contractor is reporting to you on a monthly basis on cost performance using CPI. History has shown that the CPI on a project often becomes stable when what percent of the work is complete?
a. 15%-20%
b. 25%-30%
c. 30%-45%
d. 30% -50%

© January 2016 AME Group, Inc. author Aileen Ellis, PMP, PgMP
aileen@amegroupinc.com 719-659-3658

A170. You have been managing a large mapmaking project for the government. Your customer is asking for multiple scope changes. You are looking at these requested changes and trying to determine the true magnitude of these changes. You are most likely to review what document?
a. scope management plan
b. WBS
c. project charter
d. cost management plan

A171. You have spent months planning your project and you and your team are ready to start execution. Direct and manage project work is implementing the project management plan and any approved changes made to the plan. Which of the following is not an input to direct and manage project work?
a. approved corrective action
b. approved preventive action
c. approved defect repair
d. approved contract changes

A172. You work for a large company that has existed for over 100 years. Your business is building and maintaining the railroad systems for the country. Projects have always been managed using a functional structure and you, as a new project manager, are pushing to move to a projectized structure. Which of the following is a disadvantage of a projectized structure?
a. higher potential for conflict
b. more complex to manage
c. extra administration required
d. less efficient use of resources

A173. The procurement professionals in your organization work in a centralized organization. A consultant has recommended that you move to decentralized contracting. All of the following are positives of decentralized contracting except:
a. more loyalty to the project
b. easier access to contracting expertise
c. more in depth understanding of the needs of the project
d. clearly defined career paths for contracting professionals

A174. Deviations from the project management plan may indicate:
a. the project team has apathy for the project
b. poor teamwork
c. potential impacts of threats and opportunities
d. the need for more quality inspectors

A175. Your organization has just won a large contract. Management says start work immediately. For you this means to get a project charter approved. Management tells you there is no time for this. What should you do first?
a. explain the risks of proceeding without a charter
b. begin work on planning and at the same time push until you get the charter defined and approved
c. say you will skip the charter but demand that management allows you time to create a WBS
d. assume the contract is the charter and begin work

A176. When an organization identifies an opportunity to which it would like to respond, it often initiates a:
a. project scope statement
b. feasibility study
c. work breakdown structure
d. project management plan

A177. The cost of proposal preparation is normally at:
a. no direct cost to the buyer
b. a direct cost to the buyer only if the buyer does not buy from the seller
c. a direct cost to the buyer only if the buyer does buy from the seller
d. a direct cost to the buyer regardless of whether the buyer buys from the seller

A178. Based on the diagram the project is currently?
a. ahead of schedule and under budget
b. ahead of schedule and over budget
c. behind schedule and under budget
d. behind schedule and over budget

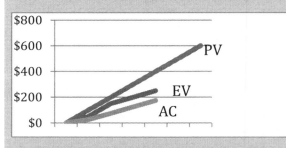

A179. The theory that high levels of trust, confidence, and commitment to workers on the part of management leads to a high level of motivation and productivity on the part of workers is:
a. Vroom's Expectancy theory
b. Ouchi's Theory Z
c. McGregor's Theory X
d. Herzberg's Hygiene Theory

A180. Your quality manager and operations manager are arguing about how much money should be spent on quality. The real question is how to define optimal quality. Marginal analysis states that optimal quality is reached when:
a. the incremental revenue from improvement equals the incremental cost to obtain it
b. quality has the same priority as cost and schedule
c. more money is spent proactively on quality than reactively on quality
d. nothing more can be done to improve quality

A181. The performance measurements on your project are good and holding steady but your project seems completely out of control. The project CPI is 1.04 and the project SPI is 1.03. You have 405 team members in 30 different countries. You know that your focus should be on communications yet all of your time is spent on managing changes. All of the changes are catching you by surprise. Your team is closing out phase four of an eight phase project. One likely lesson learned is that more effort should have been placed on:
a. identifying a project manager for every country
b. planning for delays related to the number of countries involved
c. planning for cost overruns related to the number of countries involved
d. identifying stakeholders

A182. As a house builder you often take on more work than you can handle. For years you have delivered homes late, but you continue to be profitable. Your current project is running 90 days late and the home buyer states that she is going after punitive damages. Punitive damages represent:
a. the exact amount due to the injured party for his loss
b. the amount agreed to in advance
c. the specific performance stated in the contract
d. the amount above what would barely compensate the injured party for his loss

A183. Herzberg's hygiene theory stresses:
a. some job factors lead to satisfaction whereas others can only prevent dissatisfaction
b . some job factors lead to satisfaction and to dissatisfaction
c. some job factors lead to satisfaction in some people and dissatisfaction in other people
d. job satisfaction and dissatisfaction exist on the same continuum.

A184. On your factory floor much space is occupied by work in progress. Management has decided to try a pull system. Therefore, workers do not automatically receive work in progress from a previous station but need to pull when they need inventory. Another name for this system is:
a. Kanban
b. Kaizen
c. Utility Theory
d. Marginal Analysis

A185. Your manager has limited knowledge of project management but understands the basic idea that it is important to manage the critical path. You have one critical path on your project and seven near critical paths. Your manager has only had a basic course on project management and never heard of the idea of near critical path. You explain the more near critical paths you have, the more:
a. float you have on your activities
b. cost you have on your project
c. risk you have on your project
d. people working on the project

A186. Your management is heavily involved in making choices of where to concentrate resources on your project, anticipating potential project issues and dealing with these issues before they become critical. You remind your manager that on a project these type of roles are handled by:
a. the sponsor
b. the project manager
c. the team
d. the functional managers

A187. A project manager has been managing a long term training project. The training is over and she is trying to close out her project. The situation is not good. All of the requirements have been met but the customer is not satisfied. The customer is stating that the results of the training are not what they expected. One likely cause of this is:
a. the instructors were not qualified
b. the customer's expectations were not turned into requirements
c. the customer is trying to exploit the contract
d. the training did not go into enough detail

A188. The project manager has submitted several contested changes to the customer.
These contested changes, often called claims or disputes, are getting in the way of progress. The preferred method to settle claims and disputes is:
a. mediation
b. arbitration
c. litigation
d. negotiation

A189. Your company, Hausmann Associates, is in the final stages of the design/build of a semiconductor factory for a major customer. At the last customer meeting, the company finance manager mentioned the possibility of building another factory in the near future. This is an opportunity your company wants. The most likely strategy you are to use is:
a. exploit
b. mitigate
c. transfer
d. avoid

A190. The theory that people choose behaviors that they believe will lead to desired rewards or outcomes is:
a. Maslow's Hierarchy
b. McGregor's Theory Y
c. Vroom's Expectancy Theory
d. Ouchi's Theory Z

A191. As the project manager of a small start-up company it is always important to understand your working capital. Working capital is defined as:
a. current assets minus current liabilities
b. present value of inflows minus present value of outflows
c. price minus cost
d. price minus profit

A192. One of the key resources on your project is being pulled to a higher priority project. Their activity (Activity A) has an early finish of 12 days and a late finish of 10 days. This means:
a. Activity A has -2 days of total float
b. Activity A has a lag of 2 days
c. Activity A has a duration of 2 days
d. Activity A has a +2 days of float

A193. You are heavily involved in the sale of construction services to a large manufacturing firm. During the negotiation, your organization's contracts manager takes over and pushes for the contract type to be cost plus percentage cost instead of the originally planned cost plus fixed fee. You realize that your contract's manager may be assuming:
a. the contract will run over the estimated costs
b. the contract will run under the estimated costs
c. the buyer is taking too much risk
d. the buyer needs the seller to take more risk before they will sign the contract

A194. You are the project manager for a large construction company. Risk management is a large part of what you manage. Your management tells you to focus on the business risks and they will focus on the pure risks. How is your organization most likely to deal with pure risks?
a. hire more staff
b. build contingency into the schedule
c. build contingency into the budget
d. buy insurance

A195. The control limits on a control chart provide us information on:
a. the amount of expected variation expected
b. the amount of allowed variation expected
c. the tolerances set by the customer
d. the specifications set by the customer

A196. You have been put in charge of a team comprised of very experienced members. The team has been very successful in the past. Your least likely leadership style in this situation is:
a. consensus
b. consultative
c. autocratic
d. facilitating

A197. The project is to transfer technology developed in your factory in Scotland to an operations facility in China. There are approximately 3,000 stakeholders on the project living in 12 different countries. Your sponsor is very involved and communicates regularly with you, the project management team, and the key stakeholders. Your CPI is .95 and the project is running 14 weeks behind schedule. Based on this scenario what should you be most concerned about?
a. schedule
b. cost
c. stakeholder management
d. sponsor management

A198. You are reviewing the latest data collected on your control chart. The piece of equipment is cutting pipe. The process mean is a length of 42.35 meters. The upper control limit is 42.83 meters. The lower control limit is 41.87. The latest data in sequence is: 41.92, 42.38, 42.75, 42.32, 42.01, 41.97, 41.88, 42.30, 42.09, 41.95. From this data we can state:
a. the process is out of control
b. the process is in control
c. the tolerance limits should be tighter
d. the tolerance limits should be wider

A199. The pessimistic time to complete Activity A is 22 days. The optimistic time is 10 days. The standard deviation for Activity A is:
a. 1 day
b. 2 days
c. 6 days
d. 12 days

A200. You are managing multiple projects for your customer, the British Government. Each contract seems to be a different type such as Time and Materials, Cost Reimbursable, and even some Fixed Price contracts. The corporate accountant calls you to state that you are about to hit your PTA (point of total assumption) on one of the contracts. The accountant is talking about which contract type?
a. Time and Materials
b. cost plus fixed fee
c. cost plus incentive
d. fixed price incentive

© January 2016 AME Group, Inc. author Aileen Ellis, PMP, PgMP
aileen@amegroupinc.com 719-659-3658

SAMPLE TEST

Solutions

A001. b.   PMBOK® Guide: Section 1.5.2

Y   b. Projects often fail when the project's objectives are not aligned to the strategic plan of the organization. Therefore, we need to ensure that the project stays aligned to the organization's strategic plan.

N   a. We should never update a document as quickly as possible. We need to ensure that the new project objectives are aligned with the organization's strategic plan.

N   c We cannot always reject changes to the project objectives. At times these changes may make sense.

N   d. We cannot update the project plan based on the new project objectives unless the charter is updated first. The project objectives are found in the project charter.

A002. b.   PMBOK® Guide: Chapter 11 - Introduction

Y   b. A tolerance represents the point at which the organization will stand no more risk. This is represented in the question at the point when Alarm #2 rings.

N   a. A risk appetite is the degree of uncertainly an entity is willing to take on in anticipation of a reward.

N   c. The ringing of Alarm #1 tells us we have reached a threshold and we have specific interest in this. We are going to change our behavior at this threshold.

N   d. A workaround is an unplanned response to a risk event. The alarm ringing is a planned, not an unplanned response.

A003. c.   PMBOK® Guide: Section 10.1.2.4

Y   c. During the acquire project team process (as part of executing) we negotiate for the team members we need. During the develop project team process (as part of executing) we provide training and team building.

N   a. During initiating most of the work is being accomplished by the project manager, the sponsor, and a very limited number of team members.

N   b. During planning we may have a planning team (a limited team). There is nothing in the question to make us believe we are talking about a planning team.

N   d. We negotiate for team members and provide team building as part of executing, not monitoring and controlling.

A004. d.   PMBOK® Guide: Section 4.1

Y   d. The project charter at a minimum defines the project objectives. We cannot proceed with planning until we have agreed on the project objectives.

N   a., b., and c. It is important to have the charter developed and approved before we start planning. How can we plan if we are unsure of the project objectives. Also, we need a sponsor to provide the financial resources for the project. The sponsor needs to sign the charter.

A005. d.   PMBOK® Guide: Chapter 8 - Quality Introduction

Y   d. The question asks the first thing to do. We may want to do everything on the list, but what do we do first? We address the immediate problem first.

N   a and b. These are both great ideas, we just do not do them first.

N   c. It is our responsibility as the project manager to address these issues.

A006. b.   PMBOK® Guide: Section 8.1.2.3

Y   b. Variations inside the control limits on a control chart provide us information related to common causes.

© January 2016 AME Group, Inc. author Aileen Ellis, PMP, PgMP
aileen@amegroupinc.com 719-659-3658

N   a., c. and d. Variation outside the control limits may be called special cause variation or assignable cause variation and may be associated with unnatural patterns.

Figure for A007-009

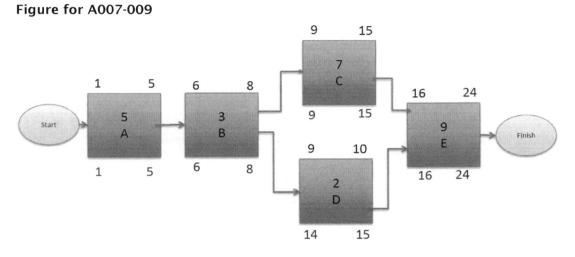

A007. b.   **PMBOK® Guide 5.4.2.1 and 6.3.2.1**

Lets do a forward pass to calculate the project duration. Remember the project and the critical path duration are the same. The project duration is 24 days. Answer b.

A008.   **d.**   **PMBOK® Guide 5.4.2.1 and 6.3.2.1**
Now lets do a backward pass to calculate the float of D.

Now let's calculate the float of D. The float (or you could call it total float or slack or total slack) of D=
late finish of D-early finish of D= 15-10=5. D has 5 days of float.

Let's calculate the other floats.
Float of A= late finish of A-early finish of A= 0
Float of B= late finish of B-early finish of B= 0
Float of C= late finish of C-early finish of C= 0
Float of E= late finish of E-early finish of E= 0

A009. d.   **PMBOK® Guide 5.4.2.1 and 6.3.2.1**
The activities on the critical path are A-B-C-E since they each have zero float.

A010. d.   **PMBOK® Guide: Section 10.1**
Y   d. When you see a question that asks what process may have prevented an issue, in general we are looking for a planning process, not a controlling process. Often the issues we see during executing and monitoring and controlling were caused, or at least not prevented, during planning.
N   a. and b. Controlling processes do not prevent issues. They help us determine corrective or preventative actions. Etc.
N   c. Manage communications at first sounds like a good answer. In this process though we just follow the communications plan. If the plan has errors, this process will just follow the errors.

A011. d.   Garrett World Class Contracting page 128
Y   d. A letter of intent is a pre-contract agreement that often unofficially encourages sellers to start work.
N   a. A purchase order is the simplest form of a fixed price contract. The statement is asking about what you would use before you can award a contract.
N   b. A request for proposal is a document used to request proposals from sellers. This document will not get the seller to start work.
N   c. A purchase agreement sets the terms and conditions that apply to transactions between parties. The seller in general though will not start work until there is a contract.

A012. b.   PMBOK° Guide: Section 11.4.2.2
Y   b. The network diagram is the part of the model used for schedule risk analysis. One reason for this is that the network diagram shows path convergence. The duration estimates are also required since the output will show the probability of achieving time objectives.
N   a. There is no such thing as a work breakdown schedule. There is a work breakdown structure, though it is not used for schedule risk analysis.
N   c. Duration estimates alone are not enough for schedule risk analysis. We need a diagram that shows the entire schedule including path convergence.
N   d. The schedule management plan is a plan that describes how we will manage changes to the project schedule. It is a plan, not a model.

A013. c.   PMBOK° Guide: Section 4.5
Y   c. Often an indicator that one or more key stakeholders were not involved early on is a higher than expected number of change orders.
N   a. The question states that your sponsor is very involved.
N   b. The question states that you have a project plan including baselines.
N   d. The question states the project will involve working with the city, the county, the police department, and several suppliers. All of these stakeholders should be identified early in the project.

A014. c.   PMBOK® Guide: Section 9.1.2.1
Y   c. RAMs (responsibility assignment matrixes) show who is responsible for what activity. It is critical that only one person be accountable for each activity.
N   a. An organizational breakdown structure shows the organization's departments and which work packages are assigned to which departments.
N   b. An organizational chart shows reporting relationships.
N   d. A resource calender shows when specific resources are available.

A015. d.   PMBOK® Guide: Section 8.1.2.3
Y   d. Pareto diagrams help us set priority.
N   a. Cause and effect diagrams help us find the root cause of certain negative effects.
N   b. Flowcharts help us visualize the steps to transform an input(s) into a desirable output.
N   c. Checksheets are used to visibly collect data.

A016. d.   PMBOK® Guide: Section 7.2.2.2
Y   d. Analogous estimating is often used when little information is available about the project. In this method we use a past similar project as the basis for our estimate. This method is often quicker, less costly but less accurate.
N   a. Vendor bid analysis involves using vendor bids as the basis of our estimates.
N   b. Parametric estimating involves using statistical relationships between variables to create cost estimates.

© January 2016 AME Group, Inc. author Aileen Ellis, PMP, PgMP
aileen@amegroupinc.com 719-659-3658

N   c. Bottom-up estimating involves estimating the cost of work packages (or activities) and rolling these estimates up to create a cost estimate for the project.

A017. d.   PMBOK° Guide: Section 6.3.2.3

Y   d. Lag time is delay time; this is the time needed for the concrete to cure.

N   a. Total float is the total amount of time that a scheduled activity may be delayed from its early start without delaying the project finish date. This question has nothing to do with float.

N   b. Free float is the amount of time that a schedule activity can be delayed without delaying the early start of any immediately following schedule activity. The question has nothing to do with free float.

N   c. Lead is a modification of a logical relationship that allows an acceleration of the successor activity. This question is the exact opposite of a lead.

A018.   PMBOK° Guide: Sections 6.4 and 9.2

Y   b. This statement describes plan human resource management and estimate activity resources very well.

N   a. Plan human resource management and estimate activity resources are very different processes. Plan human resource management is related to people; estimate activity resources is related to all resources such as people, equipment, and materials.

N   c. This statement is reversed. Plan human resource management leads to acquire project team and estimate activity resources leads to estimate costs.

N   d. This statement is reversed. The project organization chart is an output of plan human resource management and the resource breakdown structure is an output of estimate activity resources.

A019. b.   PMBOK° Guide: Figure 4-1

Y   b. Change requests are an output of monitor and control project work.

N   a. The project management plan is an output of develop project management plan.

N   c. Approved change requests are an output of perform integrated change control.

N   d. All requested changes should be approved or rejected and approved changes implemented before close project.

A020. a.   PMBOK° Guide: Section 4.5

Y   a. Every change should go through the change control process. In this example we may decide to cancel the project versus implement the change.

N   b., c., and d. Elements of perform integrated change control include: controlling factors that create changes to make sure those changes are beneficial, determining when a change has occurred, and managing the approved changes.

A021. a.   PMBOK° Guide: Section 5.1

Y   a. The effort spent on project management should be appropriate based on the size, risk, and importance of the project.

N   b. As project managers, we should not follow this methodology explicitly. We need to work with the PMO to tailor the methodology for our project.

N   c. The methodology should not be ignored. It should be tailored for our project.

N   d. This answer is good but we need to work with the PMO since we have been instructed to follow the methodology.

A022. c.   PMI° Code of Ethics and Professional Conduct

Y   c. The PMI° Code of Ethics and Professional Conduct is applicable for both PMI° members and individuals who have applied for or received certification through PMI° regardless of their membership in PMI°.

N   a. The *PMBOK® Guide* is a standard, not a regulation. It does not have to be followed. It is suggested that the project management team tailor the information in the *PMBOK® Guide* to their specific project.

N   b. PMI® publishes a tremendous amount of information. It is the responsibility of the project management team to determine what is appropriate for any given project.

N   d. PMI® standards are standards, not regulations. They do not have to be followed.

A023. d.   PMBOK® Guide: Section 10.2.3.1

Y   d. The communications management plan describes many things, including the person or group who will receive information.

N   a. Be careful with any answer that contains the word all. It is unlikely that any report would go to all stakeholders. Remember that stakeholders can include many groups of people, both internal and external. It is highly unlikely that all of these groups would be getting a performance report.

N   b. "Key stakeholders" is certainly a better answer than all stakeholders, but still, we communicate based on the communications plan.

N   c. Team members may be true but we don't know until we look at the communications plan.

A024. b.   PMBOK® Guide: Section 9.1.3.1

Y   b. The staffing management plan should include items such as staff acquisition, timetables, release criteria, training needs, recognition and rewards, compliance and safety.

N   a. The project management plan is a true statement but look for an answer that is a little more specific.

N   c. The project organization chart is a visual display of the project team members and their reporting relationships.

N   d. The communication management plan documents the project communication needs and how those needs will be addressed.

A025. c.   Any Text Book on Quality or Six Sigma

Y   c. With three sigma, defects occur about 3 times in a thousand and with six sigma, defects occur about 3.3 times in a million. Six sigma for many organizations is a measure of quality that strives for near perfection.

N   a. Six sigma is much more than twice as stringent as three sigma. With three sigma, defects occur about 3 times in a thousand and with six sigma, defects occur only about 3.3 times in a million.

N   b. Control limits are often set at plus or minus three sigma not six sigma (PMBOK Guide 8.1.2.3).

N   d. When people say three sigma they really mean plus or minus three standard deviations on each side of the mean.

A026. c.   PMBOK® Guide: Section 7.4.3.4

Y   c. A revised cost baseline may need to be created to provide a realistic basis for performance measurement.

N   a. Your cost management plan is updated if approved changes impact the management of costs. This scenario does not affect the management of costs and therefore the cost management plan is not updated.

N   b. A revised project schedule is created when we can no longer measure schedule performance. The question relates to cost performance, not schedule performance.

N   d. The WBS is updated when approved changes have an effect upon the project scope. This scenario does not imply a change in scope and therefore the WBS is not updated.

A027. c.   Any statistics book

Y   c. The variance is defined as the square of the standard deviation. One standard deviation = (P-O)/6. = (24-12)/6= 2 days. The variance is (2 days) 2 = 4 days.

N   a and b. These are distractor answers.

N   d. 2 days is the standard deviation, not the variance.

A028. b.   PMBOK® Guide: Section 5.3

Y   b. A WBS shows the hierarchy of deliverables. It does not show sequence. A network diagram or schedule shows sequence.

N   a. The WBS is deliverable oriented. Each level shows the progressive level of detail.

N   c. The output of building the WBS is the WBS. A secondary effect is that the work it takes to build the WBS also builds the team.

N   d. With more investigation you will find that the WBS is an input to many of the planning processes that follow it.

A029. a.   PMI® Code of Ethics and Professional Conduct

Y   a. The four core values described in the PMI® Code of Ethics and Professional Conduct are: responsibility, respect, fairness, and honesty. A conflict of interest occurs when we are in a position to influence an outcome when such outcomes could affect one or more parties with whom we have competing loyalties.

N   b., c., and d. The four core values described in the PMI® Code of Ethics and Professional Conduct are: responsibility, respect, fairness, and honesty.

A030. c.   PMBOK® Guide: Table 3-1

Y   c. Manage stakeholder engagement is a process of the executing group, not the monitoring and controlling group.

N   a. Validate scope is a process of the monitoring and controlling process group.

N   b. Control risk is a process of the monitoring and controlling process group.

N   d. Control stakeholder engagement is a process of the monitoring and controlling process group.

A031. c.   Garrett World Class Contracting, page 123

Y   c. A purchase agreement sets the terms and conditions that apply to transactions between parties. It is often used when the parties do not know the exact quantity or exact products that will be exchanged. This agreement reduces the time to form a contract since the terms and conditions are already in place each time.

N   a. A purchase order is the simplest form of a firm fixed price contract. You will not want to use a firm fixed price contract since you do not know the exact quantity or exact products you are buying.

N   b. A request for proposal is a document used to request proposals from sellers.

N   d. A letter of intent is a pre-contract agreement that often unofficially encourages sellers to start work.

A032. c.   PMBOK® Guide: Section 11.5.3.2

Y   c. A secondary risk is a risk that emerges as the direct result of implementing a risk response.

N   a. A fallback plan is a plan if the contingency plan does not work.

N   b. A contingency plan is developed in advance as part of active acceptance.

N   d. A workaround is an unplanned response to a risk event.

A033. c.   PMBOK® Guide: Section 13.2.2.3

Y   c. The stakeholder engagement matrix shows both the current level and the desired level of engagement.

N   a. The communications management plan describes who gets what communication, when, how often, and in what form.

N   b. The stakeholder register shows a list of stakeholders as well as assessment and classification information.

N   d. The requirements documentation shows the requirements for the project. In the question it is clear that the issue is not with requirements but with the lack of involvement of the stakeholders.

A034. b.   *PMBOK® Guide*: Section 6.5.2.4

Y   b. PERT = (optimistic + 4* most likely + pessimistic)/6 =(80+(4*100)+150)/6 = 105 hours.

N   a., c., and d. Use the formula:
PERT = (optimistic + 4* most likely + pessimistic)/6 to find the correct answer.

A035. c.   PMBOK® Guide: Section 8.1.2.5

Y   c. Design of experiments is a statistical method that helps identify which factors may influence specific variables of a product or process under development or in production.

N   a. Pareto charts help rank order to guide corrective action.

N   b. Control charts help determine whether or not a process is stable or has predictable performance.

N   d. An inspection is the examination of a work product to determine whether it conforms to standards.

A036. a.   PMBOK® Guide: Section 7.1.3.1

Y   a. Cost estimates should be provided to a prescribed precision ($100, $1000) based on the activities and magnitude of the project.

N   b. Control thresholds set the agreed amount of variance allowed over time on a project.

N   c. Earned value rules define several items including the level of the work breakdown structure at which EV analysis will be performed.

N   d. Report formats define the format of various cost reports.

A037. a.   See Wikipedia –Work Breakdown Structure

Y   a. The 80 hour rule is a heuristic. It is a rule of thumb that states that each work package should require 80 hours of effort or less.

N   b. PMI has no regulations on the number of effort hours that should be required to complete a work package.

N   c. A constraint limits the project team's options. Management made a suggestion. Suggestions are not constraints.

N   d. Ground rules are often developed by teams to list acceptable and unacceptable behaviors to improve relationships.

A038. d.   PMBOK® Guide: Section 8.1.2.3

Y   d. Control charts help us see over time if a process is stable and/or has predictable performance.

N   a. Cause and effect diagrams help us determine the root causes for certain effects.

N   b. Histograms show the shape of a distribution. They do not show the time.

N   c. Scatter diagrams seek to explain correlations or the lack of correlations.

A039. d.   PMBOK® Guide: Section 4.5

Y   d. Perform integrated change control is the process that maintains baseline integrity. This is where we need to address the approved changes and assure that all the approved changes get into the baseline.

N   a. Develop project management plan is the process of documenting the actions required to plan and manage the project. This answer is true but not the best answer. Look for a more specific answer.

N   b. Direct and manage project work is about implementing the work of the project plan.

N   c. Monitor and control project work is the process of measuring the work against the project plan and initiating corrective action. Requested changes, not approved or rejected changes, come out of this step.

A040. b.   PMBOK° Guide: Chapter 7 and Chapter 12

Y   b. Cost is the amount spent to deliver a product or service. Price is the amount charged to a customer. The price may or may not be related to the cost. Often the price is market driven. This idea is not in the book. Hopefully, you were able to eliminate the other answers so as to be left with this one. Of course, practical experience may have helped also.

N   a., c., and d. These statements are all true.

A041. a.   PMBOK° Guide: Section 12.2.2.1

Y   a. Often before the bidder conference we allow bidders to submit questions on the requirements. During the conference we make sure that every bidder hears every question and every answer.

N   b. Weighted criteria is often used as part of the proposal evaluation techniques. This does nothing to ensure that all the bidders understood the requirement.

N   c. Analytical techniques are used to ensure that the bidder can meet the requirement, etc.

N   d. Procurement negotiations are used to clarify the requirements, etc. In general, negotiations won't ensure that every bidder receives fair treatment.

A042. a.   PMBOK° Guide: Section 11.5.2.1

Y   a. A contingency reserve is not a change to how we are going to do the work of the project and thus is associated with acceptance, not mitigation. Be careful of the word except.

N   b., c., and d. Mitigation is the lowering of the probability or impact of an adverse risk event. The examples listed are all examples of mitigation. Be careful of the word except.

A043. a.   PMBOK° Guide: Chapter 10 - Introduction

Y   a. Formal written communication examples include project reports, project plans, etc.

N   b. An informal written example would be an e-mail.

N   c. A formal verbal example would be a project presentation.

N   d. An informal verbal example would be an ad hoc discussion.

A044. b.   PMBOK° Guide: Section 9.3.2.6

Y   b. Zero sum rewards are win-lose rewards that only a limited number of project team members can achieve such as team member of the month.

N   a. Zero sum rewards may or may not cost money.

N   c. Not everyone, at least not at the same time, can win a zero sum reward. They are for a limited number of team members.

N   d. This statement is just the opposite of a zero sum reward.

A045. a.   PMBOK° Guide: Section 8.1.2.3

Y   a. Pareto charts show how many defects (or missed questions) were generated by type or category of identified cause and help rank order to guide corrective action.

N   b. Cause and effect diagrams help us understand how various factors may be linked to potential problems.

N   c. Flow charts show how items in a system relate.

N   d. Scatter diagrams are used to show the possible relationship between two variables.

A046. d.   PMBOK° Guide: Section 12.1.1.9

Y   d. Fixed price is the contract type in which the buyer has the lowest financial risk because the buyer knows exactly what the price of the contract will be if there are no approved change orders.

N   a. Time and materials contracts in general are a higher risk for the buyer since this contract type is open ended. The full value of the agreement and the exact quantity of items to be delivered are not defined.

N   b. and c. Cost plus percentage of cost and cost plus fixed fee generally are a higher risk for the buyer because in these contract types the buyer must reimburse the seller for all allowable costs plus a fee. The buyer does not know the total price of the contract at the time of contract award.

A047. a.   Northcote Parkinson, Parkinson's Law: The Pursuit of Progress, London, John Murray (1958)

Y   a. Parkinson's theory states that people will expand the work to fill the time allowed. In the question, more paths are becoming critical because people are expanding the work to fill the time and thus using up the float.

N   b. This could be lazy team members but lazy team members is not likely to be an answer on the exam.

N   c. Critical chain is a network analysis technique that modifies the project schedule to account for limited resources. There is nothing in the question to lead us to critical chain.

N   d. The critical path method calculates theoretical early and late start and finish dates. This is a network analysis technique. This answer does not address the issue in the question of additional critical paths.

A048. a.   PMBOK® Guide: Section 5.4.3.1

Y   a. The WBS dictionary describes the details of each work package. This detailed explanation should help lower the probability of different interpretations of the work packages.

N   b. A detailed WBS means that you decompose the WBS to a tremendous amount of detail. This may help, but look for a better answer. The WBS lists the work packages but does not define them.

N   c. A work authorization system authorizes when and in what sequence activities should occur. This system is very useful on large construction as well as other projects.

N   d. The control accounts are part of every WBS. Having control accounts will not help define the work packages because the control accounts are above the work packages.

A049. b.   Do web search on mathematical models for project selection

Y   b. Mathematical models that use linear, nonlinear, dynamic, integer, or multi-objective programming algorithms are used in project selection.

N   a., c., and d. Benefit contribution, comparative approaches, and economic models are all examples of benefit measurement methods used in project selection.

A050. a.   PMBOK° Guide: Table 3-1

Y   a. Integrated change control is part of the monitoring and controlling process group, not the executing process group.

N   b., c., and d. These processes are all part of the executing process group.

A051. d.   Garrett World Class Contracting, page 114

© January 2016 AME Group, Inc. author Aileen Ellis, PMP, PgMP
aileen@amegroupinc.com 719-659-3658

Y   d. The point of total assumption is the point where the sharing relationship changes to a share ratio to 0/100. At this point the seller picks up 100 % of the cost risk.

N   a. Contract award is the point when the buyer and the seller sign the contract.

N   b. Contract breach is the failure without legal excuse to perform a promise of the contract.

N   c. Contract termination is the end of the contract while at least one party still has open obligations.

A052.   a.   PMBOK® Guide: Figure 2-9

Y   a. Early in the project, we have not invested a lot and thus the amount at stake is low. The further we get into a project, the more has been invested, and thus the more is at stake. This is not explained clearly in the PMBOK® Guide.

N   b. The level of uncertainty is highest at the beginning of the project. The certainty of completion generally gets higher as the project continues and thus the level of uncertainty decreases.

N   c. Early in the project, we have not invested a lot and thus the amount at stake is low. The further we get into a project, the more has been invested, and thus the more is at stake.

N   d. The risk of failing to achieve the objectives is highest at the start and gets lower as the project continues.

A053.   c.   Statistical Process Control textbooks or Web Search

Y   c. One standard deviation is equal to the absolute value of ((upper control limit-lower control limit)/6). Therefore, one standard deviation = (63-57)/6= 6/6= 1 centimeter. The mean is 60 centimeters. 58 centimeters is – 2 standard deviations from the mean, and 62 centimeters is + 2 standard deviations from the mean. We are looking for the answer that represents +/- 2 standard deviations from the mean. 95.5 % of the data will fall within +/- 2 standard deviations.

N   a. 68.3% of the data represents +/- 1 standard deviation. That range would be the mean of 60 centimeters plus 1 centimeter and the mean minus 1 centimeter (61 -59 centimeters).

N   b. This is a distractor answer.

N   d. 99.7 % of the data will fall in the range of +/- 3 standard deviations, which is 57-63 centimeters.

A054.   d.   Verma, *Human Resource Skills for the Project Manager*, page 70

Y   d. Theory Y is a positive view management has of workers.

N   a., b., and c. These statements are all a negative view of workers from management. Therefore, these statements represent the McGregor's Theory X not Theory Y.

A055.   a.   PMBOK® Guide: Section 5.2.2.3

Y   a. Storyboarding is an example of a prototyping technique.

N   b. Benchmarking is used to identify best practices by comparing our practices to those of others.

N   c. Examples of facilitated workshops include JAD sessions and QFD sessions.

N   d. Brainstorming is used to collect ideas often from a large diverse group of people.

A056.   a.   PMBOK® Guide: Table 7-1 right hand column

Y   a. A SPI of less than one means that you are running behind schedule. You should put your focus on the schedule.

N   b. A CPI of 1.2 means that you are running under budget. This is a good thing.

N   c. and d. We should always be concerned about our stakeholders and our management. There is nothing in the question though that states we need to focus more on our stakeholders or our manager. The question does state that we have an SPI that is less than one. The SPI is measurable.

A057. b.   PMBOK® Guide: Section 6.6.2.7

Y   b. Fast-tracking is a technique in which we allow activities to overlap or be completed in parallel that we would prefer to be done in series.

N   a. Crashing is a schedule compression technique that involves adding resources to activities on the critical path. This is not the right answer since it involves adding resources.

N   c. Resource leveling is not a schedule compression technique. In fact, the schedule often gets longer when resource leveling is done.

N   d. Project management software certainly can help with develop schedule but it is not a schedule compression technique.

A058. a.   PMBOK® Guide: Section 5.4.3.1

Y   a. The scope management plan describes how we will define and manage scope. The scope itself is not defined in the scope management plan.

N   b. There are three documents that make-up the scope baseline including the scope statement.

N   c. There are three documents that make-up the scope baseline. The WBS is one of them.

N   d. There are three documents that make-up the scope baseline. The WBS dictionary is one of them.

A059. b.   PMBOK® Guide: Section 4.5

Y   b. The configuration management system is a subsystem of the overall project management system. It is a collection of formal documented procedures used to apply technical and administrative direction and surveillance to: identify and document the functional and physical characteristics of a product, result, service, or component; control any changes to such characteristics; record and report each change and its implementation status; and support the audit of the products, results, or components to verify conformance to requirements.

N   a. The change control system is a collection of formal documented procedures that define how project deliverables and documentation will be controlled, changed, and approved. In most application areas the change control system is a subset of the configuration management system.

N   c. A change control board is responsible for meeting and reviewing the change requests and approving or rejecting those changes.

N   d. The project team uses stakeholders with expert judgment on the change control board to control and approve all requested changes to any aspect of the project.

A060. a.   PMBOK® Guide: Table 3-1

Y   a. The cost estimates are an output of estimate costs and an input of determine budget. Therefore, estimate costs is likely to occur before determine budget.

N   b. Qualitative risk analysis is the process of prioritizing risk for quantitative analysis. It makes sense that qualitative risk analysis would come before quantitative risk analysis.

N   c. We must plan our procurements before we can conduct our procurements.

N   d. Requirements documentation, which is an output of collect requirements is an input into define scope. Therefore, we work on requirements before scope.

A061. c.   PMBOK® Guide: Figure 12-1

Y   c. Control procurements is the process of managing procurement relationships, monitoring contract performance, and making changes and corrections as needed.

N   a. Plan procurements is the process of documenting project purchasing decisions, specifying the approach, and identifying potential sellers. This is too early for the contract change control system.

© January 2016 AME Group, Inc. author Aileen Ellis, PMP, PgMP
aileen@amegroupinc.com 719-659-3658

N   b. Conduct procurements is the process of obtaining seller responses, selecting a seller, and awarding a contract. This is too early for the contract change control system.

N   d. Close procurements is the process of completing each project procurement. This is too early for the contract change control system.

A062. d.   PMBOK Guide: Chapter 11 - Introduction

Y   d. Perform quantitative risk analysis looks at overall project risk.

N   a. Perform qualitative risk analysis looks at individual risks from a subjective standpoint.

N   b. Monitor and control project risks is the process of implementing risk responses, etc.

N   c. Plan risk responses is the process of development options to enhance opportunities and reduce threats.

A063. b.   PMBOK® Guide: Section 6.2.2.2

Y   b. Rolling wave planning is a tool and technique of define activities. With this tool and technique we plan near term work in detail and long term work at a higher level.

A064. d.   Verma, *Human Resource Skills for the Project Manager,* Figure 7-9

Y   d. Expert power is derived from one's knowledge, not one's position.

N   a., b., and c. Formal, reward, and penalty power may all be associated or derived from one's position in the organization.

A065. d.   Any Text Book on Statistics

Y   d. We may decide to test samples instead of populations for either attribute sampling or for variable sampling. This is not the reason to test samples.

N   a., b., and c. The three main reasons that organizations test samples instead of populations are: the testing may be destructive, the testing is expensive, and the testing takes a long time.

A066. a.   *Earned Value Management*, Fleming and Koppelaman

Y   a. The performance measurement baseline is split into the distributed budget and the undistributed budget.

N   b. The contract budget is split into the performance measurement baseline and the management reserve. The contingency reserve is part of the performance measurement baseline.

N   c. The contract price is split into the cost and profit.

N   d. The cost accounts are split into the planning packages and the work packages.

A067. a.   Wikipedia on Concurrent Engineering

Y   a. Fast tracking is about overlapping activities while concurrent engineering is moving implementers to an earlier phase of the project.

N   b. Fast tracking is about overlapping activities. Crashing, not concurrent engineering, is adding resources to the critical path.

N   c. Concurrent engineering, not fast tracking, is about moving implementers to an earlier phase of the project. Crashing, not concurrent engineering, is about adding resources to the critical path.

N   d. Fast tracking is overlapping phases as well as overlapping activities.

A068. b.   PMBOK® Guide: Section 5.2.3.1 (constraints)

Y   b. The contract provisions will generally be the constraints when a project is done under contract.

N   a. and c. The customer and the performing organization may request constraints.

N   d. The project manager must manage to the constraints but probably does not issue constraints.

A069. b.   **PMBOK® Guide: Figure 4-1**

Y   b. Direct and manage project work is the process of performing the work defined in the project management plan including all approved changes.

N   a. Change requests are not an input or output of develop project management plan.

N   c. Change requests are an output of monitor and control project work.

N   d. Perform integrated change control has change requests as an input and change requests status updates as an output.

A070. c.   **PMBOK® Guide: Section 1.4.2**

Y   c. Senior management is responsible for setting priorities across projects and programs. Senior management manages the portfolios.

N   a. The customer may not be the best choice since each project or program may have a different customer.

N   b. The project sponsor may not be the best choice since each project or program may have a different sponsor.

N   d. The project managers have authority to manage to the objectives set for their own project but not the authority to set priorities across projects.

A071.   **d. Garrett World Class Contracting**

Contract type	Cost Plus Incentive
Overrun or under run? How much?	Overrun of $5,000
Will the seller's fee be increased or decreased for an overrun?	Decreased by the seller's % of the overrun. (go to share ratio-take 2nd %)
Decreased by how much?	40% of $5,000= $2,000
Seller fee=target fee-adjustment	Seller fee= $8,000-$2,000 Seller fee= $6,000
Is fee between max and min fee?	Yes, so Seller fee=$6,000

A072. d.   **PMBOK® Guide: Chapter - 11 Introduction**

Y   d. The risk event is what might occur, not the impact of it.

N   a. The project will finish three weeks late is the impact, not the event.

N   b. The uncertainty that the project may run over budget is the impact, not the event.

N   c. The degradation in quality is the impact, not the risk event.

A073. a.   **PMBOK® Guide: Section 10.1.2.3**

Y   a. Encode means to translate the thoughts or ideas into a language that is understood by others. The sender does this.

N   b., c., and d. The sender encodes the initial message and the receiver decodes the initial message.

A074. a.   **Verma, *Human Resource Skills for the Project Manager*, Table 4-1**

Y   a. Smoothing involves emphasizing areas of agreement and avoiding points of disagreement.

N   b. Collaborating is the technique we use to manage conflict when we incorporate multiple ideas and viewpoints into the solution.

N   c. Withdrawing involves pulling away from a conflict.

N   d. Forcing involves making the other party do it your way.

© January 2016 AME Group, Inc. author Aileen Ellis, PMP, PgMP
aileen@amegroupinc.com 719-659-3658

A075. d.   Any Text book on Quality
Y   d. Common causes are also called random causes and they represent normal process variation.
N   a. and b. Special causes are also known as unusual events.
N   c. Control limits represent the level of control we have over our processes.

A076. d.   PMBOK° Guide: Section 13.1.2.1
Y   d. The salience model classifies stakeholders based on power, urgency, and legitimacy.

A077. d.   Standard practice of projects
Y   d. After we finish planning and before we move to executing we want to hold a kick-off meeting.
N   a. Celebrate as a team should occur at the end of the project.
N   b. Recommended preventive action is an output of monitor and control project work. We are still in planning, not monitoring and controlling.
N   c. Recommended corrective action is an output of monitor and control project work. We are still in planning, not monitoring and controlling.

A078. d.   PMBOK° Guide: Chapter 5 - Introduction
Y   d. Completion of the product scope, not the project scope, is measured against the product requirements.
N   a., b., and c.   Completion of the project scope is measured against the project management plan, the scope statement, and the WBS.

A079. d.   PMBOK® Guide: Section 4.1.3.1
Y   d. In this question we need to look at the list given. Then determine which documents on this list will be updated based on a change in objectives then put those documents in sequence. In reality all of these documents. The project charter is the first document in sequence that will be updated based on a change in objectives.
N   a. The project management plan may be updated, but it will not be updated first. What document comes before it in sequence?
N   b. The WBS most likely will be updated but it will not be updated first.
N   c. The scope statement most likely will be updated but it will not be updated first.

A080. d.   PMBOK° Guide: Section 2.1.3
Y   d. In a functional organization the worker has one and only one supervisor. Every person in a functional organization works in their function. As an example: engineers work in an engineering group, sales people work in a sales group.
N   b. A composite organization involves multiple structures at various levels. In the functional part of the composite, the worker has only one supervisor; in the matrix part, the worker may have more than one supervisor.
N   a. and c. In a matrix (weak, balanced, or strong) the worker has a functional manager and at least one project manager.

A081. d.   PMBOK Guide: Section 13.1 (implied)
Y   d. The manufacturing manager at the facility in Ireland is a key stakeholder. The statement that you do not know this person implies that he was overlooked during stakeholder identification.
N   a. The question states that your sponsor is fully engaged.
N   b. The question states that you have a full project plan including baselines.
N   c. There is nothing in the question to tell us that our team is too large and that we are having issues managing the team.

A082. c.   *PMP® Exam content outline- June 2015*
Y   c. Performing a project assessment in order to evaluate the feasibility of the project is often performed before the other tasks listed.

A083. b.
Y   b. For a benefit to have value it must be realized in a timely manner even if this is after the project closeout.

A084. b.
Y   b. Organizational strategy is the result of the strategic planning cycle where the vision and the mission of the organization are translated into a strategic plan.
N   a., c. and d. All three of these answers are reactive not proactive. Organizational strategy should drive these three ideas, not the other way around.

A085. c.   *PMBOK® Guide Section 2.1.4*
Y   c. Templates are considered part of the organizational process assets.

A086. b.
Y   b. Just-in-time means to produce, deliver or purchase only the materials required, in only the amounts required, only when required. To successfully adopt JIT, you must know **what you need, how many,** and **when**. The best way to monitor these three elements of JIT is to ensure that each "next-process" takes only the necessary items, in the necessary quantity and only when required, from the "previous-process". This is called a "Pull" system.

A087. c.   *PMBOK® Guide Section 8.3*
Y   c. During control quality we test to determine if we built the product correctly.
N   d. During validate scope the customer tests the product to determine if we have built the correct product.

A088. a.
Y   a. Relying on human memory is often the riskiest ways to capture knowledge. People forget or they change positions or leave the organization.

A089. a.
Y   a. Searchable databases are a technology used to apply the transfer of knowledge.
N   b., c. and d. These are methods for assessing the value or benefits of knowledge transfer and not technologies for applying transferred knowledge.

A090. a.
Y   a. A KPI measures if the project is successful. If the success of the call center will be measured by tracking the number of new customers than this is a KPI.
N   b. and c. The terms key success factors and critical success factors (CSF) mean exactly the same thing. They are factors that must go right for an organization to achieve its mission.
N   d. Cost performance index (CPI) is the earned value divided by the actual cost. The CPI is not related to this question.

A091. c.   **Wikipedia Business acumen**
Y   c. Nicholas needs to understand the business and how his behavior and actions may affect other business units. This is called business acumen.

A092. d.   **Wikipedia-*Hofstede's cultural dimensions theory***

Y   d. A society scoring low on Hofstede's dimension of individualism believes Collectivism. An example would be the belief in keeping opinions to oneself so as to maintain harmony.

N   a., b. and c. A society scoring high on Hofstede's dimension of individualism believes in individualism over collectivism. Examples would be the belief in social mobility, direct communication, and the "I" being more important than the "we".

A093. b. *Wikipedia Emotional Intelligence*

Y   b. A person who struggles with self-regulation often has trouble controlling and redirecting one's disruptive emotions and impulses and adapting to changing circumstances.

A094. d.   *PMI® Practice Standard for Configuration Management 2007*

Y   d. Tools and techniques are not kept under configuration management control.

N   a. b. and c. Often we keep physical items, documents forms and records under configuration control.

A095. c.   *PMBOK® Guide 2.2.2*

Y   c. The project governance framework should provide the project manager with structure, processes, and decision-making models for the project.

A096. b.   *PMBOK® Guide section X3.6*

Y   b. In the consultation decision making style the manager asks team members for input but makes it clear up front that the manager will make the decision alone after he hears input from his team.

A097. d. *PMBOK® Guide Section 8.3.3.8*

Y   d. The primary reason we collect lessons learned is to improve project estimating and performance on current and future projects.

N a. I would eliminate answer (a) since the answer has a tone of "blame" to it.

A098. c.   PMBOK® Guide: Section 7.4.2.2

Y   c. EAC=BAC/CPI. Therefore, BAC=EAC*CPI= \$100,000*1.2= \$120,000.

N   a., b., and d. These are distractor answers.

A099. b.   PMBOK® Guide: Sections 6.6.2.2 and 6.6.2.3

Y   b. The critical path is time constrained. The critical chain is resource constrained.

N   a. The critical path is time constrained. The critical chain is resource constrained. They are very different.

N   c. The critical path assumes unlimited resources while the critical chain assumes limited resources.

N   d. The critical path method has been around for decades while the term critical chain was created in the 1990's.

A100. b.   PMBOK® Guide: Section 5.3.3.1

Y   b. The project scope statement describes the project boundaries and states explicitly what is excluded from the project.

N   a. The WBS defines the total scope of the project, but does not state what is excluded.

N   c. The scope management plan provides guidance on how the project scope will be defined, documented, verified, managed, and controlled.

N   d. The project management plan describes how the project will be executed, monitored and controlled, and closed.

A101. b.   PMBOK® Guide: Section 8.3.3.2

Y   b. Control quality is the process in which changed or repaired items are inspected.

N   a. Validate scope is the process in which the customer accepts or rejects the project deliverables. Validate scope is about acceptance, not correctness.

N   c. Approved change requests, including those related to defect repair, are an input to direct and manage project work.

N   d. Monitor and control project work has change requests, including those related to defect repair as an output.

A102. a.   PMBOK° Guide: Section 12.4

Y   a. Completion is the normal end of a contract after all the work is completed. Termination is the early end of the contract before some aspect of the contract is complete.

N   b. Termination for cause means the contract terminates because one of the parties is not meeting at least one of its obligations.

N   c. Termination by mutual agreement means the contract ends because both parties feel it is in their best interests to end the contract even though there are still open obligations.

N   d. Termination for convenience means that one of the parties, usually the buyer, has the right granted to them in the contract to end the contract because it is convenient for them.

A103. d.   PMBOK° Guide: Section 11.2.2.2

Y   d. The Delphi technique is an information-gathering technique in which experts participate anonymously. The Delphi technique helps reduce bias in data and prevents anyone from having an undue influence on the outcome.

N   a. During brainstorming some people may have an undue influence. Sometimes the loudest person in the room influences the outcome.

N   b. SWOT analysis ensures a look at a project from its strengths, weaknesses, opportunities, and threats perspective.

N   c. Root cause analysis is an analytical technique. It is not related to preventing people from dominating meetings and having an undue influence.

A104. b.   PMBOK° Guide: Table 7-1

Y   b. An index less than one is not good. An index greater than one is good. A CPI of .8 means that we are over budget. An SPI of 1.1 means that we are ahead of schedule.

N   a. The project is ahead of schedule. For it to be under budget, the CPI would need to be less than one.

N   c. If we were behind schedule, our SPI would be less than one. If we were under budget, our CPI would be greater than one.

N   d. If we were behind schedule, our SPI would be less than one. We are over budget.

A105. d.   PMBOK° Guide: Section 8.1.2.3

Y   d. Pareto charts show how many defects were generated by type or category of identified cause and help rank order in order to guide corrective action.

N   a. Control charts help us understand the limits of our process.

N   b. Process flowcharts help show how various elements of a system interrelate.

N   c. Cause and effect diagrams illustrate how various factors might be linked to potential problems.

A106. b.   PMBOK° Guide: Section 7.2.2.3

Y   b. The PM should create the model with inputs from other stakeholders. The question is asking for the exception.

N   a. The historical information going into the estimate should be accurate. We want this to be true.

N   c. The parameters used in the model are readily quantifiable. We want this to be true.

© January 2016 AME Group, Inc. author Aileen Ellis, PMP, PgMP
aileen@amegroupinc.com 719-659-3658

N   d. The model is scalable. We want this to be true.

A107. a.   PMBOK° Guide: Section 4.6
Y   a. Formal acceptance and handover of the final product or service to the customer should include receipt of a formal statement that the terms of the contract have been met and be part of close project or phase.
N   b. During control contracts administration each party makes sure that the other party meets their obligations. Final receipt that all the work is complete does not happen here.
N   c. Formal acceptance of the project scope and deliverables is achieved through validate scope. Validate scope would occur before close project.
N   d. Control quality involves monitoring specific project results to determine whether they comply with relevant quality standards, and identifying ways to eliminate causes of unsatisfactory results. Control quality is about correctness more than acceptance.

A108. a.   PMBOK° Guide: Section 2.1.1
Y   a. A regulation is a government imposed requirement and thus no reflection of the organizational culture.
N   b., c., and d. Shared values, policies, procedures, views of authority relationships, work ethic, and work hours are all representative of organizational cultures and styles.

A109. a.   PMBOK° Guide: Chapter 10 - Introduction
Y   a. Horizontal communication is with your peers.
N   b., c., and d. These are all examples of vertical communication.

A110. c.   PMBOK° Guide: Section 9.3.2.3
Y   c. Forming, storming, norming, performing is the correct order.
N   a., b., and d. see solution c. during forming, team members are polite. During storming, team members confront each other. During norming, people confront issues, not people. During performing, the team members settle down and are productive as a team. and productive effort.

A111. c.   PMBOK° Guide: Section 8.1.2.5
Y   c. Design of experiments (DOEs) plays a role in optimization of products and processes. DOEs allow you to systematically change all the important factors for a product or process to provide the optimal conditions.
N   a. Benchmarking involves comparing actual or planned project performance practices to those of other projects to generate ideas for improvement and to provide a basis to measure performance.
N   b. Control charts help us understand the limits of our process.
N   d. Run charts show history and the pattern of variation.

A112. a.   PMBOK° Guide: Table 7-1
Y   a. EAC=BAC/CPI. CPI =BAC/EAC= $100,000/$120,000= .83CPI= .83
N   b., c., and d. These are distractor answers.

A113. c.   PMBOK° Guide A1.6
Y   c. A large part of the project budget is spent during the executing process group.

A114. b.   PMBOK° Guide: Chapter 5 - Introduction
Y   b. Some project deliverables will be related to product scope and some will be related to project scope. An example of a deliverable related to project management would be the project management plan.

N   a. Product scope is defined first. This is a driver or input into defined the project scope.

N   c. The project life cycle is a subset of the product life cycle. Think of the product as a book and the project is to write the book. Writing the book is the subset. After we write the book we need to manufacture it, distribute it, do revisions on the book (more projects), and maybe eventually pull the book out of the market.

N   d. The configuration management system helps us define, manage, and control changes to the product. The change control system helps us do the same thing to the project.

A115. c.   PMBOK® Guide: Section 4.5 (not clearly expressed in PMBOK® Guide)

Y   c. Evaluate the change request is the first thing we do when a change request comes to us, regardless from whom the change request came.

N   a. and b. We don't want to meet with our management or sponsor until we have information about the impact of the requested change and we are able to recommend alternatives.

N   d. Every change request must be evaluated, even if it comes from the customer. We do not make any changes unless an evaluation has been completed.

A116. c.   PMBOK® Guide: Section 11.4.2.2

Formula EMV= amount at stake* risk probability

Amount at Stake	Risk Probability	Expected Monetary Value
$ 40,000	20%	$40,000*20%= $8,000
$ 10,000	30%	$10,000*30%= $3,000
($20,000)	50%	-$20,000*50%= -$10,000
		EMV of Venture Total= $1,000

A117. a.   PMBOK® Guide: Table 7-1

Y   a. SV= EV-PV. If this answer is a positive number, meaning if EV > PV, then your project is running ahead of schedule.

N   b. The EV would be less than PV if the project was behind schedule.

N   c. and d. AC is required information to determine cost variances since CV=EV-AC.

A118. c.   PMBOK® Guide: Section 7.4.2.4

Y   c. Trend analysis examines project performance over time to determine if performance is improving or deteriorating

N   a. Variance analysis compares actual project performance to planned performance.

N   b. Earned value analysis compares actual cost and schedule performance to planned performance.

N   d. Cost-benefit analysis compares the cost of a project to the benefits of the project. In general we only work on projects with benefits that outweigh costs.

A119. b.   PMBOK® Guide: Section 5.5

Y   b. Validate scope is the process that would be performed after a project is terminated. During validate scope we establish and document the level and extent of completion. When a project is terminated we want to see if there are any deliverables we can turn over to the customer.

N a. Control quality is about correctness, not acceptance.

N c. Close contracts is about acceptance of the work of our suppliers, not about our customer accepting the work of the project (PMBOK® Guide: Section 12.4).

N d. Control scope is the process concerned with scope changes, not project terminations.

A120. c.   PMBOK® Guide: Section 11.6.2.5

Y c. Reserve analysis during monitoring and controlling project risk compares the amount of contingency reserve remaining versus the amount of risk remaining.

N a. Earned value analysis compares plan versus actual on cost performance through the CPI.

N b. Earned value analysis compares plan versus actual on schedule performance through the SPI.

N d. Earned value analysis compares the amount of money remaining versus the amount of work remaining through the TCPI (to complete performance index).

A121. c.   PMBOK® Guide: Table 7-1

Y c. CV=EV-AC. If the answer is a negative number, meaning if your AC is higher than your EV, then your project is running over budget.

N a. and b. PV is required information to determine schedule variance since SV=EV-PV.

N d. The AC would be less than the EV if your project was under budget.

A122. d.   PMBOK® Guide: Section 8.1.2.3

Y d. Quality audits are tools of perform quality control, not plan quality.

N a., b., and c. These are all examples of tools to plan quality.

A123. c.   PMBOK® Guide: Section 5.6

Y c. Scope creep is another name for uncontrolled changes.

N a. Cost growth is a change to the cost of a project/contract because of an approved change in scope.

N b. Schedule growth is a change to the schedule of a project/contract because of an approved change in scope.

N d. Scope changes are approved changes to the project scope.

A124. b.   PMBOK® Guide: Table 7-1

Y b. CPI=EV/AC. If you are running on budget your EV=AC which means your CPI=1.

N a. CPI= 0. We do not think of indexes as being zero. If our "cost variance" was zero that would mean that we are operating right on budget.

N c. CPI>1 when the project is running under budget.

N d. CPI<1 when the project is running over budget.

A125. b.   PMBOK® Guide: Section 5.4

Y b. The WBS is a deliverable oriented document. If something is in scope it is in the WBS. If something is out of scope it is not in the WBS.

N a. The scope management plan describes the processes to determine, verify, and control scope. There is nothing in the plan that describes what is in or not in scope.

N c. The project charter is a document that states we have an approved document. It is not specific about the scope of the project. The scope of the project has not been defined yet.

N d. The integrated change control system contains the procedures for making changes. It does not contain the scope of the project.

A126. c.   PMBOK® Guide: Section A1.5.11

Y   c. The schedule baseline is an output of develop schedule.

A127. d.   PMBOK® Guide: Section 2.1.3

Y   d. In a projectized structure there is often less efficient use of resources. As an example, the project may require an accounting person for half time, yet if the organization is projectized, the accounting person will be full-time on the project.

N   a. A higher potential for conflict is a negative of the matrix structure not the projectized structure.

N   b. A matrix structure is more complex to manage, not a projectized structure.

N   c. A matrix structure requires extra administration, not a projectized structure.

A128. d.   PMBOK® Guide: Table 7-1

Y   d. EAC= (BAC/CPI) is the formula when current variances are seen as typical of future variances and we should use the present CPI to predict the future.

N   a. and c. In these situations, use the formula: EAC=AC+ETC.

N   b. In this situation, use the formula: EAC=AC+(BAC-EV).

A129. d.   PMBOK® Guide: Section 4.2.1.4

Y   d. Project plan templates may include guidelines for tailoring an organizations standard processes.

N   a., b., and c. These examples are all enterprise environmental factors not organizational process assets.

A130. a.   PMBOK® Guide: Section X3.6

Y   a. Risk management is not an element of decision-making.

A131. d.   PMBOK® Guide: Section 12.1.1.9

Y   d. Time and materials contracts are often used when the buyer is purchasing services. When the buyer needs a contractor quickly, time and materials are often used since they can be set-up quickly without a definite quantity specified.

N   a. and b. Fixed price contracts are used when the product is well defined. Often in an emergency we do not have time to define the product well before the seller must start working.

N   c. The cost plus incentive contract is a complex contract to set-up and thus often not used in an emergency.

A132. b.   PMBOK® Guide: Table 7-1

Y   b. EAC is the forecast of the most likely total cost of the work based on project performance and risk quantification.

N   a. EV is the earned value; it is a measure of work actually completed.

N   c. BAC is the budget at completion and is equal to the total cumulative PV at completion.

N   d. PV is the planned value; it is the budgeted cost for the work scheduled to be completed at a given time.

A133. d.   PMBOK® Guide: Section 8.1.2.4

Y   d. Benchmarking is a tool for plan quality as well as perform quality assurance. Benchmarking involves finding best practices and providing a basis for measuring performance.

N   a. Control charts are used to determine whether or not a process is stable.

N   b. and c. Pareto charts and scatter diagrams are all tools of control quality, not plan quality. The question tells us we are in planning. Therefore, these answers cannot be correct.

A134. d.   PMBOK® Guide: Figure 7-1

Y   d. Cost forecasts are an output of the process control costs.

© January 2016 AME Group, Inc. author Aileen Ellis, PMP, PgMP
aileen@amegroupinc.com 719-659-3658

A135. c.   PMBOK® Guide: Figure 5-1

Y   c. The project charter and the stakeholder register are the two key inputs into collect requirements.

A136. a.   PMBOK® Guide: Figure 11-1

Y   a. From the list, risk identification comes first.

N   b. We cannot plan risk responses until we have identified and analyzed the risks.

N   c. Risk qualification happens after risk identification.

N   d. Risk quantification happens after risk qualification, which happens after risk identification.

A137. a.   PMBOK® Guide: Table 7-1

Y   a. CV= EV-AC. If your project is running over budget, your AC will be greater than your EV and your CV will be negative.

N   b. Your CV will be positive if your project is running under budget.

N   c. Your CV will be 0 if your project is running right on budget.

N   d. Your CV will be 1 if your project is running $1 under budget.

A138. d.   PMBOK® Guide: Section 9.4.2.3

Y   d. Forcing involves pushing one viewpoint at the expense of another. This is the technique often used in an emergency situation. Hard feelings may come back in other forms after forcing.

N   a. Problem solving treats conflict as a problem to be solved. This technique provides ultimate resolution but takes time.

N   b. Compromising is giving something to receive something. Both parties get some degree of satisfaction.

N   c. Withdrawal involves giving up, pulling out, or retreating. This technique does not solve the problem.

A139. d.   PMBOK® Guide: Table 7-1

Y   d. The BAC for your project is your total project budget. The question says you have a budget of $200/month for six months. Your total project budget is $1,200.

Y   a., b., and c. These are distractor answers.

A140. c.   PMBOK® Guide: Section 1.3 (not explicit in book)

Y   c. A project creates unique products, services, or results. This is one of the ideas that separates projects from operations. Be careful of the word except in questions.

N   a. Most projects within a given organization will have similar project life cycles.

N   b. Most projects within a given organization will have similar project deliverables by phase.

N   d. Most projects within a given organization will have standard WBS templates.

A141. c.   PMBOK® Guide: Section 1.3

Y   c. As one element of the competing constraints changes at least one other element is likely to change.

N   a. A change is not always a growth. If we de-scope the project, the cost may go up or down, based on the de-scope.

N   b. A change is not always a growth. If we de-scope the project, the schedule may get shorter or longer, depending on the de-scope.

N   d. If we change one constraint, at least one other element is likely to change.

A142. d.   PMBOK® Guide: Section 12.4.2.1

Y   d. A procurement audit is a structured review of the procurement process.

N   a. The quality process identifies any weaknesses in the seller's work processes or deliverables.

N   b. A quality audit, not procurement audit, is used to identify inefficient and ineffective policies, processes, and procedures.

N   c. A risk audit, not procurement audit, examines and documents the effectiveness of risk responses.

A143. d.   PMBOK° Guide: Section 11.5.2.3

Y   d. A risk trigger is a warning sign that a risk event is about to occur or has just occurred.

N   a. A risk event is what might happen.

N   b. The risk impact is the severity of the consequences.

N   c. The risk score is the risk probability multiplied by the risk impact. The higher the risk score, the higher the priority.

A144. b.   Not explicit in PMBOK® Guide

Y   b. Team member knowledge is useful but generally less reliable than documented performance. The idea here is to base your cost estimates on documented performance, not on someone's memory.

N   a. and d. The information is useful, but not the most reliable.

N   c. This statement is reversed.

A145. d.   PMBOK° Guide: Section 1.4.1

Y   d. The program manager, not the project manager, handles priorities across a program.

A146. d.   PMBOK° Guide: Section 8.3.3.4

Y   d. Formal acceptance, not quality control, validates the customer's acceptance criteria has been met. Quality control is about correctness, not acceptance.

N   a., b., and c. These statements are all true. The question is looking for the false statement.

A147. c.   PMBOK° Guide: Table 7-1

Y   c. The planned value (PV) is the budgeted cost of work scheduled. You have $200/month budget and you are at the end of month four. Therefore, your PV= $ 800.

N   a., b., and d. These are distractor answers.

A148. a.   PMBOK® Guide: Section 6.2.2.2

Y   a. Rolling wave planning is a technique in which the project team waits for clarification before completely decomposing deliverables. If a deliverable won't be produced for a long time, it may not make sense to do complete decomposition early on in the project.

N   b. Templates contain a defined structure for collecting, organizing, and presenting information.

N   c. Define activities decomposes work packages into the activity list.

N   d. Product analysis allows the project scope statement to be developed based on the scope of the product.

A149. b.   PMBOK° Guide: Table 7-1

Y   b. You have a CPI that is less than one. You are therefore running over budget and need to put your focus on cost first.

N   a. The question says you are two weeks behind schedule. This is noise. You do not know if it is a two week or ten year project. You need to know your SPI before deciding to put your focus on schedule.

© January 2016 AME Group, Inc. author Aileen Ellis, PMP, PgMP
aileen@amegroupinc.com 719-659-3658

N   c. Stakeholder management is the step responsible to manage communication, satisfy the needs and resolve issues of stakeholders. There is nothing in the question that states we need to put more focus on stakeholder management. 30 stakeholders is noise.

N   d. There is no information in the question to lead us to believe we need a larger focus on conflict management. 30 stakeholders is noise.

A150. b.   PMBOK° Guide: Section 1.4

Y   b. Portfolios are groups of projects or programs that may or may not be related. It is the responsibility of senior management to oversee the management of portfolios.

N   a. Projects are a subset of programs. Projects and programs are a subset of portfolios.

N   c. Portfolios are a group of projects or programs that may or may not be related. All projects in a program are related.

N   d. Projects are a subset of programs and are usually smaller than programs.

A151. b.   PMBOK° Guide: Section 7.4.2.1(not explicit)

Y   b. You have a CPI that is less than one. You are therefore running over budget and need to put your focus on cost first.

N   a. The question says you are two weeks behind schedule. This is noise. You do not know if it is a two week or ten year project. You need to know your SPI before deciding to put your focus on schedule.

N   c. Stakeholder management is the step responsible to manage communication, satisfy the needs and resolve issues of stakeholders. There is nothing in the question that states we need to put more focus on stakeholder management. 30 stakeholders is noise.

N   d. There is no information in the question to lead us to believe we need a larger focus on conflict management. 30 stakeholders is noise.

A152. a.   Meredith et al. *Project Management: A Managerial Approach*

Y   a. The investment was made at the start of the project. Therefore, the present value (PV) of the investment is a negative $80,000.

The Present Value of $50,000 received at the end of year 1:

$PV = FV/(1+i)^t$

$PV = $50,000/(1..08)^1$

PV= $46,296.29

The Present Value of $30,000 received at the end of year 2:

$PV = FV/(1+i)^t$

$PV = $30,000/(1.08)^2$

PV= $25,720.16

Therefore, the NPV for Project A= $46,296.29+$25,720.16-$80,000
NPV for Project A= -$7,983.55
The answer is negative because the benefits are of less value than the investment.

A153. c.   PMBOK° Guide: Section 4.5

Y   c. Evaluating the change request is the first thing we do when a change request comes to us, regardless from whom the change request came.

N   a. and b. We don't want to meet with our management or sponsor until we have information about the impact of the requested change and are able to recommend alternatives.

N   d. Every change request must be evaluated, even if it is mandated by the government. We may decide to cancel the project instead of making the change on the project. We do not make any changes unless an evaluation has been completed.

A154. a.   Any Accounting Textbook or Web Search
Y   a. Sunk costs are costs that have already been expended but cannot be recouped. We should not take these into account during project selection.

N   b. Opportunity costs represent the opportunity we pass over when selecting one project instead of another. We should take these into account during project selection.

N   c. In general we want the present value of inflows to be greater than the present value of outflows (a positive net present value) when selecting projects. Thus, we should take into account net present value.

N   d. In general we want the payback period (the time required for the project to repay its initial investments) to be as short as possible. Thus, we should take into account the payback period.

A155. b.   Any Statistical Quality Control Text
Y   b. A data point may fall outside the control limits but still be inside the tolerances.

N   a. In general, tolerances should be wider than control limits. We want our control to be tighter than the customer or market requires.

N   c. The customer or market sets the tolerances - what is acceptable.

N   d. Our process or equipment usually sets the control limits. The control limits show how well we can control the process.

A156. b.   PMBOK® Guide: Section 12.1.2.1
Y   b. $100*W= $900+$10*W. ($100-$10)*W= $900. $90* W = $900. W= 10 weeks. At 10 Weeks the cost to rent will equal the cost to purchase.

N   a., c., and d. These are distractor answers.

A157. d.   PMBOK® Guide: Table 7-1
Y   d. We need to determine our four critical terms: BAC, PV, AC, and EV.
The BAC is given. It is the project budget of $100,000.
The PV is a measure of how much work should be complete. The question says that we are exactly 18 months into a 3 year project. This means that we should have half of the work complete. The PV= ½ (total budget)= ½ ($100,000)= $50,000.
The AC is a measure of how much money has been spent to date. The question states that 30% of the budget has been spent. Therefore, AC= 30% ($100,000)= $30K.
The EV is a measure of how much work is complete. The question states that 40% of the work is complete. Therefore, EV= 40% ($100,000)= $40K.
The Schedule Variance= SV= EV-PV= $40,000-$50,000= Negative $10,000. Therefore, the project is behind schedule.
The Cost variance= CV= EV-AC= $40,000=$30,000= $10,000. Since this is a positive number the project is running under budget.

A158. a.   Meredith et al. *Project Management: A Managerial Approach*
Y   a. Project A with a payback period of 8 months has the shortest payback period, everything else being equal then this is the best project.

N   b., c., and d. Project A has a shorter payback period than the others. Payback period for a project is the amount of time it takes a project to pay back its initial investment. Everything else being equal, the shorter the better.

A159. d.   PMBOK® Guide: Section 13.3 (not explicit)

Y d. If the question tells you that you are experiencing more changes than normal, that the changes are costing more money than expected or that the product may be rejected even though requirements are being met, look for an answer that relates to not engaging a key stakeholder or not engaging a key stakeholder early enough.

A160. c. Project Risk - Wideman

Y c. Utility theory assumes that any decision is made on the basis of the utility maximization principle, according to which the best choice is the one that provides the highest utility (satisfaction) to the decision maker.

N a. Maslow's Hierarchy of Needs is related to motivation, not a person's view of risk.

N b. Herzberg's Hygiene theory is related to motivation, not a person's view of risk.

N d. Vroom's expectancy theory is related to motivation, not a person's view of risk.

A161. b. Verma, *Human Resource Skills for Project Manager,* page 233

Y b. Referent power refers to the potential influence one has due to the strength of the relationship between the leader and the followers.

N a. Expert power is derived from one's knowledge.

N c. Penalty power refers to the negative things a project manager might do.

N d. Formal power, often called legitimate power, is derived from one's position in an organization.

A162. d. PMBOK® Guide: Section 13.3

Y d. If the project's product is being put on the shelf at this point, we probably should have put more effort into managing our relationship with our stakeholders and understanding their requirements.

N a. Since the SPI is above 1.0 we did not need to put more focus on the schedule.

N b. Since the CPI is above 1.0 we did not need to put more focus on managing the budget.

N c. The issue in the question is that the product is being put on the shelf. There is nothing in the question that states we had issues with our team members.

A163. a. Wikipedia search on problem solving

Y a. Problem solving is a combination of problem identification, alternative identification, and decision-making. Risk management is not one of the three elements.

A164. b. Verma, *Human Resource Skills for Project Managers*: Table 4-1 and PMBOK® Guide: Section 9.4.2.3

Y b. Forcing involves pushing one viewpoint at the expense of another. This is the technique often used in an emergency situation. Hard feelings may come back in other forms after forcing.

N a. Compromising is giving something to receive something. Both parties get some degree of satisfaction.

N c. Confronting, also called problem solving, treats conflict as a problem to be solved. This technique provides ultimate resolution.

N d. Withdrawal involves giving up, pulling out, or retreating. This technique does not solve the problem.

A165. d. PMBOK® Guide: Section 8.1.2.6

Y d. This statement is a definition of attribute sampling but not a reason to do sampling.

N a., b., and c. All of the statements are reasons to do sampling over testing the entire population. Notice the question is asking for the *exception*.

A166. b. Any Accounting Text Book

Y   b.   Indirect costs such as overhead and general and administrative are hard, if not impossible for the project manager to influence.

N   a.   Direct costs are incurred for the exclusive benefit of the project. The project manager should be controlling direct costs.

N   c. and d.   Variable costs change based on the size of certain elements of the project. Fixed costs do not change based on the size of certain elements of a project. Project managers control direct costs, regardless of whether they are variable or fixed.

A167.   c.   Wikipedia search on graphical evaluation review technique

Y   c.   Graphical evaluation review technique allows for conditional statements.

N   a.   The arrow diagramming technique does not allow for conditional statements, such as "if-then".

N   b.   The precedence diagramming technique does not allow for conditional statements, such as "if-then".

N   d.   Fast tracking is a technique of overlapping activities or phases.

A168.   b.   PMBOK° Guide: Section 5.4.3.1

Y   b.   Create WBS has the WBS dictionary as an output.

N   a.   Define scope has the scope statement as an output not the WBS dictionary.

N   c.   Define activities has the activity list as an output not the WBS dictionary.

N   d.   Develop project management plan has the project management plan as an output.

A169.   a.   *Earned Value Management*, Fleming and Koppelaman

Y   a.   The cumulative CPI has been proved to stabilize once the project is approximately 20% complete.

N   b., c., and d.   The cumulative CPI would stabilize before this.

A170.   b.   PMBOK° Guide: Section 5.4

Y   b.   The WBS is a deliverable oriented document. If something is in scope it is in the WBS. If something is out of scope it is not in the WBS.

N   a.   The scope management plan describes the processes to determine, validate, and control scope. There is nothing in the plan that describes what is in or not in scope.

N   c.   The project charter is a document that states we have an approved document. It is not specific about the scope of the project. The scope of the project has not been defined yet.

N   d.   The integrated change control system contains the procedures for making changes. It does not contain the scope of the project.

A171.   d.   PMBOK° Guide: Sections 4.3 and 12.3.2.1

Y   d.   Contract changes are handled in the control procurements process, not the direct and manage project work process.

N   a.   Approved corrective actions are implemented during direct and manage project work.

N   b.   Approved preventive actions are implemented during direct and manage project work.

N   c.   Approved defect repairs are implemented during direct and manage project work.

A172.   d.   PMBOK° Guide: Section 2.1.3

Y   d.   In a projectized structure there is often a less efficient use of resources. As an example, the project may require an accounting person for half time, yet if the organization is projectized, the accounting person will be full-time on the project.

N   a.   A higher potential for conflict is a negative of the matrix structure not the projectized structure.

N   b.   A matrix structure is more complex to manage, not a projectized structure.

N   c.   A matrix structure requires extra administration, not a projectized structure.

A173. d.   Web search on centralized versus decentralized contracting

Y   d.   Clearly defined career paths for contracting professionals is a positive of centralized, not decentralized contracting.

N   a. More loyalty to the project is a positive decentralized contracting.

N   b. Easier access to contracting expertise is a positive of decentralized contracting.

N   c. If procurement people are part of the project team, they are likely to have a more in depth understanding of the needs of the project.

A174. c.   PMBOK° Guide: Section 11.6.2.3

Y   c. Deviations from the baseline plan may indicate the potential impact of threats or opportunities. If the deviations are positive, it may be the result of opportunities. If the deviations are negative, it may be the result of threats.

N   a. Apathy is often demonstrated through a total lack of conflict.

N   b. Unproductive meetings are a sign of poor teamwork.

N   d. In general, the people doing the work should inspect the quality of the work.

A175. a.   PMBOK° Guide: Section 4.1

Y   a. The charter is the document that states we have an approved project and assigns the project manager. We do not want to proceed without this document as the probability of project success goes down.

N   b. Starting work on planning without a charter raises the risk on project failure.

N   c. As a project manager we cannot demand anything of our management. In general, the word demand will not be found in the right answers on the test unless the question is asking what not to do.

N   d. The contract is not the charter. The contract is an input to creating the charter.

A176. b.   Wikipedia search on feasibility study

Y   b. A feasibility study is often initiated to help an organization decide whether it should undertake a project.

N   a. A project scope statement is developed after a project has been chartered but not to help decide if a project should be undertaken.

N   c. The work breakdown structure defines the total scope of the project. It is developed long after a project has been chartered.

N   d. The project management plan is a formal approved document that describes how the project will be executed, monitored, and controlled. It is developed long after the project is chartered.

A177. a.   Wikipedia search on business proposals

Y   a. The cost of the proposal is normally at no direct cost to the buyer.

N   b., c., and d. The cost of the proposal is normally at no direct cost to the buyer, regardless of whether the buyer buys for the seller.

178.   c.   PMBOK Guide: Table 7-1

Y   c. The project is behind schedule and under budget. To solve these problems always begin with the earned value (EV). Since the earned value (EV) is less than the planned value (PV) the project is running behind schedule. Another way to say this is that we have less work complete than scheduled. Since the earned value (EV) is greater than the actual cost (AC) the project is running under budget. Another way to say this is that we have more work complete than money spent.

A179. b.   Verma, *Human Resource Skills for the Project Manager,* page 65-73

Y   b. Ouchi's Theory Z is based on Japanese styles and philosophies and states that high levels of trust, confidence, and commitment to workers on the part of management leads to a high level of motivation and productivity on the part of workers.

N   a. Vroom's Expectancy Theory states that people choose behaviors that they believe will lead to desired results and that they will be rewarded attractively for those results.

N   c. McGregor's Theory X describes management's view that most workers dislike their work and try to avoid it.

N   d. Herzberg's Hygiene Theory states that some job factors lead to satisfaction, whereas others can only prevent dissatisfaction and are not sources of satisfaction. Hygiene factors related to the work itself, if provided appropriately, prevent dissatisfaction. Motivational factors related to the work itself can increase job satisfaction.

A180. a.   Web search on Marginal Analysis

Y   a. Marginal analysis states that optimal quality is reached at the point where the incremental revenue equals the incremental cost to achieve the improvement.

N   b. In theory, quality should have the same priority as cost and schedule.

N   c. The cost of quality looks at the money spent proactively (cost of conformance) and reactively (cost of non-conformance).

N   d. There is almost always more than can be done to improve quality, but this improvement comes at a cost.

A181. d.   PMBOK° Guide: Chapter 13

Y   d. Often the underlying reason for "too many" change requests is the lack of identification of all stakeholders. If we do not identify a stakeholder, we do not identify their requirements and therefore we are likely to experience many change requests.

N   a. There is nothing in the question to lead up to believe that the issue of too many change requests is because of a lack of a project manager in each country. Do not read information into the question that is not there.

N   b. The SPI is 1.03. The project is ahead of schedule.

N   c. The CPI is 1.04. The project is running under budget.

A182. d. Garrett World Class Contracting, page 59

Y   d. Punitive damages are often set to punish the other party and represent the amount above what would barely compensate the injured party for his loss.

N   a. Compensatory damages are the exact amount due to the injured party for his loss.

N   b. Liquidated damages represent the amount agreed to in advance.

N   c. In most cases, the injured party is awarded damages (money). At times though a party is forced to perform the specifics of the contract.

A183. a.   Verma, *Human Resource Skills for the Project Manager,* page 64

Y   a. Some job factors called motivational factors lead to satisfaction, whereas others, called hygiene factors, can only prevent dissatisfaction.

N   b., c., and d. If provided appropriately, hygiene factors can prevent dissatisfaction but cannot lead to satisfaction. Motivational factors related to the work itself can lead to job satisfaction, but cannot prevent dissatisfaction. They are not on the same continuum.

A184. a.   Web Search on Kanban

Y   a. Kanban is a signaling system through which just in time (JIT) is managed.

N   b. Kaizen is another name for continuous improvements.

N   c. Utility theory is a measure of someone's willingness to take a risk based on their satisfaction meter.

N   d. Marginal analysis states that optimal quality is reached at the point where the incremental revenue equals the incremental cost to achieve the improvement.

© January 2016 AME Group, Inc. author Aileen Ellis, PMP, PgMP
aileen@amegroupinc.com 719-659-3658

A185. c.   PMBOK° Guide: Section 6.6.2.2

Y   c. The more near critical paths you have the more risk you have that you may miss your schedule.

N   a. The more near critical paths you have the less float you have on your activities.

N   b. There is no way to know from this question how schedule affects cost.

N   d. Paths being critical or non-critical is not determined by the number of people working on the project.

A186. b.   PMBOK° Guide: Section 2.2.1

Y   b. The items listed are all project integration activities and thus the responsibility of the Project Manager.

N   a. The sponsor provides the financial resources for the project.

N   c. The team is responsible to analyze and understand the project scope, document specific criteria of the product requirements, prepare the WBS, etc.

N   d. The functional managers provide the people we need in a matrix organization.

A187. b.   PMBOK° Guide: Section 5.2

Y   b. Stakeholders needs, wants, and expectations must be analyzed and converted into requirements. Often unidentified expectations or unquantifiable expectations can put customer satisfaction at risk.

N   a. There is nothing in the question to tell us that the instructors were not qualified. In fact, the requirements were met, so this is not the likely explanation.

N   c. There is nothing in the question to make us believe that the customer is trying to exploit the contract. In fact, this is not a likely "type" of right answer on the test.

N   d. There is nothing in the question to tell us that the training did not go into enough detail. In fact, the requirements were met, so this is not the likely explanation.

A188. d.   PMBOK° Guide: Section 12.4.2.2

Y   d. Negotiation between the two parties is the preferred method of settlement of claims and disputes.

N   a. Mediation involves bringing in a third party to help reach a settlement on the claim or dispute.

N   b. Arbitration involves bringing in a third party to make a decision regarding the claim or dispute.

N   c. Litigation involves using the courts to settle a claim or dispute. This is the least desirable option.

A189. a.   PMBOK® Guide: Section 11.5.2

Y   a. Exploit is the strategy used to make sure that opportunities are realized.

N   b. Mitigate is a strategy to deal with threats, not opportunities.

N   c. Transfer is a strategy to deal with threats, not opportunities.

N   d. Avoid is a strategy to deal with threats, not opportunities.

A190. c.   Verma, *Human Resource Skills for the Project Manager*, page 65-73

Y   c. Vroom's Expectancy Theory states that people choose behaviors that they believe will lead to desired results and that they will be rewarded attractively for those results.

N   a. Maslow's Hierarchy is a model of motivation that suggests that each of us has a hierarchy of five types of needs. The bottom level is physiological needs. Level two is safety, level three is social, level four is esteem, and the top level is self-actualization.

N   b. McGregor's Theory Y describes management's view that most workers are self-disciplined, can direct and control themselves, desire responsibility, and accept them willingly.

N   d. Ouchi's Theory Z is based on Japanese styles and philosophies and states that high levels of trust, confidence, and commitment to workers on the part of management leads to a high level of motivation and productivity on the part of workers.

A191. a.   Any Accounting book

Y   a. Your working capital is your current assets minus your current liabilities. Working capital is a measure of how much liquid assets a company has to build the business.

N   b. Net present value is the present value of inflows minus the present value of outflows. NPV is used in capital budgeting to analyze the profitability of an investment or project.

N   c. Profit is equal to price minus cost. This is a procurement idea. The profit the seller receives is equal to the price they charge minus their costs.

N   d. Cost is equal to price minus profit. This is a procurement idea. A seller's cost is equal to the price they charge minus the profit they make.

A192. a.   PMBOK® Guide: Section 6.6.2.2

Y   a. Total float = late finish –early finish= 10 -12 =-2 days

N   b. and c. There is not enough information to know if there is a lag or to know the duration of Activity A.

N   d. Total float = late finish –early finish= 10 -12 =-2 days. Answer d. shows a positive 2 days.

A193. a.   Garrett, World Class Contracting, page 110

Y   a. On a cost plus fixed fee contract the seller's profit remains the same when the contract runs over the estimated costs. On a cost plus percentage cost contract the seller's profit goes up if the contract overruns the estimated costs. Your contract's manager is probably assuming the contract will overrun the estimated costs and is pushing for the cost plus percentage cost so as to obtain the extra profit.

N   b. On a cost plus percentage cost contract the seller's profit goes down if the contract runs under the estimated costs. If your contract's manager is assuming the contract will under run the estimated cost, he would not push for a cost plus percentage cost contract because this will provide for a lower profit. On a cost plus fixed fee, the seller's profit does not go down if the contract runs under its estimated costs.

N   c. The cost plus percentage cost has more buyer risk than the cost plus fixed fee.

N   d. The cost plus percentage cost provides the seller with less risk, not more risk, than the cost plus fixed fee.

A194. d. Project Risk - Wideman

Y   d. A pure risk is another name for an insurable risk. Most organizations buy insurance to shift the risk to another party.

N   a., b., and c. A pure risk is another name for an insurable risk. Most organizations buy insurance to shift the risk to another party.

A195. a.   PMBOK® Guide: Section 8.1.2.3

Y   a. The control limits on a control chart tell us the amount of variation expected.

N   b., c., and d. The specification limits. Sometimes called the tolerance limits tell us how much variation the customer will accept.

A196. c.   Verma, *Human Resource Skills for the Project Manager*, page 218

Y   c. Autocratic style refers to the project manager making a decision without input from others. You are less likely to use this style with a very senior group of people.

N   a. Consensus refers to sharing problems with team members in a group and then reaching a decision by consensus.

© January 2016 AME Group, Inc. author Aileen Ellis, PMP, PgMP
aileen@amegroupinc.com 719-659-3658

N b. Consultative in a group refers to group decision-making where the project manager invites ideas and suggestions of team members in a meeting and the project manager makes the final decision.

N d. Facilitating refers to coordinating the work of the team.

A197. b. PMBOK° Guide: Section 7.4.2.1

Y b. A CPI=.95 is a quantitative idea. This is where we should put our focus.

N a. The question states that the CPI= .95 and the project is 14 weeks behind schedule. Both items sound bad. How do we decide? We look for the quantitative answer. The project is 14 weeks behind schedule. I am saying this is qualitative, not quantitative because we do not know how long the schedule is. What if the schedule is 15 years? 14 weeks may not be that bad.

N c. While we have many stakeholders there is nothing in the question to state that we have an issue that needs to be resolved.

N d. The question states that the sponsor is communicating. Everything looks good with the sponsor.

A198. a. PMBOK° Guide: Section 8.1.2.3 (bullet on control charts)

Y a. Looking at the data we see that we have 7 points in a row that are below the mean. The process is out of control. Make sure you know the rule of 7 for the

N c. and d. The question tells us nothing about the tolerances (specifications).

A199. b. Statistical Process Control textbook or Web Search

Y b. One standard deviation is approximately equal to the absolute value of $((p-o)/6)$. Therefore, one standard deviation = $(22-10)/6= 12/6= 2$ days.

N a., c., and d. One standard deviation is approximately equal to the absolute value of $((p-o)/6)$.

A200. d. Garrett, World Class Contracting, page 114

Y d. The point of total assumption is the point where the sharing relationships changes for the share ratio to 0/100. At this point the seller picks up 100 % of the cost risk. In a fixed price incentive the buyer and seller share the risk according to the share ratio. If the seller continues to overrun eventually the seller hits the PTA. The PTA is caused by the price ceiling.

N a. Time and materials contracts do not have a point of total assumption. There is no share ratio in the Time and materials contract. The seller is reimbursed a fixed price per hour or day (the time portion of the contract) and at cost for materials.

N b. The cost plus fixed fee has no point of total assumption. There is no share ratio in a cost plus fixed fee. The seller is reimbursed 100 % for overruns as long as the overruns are allowable. The buyer has 100% of the cost risk.

N c. The cost plus percentage cost has no point of total assumption. There is no share ratio in a cost plus percentage cost. The seller is reimbursed 100 % for overruns as long as the overruns are allowable. The buyer has 100% of cost risk.

REFERENCES

Ferraro, Gary P. *The Cultural Dimension of International Business.* 3rd ed. Upper Saddle River, N.J.: Prentice Hall, 1998

Fleming, Quentin W. and Koffleman, Joel M. *Earned Value Project Management.* 4th ed., Newtown Square Penn.: Project Management Institute. 2010

Frame, J. Davidson. *Managing Projects in Organizations: How to Make the Best Use of Time, Techniques and People.* Rev. ed. San Francisco: Jossey-Bass, 1995

Maslow, Abraham H. *Motivation and Personality.* New York: Harper and Row, 1954

McGregor, Douglas. *The Human Side of Enterprise.* New York. McGraw-Hill, 1960

Meredith, Jack R., and Samuel J. Mantel, Jr. *Project Management: A Managerial Approach*, 5th ed. New York: John Wiley and Sons, 2003

Project Management Institute *A Guide to the Project Management Body of Knowledge*, Fifth Edition (PMBOK® Guide). Newtown Square Penn.: Project Management Institute. 2012

Project Management Institute. *PMI® Code of Ethics and Professional Conduct.*

Project Management Institute. *PMP® Exam Content Outline June 2015* (for Exam beginning January 12, 2016)

Rosen, Robert, Patricia Digh, Marshall Singer, and Carl Phillips. *Global Literacies: Lessons on Business Leadership and National Cultures.* New York: Simon & Schuster, 2000

Verma, Vijay K. *Human Resource Skills for the Project Manager.* Volume 2 of T*he Human Aspects of Project Management.* Upper Darby, Penn.: Project Management Institute, 1996

Verma, Vijay K. *Organizing Projects for Success* Volume 1 of T*he Human Aspects of Project Management.* Upper Darby, Penn.: Project Management Institute, 1996

Walker, Danielle Medina and Thomas Walker, Joerg Schmitz, *Doing Business Internationally: The Guide to Cross-Cultural Success.* New York: McGraw-Hill 2003

Wideman, R. Max, *Project and Program Risk Management: A Guide to Managing Project Risks and Opportunities.* , Newtown Square Penn.: Project Management Institute. 1992

Final Comments:

Congratulations to you on making the commitment to obtain your PMP® Certification. This designation, and the knowledge gained by achieving it, will set you apart from your peers and help you achieve higher levels in the performance of your work.
Aileen. hopes this book benefits you greatly on your path to success. Please send any comments or suggestions for improvement directly to the author at aileen@aileenellis.com Finally, good luck in all your future endeavors.

Available at amazon.com in both print and e-book format.

Available at amazon.com in both print and e-book format.

Made in the USA
Middletown, DE
31 January 2016